THE AMAZING GRILLA GRILLS WOOD PELLET GRILL

COOKBOOK

600 DELICIOUS, EASY AND YUMMY RECIPES FOR WHOLE FAMILY TO MASTER THE BBQ

DAVID BLAKE

Copyright © 2021 by David Blake All rights reserved worldwide.

No part of this book may be reproduced or transmitted in any form or by any means, electronic or mechanical, including photo- copying, recording or by any information storage and retrieval system, without written permission from the publisher, except for the inclusion of brief quotations in a review.

Warning-Disclaimer: The purpose of this book is to educate and entertain. The author or publisher does not guarantee that anyone following the techniques, suggestions, tips, ideas, or strategies will become successful. The author and publisher shall have neither liability or responsibility to anyone with respect to any loss or damage caused, or alleged to be caused, directly or indirectly by the information contained in this book.

CONTENTS

INTRODUCTION 11
  How the Grilla Grills Wood Pellet Grill Works 11
  The Benefits of Choosing the Grilla Grills Wood Pellet Grill 12
  Hints on Using Your Grilla Grills Wood Pellet Grill 13
  Cleaning Methods for the Grilla Grills Wood Pellet Grill 14

BAKING RECIPES 15
  Blueberry Pancakes 15
  Chocolate Lava Cake With Smoked Whipped Cream 15
  Baked Wood-fired Pizza 15
  Pull-apart Dinner Rolls 16
  Baked Chocolate Coconut Brownies 16
  Mint Butter Chocolate Chip Cookies 16
  Pizza Bites 17
  Spiced Carrot Cake 17
  Green Bean Casserole Circa 1955 18
  Double Vanilla Chocolate Cake 18
  Carrot Cake 18
  Caramel Bourbon Bacon Brownies 19
  Old Fashioned Cornbread 19
  Smoked, Salted Caramel Apple Pie 19
  Smoky Pimento Cheese Cornbread 20
  Beer Bread 20
  Baked Buttermilk Biscuits 20
  Baked Potatoes & Celery Root Au Gratin 21
  Lemon Chicken, Broccoli, String Beans Foil Packs 21
  Smoked Cheesy Alfredo Sauce 21
  Tarte Tatin 22
  Sweet And Spicy Baked Pork Beans 22
  Marbled Brownies With Amaretto & Ricotta 22
  Maple Syrup Pancake Casserole 22
  Smoker Wheat Bread 23
  Strawberry Basil Daiquiri 23
  Grilled Beer Cheese Dip 23
  Baked Brie 24
  Skillet Buttermilk Cornbread 24
  Pretzel Rolls 24
  Chili Cheese Fries 25
  Spiced Lemon Cherry Pie 25
  Cinnamon Pull-aparts 25
  Savory Cheesecake With Bourbon Pecan Topping 26
  Blueberry Sour Cream Muffins 26
  Donut Bread Pudding 27
  Crescent Rolls 27
  Smoked Blackberry Pie 27
  Baked Cast Iron Berry Cobbler 27
  Baked Green Chile Mac & Cheese By Doug
  Scheiding 28
  Basil Margherita Pizza 28
  Sopapilla Cheesecake By Doug Scheiding 28
  Focaccia 29
  Baked Pear Tarte Tatin 29
  Baked Bourbon Maple Pumpkin Pie 30
  Smokin' Lemon Bars 30
  Bananas Rum Foster 31
  Smoked Lemon Tea 31
  Baked Molten Chocolate Cake 32
  The Dan Patrick Show Pull-apart Pesto Bread 32
  Vanilla Cheesecake Skillet Brownie 32
  Double Chocolate Chip Brownie Pie 32
  Caramelized Bourbon Baked Pears 33
  Eggs Ham Benedict 33
  Pumpkin Bread 33
  Quick Baked Dinner Rolls 34
  Baked Pumpkin Pie 34
  Delicious Peanut Butter Cookies 34
  Delicious Pellet Grill Cornbread 34
  Baked Chocolate Brownie Cookies With Egg Nog 35
  Butternut Squash Macaroni And Cheese 35
  Traeger Baked Protein Bars 35
  Sourdough Pizza 36

Rosemary Cranberry Apple Sage Stuffing 36
Ultimate Baked Garlic Bread 36
Sweet Cheese Muffins 36
Smoky Apple Crepes 37
Cake With Smoked Berry Sauce 37
Chicken Pot Pie 38
Garlic Lemon Pepper Chicken Wings 38
Garlic Cheese Pull Apart Bread 38
Anzac Coconut Biscuits 39
Grilled Apple Pie 39
Traeger Baked Focaccia 39
Blueberry Bread Pudding 40
Vanilla Chocolate Bacon Cupcakes 40
Dark Chocolate Brownies With Bacon-salted Caramel 40
Baked Irish Creme Cake 41
S'mores Dip Skillet 41
Cast Iron Pineapple Upside Down Cake 41
Baked Cheesy Parmesan Grits 42
Eyeball Cookies 42
Smoked Lemon Cheesecake 42
Pound Cake 43
Grilled Bourbon Pecan Pie 43
Crème Brûlée 43
Chocolate Peanut Cookies 44
Bacon Chocolate Chip Cookies 44
Pineapple Cake 44
Chocolate Almond Cake 45
Cornbread Chicken Stuffing 45

PORK RECIPES 46

Fast Ribs 46
Grilled Lasagna With Cold-smoked Mozzarella 46
Baked Honey Glazed Ham 46
Hawaiian Pulled Pork 47
Chinese Alcoholic Bbq Pork Tenderloin 47
Traeger Smoked Sausage 47
Bbq Pulled Pork With Sweet & Heat Bbq Sauce 48
Bacon Onion Ring 48
St. Louis Bbq Ribs 48
Pig On A Stick With Buffalo Glaze 49
Apple & Bourbon Glazed Ham 49
Amazing Bacon Cheese Fries 49
Baked Sage & Sausage Stuffing 50
Pretzel Bun With Pulled Pork 50
Bbq Brown Sugar Bacon Bites 50
Pulled Pork Stew 51
Grilled Prosciutto Wrapped Asparagus 51
Smoked Chili Con Queso By Doug Scheiding 51
Apple-smoked Bacon 52
Delicious Pulled Pork Poutine 52
Anytime Pork Roast 52
Crown Roast Of Pork 52
Smoked Bologna 53
Smoked Pork Loin 53
Turkey Stuffing Bacon Balls 53
Dry Rub Grilled Ribs 53
Grilled Sweet Pork Tenderloin 54
Korean Pulled Pork Lettuce Wraps 54
Jalapeno Cheddar Smoked Sausages 54
Brats In Beer 55
Smoked Pork Tenderloin 55
Honey Glazed Pork Chops 55
Smoked Traeger Pulled Pork 55
Roasted Pork With Balsamic Strawberry Sauce 56
Southern Sugar-glazed Ham 56
Pulled Pork Shoulder And Chicken 57
Bbq Pork Belly 57
Roasted Ham With Apricot Sauce 57
Braised Pork Carnitas 57
Apple Bacon Smoked Ham 58
Baked Candied Bacon Cinnamon Rolls 58
Grilled Pork Loin 58
Baked Maple And Brown Sugar Bacon 59
Traeger Pork Chops 59
Smoked Porchetta With Italian Salsa Verde 59
Smoked Curry Ketchup Pork Ribs 60
Pulled Pork Taquitos With Sour Cream 60
Home-cured Picnic Ham With Mustard Caviar 61
Spiced Pork Belly 61
Grilled Lemon Pepper Pork Tenderloin 61
Grilled Raspberry Chipotle Pork Ribs 62
Smoked Apple Pork Belly 62
Spiced Grilled Pork Chops 62
Prosciutto Wrapped Dates With Marcona Almonds ... 62

Smoked Porchetta 63	Bourbon Chile Glazed Ham................................. 69
Traeger Pulled Pork Sandwiches.......................... 63	Bacon Wrapped Asparagus 69
Balsamic Brussels Sprouts With Bacon................ 64	Smoked Rack Of Pork 69
Grilled Sugar Snap Peas And Smoked Bacon 64	Smoked Bacon Roses 70
Delicious Smoked Bone-in Pork Chops 64	Smoked Pork Tomato Tamales 70
Old-fashioned Roasted Glazed Ham..................... 65	Bbq Pork Chops 71
Smoked Chorizo & Arugula Pesto 65	Cuban Onion Pork Sandwich............................... 71
Mini Sausage Rolls 65	Sweet And Spicy Pork Roast 72
Everything Pigs In A Blanket 66	Bbq Pork Belly Burnt Ends 72
Bbq Pulled Pork Hash 66	Smoked Pig Shots 72
Smoked Baby Back Ribs 66	Bbq Sweet & Smoky Ribs..................................... 73
St Louis Style Bbq Ribs With Texas Spicy Bbq Sauce.66	Hickory Smoked Pork Shoulder........................... 73
Sweet Smoked Country Ribs 67	Lip-smackin' Pork Loin.. 73
Texas Grilled Ribs 67	Simple Smoked Baby Backs 74
Whiskey- & Cider-brined Pork Shoulder.............. 67	Beer Pork Belly Chili Con Carne 74
Kodiak Cakes Candied Bacon Crumble Brownies 68	Championship Ribs With Kansas City Style 74
Bacon Weave Smoked Country Sausage............... 68	Unique Carolina Mustard Ribs............................. 75
Cajun Double-smoked Ham 68	Bbq Pork Shoulder Roast With Sugar Lips Glaze 75
Grilled Stuffed Pork Chops 69	

SEAFOOD RECIPES **76**

Cajun-blackened Shrimp..................................... 76	Tequila & Lime Shrimp With Smoked Tomato Sauce 82
Bacon Wrapped Shrimp....................................... 76	Smoked Lobster Scampi 82
Simple Glazed Salmon Fillets 76	Swordfish With Sicilian Olive Oil Sauce 83
Lemon Herb Grilled Salmon 76	Spiced Smoked Swordfish 83
Lobster Tail... 77	Grilled Pepper Lobster Tails 83
Salmon Cakes With Homemade Tartar Sauce 77	Lime Mahi Mahi Fillets 84
Smoked Salt Cured Lox 77	Florentine Shrimp Al Cartoccio 84
Grilled Tuna Steaks With Lemon & Caper Butter 78	Cedar Smoked Garlic Salmon 84
Grilled Albacore Tuna With Potato-tomato Casserole 78	Lemon Lobster Rolls 85
Shrimp Cabbage Tacos With Lime Cream 78	Grilled Shrimp Brochette 85
Smoked Honey Salmon....................................... 79	Sweet Smoked Salmon Jerky 85
Whole Vermillion Red Snapper........................... 79	Garlic Blackened Salmon..................................... 85
Cold-smoked Salmon Gravlax 79	Spicy Shrimp Skewers.. 86
Roasted Halibut With Spring Vegetables 79	Garlic Pepper Shrimp Pesto Bruschetta 86
Mango Rice Wine Thai Shrimp 80	Mexican Mahi Mahi With Baja Cabbage Slaw.......... 86
Kimi's Simple Grilled Fresh Fish 80	Citrus-smoked Trout 87
Grilled Whole Steelhead Fillet 80	Vodka Brined Smoked Wild Salmon 87
Bacon Wrapped Scallops...................................... 80	Sweet Mandarin Salmon...................................... 87
Grilled Lemon Shrimp Scampi 81	Grilled Lobster Tails With Smoked Paprika Butter 87
Grilled Crab Legs With Herb Butter 81	Garlic Blackened Catfish 88
Mezcal Shrimp With Salsa De Molcajete 81	Cider Hot-smoked Salmon 88
Spicy Lime Shrimp... 82	

Baked Steelhead 89
Thai-style Swordfish Steaks With Peanut Sauce 89
Smoked Cedar Plank Salmon 89
Smoke-roasted Halibut With Mixed Herb Vinaigrette 90
Grilled Tilapia With Blistered Cherry Tomatoes 90
Coconut Shrimp Jalapeño Poppers 90
Oysters Margarita 91
Alder Smoked Scallops With Citrus & Garlic Butter Sauce 91
Barbecued Scallops 92
Baked Whole Fish In Sea Salt 92
Traeger Smoked Salmon 92
Grilled Artichoke Cheese Salmon 92
Traeger Jerk Shrimp 93
Wood-fired Halibut 93
Smoked Fish Chowder 93
Seared Bluefin Tuna Steaks 94
Barbecued Shrimp 94
Planked Trout With Fennel, Bacon & Orange 94
Oysters In The Shell 95
Teriyaki Smoked Honey Tilapia 95
Bbq Roasted Salmon 95
Honey Balsamic Salmon 95
Smoked Sugar Halibut 96
Cured Cold-smoked Lox 96
Delicious Smoked Trout 96
Lemon Shrimp Scampi 97
Smoky Crab Dip 97
Peper Fish Tacos 97
Grilled Blackened Saskatchewan Salmon 97
Seared Ahi Tuna Steak With Soy Sauce 98
Honey-soy Garlic Salmon 98
Grilled Salmon Steaks With Dill Sauce 98
Smoked Trout 99
Grilled Trout With Citrus & Basil 99
Bbq Oysters 99
Smoked Mango Shrimp 99
Pacific Northwest Salmon 100
Traeger Crab Legs 100
Prosciutto-wrapped Scallops 100
Traeger Baked Rainbow Trout 101
Garlic Bacon Wrapped Shrimp 101
Moules Marinières With Garlic Butter Sauce 101
Charleston Crab Cakes With Remoulade 101
Grilled Salmon 102
Grilled Garlic Lobster Tails 102
Spicy Crab Poppers 102
Flavour Fire Spiced Shrimp 103

VEGETABLES RECIPES 104

Roasted Hasselback Potatoes By Doug Scheiding 104
Roasted Mashed Potatoes 104
Broccoli-cauliflower Salad 104
Roasted Potato Poutine 104
Salt Crusted Baked Potatoes 105
Grilled Street Corn 105
Roasted Asparagus 105
Twice-smoked Potatoes 105
Bacon Wrapped Corn On The Cob 106
Grilled Asparagus And Hollandaise Sauce 106
Traeger Smoked Coleslaw 106
Grilled Corn On The Cob With Parmesan And Garlic 107
Smoked Asparagus Soup 107
Smoked Pico De Gallo 107
Traeger Baked Potato Torte 107
Smoked Macaroni Salad 108
Roasted Pumpkin Seeds 108
Stuffed Jalapenos 108
Roasted Olives 109
Grilled Asparagus And Spinach Salad 109
Red Potato Grilled Lollipops 109
Baked Breakfast Mini Quiches 109
Butternut Squash 110
Steak Fries With Horseradish Creme 110
Baked Winter Squash Au Gratin 110
Parmesan Roasted Cauliflower 110
Smoked Parmesan Herb Popcorn 111
Baked Heirloom Tomato Tart 111
Grilled Ratatouille Salad 111
Roasted Artichokes With Garlic Butter 111
Chef Curtis' Famous Chimichurri Sauce 112

Roasted Garlic Herb Fries..112	Tater Tot Bake..120
Grilled Zucchini Squash Spears 112	Smoked & Loaded Baked Potato 120
Potluck Salad With Smoked Cornbread...................113	Roasted Tomatoes 121
Smoked Pickled Green Beans 113	Braised Creamed Green Beans 121
Sweet Potato Marshmallow Casserole 113	Blt Pasta Salad 121
Roasted Sheet Pan Vegetables..................................114	Grilled Chili-lime Corn..122
Roasted Sweet Potato Steak Fries.............................114	Smoked Beet-pickled Eggs 122
Baked Loaded Tater Tots 114	Smoked Mashed Potatoes...122
Smoked Mushrooms 115	Carolina Baked Beans 123
Roasted New Potatoes 115	Baked Garlic Duchess Potatoes 123
Grilled Asparagus & Honey-glazed Carrots...............115	Roasted Fall Vegetables 123
Baked Bacon Green Bean Casserole 115	Skillet Potato Cake 123
Baked Sweet Potatoes..116	Baked Artichoke Parmesan Mushrooms 124
Mashed Red Potatoes...116	Grilled Broccoli Rabe 124
Smoked Jalapeño Poppers 116	Baked Sweet And Savory Yams By Bennie Kendrick..124
Roasted Vegetable Napoleon 116	Spicy Asian Brussels Sprouts 124
Portobello Marinated Mushroom 116	Grilled Beer Cabbage..125
Roasted Jalapeño Poppers 117	Baked Stuffed Avocados 125
Roasted Green Beans With Bacon............................117	Roasted New Potatoes With Compound Butter........125
Double-smoked Cheese Potatoes.............................117	Green Bean Casserole 126
Whole Roasted Cauliflower With Garlic Parmesan Butter..118	Sicilian Stuffed Mushrooms 126
	Roasted Tomatoes With Hot Pepper Sauce.............126
Roasted Jalapeno Cheddar Deviled Eggs...............118	Christmas Brussel Sprouts 126
Roasted Beet & Bacon Salad......................................118	Smoked Bbq Onion Brussels Sprout 127
Grilled Fingerling Potato Salad 119	Grilled Cabbage Steaks With Warm Bacon Vinaigrette 127
Butter Braised Green Beans 119	
Roasted Pickled Beets 119	Baked Kale Chips 127
Traeger Grilled Whole Corn 120	Cast Iron Potatoes 128
Baked Sweet Potato Casserole With Marshmallow Fluff..120	Roasted Red Pepper White Bean Dip 128
	Roasted Do-ahead Mashed Potatoes......................128

POULTRY RECIPES..129

Bbq Breakfast Sausage...129	Grilled Honey Chicken Wings...................................133
Duck Breast With Pomegranate Sauce 129	Grilled Cheesy Chicken..133
Buttered Thanksgiving Turkey 129	Cranberry Turkey Breast 133
Savory Smoked Chicken Breasts 130	Roasted Rosemary Orange Chicken 134
Traeger Bbq Half Chickens 130	Buffalo Wings...134
Spiced Smoked Chicken Quarters 130	Spatchcocked Chicken With White Barbecue Sauce.134
Chicken Lollipops 131	Bbq Chicken Tostada 135
Buffalo Chicken 131	Smoked Turkey Wings..135
Bbq Chicken Drumsticks...132	Spatchcocked Turkey..135
Bbq Chicken Breasts 132	Lemon Rosemary Beer Can Chicken 135
Smoked Turkey Jerky...132	Fig Glazed Chicken Stuffed Cornbread 136

Asian Chicken Sliders 136	Bbq Chicken Thighs 147
Bbq Chicken Legs 137	Smoked Maple Syrup Thanksgiving Turkey 147
Bbq Smoked Turkey Jerky 137	Grilled Chicken Wings 147
Applewood-smoked Whole Turkey 137	Smoked Drumsticks 148
Jalapeño- & Cheese-stuffed Chicken 137	Oktoberfest Pretzel Mustard Chicken 148
Smoked Whiskey Peach Pulled Chicken 138	Grilled Whole Chicken Stuffed Sausage And Apple . 148
Italian Grilled Chicken Saltimbocca 138	Savory Grilled Chicken Burrito Bowls 148
Apple Bacon Lattice Turkey 138	Chicken Tenders 149
Buffalo Chicken Wraps 139	Smoked Boneless Chicken Thighs 149
Roasted Whole Chicken 139	Crispy Spiced Chicken Wings 149
Cider-brined Turkey 139	Chicken Breast Calzones 150
Chicken On A Throne 140	Cheese Chicken Cordon Bleu 150
Roasted Christmas Goose 140	Chicken Nachos 150
Bbq Turkey Drumsticks 140	Lemon & Herb Chicken 150
Smoked Honey Chicken Drumsticks 141	Grilled Parmesan Chicken Wings 151
Nashville Spiced Smoked Chicken 141	Roasted Beer Can Chicken 151
Roasted Tin Foil Dinners 141	Traeger Mandarin Wings 151
Green Chile Chicken Enchiladas 141	Juicy Jerk Chicken Kebabs 152
Grilled Chipotle Chicken Skewers 142	Chicken Egg Rolls With Buffalo Sauce 152
County Fair Turkey Legs 142	Traditional Smoked Thanksgiving Turkey 152
Smo-fried Chicken 142	Savory Jerk Chicken Wings 153
Cajun Brined Maple Smoked Turkey Breast 143	Italian Grilled Barbecue Chicken Wings 153
Cornish Game Hen 143	Lemon Cajun Chicken Carbonara 153
Mandarin Chicken Breast 143	Wild West Wings 154
Chicken Corn Fritters 144	Marinated Grilled Honey Chicken Wings 154
Delicious Smoked Turketta 144	Smoked Beer Brine Hens 154
Buffalo Chicken Wings 144	Green Goddess Chicken Legs 154
Roasted Honey Bourbon Glazed Turkey 145	Baked Prosciutto-wrapped Chicken Breast With
Grilled Hand Pulled Chicken 145	Spinach And Boursin 155
Beer Chicken 145	Smoked Deviled Eggs 155
Dry Brine Traeger Turkey 146	Loaded Chicken Fries 155
Cornish Game Hens 146	Grilled Greek Chicken With Garlic & Lemon 156
Jamaican Jerk Chicken Quarters 146	Peanut Butter Chicken Wings 156
Turkey & Bacon Kebabs With Ranch-style Dressing 146	Bbq Turkey Breast With Meat Church Holy Cow 156

BEEF LAMB AND GAME RECIPES 157

Brined Smoked Brisket 157	Texas Pepper Beef Ribs 159
Pastrami 157	Reverse Seared Rib-eye Caps 159
Flavour Texas Smoke Beef 157	Flavour Memphis Bbq Beef Brisket 159
Bbq Brisket With Traeger Coffee Rub 157	Smoked New York Steaks 160
Three Ingredient Pot Roast 158	Ancho Pepper Rubbed Brisket 160
Garlic Leg Of Lamb Roast 158	Braised Mediterranean Beef Brisket 160
Flavour Bbq Brisket Burnt Ends 159	Garlic Standing Rib Roast 161

Traditional Tomahawk Steak..................................161	Citrus Grilled Lamb Chops......................................174
Bbq Beef Sandwich 161	Moked Christmas Crown Roast Of Lamb................174
Beef Brisket With Chophouse Steak Rub..................162	Green Chile Cheese Beef Sliders..............................174
Savory Whiskey Grilled Elk Steaks..........................162	Savory Teriyaki Smoked Steak Bites 175
Sweetheart Steak 162	3-2-1 Bbq Beef Cheeks 175
Smoked Red Wine Beef Roast 162	Standing Venison Rib Roast....................................175
Pulled Beef 163	Reverse-seared Steaks 176
Reuben Sandwich 163	Bison Meatballs 176
The Perfect T-bones 163	Smoked Beer Corned Beef 176
Reverse-seared Tri-tip...164	Beer Braised Beef Sandwiches 177
Chorizo Cheese Stuffed Burgers..............................164	Venison Carne Asada...177
Smoked Pheasant 164	Bbq Beef Short Ribs With Traeger Prime Rib Rub...178
Smoked Spiced Pulled Beef Chuck Roast.................164	Baked Venison Tater Tot Casserole 178
Cheddar Bacon Beef Burgers 165	Mustard Garlic Crusted Prime Rib 178
Smoked Tri-tip...165	Bbq Brisket Tacos..178
Smoked Duck Breast Bacon.....................................165	Pan Seared Parsley Ribeye Steak 179
Smoked Chicken Steak Sandwiches.........................166	Classic Poor Man's Burnt Ends................................179
Whiskey Bourbon Bbq Cheeseburger 166	Venison Steaks 179
Grilled Tomahawk Steak 167	Traeger Tri-tip Roast...179
Roasted Prime Rib 167	Beef Caldereta Stew..180
Hickory Smoked Prime Rib 168	Bbq Sweet Pepper Meatloaf 180
Beer Chili Bratwurst..168	Smoked Meatball Egg Sandwiches..........................180
Bistecca Alla Fiorentina With Mushroom Ragout ...168	Savory Chili Mac And Cheese 181
Italian Meatballs 169	Lemon Tomahawk Steak...181
Sweet Heat Burnt Ends 169	Herb Grilled Venison Stew 182
Texas Shoulder Clod 170	Fajita Style Mexican Hot Dogs 182
Hot Coffee-rubbed Brisket 170	Spicy Smoked Chili Beef Jerky................................182
Roasted Mustard Crusted Prime Rib 170	Smoked Beer Brisket...183
Rosemary-smoked Lamb Chops..............................170	Smoked Corned Beef Reuben..................................183
Santa Maria Tri-tip With Pico De Gallo 171	Smoked Longhorn Brisket......................................183
Slow Smoked Rib-eye Roast 171	Bacon Burger 184
Savory Reverse Seared Ny Steak 171	Smoked Cheese Beef Burgers 184
Grilled Loco Moco Burger..172	Duck Fat Fries (confit) 184
Smoked Prime Rib 172	Smoked Longhorn Cowboy Tri-tip 185
Savory Bacon Mac And Cheese Stuffed Sliders.........172	Garlic Beef Meatballs 185
Smoked Sirloin Roast Beef.......................................173	Smoked Corned Beef Brisket 185
Smoked Corned Beef & Cabbage 173	Flavour Smoked Corned Beef Brisket Hash............186
Texas Smoked Beer Leftover Rib Meat 173	Smoked Garlic Meatloaf..186
Bbq Bacon Meatballs 174	

APPETIZERS AND SNACKS..187

Chicken Wings With Teriyaki Glaze 187	Bacon Pork Pinwheels (kansas Lollipops) 187
Bacon-wrapped Jalapeño Poppers...........................187	Bayou Wings With Cajun Rémoulade 188

Pulled Pork Loaded Nachos 188
Citrus-infused Marinated Olives 189
Chorizo Queso Fundido 189
Grilled Guacamole 189
Pigs In A Blanket 190
Simple Cream Cheese Sausage Balls 190
Deviled Eggs With Smoked Paprika 190
Smoked Cashews 191
Pig Pops (sweet-hot Bacon On A Stick) 191
Chuckwagon Beef Jerky 191
Smoked Cheese 192
Roasted Red Pepper Dip 192
Delicious Deviled Crab Appetizer 192
Smoked Turkey Sandwich 193
Sriracha & Maple Cashews 193
Jalapeño Poppers With Chipotle Sour Cream 193
Cold-smoked Cheese 194

COCKTAILS RECIPES 195

Smoked Berry Cocktail 195
Smoking Gun Cocktail 195
Traeger Smoked Daiquiri 195
In Traeger Fashion Cocktail 195
Smoked Apple Cider 196
Grilled Blood Orange Mimosa 196
Sunset Margarita 196
Ryes And Shine Cocktail 196
Grilled Peach Sour Cocktail 197
Zombie Cocktail Recipe 197
Smoked Hot Buttered Rum 197
Strawberry Mule Cocktail 197
Garden Gimlet Cocktail 198
Grilled Hawaiian Sour 198
Smoked Pomegranate Lemonade Cocktail 198
Smoked Mulled Wine 198
Batter Up Cocktail 199
Smoked Ice Mojito Slurpee 199
Grilled Frozen Strawberry Lemonade 199
Smoked Sangria 199
Smoked Pumpkin Spice Latte 200
Fig Slider Cocktail 200
Bacon Old-fashioned Cocktail 200
Smoked Salted Caramel White Russian 201
Smoky Scotch & Ginger Cocktail 201
A Smoking Classic Cocktail 201
Cran-apple Tequila Punch With Smoked Oranges ... 201
Smoked Cold Brew Coffee 202
Smoked Hibiscus Sparkler 202
Smoked Jacobsen Salt Margarita 202
Smoked Barnburner Cocktail 203
Smoked Pineapple Hotel Nacional Cocktail 203
Dublin Delight Cocktail 203
Grilled Peach Mint Julep 204
Smoked Irish Coffee 204
Smoked Texas Ranch Water 204
Traeger Old Fashioned 204
Traeger Boulevardier Cocktail 205
Grilled Rabbit Tail Cocktail 205

RECIPE INDEX 206

INTRODUCTION

How the Grilla Grills Wood Pellet Grill Works

Because pellet grills can perform so many cooking functions and require little to no monitoring, you might expect them to operate using complicated technology. In reality, wood pellet smokers are simple, straightforward cooking tools that are easy and safe to operate.

The following parts of a pellet grill work together to help you achieve a delicious, evenly cooked meal:

1. **Wood Pellets:** Pellets are small cylindrical food-grade wood that act as fuel for a pellet grill. Some wood pellets come from flavored woods, like apple or hickory, which add layers of flavor to food.

2. **Hopper:** The hopper is the vessel that holds the pellets, keeping them dry until they are ready for use.

3. **Auger:** Once you start the grill, the auger moves wood pellets from the hopper onto the firepot.

4. **Firepot:** The firepot is exactly what you expect — the place where the fire ignites, using the wood pellets for fuel.

5. **Induction fan:** The induction fan keeps the fire going and circulates the heat and smoke throughout your pellet grill and into your food.

6. **Controller:** The controller is on the outside of the pellet grill, and it is where you set and monitor the cooking temperature and pellet grill heating. Every smoker is different, so keep in mind some models may offer more precise control than others.

7. **Drip tray:** You'll find the drip tray between the cooking grates and the grill's inner workings. This tray collects any grease or food drippings, so they don't fall into the fire, and keeps food safe from direct heat.

To use a pellet grill, you fill the hopper with wood pellets marked safe for pellet grills. Follow manufacturer guidelines and be careful not to overfill or underfill your smoker. Once the pellets are in the hopper, use the digital controller to set your desired temperature. The induction fan will keep the fire going while your pellets move through the auger into the firepot. As the wood pellets ignite, the hot smoke circulates back through the grill to create a flavorful cooking chamber.

The Benefits of Choosing the Grilla Grills Wood Pellet Grill

1. Amazing Versatility

One of the best features of having a pellet grill is its versatility.

A traditional charcoal grill or gas grill simply doesn't compare when cooking with pellets, as with this grill you are also able to smoke, braise, bake, roast, and sear your food.

This means you can have the chance to cook a lot more varieties of food and try out different recipes and cooking styles, including smoked meat which totally eliminates the need for a separate smoker.

The temperature is also a benefit of using a pellet grill as they mostly feature precision temperature control systems which can range from around 180 degrees to 500 degrees.

2. ADDS GREAT FLAVOR

If you haven't already heard, one of the main benefits of having a pellet grill is the quality and flavor food that you can prepare when using it.

Sometimes, when using more traditional grills, they can tend to leave quite a smoky or chemical taste on the meat after it's been smoked. With pellet grills, however, the addition of smoking with pellets can make a big difference to the final flavor.

This is because the wood pellets used really help to flavor the meat, a whole lot better than when cooking over gas and charcoal.

Wood pellets also come in various different flavors, such as apple, peach, mesquite, pecan, oak, cherry, maple and hickory, which can all really make a difference to your meals.

These pellets can also be mixed and matched as you like, allowing you to discover the perfect flavor for your taste buds.

In fact, many professional chefs opt for wood when cooking as it provides the best flavor possible. Therefore, if it is top flavor you are after, a pellet grill is your best option.

3. EASY TO USE

When it comes to cooking with a pellet grill, there are more advantages yet again.

Although some people may at first seem intimidated by their versatile design, they are actually not difficult to operate at all and in fact very easy to use.

Quite a few of the more recent grill styles have integrated one button start up controls, which means they will be super easy to get working.

As previously mentioned, the temperature control systems on a pellet grill is a lot better than more traditional ones.

These grills will be able to control the temperature throughout the entire cooking process, meaning all you will have to do is place the meat down and let the grill do its job.

They work similar to a convection oven, in that you won't need to fear your food ever being cooked uneven. This definitely helps to give the BBQ chef complete peace of mind!

Most pellet grills also feature flare prevention, which can stop any troubling flare-ups from occurring.

Hints on Using Your Grilla Grills Wood Pellet Grill

1. Allow yourself some time to get acquainted with your new grill/smoker.

Allow yourself some time to get acquainted with your new grill/smoker. We know you'll be anxious to try it out, but don't be overly ambitious. Instead of a whole brisket, which could take 15 hours or more, or a budget-busting prime rib roast, start with chicken (parts, such as breasts or wings, or a whole bird), pork loin tenderloin, or blade (shoulder) steaks, Cornish hens, salmon steaks or fillets, or other relatively inexpensive cuts that can be completed in 2 hours or less.

2. Identify any hot spots—most grills have them.

Identify any hot spots—most grills have them. Preheat your grill to medium-high as directed by the owner's manual, then lay slices of cheap white bread shoulder to shoulder across the grate. Watch carefully, then flip after a few minutes. Take a photo of the results. The darkest bread will indicate where the temperature might be hotter. (Print the photo out and add it to your owner's manual for reference.)

3. Don't let your meat come to room temperature before cooking.

Whatever meat you select, put it on the preheated grill/smoker straight from the refrigerator. Do not, as many recipes suggest, allow it to come to room temperature before cooking.

As Steven often notes, high-end steak houses do not leave their meats out at room temperature. (The danger area is 40 to 140 degrees.) The heat of the grill is sufficient to raise the internal temperature of the meat by those few degrees.

4. Invest in a good meat thermometer.

A laser-type thermometer such as this one will give you a more accurate temperature reading at grill level than a built-in dome thermometer. Determine the temperature range of your grill model from lowest to highest (180 degrees to 500+, for example).

5. **Take advantage of your pellet grill's searing capabilities.**

Many pellet grills feature searing capabilities, meaning they can reach temperatures over 500 degrees. Again, check your owner's manual for information

Cleaning Methods for the Grilla Grills Wood Pellet Grill

A clean grill is a safe appliance that makes delicious food as a bonus. Before you begin your search for kitchen items to clean your grill, you should know some general grill cleaning tips.

1. Clean and scrape grates while they're still warm: Warm residue is easier to clean than dry, stuck-on grease. If you go with this method, be extra careful while handling your grill grates. Use protective gloves and be sure the DIY grill cleaner you're using isn't flammable if you're working with a warm grill.

2. Give it a quick clean after every use: You don't need to do a deep clean every time you grill out. But a once-over scrub after using it can save you from painstaking scraping later.

3. Do deep cleans depending on your usage: In general, you should do a deep clean every couple of months. If you use your grill more often, consider a deep clean once a month. If you hardly use your grill — but let's be real, we're using it all the time — every few months will suffice.

4. Deep clean a cool grill: If you have to get deep into your grill to clean it, make sure it's had a chance to cool. If you're cleaning up charcoal or pellet ash, be sure the material isn't still warm before taking a shop vacuum to it.

Along with those grill cleaning tips, some preventive measures can save you from dealing with a gunked-up grill. Be sure to:

➢ Cover surfaces with aluminum foil.
➢ Use a grill pan or basket.
➢ Use cooking oil, either on the grates or the food itself.
➢ Clean out ashes from pellets or charcoal.
➢ Use a grill cover when you aren't cooking.

BAKING RECIPES

Blueberry Pancakes

Servings: 4
Cooking Time: 10 Minutes

Ingredients:
- 2 Cups Blueberries, Fresh
- 1 Cup Pancake Mix
- 1/2 Cup Sugar
- 3/4 Cup Water, Warm

Directions:
1. Supply your smoker with wood pellets and follow the start-up procedure. Preheat the grill, with the lid closed, to 350° F.
2. Place the cast iron griddle on the grates of your grill.
3. In a large bowl, pour water, pancake mix and 1/2 cup of the blueberries and mix until combined.
4. Pour the batter onto the griddle in 4 equal parts. Cook with the lid closed for about 6 minutes, or until the edges of the pancakes are slightly cooked. Flip each pancake and continue cooking for another 4 minutes.
5. Pour the hot blueberry sauce over your freshly cooked pancakes and enjoy!

Chocolate Lava Cake With Smoked Whipped Cream

Servings: 4
Cooking Time: 45 Minutes

Ingredients:
- 1 Pint heavy whipping cream
- 9 Tablespoon Butter
- 220 G Semisweet Chocolate
- 1 1/4 Cup powdered sugar
- 2 Large eggs
- 2 egg yolk
- 6 Tablespoon flour
- 1 Tablespoon Bourbon Vanilla
- Powdered Sugar
- cocoa powder

Directions:
1. Supply your smoker with wood pellets and follow the start-up procedure. Preheat the grill, with the lid closed, to 180° F.
2. For the Smoked Whipped Cream: Add cream to a shallow, aluminum baking pan. Place the pan on the grill and smoke for 30 minutes.
3. Pour the smoked cream into a large mixing bowl and refrigerate for later use. Grill: 180 °F
4. Increase the grill temperature to 375°F and preheat. Grill: 375 °F
5. Brush 4 small soufflé cups with 1 tablespoon melted butter.
6. Melt the chocolate and remaining butter in a heatproof bowl over simmering water, stir until smooth.
7. Stir in powdered sugar. Add eggs and egg yolks, stirring continuously. Whisk in flour until blended completely.
8. Pour batter into the prepared soufflé cups. Place them on the Traeger and bake for 13-14 minutes, or until the sides are set. Grill: 375 °F
9. For the Whipped Cream: Remove the chilled smoked cream from the refrigerator, add the bourbon vanilla and whip until airy.
10. Add confectioners sugar and continue whipping until whipped cream forms stiff peaks.
11. Dust lava cakes with confectioners sugar and cocoa, top with a dollop of smoke-infused whipped cream. Enjoy!

Baked Wood-fired Pizza

Servings: 6
Cooking Time: 12 Minutes

Ingredients:
- 2/3 Cup warm water (110°F to 115°F)
- 2 1/2 Teaspoon active dry yeast
- 1/2 Teaspoon granulated sugar
- 1 Teaspoon kosher salt
- 1 Tablespoon oil
- 2 Cup all-purpose flour
- 1/4 Cup fine cornmeal
- 1 Large grilled portobello mushroom, sliced
- 1 Jar pickled artichoke hearts, drained and chopped
- 1 Cup shredded fontina cheese
- 1/2 Cup shaved Parmigiano-Reggiano cheese, divided
- To Taste Roasted Garlic, minced
- 1/4 Cup extra-virgin olive oil
- To Taste banana peppers

Directions:
1. In a glass bowl, stir together the warm water, yeast and sugar. Let stand until the mixture starts to foam, about 10 minutes. In a mixer, combine 1-3/4 cup flour, sugar and salt. Stir oil into the yeast mixture. Slowly add the liquid to the dry ingredients while slowly increasing the mixers speed until fully combined. The dough should be smooth and not sticky.
2. Knead the dough on a floured surface, gradually adding the remaining flour as needed to prevent the dough from sticking, until smooth, about 5 to 10 minutes.
3. Form the dough into a ball. Apply a thin layer of olive oil to a large bowl. Place the dough into the bowl and coat the dough ball

with a small amount of olive oil. Cover and let rise in a warm place for about 1 hour or until doubled in size.
4. When ready to cook, set smoker temperature to 450°F and preheat, lid closed for 15 minutes.
5. Place a pizza stone in the grill while it preheats.
6. Punch the dough down and roll it out into a 12-inch circle on a floured surface.
7. Spread the cornmeal evenly on the pizza peel. Place the dough on the pizza peel and assemble the toppings evenly in the following order: olive oil, roasted garlic, fontina, portobello, artichoke hearts, Parmigiano-Reggiano and banana peppers.
8. Carefully slide the assembled pizza from the pizza peel to the preheated pizza stone and bake until the crust is golden brown, about 10 to 12 minutes. Enjoy!

Pull-apart Dinner Rolls

Servings: 8
Cooking Time: 10 Minutes

Ingredients:
- 1/4 Cup warm water (110°F to 115°F)
- 1/3 Cup vegetable oil
- 2 Tablespoon active dry yeast
- 1/4 Cup sugar
- 1/2 Teaspoon salt
- 1 egg
- 3 1/2 Cup all-purpose flour
- cooking spray

Directions:
1. Supply your smoker with wood pellets and follow the start-up procedure. Preheat the grill, with the lid closed, to 400° F.
2. In the bowl of a stand mixer, combine warm water, oil, yeast and sugar. Let mixture rest for 5 to 10 minutes, or until frothy and bubbly.
3. With a dough hook, mix in salt, egg and 2 cups of flour until combined. Add remaining flour 1/2 cup at a time (dough will be sticky).
4. Prepare a cast iron pan with cooking spray and set aside.
5. Spray your hands with cooking spray and shape the dough into 12 balls.
6. After shaped, place in the prepared cast iron pan and let rest for 10 minutes. Bake in Traeger for about 10 to 12 minutes, or until tops are lightly golden. Enjoy! Grill: 400 °F

Baked Chocolate Coconut Brownies

Servings: 4
Cooking Time: 25 Minutes

Ingredients:
- 1/2 Cup gluten-free or all-purpose flour, such as Bob's Red Mill
- 1/4 Cup unsweetened alkalized cocoa powder
- 1/2 Teaspoon sea salt
- 4 Ounce semisweet chocolate, coarsely chopped
- 3/4 Cup unrefined coconut oil
- 1 Cup raw cane sugar
- 4 eggs
- 1 Teaspoon vanilla extract
- 4 Ounce semisweet chocolate chips, optional

Directions:
1. Supply your smoker with wood pellets and follow the start-up procedure. Preheat the grill, with the lid closed, to 350° F.
2. Grease a 9x9 inch baking pan and line with parchment paper.
3. Combine the flour, cocoa powder and salt in a medium bowl. Set aside.
4. In a double boiler or microwave, melt the chopped chocolate and coconut oil. Let cool slightly.
5. Add the sugar, eggs and vanilla. Whisking until well combined.
6. Whisk in the flour mixture and fold in the chocolate chips. Pour into the prepared pan.
7. Place on the grill and bake until a toothpick inserted in the center of the brownies comes out clean, about 20 to 25 minutes. This will yield a somewhat gooey brownie. Continue to bake for 5 to 10 minutes if you prefer a drier brownie. Grill: 350 °F
8. Let the brownies cool completely, then cut into squares. Store in an airtight container at room temperature for up to 3 days. Enjoy!

Mint Butter Chocolate Chip Cookies

Servings: 24
Cooking Time: 12 Minutes

Ingredients:
- 1/2 Cup Butter, Melted
- 1 Package Chocolate Chip Cookie Mix
- 8-10 Drop Food Coloring
- 1/2 Tsp Mint, Extract

Directions:
1. Supply your smoker with wood pellets and follow the start-up procedure. Preheat the grill, with the lid closed, to 350° F.
2. Follow the directions on the back of the Chocolate Chip Cookie mix and also add the mint extract and green food coloring. Mix until combined.
3. On a baking sheet lined with parchment paper, drop balls of dough about 2 tbsp in size onto the pan.
4. Place in your Grill and bake for 10-12 minutes. Let cool for a couple minutes before removing from the pan. Enjoy!

Pizza Bites

Servings: 6
Cooking Time: 20 Minutes

Ingredients:
- 4 1/2 Cup Bread Flour
- 1 1/2 Tablespoon sugar
- 2 Teaspoon Instant Yeast
- 2 Teaspoon kosher salt
- 3 Tablespoon extra-virgin olive oil
- 15 Fluid Ounce Water, Lukewarm
- 8 Ounce Pepperoni, sliced
- 1 Cup pizza sauce
- 1 Cup mozzarella cheese
- 1 Whole egg, for egg wash
- 1 As Needed salt

Directions:
1. For the Pizza Dough: Combine flour, sugar, salt, and yeast in food processor. Pulse 3 to 4 times until incorporated evenly. Add olive oil and water. Run food processor until mixture forms ball that rides around the bowl above the blade, about 15 seconds. Continue processing 15 seconds longer.
2. Transfer dough ball to lightly floured surface and knead once or twice by hand until smooth ball is formed. Divide dough into three even parts and place each into a 1 gallon zip top bag. Place in refrigerator and allow to rise at least one day.
3. At least two hours before baking, remove dough from refrigerator and shape into balls by gathering dough towards bottom and pinching shut. Flour well and place each one in a separate medium mixing bowl. Cover tightly with plastic wrap and allow to rise at warm room temperature until roughly doubled in volume.
4. When ready to cook, set the grill temperature to 350°F and preheat, lid closed for 15 minutes.
5. After the first rise remove the dough from the fridge and let come to room temperature. Roll dough on a flat surface. Cut dough into long strips 3" wide by 18" long.
6. Slice pepperoni into strips.
7. In a medium bowl combine the pizza sauce, mozzarella and pepperoni.
8. Spoon 1 TBSP of the pizza filling onto the pizza dough every two inches, about halfway down the length of the dough. Dip a pastry brush into the egg wash and brush around pizza filling. Fold the half side of the dough (without the pizza filling) over the other half that contains the pizza filling.
9. Press down between each pizza bite slightly with your fingers. With a ravioli or pizza cutter, cut around each filling- creating a rectangle shape and sealing the crust in.
10. Transfer each pizza bite onto a parchment lined cookie sheet. Cover with a kitchen towel and let them rise for 30 minutes.
11. When ready to cook, preheat the grill to 350 ℉ with the lid closed for 10-15 minutes.
12. Brush the bites with remaining egg wash, sprinkle with salt and place directly on the sheet tray. Bake 10-15 minutes until the exterior is golden brown.
13. Remove from grill and transfer to a serving dish. Serve with extra pizza sauce for dipping and enjoy!

Spiced Carrot Cake

Servings: 10
Cooking Time: 35 Minutes

Ingredients:
- 1/2 Cup Apple Sauce, Unsweetened
- 2 Tsp Baking Powder
- 1 Tsp Baking Soda
- 1 1/2 Cups Brown Sugar
- 1/2 Cup Butter, Room Temp
- 3/4 Cup Canola Oil
- 3 Cups Carrot, Grated
- 1 1/2 Tsp Cinnamon, Ground
- 2 (8-Ounce) Packages Cream Cheese, Room Temperature
- 4 Egg
- 2 Cups Flour, All-Purpose
- 1/2 Tsp Ginger, Ground
- 1/4 Tsp Nutmeg, Ground
- 1/2 Tsp Salt
- 1/2 Cup Sugar
- 3 Cups Sugar, Icing

Directions:
1. Supply your smoker with wood pellets and follow the start-up procedure. Preheat the grill, with the lid closed, to 350° F.
2. Line the bottom of 2 9-inch cake pans with parchment paper and spray the sides with cooking spray. Set aside.
3. In a large bowl, combine flour, baking powder and soda, spices and salt.
4. In a smaller bowl, combine oil, eggs, sugars, and applesauce and whisk together. Add carrots and stir until well combined.
5. Pour the wet ingredients into the dry. Stir until combined but take care not to over mix. Pour the batter evenly between the two cake pans. Bake for about 35 minutes in your Grill, rotating the cake pans halfway between the cook. Remove once a toothpick is inserted in the middle of the cake and comes out clean.
6. While the cake is cooling, prepare the frosting. Beat the cream cheese until smooth with a hand mixer. Add the butter and icing sugar and mix until fully combined.
7. On a clean plate or cake stand, place one half of the cake and top with a good layer of cream cheese frosting. Place the second half on top and cover with the remaining frosting. Icing tip: try not to lift your knife while icing. Instead make long, smooth strokes. Lifting the knife often make cause crumbs to get into your icing. Top with pecans if desired.

Green Bean Casserole Circa 1955

Servings: 6
Cooking Time: 30 Minutes

Ingredients:
- 1 1/2 Pound Green Beans, fresh
- 1 Can cream of mushroom soup
- 1/2 Cup milk
- 2 Teaspoon soy sauce
- 1/2 Teaspoon Worcestershire sauce
- 1/2 Teaspoon black pepper
- 1.334 Cup French's Original Crispy Fried Onions
- 1/4 Cup red bell pepper, diced

Directions:
1. In a mixing bowl, combine the beans (trimmed and cooked until tender, or may use 2 16 oz. cans), soup, milk, soy sauce, Worcestershire sauce, black pepper, 2/3 cup of the onion rings, and red pepper, if using. Transfer to a 1-1/2 quart casserole dish.
2. Supply your smoker with wood pellets and follow the start-up procedure. Preheat the grill, with the lid closed, to 375° F.
3. Cook the casserole until the filling is hot and bubbling, 25 to 30 minutes. Top with the remaining onions and cook for 5 to 10 minutes more, or until the onions are crisp and beginning to brown. Grill: 375 °F

Double Vanilla Chocolate Cake

Servings: 12
Cooking Time: 40 Minutes

Ingredients:
- 1 1/2 Tsp Baking Soda
- 1/2 Cup Butter, Melted
- 1 Cup Buttermilk, Low Fat
- 1 Jar Chocolate Icing, Prepared
- 3/4 Cup Cocoa, Powder
- 1 Cup Coffee, Hot
- 2 Large Egg
- 1 3/4 Cups Flour, All-Purpose
- 3/4 Tsp Salt
- 2 Cups Sugar
- 1 Tbsp Vanilla

Directions:
1. Supply your smoker with wood pellets and follow the start-up procedure. Preheat the grill, with the lid closed, to 350° F.
2. Stir together flour, sugar, cocoa, baking soda and salt in a large bowl. Combine eggs, buttermilk, butter and coffee and mix until smooth. Add in hot coffee and stir until combined and the dough is runny.
3. Pour the batter into two prepared baking pans and bake on the top rack of your for 40 minutes, turning the pans 180 degrees halfway through.
4. Allow to cool and then frost with chocolate icing.

Carrot Cake

Servings: 4-6
Cooking Time: 60 Minutes

Ingredients:
- 8 carrots, peeled and grated
- 4 eggs, at room temperature
- 1 cup vegetable oil
- ½ cup milk
- 1 teaspoon vanilla extract
- 2 cups sugar
- 2 cups self-rising or cake flour
- 2 teaspoons baking soda
- 1 teaspoon salt
- 1 cup finely chopped pecans
- Nonstick cooking spray or butter, for greasing
- 8 ounces cream cheese
- 1 cup confectioners' sugar
- 8 tablespoons (1 stick) unsalted butter, at room temperature
- 1 teaspoon vanilla extract
- ½ teaspoon salt
- 2 tablespoons to ¼ cup milk

Directions:
1. For the cake:
2. Supply your smoker with wood pellets and follow the start-up procedure. Preheat, with the lid closed, to 350°F.
3. In a food processor or blender, combine the grated carrots, eggs, oil, milk, and vanilla, and process until the carrots are finely minced.
4. In a large mixing bowl, combine the sugar, flour, baking soda, and salt.
5. Add the carrot mixture to the flour mixture and stir until well incorporated. Fold in the chopped pecans.
6. Coat a 9-by-13-inch baking pan with cooking spray.
7. Pour the batter into prepared pan and place on the grill grate. Close the lid and smoke for about 1 hour, or until a toothpick inserted in the center comes out clean.
8. Remove the cake from the grill and let cool completely.
9. For the frosting:
10. Using an electric mixer on low speed, beat the cream cheese, confectioners' sugar, butter, vanilla, and salt, adding 2 tablespoons to ¼ cup of milk to thin the frosting as needed.
11. Frost the cooled cake and slice to serve.

Caramel Bourbon Bacon Brownies

Servings: 16
Cooking Time: 60 Minutes

Ingredients:
- 2 Cup All-Purpose Flour
- 1/4 Cup Bourbon
- 1 Cup Brown Sugar
- 1 Cup Canola Oil
- Caramel Sauce
- 1.5 Cup Cocoa Powder
- 1 Tablespoon Hickory Honey Sea Salt
- 2 Tablespoon Instant Coffee
- 6 Large Eggs
- 1/2 Teaspoon Smoked Infused Hickory Honey Sea Salt
- 1 Cup Powdered Sugar
- 6 Slices Bacon, Raw
- 4 Tablespoons Water
- 3 Cups White Sugar

Directions:
1. Supply your smoker with wood pellets and follow the start-up procedure. Preheat the grill, with the lid closed, to 400° F.
2. In a large mixing bowl, whisk together the cocoa, powdered sugar, white sugar, instant coffee and flour.
3. To the flour mixture, add the eggs, oil and water until just combined.
4. Spray the 9 x 13 pan well with cooking spray.
5. Pour half the batter in the pan, drizzle with caramel.
6. Pour other half of batter on top and drizzle with caramel again and add candied bacon to the top.
7. Bake the brownies in the smoker for 1 hour, or until a toothpick inserted in the center of the pan comes out clean.
8. Remove from the smoker and allow to cool before slicing.

Old Fashioned Cornbread

Servings: 4
Cooking Time: 25 Minutes

Ingredients:
- 1 Cup all-purpose flour
- 1 Cup Cornmeal
- 1 Tablespoon sugar
- 2 Teaspoon baking powder
- 1/2 Teaspoon salt
- 3 Tablespoon butter
- 1 Cup milk
- 1 Whole egg, lightly beaten

Directions:
1. In a mixing bowl, combine the flour, cornmeal, sugar, baking powder, and salt.
2. Melt the butter in a small saucepan. Remove from the heat, and stir in the milk and the egg. (Make sure the mixture isn't hot or the egg will curdle.)
3. Add the milk-egg mixture to the dry ingredients and stir to combine. Do not overmix.
4. Spread the batter evenly in a greased 8 or 9-inch square baking pan or pie plate.
5. Supply your smoker with wood pellets and follow the start-up procedure. Preheat the grill, with the lid closed, to 375° F.
6. Bake the cornbread until it begins to pull away from the sides of the pan and the top is beginning to brown, 25 to 35 minutes. Cut into squares (or wedges, if you used a pie plate) for serving. Grill: 375 °F

Smoked, Salted Caramel Apple Pie

Servings: 4
Cooking Time: 60 Minutes

Ingredients:
- 1 Cup cream
- 1 Cup brown sugar
- 3/4 Cup Light Corn Syrup
- 6 Tablespoon butter
- 1 Teaspoon sea salt
- 1 Pastry for Double-Crust Pie
- 6 Granny Smith Apples, Cut Into Wedges

Directions:
1. Supply your smoker with wood pellets and follow the start-up procedure. Preheat the grill, with the lid closed, to 180° F.
2. Fill a large pan with ice and water. Pour the cream into a smaller, shallow pan. Place the pan with the cream in the ice bath and place them both on the Traeger to smoke for 15-20 minutes. Grill: 180 °F
3. To make the caramel, combine the sugar and corn syrup in a saucepan and cook over medium heat, stirring constantly until it coats the back of your spoon and starts to turn a copper color, then stir in butter, salt, and smoked cream.
4. To assemble the pie, gather the pie crust, salted caramel, and apples. Place one of the pie crusts into the pie plate and fill with apple slices. Pour caramel over the apples. Lay the top crust over the filling, then crimp the top and bottom crusts together.
5. Make slits in the top crust to release the steam and finish by brushing with egg or cream. Sprinkle with raw sugar and sea salt.
6. When ready to bake, set the Traeger to 375°F and preheat, lid closed for 15 minutes.
7. Place the pie on the grill and bake for 20 minutes. Grill: 375 °F
8. Reduce heat to 325°F and cook for 25 more minutes. When ready, the crust should be golden brown and the filling, bubbly. Grill: 325 °F
9. Remove the pie from the grill and let cool. Serve with vanilla ice cream. Enjoy!

Smoky Pimento Cheese Cornbread

Servings: 4
Cooking Time: 30 Minutes

Ingredients:
- 2 Tsp Baking Powder
- 2 Cups Buttermilk, Low Fat
- 1/2 Cup Cornmeal, Yellow
- 2 Egg
- 1 1/2 Cups Flour, All-Purpose
- 16 Oz Pimento Cheese Spread
- 2 Tbsp Bacon Cheddar Seasoning
- 1/4 Cup Sugar

Directions:
1. Supply your smoker with wood pellets and follow the start-up procedure. Preheat the grill, with the lid closed, to 350° F. Place a cast iron skillet in the grill to preheat.
2. In a bowl, mix together the eggs, buttermilk, Bacon Cheddar Seasoning, and pimento cheese spread. Add in the sugar, baking powder, cornmeal and flour. Mix until well combined.
3. With cooking gloves, carefully remove the cast iron skillet from the grill, grease it, and add the cornbread batter.
4. Grill for 25-30 minutes, or until the cornbread is golden and pulling away from the edges of the skillet.

Beer Bread

Servings: 4
Cooking Time: 60 Minutes

Ingredients:
- 400 g all-purpose flour
- 2 Tablespoon sugar
- 1 Tablespoon baking powder
- 1 Teaspoon salt
- 12 Ounce beer
- 2 Tablespoon honey
- 6 Tablespoon butter, melted

Directions:
1. Supply your smoker with wood pellets and follow the start-up procedure. Preheat the grill, with the lid closed, to 350° F.
2. Spray a loaf pan (9x5x3 inches) (55x12x20 cm) with nonstick cooking spray and set aside.
3. Put the flour, sugar, baking powder, and salt in a large mixing bowl. Whisk with a wire whisk to combine and aerate. Add the beer and honey and stir with a wooden spoon until the batter is just mixed. (Do not overmix.) If desired, gently stir in one or more of the optional add-ins.
4. Pour half of the melted butter in the prepared loaf pan and spoon in the batter. Pour the remainder of the butter over the top of the loaf.
5. Put the loaf pan directly on the grill grate and bake until a wooden skewer or toothpick inserted in the center of the loaf comes out clean, 50 to 60 minutes, and the bread is golden-brown. (Note: If using a glass loaf pan, the baking time might be shorter.)
6. Let the loaf cool slightly in the pan before removing from the pan. Leftovers make great toast.
7. Optional Add-ins: Bacon, cooked and crumbled, 1 cup (100 g) Grated Cheese, Red Bell Pepper and Onion, diced and sauted in Butter (1/4 cup each), Green Onions, minced, Dried Herbs such as Dill, Rosemary, Mixed Italian Herbs, etc,.Cracked Black Pepper, Your favorite Barbecue Rub, such as Traeger's Pork and Poultry Shake, Ground Cinnamon, Dry Ranch Dressing Mix, Coarse-grained Mustard.

Baked Buttermilk Biscuits

Servings: 4
Cooking Time: 15 Minutes

Ingredients:
- 2 Cup all-purpose flour
- 1/4 Cup butter
- 3/4 Cup buttermilk

Directions:
1. Supply your smoker with wood pellets and follow the start-up procedure. Preheat the grill, with the lid closed, to High heat. Spoon the flour into a measuring cup and level with a knife.
2. Put the flour into a mixing bowl. Using a pastry blender, cut the butter into the flour until the mixture resembles coarse crumbs.
3. With a fork, gently stir in just enough of the buttermilk so the dough leaves the sides of the bowl. (You may not need all the buttermilk.) For the most tender biscuits, do not overmix.
4. Lightly flour a work surface as well as your hands. Tip the dough onto the floured surface and gently bring together using your fingertips. (Re-flour your hands or the board if the dough is too sticky.) Knead two or three times, just to bring the dough together.
5. With a floured rolling pin, lightly and quickly roll the dough out to a thickness of about 1/2". Using a 1-1/2" floured cutter, cut out as many biscuits as you can. (Do not twist the cutter; push it straight down.) You can reroll the scraps if desired, but the "second string" biscuits will be tougher.
6. Transfer the biscuits to an ungreased baking sheet. Using a pastry brush, brush the tops with melted butter. Bake until golden brown, 10 to 15 minutes. Enjoy! Grill: 500 °F

Baked Potatoes & Celery Root Au Gratin

Servings: 2
Cooking Time: 60 Minutes

Ingredients:
- 5 Tablespoon butter, softened
- 2 Large leeks, white parts only, cleaned and sliced into half moons
- kosher salt
- freshly ground black pepper
- 5 Small Yukon Gold potatoes, sliced 1/4 inch thick
- 2 Whole celery root, peeled and sliced 1/4 inch thick
- 2 Cup cream
- 1 Tablespoon minced sage
- 1 Cup shredded Gruyere or other hearty Swiss cheese, divided

Directions:
1. Supply your smoker with wood pellets and follow the start-up procedure. Preheat the grill, with the lid closed, to 400° F.
2. Butter a 9x13 baking dish with 1 tablespoon of the softened butter. In a medium frying pan over medium heat, melt the remaining butter. Add the leeks and a generous pinch of salt and pepper and cook, stirring often until softened, about 5 minutes.
3. Remove from the heat and allow to cool. Place the potato and celery root slices into a large mixing bowl. Add the cream, leek mixture, minced sage, 1 teaspoon salt, 1/2 teaspoon pepper and 1 cup cheese. Stir gently to coat.
4. Arrange a layer of potato and celery root slices so they're slightly overlapping in the prepared baking dish. Repeat two more times so there are three layers of potatoes. Pour remaining cream from the bowl over the gratin, then sprinkle the top with the remaining cup of cheese.
5. Cover the dish loosely with foil and bake on the grill for 45 minutes. Remove the foil and continue baking until the top is golden and bubbly and the potatoes are tender when pierced, about 30 to 45 minutes longer. Let stand for 10 minutes before serving. Enjoy!

Lemon Chicken, Broccoli, String Beans Foil Packs

Servings: 4
Cooking Time: 20 Minutes

Ingredients:
- 2 Cups Broccoli
- 3 Tbsp Butter, Melted
- 4 Chicken, Boneless/Skinless
- 1 Garlic, Minced
- 1 1/2 Tsp Italian Seasoning, Dried
- 1 Lemon, Sliced
- Pepper
- Salt
- 1 Cup String Beans

Directions:
1. Supply your smoker with wood pellets and follow the start-up procedure. Preheat the grill, with the lid closed, to 450° F.
2. Lay four 12 x 12 inch pieces of foil out on a flat surface, then place one chicken breast in the middle of each foil.
3. Divide the broccoli and string beans between the four foil packs. Thinly slice the lemon, split them between each foil pack, and place the slices on, in and around the chicken and vegetables.
4. Mix the butter, garlic, juice of the remaining lemon, and Italian seasoning together, and then brush over the chicken and vegetables. Sprinkle with salt and pepper to taste.
5. Fold the foil over the chicken and vegetables to close the pack, and pinch the ends together so the pack will remain closed.
6. Grill for 7-9 minutes on each side. Turn off grill, remove the foil packets, and serve immediately.

Smoked Cheesy Alfredo Sauce

Servings: 2
Cooking Time: 40 Minutes

Ingredients:
- 1 Cup heavy cream
- 1 Stick butter
- 1 block Parmesan cheese
- 1 Sprig fresh sage
- 2 Pinch Nutmeg

Directions:
1. Supply your smoker with wood pellets and follow the start-up procedure. Preheat the grill, with the lid closed, to 180° F.
2. Pour the cream into a saucepan along with the butter and place on the Traeger grill grate to smoke along with the parmesan cheese.
3. Smoke for 30 minutes to 1 hour, depending on how much smoke flavor you want. Turn the heat on the Traeger up to 300°F. Grill: 180 °F
4. Shred the parmesan cheese and add it and the sage sprig into the pan with the cream and butter.
5. Whisk until the cheese has all melted and season to taste with the salt and pepper and a pinch or two of the ground nutmeg.
6. While warm, pour this sauce on anything. Enjoy!

Tarte Tatin

Servings: 6
Cooking Time: 55 Minutes

Ingredients:
- 2 Cup all-purpose flour
- 1 Teaspoon salt
- 1 Cup butter
- 5 Tablespoon cold water
- 1/4 Cup unsalted butter
- 3/4 Cup granulated sugar
- 10 Granny Smith Apples, Cut Into Wedges

Directions:
1. Supply your smoker with wood pellets and follow the start-up procedure. Preheat the grill, with the lid closed, to 350° F.
2. For the crust: Place flour and salt in a food processor and pulse to mix. Add butter a little at a time while pulsing. Once it starts to looks like cornmeal, add the water until dough start to come together. Form a round with the dough, wrap in plastic and let it cool in the refrigerator.
3. While dough cools, place a pie dish or a 10-inch round cake pan on the grill; add butter and sugar to pie dish. Let it caramelize.
4. When the sugar caramelizes and has come to a dark amber color, take off grill. Arrange apple wedges in a fan formation covering the caramel.
5. Roll the pie crust into a circle big enough to cover the pan. Prick the pie dough with a fork and cover the pan with the pie dough. Trim the crust leaving room for shrinkage.
6. Place on the grill and bake for 55 minutes until apples are soft. Let sit for 3 minutes. While pan is still hot, place a plate over pie and flip over. Grill: 350 °F
7. Serve warm, topped with ice cream or whipped cream. Enjoy!

Sweet And Spicy Baked Pork Beans

Servings: 20
Cooking Time: 120 Minutes

Ingredients:
- 1 - 21 Oz Apple Pie Filling, Can
- 1 Gallon Baked Beans
- 1 Tbs Chilli, Powder
- 1 Green Bell Pepper, Diced
- 1 10 Oz Drained Jalapeno, Can Diced
- 1 Cup Maple Syrup
- 1 Onion, Diced
- 1 Lb Pork, Pulled

Directions:
1. Supply your smoker with wood pellets and follow the start-up procedure. Preheat the grill, with the lid closed, to 350° F.
2. Place all ingredients in mixing bowl and mix well.
3. Pour bean mixture into foil pans.
4. Bake in grill till bubbling throughout – about 2 hours.
5. Rest at least 15 minutes before serving.

Marbled Brownies With Amaretto & Ricotta

Servings: 4
Cooking Time: 30 Minutes

Ingredients:
- 1 Cup Ricotta Cheese
- 1 eggs
- 1 Tablespoon Amaretto Liqueur
- 1/4 Cup sugar
- 2 Teaspoon cornstarch
- 1/2 Teaspoon vanilla extract
- 1 Brownie Mix

Directions:
1. Coat a 9- by 13-inch nonstick baking pan with cooking spray or softened butter and set aside. (If you do not have a nonstick pan, line a regular one with buttered foil or parchment paper.)
2. In a medium bowl, combine the ricotta, egg, amaretto, sugar, cornstarch, and vanilla and whisk together thoroughly. Set aside.
3. Prepare the brownie mix according to the package directions. Spread the brownie batter evenly in the prepared pan. Randomly drop dollops of the ricotta mixture over the batter. Run a plastic knife through the ricotta mixture to give the brownies a marbled look. (A plastic knife is less likely to scratch your pan's nonstick surface.)
4. Supply your smoker with wood pellets and follow the start-up procedure. Preheat the grill, with the lid closed, to 350° F.
5. Put the pan with the brownie mixture directly on the grill grate and bake, about 25 to 30 minutes. Insert a bamboo skewer or toothpick in the center of the brownies to determine if they are done: the batter should not be wet. Grill: 350 °F
6. Transfer the brownies to a wire cooling rack to cool completely. Cut into squares.

Maple Syrup Pancake Casserole

Servings: 6
Cooking Time: 60 Minutes

Ingredients:
- 2 Tbsp Butter
- 1/2 Cup Chocolate Chips
- 4 Egg
- Maple Syrup
- 12 - 14 Pancakes
- Powdered Sugar
- 1/4 Cup Sugar, Granulated
- 1 Tsp Vanilla Extract
- 1 1/2 Cup Whole Milk

Directions:
1. In a mixing bowl, whisk together flour, baking powder, sugar, and salt. Then pour in the milk, egg and melted butter; mix until smooth.
2. Supply your smoker with wood pellets and follow the start-up procedure. Preheat the grill, with the lid closed, to medium-low heat. If using a gas or charcoal grill, preheat a large cast iron skillet over medium-low heat.
3. Lightly oil the griddle, then scoop the batter onto the griddle, using approximately ¼ cup for each pancake. Cook 1 to 2 minutes per side, until golden brown. Set aside to cool for 15 minutes, then assemble the casserole.

Smoker Wheat Bread

Servings: 6
Cooking Time: 60 Minutes

Ingredients:
- As Needed extra-virgin olive oil
- 2 Cup all-purpose flour
- 1 Cup whole wheat flour
- 1 1/4 Ounce Packet, Active Dry Yeast
- 1 1/4 Teaspoon salt
- 1 1/2 Cup water
- As Needed Cornmeal

Directions:
1. Oil a large mixing bowl and set aside. In a second mixing bowl, combine the flours, yeast, and salt.
2. Push your sleeve up to your elbow and form your fingers into a claw. Mix the dry ingredients until well-combined.
3. Add the water and mix until blended. The dough will be wet, shaggy, and somewhat stringy.
4. Tip the dough into the oiled mixing bowl and cover with plastic wrap.
5. Allow the dough to rise at room temperature-- about 70 degrees-- for 2 hours, or until the surface is bubbled.
6. Turn the dough out onto a lightly floured work surface and lightly flour the top. With floured hands, fold the dough over on itself twice. Cover loosely with plastic wrap and allow the dough to rest for 15 minutes.
7. Dust a clean lint-free cotton towel with cornmeal, wheat bran, or flour. With floured hands, gently form the dough into a ball and place it, seam side down, on the towel.
8. Dust the top of the ball with cornmeal, wheat bran, or flour, and cover the dough with a second towel. Let the dough rise until doubled in size; the dough will not spring back when poked with a finger.
9. In the meantime, start the smoker grill and set temperature to 450 F. Preheat, lid closed, for 10-15 minutes.
10. Put a lidded 6- to 8-quart cast iron Dutch oven - preferably one coated with enamel, on the grill grate.
11. When the dough has risen, remove the top towel, slide your hand under the bottom towel to support the dough, then carefully tip the dough, seam side up, into the preheated pot.
12. Remove the towel. Shake the pot a couple of times if the dough looks lopsided: It will straighten out as it bakes.
13. Cover the pot with the lid and bake the bread for 30 minutes. Remove the lid and continue to bake the bread for 15 to 30 minutes more, or until it is nicely browned and sounds hollow when rapped with your knuckles.
14. Turn onto a wire rack to cool. Slice with a serrated knife. Enjoy!

Strawberry Basil Daiquiri

Servings: 2
Cooking Time: 20 Minutes

Ingredients:
- 4 strawberries, stemmed
- 6 Tablespoon granulated sugar, divided
- 6 basil leaves
- 3 Ounce white rum
- 2 Ounce lime juice
- 1 Ounce Smoked Simple Syrup
- 2 fresh basil leaves, for garnish
- 2 lime slice, for garnish

Directions:
1. Supply your smoker with wood pellets and follow the start-up procedure. Preheat the grill, with the lid closed, to 375° F.
2. Cut strawberries in half and coat in 2 tablespoons granulated sugar. Place directly on grill grate and cook for 15 to 20 minutes. Remove from heat and cool. Grill: 375 °F
3. Add 1 tablespoon granulated sugar and basil leaves to shaking tin and lightly muddle. Add strawberries and muddle again.
4. Pour in white rum, lime juice and Smoked Simple Syrup. Shake with ice.
5. Strain contents into a chilled glass and garnish with large fresh basil leaf and sliced lime. Enjoy!

Grilled Beer Cheese Dip

Servings: 6
Cooking Time: 20 Minutes

Ingredients:
- 6 Oz Beer, Can
- 8 Oz Cream Cheese
- 1 Tsp Onion Powder
- ½ Tsp Pepper
- ½ Tsp Salt
- 2 Cups Shredded Cheese

Directions:
1. Supply your smoker with wood pellets and follow the start-up procedure. Preheat the grill, with the lid closed, to 350° F. If you're using a gas or charcoal grill, set it up for medium high heat. Preheat with lid closed for 10-15 minutes.
2. In the cast iron pan add cream cheese, shredded cheese, beer, onion powder, salt and pepper. Once grill is at 350°F place cast iron skillet onto the grill and cook for about 10 minutes, stir and cook for another 5-10 minutes.
3. Top with more shredded cheese and fresh parsley. Serve with fresh baked pretzels as well.

Baked Brie

Servings: 6
Cooking Time: 8 Minutes

Ingredients:
- 16 Ounce (16 oz) brie wheel
- 1/3 Cup honey
- 1/4 Cup pecans
- Crackers
- apple, sliced

Directions:
1. Supply your smoker with wood pellets and follow the start-up procedure. Preheat the grill, with the lid closed, to 350° F.
2. Line a rimmed baking sheet with a piece of parchment or aluminum foil. Using a sharp serrated knife, slice top—the white rind—off the brie. (Le the ave the rind on the sides and bottom intact.)
3. Put the brie, cut side up, on the prepared baking sheet and drizzle with the honey. Sprinkle nuts on top.
4. Bake the brie until it is soft and oozing, but not melting, 8 to 10 minutes. Let it cool for a couple of minutes and transfer to a serving plate. Grill: 350 °F
5. Serve with crackers and sliced apple wedges. Drizzle with more honey, if desired. Enjoy!

Skillet Buttermilk Cornbread

Servings: 6
Cooking Time: 25 Minutes

Ingredients:
- 1 Cup Cornmeal
- 1 Cup all-purpose flour
- 1/3 Cup granulated sugar
- 1 Teaspoon salt
- 1 Teaspoon baking powder
- 1 1/2 Cup buttermilk
- 2 Whole eggs
- 8 Tablespoon butter, melted

Directions:
1. Grease a cast iron skillet or 9-inch square baking pan with bacon fat. Put a 10-inch well-seasoned cast iron skillet on the grill grate. If using a regular baking pan, do not preheat.
2. Supply your smoker with wood pellets and follow the start-up procedure. Preheat the grill, with the lid closed, to 400° F.
3. In a large mixing bowl, combine the cornmeal, flour, sugar, salt, and baking powder and whisk to mix thoroughly. Make a well in the center of the dry ingredients.
4. In a separate mixing bowl, whisk together the buttermilk and eggs until well-combined. Add the melted butter. Pour into the dry ingredients and mix until the batter is fairly smooth. Do not overmix.
5. Carefully pour the batter into the preheated skillet. Bake for 20 to 25 minutes, or until the top is firm and a tester inserted in the center of the cornbread comes out clean. Be careful when removing the skillet from the grill as it will be very hot. Let the cornbread cool slightly on a trivet or cooling rack before slicing into wedges or squares.

Pretzel Rolls

Servings: 6
Cooking Time: 20 Minutes

Ingredients:
- 2 3/4 Cup Bread Flour
- 1 Quick-Rising Yeast, envelope
- 1 Teaspoon salt
- 1 Teaspoon sugar
- 1/2 Teaspoon celery seed
- 1/2 Teaspoon Caraway Seeds
- 1 Cup hot water
- As Needed Cornmeal
- 8 Cup water
- 1/4 Cup baking soda
- 2 Tablespoon sugar
- 1 Whole Egg White
- Coarse salt

Directions:
1. Combine bread flour, 1 envelope yeast, salt, 1 teaspoon sugar, caraway seeds and celery seeds in food processor or standing mixer with dough hook and blend.
2. With machine running, gradually pour hot water, adding enough water to form smooth elastic dough. Process 1 minute to knead. (You could also knead it by hand for a few minutes.)
3. Grease medium bowl. Add dough to bowl, turning to coat. Cover bowl with plastic wrap, then towel; let dough rise in warm draft-free area until doubled in volume, about 35 minutes.

4. Flour a large baking sheet. Punch dough down and knead on lightly floured surface until smooth. Divide into 8 pieces. Form each dough piece into a ball.
5. Place dough balls on prepared sheet, flattening each slightly. Using serrated knife, cut X in top center of each dough ball. Cover with towel and let dough balls rise until almost doubled in volume, about 20 minutes.
6. When ready to cook, start the smoker on Smoke with the lid open until a fire is established (4-5 minutes). Turn temperature to 375 F (190 C) and preheat, lid closed, for 10 to 15 minutes.
7. Grease another baking sheet and sprinkle with cornmeal. Bring water to boil in large saucepan. Add baking soda and sugar (water will foam up). Add 3 rolls (or however many will fit comfortably in the pot) and cook 30 seconds per side.
8. Using slotted spoon, transfer rolls to prepared sheet, arranging X side up. Repeat with remaining rolls. Brush rolls with egg white glaze. Sprinkle rolls generously with coarse salt.
9. Bake rolls until brown, about 20 to 25 minutes. Transfer to racks and cool 10 minutes. Serve rolls warm or at room temperature. Enjoy!

Chili Cheese Fries

Servings: 6
Cooking Time: 10 Minutes

Ingredients:
- 1 Cup Cheddar Cheese, Shredded
- 1 Cup Chili Con Carne, Prepared
- 1 Bag French Fries
- 1 Tablespoon Olive Oil
- 1 Tablespoon Sweet Heat Rub

Directions:
1. Supply your smoker with wood pellets and follow the start-up procedure. Preheat the grill, with the lid closed, to 350° F. If you're using charcoal or gas, set it up for medium high heat.
2. Bake the fries according to manufacturer's instructions. Once the fries are done, place them in a large bowl and add the olive oil and Sweet Heat Rub. Toss the fries to coat. Once everything is well coated with the oil and seasoning, spread the fries on a baking sheet.
3. Top the fries with the chili and the shredded cheddar cheese. Place the baking sheet on the grill and grill for 7-10 minutes, or until the cheese is melted and bubbly, and the chili is warm all the way through.
4. Remove the baking sheet from the grill and serve the fries immediately.

Spiced Lemon Cherry Pie

Servings: 6-8
Cooking Time: 60 Minutes

Ingredients:
- 1/2 Teaspoon Cinnamon, Ground
- 1/2 Teaspoon Cloves, Ground
- 1/2 Cup Cornstarch
- 1 Pound Frozen Sweet Dark Cherries, Thawed
- 1 Teaspoon Water (Beaten With Egg) 1 Egg
- 1 Lemon, Juice
- 1 Lemon, Zest
- 2 Prepared Store Bought Or Homemade Pie Crust
- 1 Teaspoon Hickory Honey Sea Salt Seasoning
- 1 Cup Sugar, Granulated
- 1 Teaspoon Vanilla Extract

Directions:
1. In a large bowl, mix together the thawed cherries and their juices, sugar, cornstarch, lemon zest, lemon juice, cinnamon, clove, vanilla extract and Hickory Honey Sea Salt. Allow to sit for 30 minutes.
2. Flour a work surface and roll out one of the prepared pie crusts so that it fits a 9 inch pie tin. Fill with the cherry pie filling and refrigerate. When the pie is chilled, roll out the second pie crust, brush the edge of the first pie crust with the egg mixture, top with the second pie crust, crimp the edge with a fork, and chill. Alternatively, cut the second pie crust into strips and form a lattice pattern, attaching the strips with the egg mixture. Chill the pie for 15-30 minutes, or until the dough is very cold and firm. Brush the top of the pie with the remaining egg mixture.
3. Supply your smoker with wood pellets and follow the start-up procedure. Preheat the grill, with the lid closed, to 350° F and grill for 45 minutes to 1 hour, or until the pie crust is golden and firm and the filling is bubbly. Remove from the grill and allow to cool at room temperature for at least 4 hours to set the filling, then serve and enjoy!

Cinnamon Pull-aparts

Servings: 6
Cooking Time: 20 Minutes

Ingredients:
- 16.3 Ounce Biscuits, Homestyle, Canned
- 1 Cup packed brown sugar
- 1/2 Cup butter
- 1/4 Cup water
- 1 Teaspoon ground cinnamon
- 1/2 Cup Nuts (optional)

Directions:
1. Cut each biscuit into 4 pieces and peel each piece in half; set aside.
2. Combine brown sugar, butter and water in a large saucepan and bring to a boil; reduce heat and simmer for 1 minute. Stir in cinnamon and nuts; add biscuit quarters and mix to coat. Pour

into greased 13 by 9 inch casserole dish and spread evenly in the dish.

3. Supply your smoker with wood pellets and follow the start-up procedure. Preheat the grill, with the lid closed, to 350° F.

4. Place the casserole dish on the grill; close lid and cook for 20 to 25 minutes or until the biscuits are done. Grill: 350 °F

5. Remove from the grill and transfer to a serving platter making sure to get all the gooey syrup onto the biscuits. Serve warm. Enjoy!

Savory Cheesecake With Bourbon Pecan Topping

Servings: 6
Cooking Time: 75 Minutes

Ingredients:
- Crust
- 12 ounce Oreos
- 6 ounce melted butter
- Filling
- 24 ounces cream cheese - room temperature
- 1 cup granulated sugar
- 3 tbs cornstarch
- 2 large eggs
- 2/3 cup heavy cream
- 1 tbs vanilla
- 1 1/2 tbs bourbon
- Topping
- 3 large eggs beaten
- 1/3 cup granulated sugar
- 1/3 cup brown sugar
- 8 tbsp corn syrup dark corn syrup recommended
- 2 tbsp bourbon
- 1/2 tbsp vanilla
- 1/8 tbsp salt
- 3/4 cup rough chopped pecans (smoked pecans recommended)

Directions:

1. Supply your smoker with wood pellets and follow the start-up procedure. Preheat the grill, with the lid closed, to 350 °F.
2. Wrap foil on the bottom and up the sides of a 9" spring-form pan (outside of pan).
3. Butter the bottom & insides of the pan.
4. Crust
5. Throw ingredients in a food processor until they are finely ground.
6. Spread in 9" cheesecake pan on bottom & about ½ way upsides.
7. Filling
8. Place 8 oz of cream cheese in mixer bowl with 1/3 of sugar & cornstarch.Mix until smooth andcreamy.
9. Add another 8 oz cream cheese andbeat until smooth, then add remaining cream cheese,beating until smooth.
10. Then mix in the rest of the sugar, bourbon & vanilla.
11. Add eggs one at a time beating well after each one.
12. Add the heavy cream and mix just until smooth. Reminder: Do not over mix.
13. Pour batter into the prepared crust.
14. Topping
15. Mix all together except pecans.
16. Sprinkle pecans on top of cheesecake batter.
17. Pour topping over cheesecake batter.
18. Place in a pan big enough to hold a spring-form pan. Pour boiling water in the roasting pan to come up about ½ way up the spring-form pan.
19. Bake at 350 °F for 75 minutes until the top just barely jiggles. Carefully take the pan out of water-bath and put on cooling rack.
20. Let cool for 2 hours in pan. After 2 hours put in fridge until totally chilled then serve.

Blueberry Sour Cream Muffins

Servings: 8
Cooking Time: 25 Minutes

Ingredients:
- 2 Cup flour
- 1/2 Teaspoon salt
- 1/2 Teaspoon baking soda
- 1/2 Cup butter
- 3/4 Cup sugar, plus more for muffin tops
- 2 Large eggs
- 3/4 Cup sour cream
- 1 1/2 Teaspoon vanilla extract
- 1 1/2 Cup blueberries, fresh or thawed

Directions:

1. In a small mixing bowl, whisk together the flour, salt and baking soda.
2. In another bowl, using a wooden spoon or a mixer, beat the butter and sugar until light-colored and fluffy. Beat in the eggs, one at a time. Stir in sour cream and vanilla.
3. Add the flour mixture gradually and mix just until incorporated. Using a rubber spatula, gently fold in the blueberries.
4. Line a 12-cup muffin tin with the cupcake liners. Using an ice cream scoop or spoon, fill each muffin cup two-thirds full with the batter. Sprinkle sugar evenly over the top of each muffin.
5. Supply your smoker with wood pellets and follow the start-up procedure. Preheat the grill, with the lid closed, to 375° F.
6. Bake the muffins 25 to 30 minutes, or until a toothpick inserted comes out clean. Served warm and with butter. Grill: 375 °F

Donut Bread Pudding

Servings: 8
Cooking Time: 40 Minutes

Ingredients:
- 16 Cake Donuts
- 1/2 Cup Raisins, seedless
- 5 eggs
- 3/4 Cup sugar
- 2 Cup heavy cream
- 2 Teaspoon vanilla extract
- 1 Teaspoon ground cinnamon
- 3/4 Cup Butter, melted, cooled slightly
- Ice Cream

Directions:
1. Lightly butter a 9- by 13-inch baking pan. Layer the donuts in an even thickness in the pan. Distribute the raisins over the top, if using. Drizzle evenly with the butter.
2. Make the custard: In a medium bowl, whisk together the sugar, eggs, cream, vanilla, and cinnamon. Whisk in the butter. Pour over the donuts. Let sit for 10 to 15 minutes, periodically pushing the donuts down into the custard. Cover with foil.
3. Supply your smoker with wood pellets and follow the start-up procedure. Preheat the grill, with the lid closed, to 350° F.
4. Bake the bread pudding for 30 to 40 minutes, or until the custard is set. Remove the foil and continue to bake for 10 additional minutes to lightly brown the top. Grill: 350 °F
5. Let cool slightly before cutting into squares. Drizzle with melted ice cream, if desired. Enjoy!

Crescent Rolls

Servings: 8
Cooking Time: 12 Minutes

Ingredients:
- 1 Crescent Dough, Can

Directions:
1. Supply your smoker with wood pellets and follow the start-up procedure. Preheat the grill, with the lid closed, to 375° F.
2. Unroll the dough and separate into triangles. Roll up the triangles and place on an ungreased nonstick cookie sheet. Bake for 10 -12 minutes on your Grill. You will know that they are finished when the rolls are golden brown.

Smoked Blackberry Pie

Servings: 4-6
Cooking Time: 25 Minutes

Ingredients:
- Nonstick cooking spray or butter, for greasing
- 1 box (2 sheets) refrigerated piecrusts
- 8 tablespoons (1 stick) unsalted butter, melted, plus 8 tablespoons (1 stick) cut into pieces
- ½ cup all-purpose flour
- 2 cups sugar, divided
- 2 pints blackberries
- ½ cup milk
- Vanilla ice cream, for serving

Directions:
1. Supply your smoker with wood pellets and follow the start-up procedure. Preheat, with the lid closed, to 375°F.
2. Coat a cast iron skillet with cooking spray.
3. Unroll 1 refrigerated piecrust and place in the bottom and up the side of the skillet. Using a fork, poke holes in the crust in several places.
4. Set the skillet on the grill grate, close the lid, and smoke for 5 minutes, or until lightly browned. Remove from the grill and set aside.
5. In a large bowl, combine the stick of melted butter with the flour and 1½ cups of sugar.
6. Add the blackberries to the flour-sugar mixture and toss until well coated.
7. Spread the berry mixture evenly in the skillet and sprinkle the milk on top. Scatter half of the cut pieces of butter randomly over the mixture.
8. Unroll the remaining piecrust and place it over the top of skillet or slice the dough into even strips and weave it into a lattice. Scatter the remaining pieces of butter along the top of the crust.
9. Sprinkle the remaining ½ cup of sugar on top of the crust and return the skillet to the smoker.
10. Close the lid and smoke for 15 to 20 minutes, or until bubbly and brown on top. It may be necessary to use some aluminum foil around the edges near the end of the cooking time to prevent the crust from burning.
11. Serve the pie hot with vanilla ice cream.

Baked Cast Iron Berry Cobbler

Servings: 6
Cooking Time: 35 Minutes

Ingredients:
- 4 Cup Berries
- 12 Tablespoon sugar
- Cup orange juice
- 2/3 Cup Flour
- 3/4 Teaspoon baking powder
- 1 Pinch salt
- 1/2 Cup butter
- 1 Tablespoon Sugar, raw

Directions:

1. Supply your smoker with wood pellets and follow the start-up procedure. Preheat the grill, with the lid closed, to 350° F.
2. In a 10-inch (25-cm) cast iron or other baking pan, mix together the berries, 4 Tbsp sugar and the orange juice.
3. In a small bowl, mix together the flour, baking powder and salt. Set aside.
4. In a separate bowl, cream together the butter and granulated sugar. Add the egg and vanilla extract and mix to combine. Gradually fold in the flour mixture.
5. Spoon the batter on top of the berries and sprinkle raw sugar on top.
6. Bake the cobbler for approximately 35-45 minutes. Cool slightly and serve with whipped cream. Enjoy! Grill: 350 °F

Baked Green Chile Mac & Cheese By Doug Scheiding

Servings: 8
Cooking Time: 120 Minutes

Ingredients:
- 24 Ounce shredded cheddar cheese, divided
- 8 Ounce mozzarella cheese, shredded
- 6 Tablespoon unsalted butter
- 16 Ounce large dry elbow macaroni noodles
- 2 1/2 Cup half-and-half
- 2 Cup heavy whipping cream
- 8 Ounce cream cheese
- 16 Ounce 505 Southwestern Hatch Valley Flame Roasted Green Chile
- 2 Tablespoon Prime Rib Rub

Directions:
1. Supply your smoker with wood pellets and follow the start-up procedure. Preheat the grill, with the lid closed, to 165° F.
2. Place 16 ounces of the shredded cheddar and the 8 ounces of shredded mozzarella cheese into a shallow pan or cookie sheet and place the pan directly on the grill grate. Smoke for 30 to 40 minutes. Remove from grill and set aside. Grill: 165 °F
3. Increase the grill temperature to 300°F and place a large disposable aluminum half pan in the Traeger with the butter. Remove the pan from the grill after the butter has fully melted. Grill: 300 °F
4. Add the noodles to the pan, along with half-and-half, heavy whipping cream, 16 ounces of the cold smoked cheddar, all of the smoked mozzarella cheese and cream cheese broken into small pieces. Add the green chiles to taste (12 ounces for mild and 16 ounces for spicy) and stir to combine.
5. Place the pan in the grill and bake for 2 hours, stirring every 20 minutes. If macaroni and cheese looks like it is getting dry, add a little more half-and-half and stir to combine. Grill: 300 °F
6. During the last 20 minutes of cooking, sprinkle the remaining (unsmoked) cheddar cheese on top and add a light dusting of Traeger Prime Rib Rub. Serve hot. Enjoy!

Basil Margherita Pizza

Servings: 6
Cooking Time: 25 Minutes

Ingredients:
- Basil, Chopped
- 2 Cups Flour, All-Purpose
- Mozzarella Cheese, Sliced Rounds
- 1 Cup Pizza Sauce
- 1 Teaspoon Salt
- 1 Teaspoon Sugar
- 1 Tomato, Sliced
- 1 Cup Water, Warm
- 1 Teaspoon Yeast, Instant

Directions:
1. Combine the water, yeast, and sugar in a small bowl and let sit for about 5 minutes.
2. In a large bowl, stir together the flour and salt. Pour in the yeast mixture and mix until a soft dough forms. Knead for about 2 minutes. Place in an oiled bowl and cover with a cloth. Let the dough sit and rise for about 45 minutes or until the dough has doubled in size.
3. Roll out on a flat, floured surface (or on a pizza stone) until you"ve reached your desired shape and thickness.
4. Supply your smoker with wood pellets and follow the start-up procedure. Preheat the grill, with the lid closed, to 350° F.
5. On the rolled out dough, pour on the pizza sauce, cheese, and then tomatoes and basil. Place in your Grill and bake for about 25 minutes, or until the cheese is melted and slightly golden brown.

Sopapilla Cheesecake By Doug Scheiding

Servings: 8
Cooking Time: 45 Minutes

Ingredients:
- 2 Tablespoon softened butter
- 24 Ounce cream cheese
- 2 Cup granulated sugar, divided
- 2 Teaspoon vanilla
- 2 Can Pillsbury Butter Flake Crescent Rolls
- 1/2 Cup butter, melted
- cinnamon

Directions:
1. Coat a 9x13 inch baking dish with 2 tablespoons softened butter and set aside.

2. Supply your smoker with wood pellets and follow the start-up procedure. Preheat the grill, with the lid closed, to 350° F.
3. In a mixer, combine cream cheese, 1 to 1-1/2 cups of sugar and vanilla. Mix for 60 to 90 seconds on high with paddle attachment.
4. Take crescents out of the refrigerator. Open one can and place into the buttered 9x13 inch rectangular metal pan or glass dish. Make sure to fill in the gaps in this bottom layer of crescents.
5. Put the cream cheese mixture on the top of the crescent layer using a spatula to make it level.
6. Open the second can of crescents and put on top of the cream cheese layer, again filling in the gaps in the crescents to cover middle.
7. Pour 1/2 cup of melted butter on the top of the last layer of crescent. Start on sides first then middle.
8. Then sprinkle 1/4 cup to 1/2 cup of sugar over the entire pan followed by a light, even dusting of cinnamon.
9. Place pan directly on the grill grate and bake for 40 to 50 minutes until top is brown and starting to get crusty. Grill: 350 °F
10. Remove from grill and let cool 5 to 10 minutes. This allows the cheesecake to set which makes portioning easier. This dessert can be served warm or cold. Enjoy!

Focaccia

Servings: 6
Cooking Time: 40 Minutes

Ingredients:

- 1 Cup warm water (110°F to 115°F)
- 1/2 Ounce Yeast, active
- 1 Teaspoon sugar
- 2 1/2 Cup flour
- 1 Teaspoon salt
- 1/4 Cup extra-virgin olive oil
- 1 1/2 Teaspoon Italian herbs, dried
- 1/8 Teaspoon red pepper flakes
- As Needed coarse sea salt

Directions:

1. Measure the water in a glass-measuring cup. Stir in the yeast and sugar. Let rest for in a warm place. After 5 to 10 minutes, the mixture should be foamy, indicating the yeast is "alive." If it does not foam, discard it and start again.
2. Pour the water/yeast mixture in the bowl of a food processor. Add 1 cup of the flour as well as the salt and 1/4 cup of olive oil. Pulse several times to blend. Add the remaining flour, Italian herbs, and hot pepper flakes.
3. Process the dough until it's smooth and elastic and pulls away from the sides of the bowl, adding small amounts of flour or water through the feed tube if the dough is respectively too wet or too dry.
4. Let the dough rise in the covered food processor bowl in a warm place until doubled in bulk, about 1 hour5. Remove the dough from the food processor (it will deflate) and turn onto a lightly floured surface.
5. Oil two 8- to 9-inch round cake pans generously with olive oil. (Just pour a couple of glugs in and tilt the pan to spread the oil.) Divide the dough into two equal pieces, shape into disks, and put one in each prepared cake pan.
6. Oil the top of each disk with olive oil and dimple the dough with your fingertips. Sprinkle lightly with coarse salt, and if desired, additional dried Italian herbs.
7. Cover the focaccia dough with plastic wrap and let the dough rise in a warm place, about 45 minutes to an hour.
8. When ready to cook, start the smoker grill and set the temperature to 400F and preheat, lid closed, for 10 to 15 minutes.
9. Put the pans with the focaccia dough directly on the grill grate. Bake until the focaccia breads are light golden in color and baked through, 35 to 40 minutes, rotating the pans halfway through the baking time.
10. Let cool slightly before removing from the pans. Cut into wedges for serving.

Baked Pear Tarte Tatin

Servings: 6
Cooking Time: 45 Minutes

Ingredients:

- 2 1/2 Cup all-purpose flour
- 2 Tablespoon sugar
- butter chilled
- 8 Tablespoon cold water
- 1/4 Cup granulated sugar
- 1/4 Cup butter
- 8 Whole Bartlett Pear

Directions:

1. Supply your smoker with wood pellets and follow the start-up procedure. Preheat the grill, with the lid closed, to 350° F.
2. For the crust: Place flour and sugar in a food processor and pulse to mix. Add butter a little at a time while pulsing. Once it starts to looks like cornmeal, add the water until dough start to come together.
3. Form a round with the dough, wrap in plastic and let it cool in the refrigerator.
4. While dough cools, make the caramel sauce. In a sauce pan, add 1/4 cup granulated sugar and 1/4 cup butter. Cook butter and sugar until it becomes a dark caramel, a couple minutes.
5. Pour caramel in the bottom of 10 inch deep cake pan. While the caramel is still hot, arrange pear wedges in a fan formation covering the caramel.

6. Roll the chilled pie dough into a circle big enough to cover the pan. Prick the pie dough with a fork and cover the pan with the pie dough. Trim the crust leaving room for shrinkage.
7. Place on the grill and bake for 45 minutes or until pears are soft. The pears will be soft and most of the juice will evaporate and thicken.
8. Let sit for 3 minutes. While pan is still hot, place a plate over pie and flip over. Slowly lift the plate.
9. Serve warm, topped with vanilla ice cream or whipped cream. Enjoy!

Baked Bourbon Maple Pumpkin Pie

Servings: 6-8
Cooking Time: 60 Minutes

Ingredients:
- 1/4 Cup Cocoa Powder, Unsweetened
- 1 Tablespoon Cocoa Powder, Unsweetened
- 3 1/2 Tablespoon sugar
- 1 Teaspoon salt
- 1 1/4 Cup all-purpose flour
- 1 Tablespoon all-purpose flour
- 6 Tablespoon butter
- 2 Tablespoon vegetable oil
- 1 Large Egg Yolk
- 1/2 Teaspoon apple cider vinegar
- 1/4 Cup ice water
- 1 Large egg, beaten
- 15 Ounce Pumpkin, canned
- 1/4 Cup sour cream
- 2 Tablespoon bourbon
- 1 Teaspoon ground cinnamon
- 1/2 Teaspoon salt
- 1/4 Teaspoon ground ginger
- 1/4 Teaspoon ground nutmeg
- 1/8 Teaspoon Allspice, ground
- 1/8 Teaspoon Mace, ground
- 3 Large eggs
- 3/4 Cup maple syrup
- 2 Tablespoon sugar
- 1/2 Vanilla Bean, halved
- 1 Cup heavy cream

Directions:
1. For the Chocolate Pie Dough: Pulse cocoa powder, granulated sugar, salt, and 1-1/4 cups plus 1 Tbsp flour in a food processor to combine. Add butter and shortening and pulse until mixture resembles coarse meal with a few pea-sized pieces of butter remaining. Transfer to a large bowl.
2. Whisk together the egg yolk, vinegar, and 1/4 cup ice water in a small bowl. Drizzle half of the egg mixture over flour mixture and, using a fork, mix gently just until combined. Add remaining egg mixture and mix until the dough just comes together (you will have some unincorporated pieces).
3. Turn out dough onto a lightly floured surface, flatten slightly, and cut into quarters. Stack pieces on top of one another. Placing unincorporated dry pieces of dough between layers, and press down to combine. Repeat process twice more (all pieces of dough should be incorporated at this point). Form dough into a 1" thick disk. Wrap in plastic; chill at least 1 hour.
4. Roll out a disk of dough on a lightly floured surface into a 14" round. Transfer to a 9" pie dish. Lift up the edge and allow the dough to slump down into the dish. Trim. Leaving about 1" overhang. Fold overhang under and crimp edge. Chill in freezer 15 minutes.
5. When ready to cook, set the smoker to 350°F and preheat, lid closed for 15 minutes.
6. Line pie with parchment paper or heavy-duty foil, leaving a 1-1/2" overhang. Fill with pie weights or dried beans. Bake until crust is dry around the edge, about 20 minutes.
7. Remove paper and weights and bake until surface of the crust looks dry, 5-10 minutes.
8. Brush bottom and sides of crust with 1 beaten egg. Return to grill and bake until dry and set, about 3 minutes longer.
9. For the Pumpkin Maple Filling: Whisk together pumpkin puree, sour cream, bourbon, cinnamon, salt, ginger, nutmeg, allspice, mace (optional) and remaining 3 eggs in a large bowl; set aside.
10. Pour maple syrup and 2 tbsp sugar in a small saucepan. Scrape in the seeds from vanilla bean (reserve pod for another use) or add vanilla extract and bring syrup to a boil. Reduce heat to medium-high and simmer, stirring occasionally, until mixture is thickened and small puffs of steam start to release about 3 minutes.
11. Remove from heat and add cream in 3 additions, stirring with a wooden spoon after each addition until smooth. Gradually whisk hot maple cream into pumpkin mixture.
12. Place pie dish on a rimmed baking sheet and pour in pumpkin filling. Bake pie, rotating halfway through, until set around edge but center barely jiggles 50-60 minutes.
13. Transfer pie dish to a wire rack and let the pie cool. Slice and serve. Enjoy!

Smokin' Lemon Bars

Servings: 8-12
Cooking Time: 60 Minutes

Ingredients:
- 3/4 Cup lemon juice
- 1 1/2 Cup sugar
- 2 eggs
- 3 Egg Yolk
- 1 1/2 Teaspoon cornstarch

- Pinch sea salt
- 4 Tablespoon unsalted butter
- 1/4 Cup olive oil
- 1/2 Tablespoon lemon zest
- 1 1/4 Cup flour
- 1/4 Cup granulated sugar
- 3 Tablespoon Confectioner's Sugar
- 1 Teaspoon lemon zest
- 1/4 Teaspoon Sea Salt, Fine
- 10 Tablespoon Unsalted Butter, Cut Into Cubes

Directions:
1. When ready to cook, set grill temperature to 180°F and preheat, lid closed for 15 minutes.
2. In a small mixing bowl, whisk together lemon juice, sugar, eggs and yolks, cornstarch and fine sea salt. Pour into a sheet tray or cake pan and place on grill. Smoke for 30 minutes whisking mixture halfway through smoking. Remove from grill and set aside.
3. Pour mixture into a small saucepan. Place on stove top set to medium heat until boiling. Once boiling, boil for 60 seconds. Remove from heat and strain through a mesh strainer into a bowl. Whisk in cold butter, olive oil, and lemon zest.
4. To make a crust, pulse together the flour, granulated sugar, confectioners' sugar, lemon zest and salt in a food processor. Add butter and pulse until just mixed into a crumbly dough. Press dough into a prepared 9" by 9" baking dish lined with parchment paper that is long enough to hang over 2 of the sides.
5. When ready to cook, set the smoker to 350°F and preheat, lid closed for 15 minutes.
6. Bake until crust is very lightly golden brown, about 30 to 35 minutes.
7. Remove from grill and pour the lemon filling over the crust. Return to grill and continue to bake until filling is just set about 15 to 20 minutes.
8. Allow to cool at room temperature, then refrigerate until chilled before slicing into bars. Sprinkle with confectioners' sugar and flaky sea salt right before serving. Enjoy!

Bananas Rum Foster

Servings: 4
Cooking Time: 10 Minutes

Ingredients:
- 1/3 Cup Banana Nectar
- 4 Bananas, Quartered
- 3/4 Cup Brown Sugar
- 1/4 Cup Butter
- 1/2 Tsp Cinnamon, Ground
- 1/3 Cup Dark Rum
- Vanilla Ice Cream

Directions:

1. Supply your smoker with wood pellets and follow the start-up procedure. Preheat the grill, with the lid closed, to medium heat. If using a gas or charcoal grill, preheat a cast iron skillet.
2. Place a large skillet on the griddle, then melt butter in the skillet. Whisk in brown sugar and cinnamon, stirring until sugar dissolves.
3. Add the banana nectar and bananas. Stir to coat
4. Once the bananas begin to soften and turn brown, add the rum. Stir, then ignite the sauce with a stick lighter. After the flames subside, simmer the sauce for 2 minutes.
5. Divide the bananas among 4 scoops/bowls of vanilla ice cream, then spoon the warm sauce over the top of the ice cream. Serve immediately.

Smoked Lemon Tea

Servings: 6 - 8
Cooking Time: 60 Minutes

Ingredients:
- 8 Black Tea Bags
- 4 Cups Boiling Water
- 2 Cups Ice
- 8 Lemons
- 2 Cups Sugar
- 2 Cups Water

Directions:
1. Place the tea bags in a heat-safe pitcher. Bring 4 Cups of water to a boil and pour over tea bags. Let steep for 5-10 minutes. Remove tea bags and set pitcher aside to cool.
2. Turn on your grill and set to smoke mode. Combine 2 cups of sugar and 2 cups water in a small aluminum pan. Smoke for about 45 minutes, stirring occasionally, or until the mixture reduces to a thick, simple syrup. Remove from the grill and let it cool.
3. Supply your smoker with wood pellets and follow the start-up procedure. Preheat the grill, with the lid closed, to 450° F. If using a charcoal or gas grill, set heat to high.
4. Cut the lemons in half and sear over the flame broiler until charred, about 7 minutes. Remove from grill and set aside to cool.
5. Juice the lemons into a medium bowl. Pour lemon juice through a metal strainer into the tea pitcher to remove seeds and pulp.
6. Pour the cooled simple syrup into pitcher and stir until fully incorporated with tea and lemons. Add 2 cups of ice and refrigerate until serving.

Baked Molten Chocolate Cake

Servings: 4
Cooking Time: 20 Minutes

Ingredients:
- all-purpose flour
- butter
- 4 Ounce butter
- 6 Ounce Chocolate, Bittersweet
- 2 eggs
- 2 egg yolk
- 1/2 Cup sugar
- 1 Pinch salt

Directions:
1. Supply your smoker with wood pellets and follow the start-up procedure. Preheat the grill, with the lid closed, to 450° F.
2. Butter and flour four (6oz) ramekins. Tap out excess flour. Place ramekins on a baking sheet and reserve.
3. Melt butter and chocolate in a double boiler over simmering water. In a medium bowl, beat eggs and yolks with sugar and salt on high until thick and pale.
4. Whisk in chocolate until smooth and quickly fold into the egg mixture along with flour.
5. Spoon the batter into prepared ramekins and bake for 20 minutes or until sides are firm but centers are soft. Grill: 450 °F
6. Let cool for 1 minute, then cover each with an inverted dessert plate. Carefully turn each over, let stand 10 seconds, then unmold.
7. Serve immediately with Maple Ice Cream with Candied Bacon. Enjoy!

The Dan Patrick Show Pull-apart Pesto Bread

Servings: 8
Cooking Time: 25 Minutes

Ingredients:
- 1 Sourdough Bread, loaf
- 1/2 Cup butter, melted
- 1 Cup Pesto Sauce
- 1 1/2 Cup Italian Cheese Blend

Directions:
1. Supply your smoker with wood pellets and follow the start-up procedure. Preheat the grill, with the lid closed, to 350° F.
2. Using a serrated knife, make 1" diagonal cuts through the bread leaving the bottom crust intact. Turn the bread and make diagonal cuts in the opposite direction, creating diamonds.
3. Place the bread on a sheet of foil large enough to wrap around the entire loaf. Pour the melted butter into the cracks in the bread. Using a spoon spread the pesto into the cracks then follow with the cheese stuffing it down into each crack.
4. Fold up the edges of the foil to wrap up the loaf and transfer to a baking sheet. Place the baking sheet directly on the grill grate.
5. Bake for 15 minutes then unwrap the foil and cook for an additional 10 minutes. Remove from the grill and serve. Enjoy! Grill: 350 °F
6. Follow along as we give you a recipe each day this week from The Dan Patrick Show Game Day Recipes eBook.

Vanilla Cheesecake Skillet Brownie

Servings: 2
Cooking Time: 30 Minutes

Ingredients:
- 1 Box Brownie Mix
- 1 Package Cream Cheese
- 2 Egg
- 1/2 Cup Oil
- 1 Can Pie Filling, Blueberry
- 1/2 Cup Sugar
- 1 Tsp Vanilla
- 1/4 Cup Water, Warm

Directions:
1. Combine all brownie ingredients and mix. In a separate bowl, combine cream cheese, sugar, egg and vanilla and mix until smooth. Grease skillets and pour in brownie batter. Top with cheesecake and cherry pie filling, using a knife to blend to give it that marbled look.
2. Supply your smoker with wood pellets and follow the start-up procedure. Preheat the grill, with the lid closed, to 350°F and bake for about 30 minutes.
3. Let cool for about 10 minutes and enjoy!

Double Chocolate Chip Brownie Pie

Servings: 8-12
Cooking Time: 45 Minutes

Ingredients:
- 1/2 Cup Semisweet Chocolate Chips
- 1 Cup butter
- 1 Cup brown sugar
- 1 Cup sugar
- 4 Whole eggs
- 2 Teaspoon vanilla extract
- 2 Cup all-purpose flour
- 333/500 Cup Cocoa Powder, Unsweetened
- 1 Teaspoon baking soda
- 1 Teaspoon salt
- 1 Cup Semisweet Chocolate Chips
- 3/4 Cup White Chocolate Chips
- 3/4 Cup Nuts (optional)
- 1 Whole Hot Fudge Sauce, 8oz

- 2 Tablespoon Guinness Beer

Directions:
1. Coat the inside of a 10-inch (25 cm) pie plate with non-stick cooking spray.
2. When ready to cook, set the grill temperature to 350°F (180 C) and preheat, lid closed for 15 minutes.
3. Melt 1/2 cup (100 g) of the semi sweet chocolate chips in the microwave. Cream together butter, brown sugar and granulated sugar. Beat in the eggs, adding one at a time and mixing after each egg, and the vanilla. Add in the melted chocolate chips.
4. On a large piece of wax paper, sift together the cocoa powder, flour, baking soda and salt. Lift up the corners of the paper and pour slowly into the butter mixture.
5. Beat until the dry ingredients are just incorporated. Stir in the remaining semi sweet chocolate chips, white chocolate chips, and the nuts. Press the dough into the prepared pie pan.
6. Place the brownie pie on the grill and bake for 45-50 minutes or until the pie is set in the middle. Rotate the pan halfway through cooking. If the top or edges begin to brown, cover the top with a piece of aluminum foil.
7. In a microwave-safe measuring cup, heat the fudge sauce in the microwave. Stir in the Guinness.
8. Once the brownie pie is done, allow to sit for 20 minutes. Slice into wedges and top with the fudge sauce. Enjoy.

Caramelized Bourbon Baked Pears

Servings: 4
Cooking Time: 30 Minutes

Ingredients:
- 3 Whole Pears, fresh
- 1/4 Cup brown sugar
- 1/4 Cup bourbon
- 2 Tablespoon butter, melted
- 1 Teaspoon vanilla extract
- 1/2 Teaspoon salt

Directions:
1. Supply your smoker with wood pellets and follow the start-up procedure. Preheat the grill, with the lid closed, to 325° F.
2. Peel and core the pears. Arrange them in a buttered baking dish.
3. In a small bowl, combine the brown sugar, bourbon, butter, vanilla, cinnamon and salt. Pour the bourbon mixture over the pears.
4. Place the baking dish on the grill grate, close the lid and bake for 30-35 minutes or until the pears are fork tender. Grill: 325 °F
5. Transfer to a serving plate and spoon the caramelized bourbon mixture over the pears.
6. Serve warm over vanilla ice cream. Enjoy!

Eggs Ham Benedict

Servings: 6
Cooking Time: 15 Minutes

Ingredients:
- 1 Biscuit Dough, Tube
- 6 Egg
- 16 Ham, Sliced
- 1 Packet Hollandaise Sauce, Package

Directions:
1. Supply your smoker with wood pellets and follow the start-up procedure. Preheat the grill, with the lid closed, to 350° F.
2. Grease a muffin tin and crack an egg in each cup. Place on the grate of the for about 10 minutes or until the whites are fully cooked.
3. At the same time, place your biscuit dough on a greased pan. Follow the directions on the packaging but bake on the . Place 2 slices of ham per biscuit on the pan as well.
4. While the ham, eggs, and biscuits are cooking, prepare the Hollandaise Sauce according to the directions on the packet.
5. When everything is fully cooked, cut a biscuit in half, and stack one or two slices of ham, 1 egg and a dollop of Hollandaise sauce. Repeat for each half biscuit. Serve with fresh fruit.

Pumpkin Bread

Servings: 6
Cooking Time: 60 Minutes

Ingredients:
- 1 Cup Pumpkin, canned
- 2 eggs
- 2/3 Cup vegetable oil
- 1/2 Cup sour cream
- 1 Teaspoon vanilla extract
- 2 1/2 Cup flour
- 1 1/2 Teaspoon baking soda
- 1 Teaspoon salt
- 1/2 Teaspoon ground cinnamon
- 1/4 Teaspoon ground nutmeg
- 1/4 Teaspoon ground cloves
- 1/4 Teaspoon ground ginger
- As Needed butter

Directions:
1. In a large mixing bowl, combine the pumpkin, eggs, vegetable oil, sour cream, and vanilla and whisk to blend.
2. In a separate bowl, combine the flour, baking soda, salt, cinnamon, nutmeg, cloves, and ginger. Add the dry ingredients to the wet ingredients and stir to combine. Do not overmix.

3. If desired, stir in one or more of the optional ingredients (walnuts, dried cranberries, raisins, or chocolate chips). Butter the interiors of two loaf pans.
4. Sprinkle with flour to coat the buttered surfaces, and tap out any excess. Divide the batter evenly between the two pans.
5. When ready to cook, set the smoker to 350°F and preheat, lid closed for 15 minutes.
6. Arrange the loaf pans directly on the grill grate. Bake for 45 to 50 minutes, or until a skewer or toothpick inserted in the center comes out clean. Also, the top of the loaf should spring back when pressed gently with a finger.
7. Transfer the loaf pans to a cooling rack and let cool for 10 minutes before carefully turning out the pumpkin bread. Let the loaves cool thoroughly before slicing. Wrap in aluminum foil or plastic wrap if not eating right away. Serve and enjoy!

Quick Baked Dinner Rolls

Servings: 8
Cooking Time: 30 Minutes

Ingredients:
- 2 Tablespoon quick-rise yeast
- 1 Teaspoon salt
- 1/4 Cup sugar
- 3 1/3 Cup flour
- 1/4 Cup unsalted butter, softened
- 1 egg
- cooking spray
- 1 egg, for egg wash

Directions:
1. Combine yeast and warm water in a small bowl to activate the yeast. Let sit until foamy, about 5-10 minutes.
2. Combine salt, sugar, and flour in the bowl of a stand mixer fitted with the dough hook. Pour water and yeast into the dry ingredients with the machine running on low.
3. Add butter and egg and mix for 10 minutes gradually increasing the speed from low to high.
4. Form the dough into a ball and place in a buttered bowl. Cover with a cloth and let the dough rise for approximately 40 minutes.
5. Transfer the risen dough to a lightly floured surface and divide into 8 pieces forming a ball with each.
6. Lightly spray a cast iron pan with cooking spray and arrange balls in the pan. Cover with a cloth and let rise 20 minutes.
7. Supply your smoker with wood pellets and follow the start-up procedure. Preheat the grill, with the lid closed, to 375° F.
8. Brush rolls with egg wash and then bake for 30 minutes until lightly browned. Serve hot. Enjoy! Grill: 375 °F

Baked Pumpkin Pie

Servings: 6
Cooking Time: 50 Minutes

Ingredients:
- 4 Ounce cream cheese
- 15 Ounce pumpkin puree
- 1/3 Cup Cream, whipping
- 1/2 Cup brown sugar
- 1 Teaspoon pumpkin pie spice
- 3 Large eggs
- 1 frozen pie crust, thawed

Directions:
1. Supply your smoker with wood pellets and follow the start-up procedure. Preheat the grill, with the lid closed, to 325° F.
2. Mix cream cheese, puree, milk, sugar, and spice. One at a time, incorporate an egg to the mixture. Pour mixture into pie shell.
3. Bake for 50 minutes, edges should be golden and pie should be firm around edges with slight movement in middle. Let cool before whip cream is applied. Serve and enjoy! Grill: 325 °F

Delicious Peanut Butter Cookies

Servings: 24
Cooking Time: 15 Minutes

Ingredients:
- 1 Egg
- 1 Cup Peanut Butter
- 1 Cup Sugar

Directions:
1. Supply your smoker with wood pellets and follow the start-up procedure. Preheat the grill, with the lid closed, to High heat.
2. Combine all ingredients in a bowl. Drop tablespoon amounts of dough on a prepared baking sheet and bake in your Grill for 15-20 minutes. Allow cookies to cool for 5 minutes on the baking sheet before you enjoy!

Delicious Pellet Grill Cornbread

Servings: 6
Cooking Time: 35 Minutes

Ingredients:
- 1 cup flour
- 1 cup cornmeal
- 2 teaspoons baking powder
- 2 teaspoons salt
- 3/4 cup sugar
- 2 tablespoons honey
- 1/2 cup butter
- 1 cup sour cream

- 3 eggs
- 1 cup milk

Directions:
1. Supply your smoker with wood pellets and follow the start-up procedure. Preheat the grill, with the lid closed, to 350° F.
2. Grease a 12-inch cast iron skillet or an equivalent baking pan.
3. Add flour, cornmeal, baking powder, salt, sugar, honey, butter, sour cream, eggs, and milk into a mixing bowl.
4. Mix well then pour into pan and bake on the grill for 30-35 minutes or until the cornbread is baked through in the center.

Baked Chocolate Brownie Cookies With Egg Nog

Servings: 6
Cooking Time: 12 Minutes

Ingredients:
- 16 Ounce Bar bittersweet chocolate, finely chopped
- 4 Tablespoon unsalted butter, room temperature
- 4 eggs
- 1 1/3 Cup granulated sugar
- 1 Teaspoon vanilla extract
- 1 1/2 Cup all-purpose flour
- 1/2 Teaspoon baking powder
- 1 Cup semisweet chocolate chips

Directions:
1. Supply your smoker with wood pellets and follow the start-up procedure. Preheat the grill, with the lid closed, to 350° F.
2. Line two baking sheets with parchment paper.
3. Put the finely chopped chocolate and butter in a heatproof bowl and set over a saucepan of barely simmering water; stir occasionally until chocolate is completely melted and smooth. Set aside and allow to cool to room temperature.
4. Whisk together eggs, sugar and vanilla extract in a medium bowl. Set aside.
5. Sift together the flour and baking powder in a small bowl. Add the melted chocolate mixture to the egg mixture and stir with a rubber spatula until completely combined.
6. Add the flour mixture in three batches, folding gently into the batter with a spatula. Once all of the flour has been incorporated, stir in the chocolate chips.
7. Scoop 1-1/2 tablespoons of dough onto prepared baking sheets. Bake for 10 to 12 minutes or until they are firm on the outside. Do not over bake. Grill:350° F
8. Leave to cool completely on the baking sheets. Enjoy!

Butternut Squash Macaroni And Cheese

Servings: 2
Cooking Time: 50 Minutes

Ingredients:
- 1 Medium butternut squash
- 2 Cup macaroni, uncooked
- 1 Small yellow onion
- 1/2 Cup chicken broth
- 1 Cup milk
- salt
- pepper
- 1 Cup cheese, grated

Directions:
1. Supply your smoker with wood pellets and follow the start-up procedure. Preheat the grill, with the lid closed, to 225° F.
2. Puncture butternut squash with a fork several times and place on grill grate. Cook until tender, about 40 minutes to an hour. When cooked, scoop out meat and discard seeds. Grill: 225 °F
3. Cook elbow macaroni according to package instructions. Drain and set aside.
4. In a medium skillet, sauté chopped onion until fragrant and golden. Add broth, milk, salt, onions and butternut squash to a food processor. Puree until smooth and creamy. Add salt and pepper to taste.
5. Pour pureed sauce over cooked noodles and add the shredded cheese. Stir to melt the cheese and add milk to reach desired consistency. Serve warm. Enjoy!

Traeger Baked Protein Bars

Servings: 6
Cooking Time: 25 Minutes

Ingredients:
- 2 Cup Frozen Sweet Cherries
- 1 Cup Apricots, Frozen
- 1 Scoop Vanilla Protein Powder
- 2 Tablespoon honey
- 1 Teaspoon vanilla extract
- 1 Cup rolled oats

Directions:
1. Supply your smoker with wood pellets and follow the start-up procedure. Preheat the grill, with the lid closed, to 350° F.
2. In the bowl of a food processor, add cherries, apricots (revived in hot water for 5 minutes and drained), vanilla protein powder, honey, and vanilla. Pulse about 10 to 15 times, to break the fruit into smaller pieces and to mix all ingredients.
3. In a separate bowl, fold together oats and fruit mixture. Transfer mixture to a loaf pan or silicone mold and place in grill.
4. Bake for approximately 20 to 25 minutes. Grill: 350 °F
5. Let cool completely and cut into 8 pieces. Enjoy!

Sourdough Pizza

Servings: 4
Cooking Time: 12 Minutes

Ingredients:
- 1 1/2 Cup Fresh Sourdough Starter
- 1 Tablespoon olive oil
- 1 Teaspoon Jacobsen Salt Co. Pure Kosher Sea Salt
- 1 1/4 Cup all-purpose flour

Directions:
1. Supply your smoker with wood pellets and follow the start-up procedure. Preheat the grill, with the lid closed, to 450° F.
2. Mix together the fresh sourdough starter, one tablespoon of oil, Jacobsen salt and 1-1/4 cups of flour. Add more flour, a little at a time, as needed to form a pizza dough consistency.
3. Allow the dough to rest for 30 minutes, to allow for easier rolling. Roll the dough out into a circle, using a small amount of flour to prevent sticking.
4. Place on a pizza stone. Bake the crust for approximately 7 minutes Grill: 450 °F
5. Remove the crust from the grill; brush on remaining oil to prevent toppings from soaking into the crust. Add the desired toppings and return pizza to grill; bake until the crust browns and the cheese melts.

Rosemary Cranberry Apple Sage Stuffing

Servings: 7
Cooking Time: 45 Minutes

Ingredients:
- 10 Cups Day Old Diced Bread, Sliced Loaf
- 2 1/2 Cups Broth, Chicken
- 1 Cup Butter, Unsalted
- 1 Cup Diced Celery, Cut
- 1 1/2 Cups Fresh Cranberries
- 1 Beaten Egg
- 1 Medium Granny Smith Apple, Peel, Core And Dice
- 2 Tbsp Minced Parsley, Fresh
- 1 Tbsp Minced Rosemary, Fresh
- 2 Tbsp Roughly Chopped Sage
- Salt And Pepper
- 1 Tbsp Minced Thyme
- 2 Cups Diced Yellow Onion, Sliced

Directions:
1. Supply your smoker with wood pellets and follow the start-up procedure. Preheat the grill, with the lid closed, to 350° F.
2. Melt butter over medium heat. Add onions then celery and cook until onions start to become translucent.
3. In a large bowl, mix together bread, apples, cranberries, cooked onion and celery mixture, and fresh herbs.
4. Add half of the chicken broth to the mixture and stir.
5. Beat together eggs and the rest of the chicken broth in a small bowl. Pour into the bread mixture and stir until completely combined.
6. Add salt and pepper to taste.
7. Pour stuffing into a cast iron pan or baking dish. Cover with foil and bake on the grill for 30 minutes. Remove the foil and cook for an additional 15 minutes.
8. Serve immediately and enjoy!

Ultimate Baked Garlic Bread

Servings: 4
Cooking Time: 20 Minutes

Ingredients:
- 1 baguette
- 1/2 Cup softened butter
- 1/2 Cup mayonnaise
- 4 Tablespoon chopped Italian parsley
- 6 Clove garlic, minced
- salt
- chile flakes
- 1 Cup mozzarella cheese
- 1/2 Cup Parmesan cheese

Directions:
1. Supply your smoker with wood pellets and follow the start-up procedure. Preheat the grill, with the lid closed, to 375° F.
2. Lay baguette on a cutting board and cut it in half lengthwise.
3. In a bowl, add butter, mayonnaise, parsley, garlic, salt and chile flakes. Mix well.
4. Spread butter mixture on baguette halves and top with mozzarella and Parmesan cheese.
5. Place baguette on the grill (if you like the bread crisp, do not use foil and if you like it soft, wrap with foil). Grill for approximately 15 to 25 minutes. Serve warm. Enjoy! Grill: 375 °F

Sweet Cheese Muffins

Servings: 3
Cooking Time: 15 Minutes

Ingredients:
- 1 package butter cake mix
- 1 package Jiffy Corn Muffin Mix
- 1 cup self-rising or cake flour
- 12 tablespoons (1½ sticks) unsalted butter, softened, plus 8 tablespoons (1 stick) melted
- 3½ cups shredded Cheddar cheese
- 2 eggs, beaten, at room temperature
- 2¼ cups buttermilk
- Nonstick cooking spray or butter, for greasing
- ¼ cup packed brown sugar

Directions:
1. Supply your smoker with wood pellets and follow the start-up procedure. Preheat, with the lid closed, to 375°F.
2. In a large mixing bowl, combine the cake mix, corn muffin mix, and flour.
3. Slice the 1½ sticks of softened butter into pieces and cut into the dry ingredients. Add the cheese and mix thoroughly.
4. In a medium bowl, combine the eggs and buttermilk, then add to the dry ingredients, stirring until well blended.
5. Coat three 12-cup mini muffin pans with cooking spray and spoon ¼ cup of batter into each cup.
6. Transfer the pans to the grill, close the lid, and smoke, monitoring closely, for 12 to 15 minutes, or until the muffins are lightly browned.
7. While the muffins are cooking, make the topping: In a small bowl, stir together the remaining 1 stick of melted butter and the brown sugar until well combined.
8. Remove the muffins from the grill. Brush the tops with the sweet butter and serve warm.

Smoky Apple Crepes

Servings: 6
Cooking Time: 60 Minutes

Ingredients:
- 1/2 Cup Apple Juice
- 2 Lbs Apples
- 2 Tbsp Brown Sugar
- 5 Tbsp Butter
- 3 Tbsp Butter, Melted
- Tt Caramel
- 3/4 Tsp Cinnamon, Ground
- Tt Cinnamon-Sugar
- 3/4 Tsp Cornstarch
- 2 Eggs
- 1 Cup Flour
- 2 Tsp Lemon Juice
- Tennessee Apple Butter Seasoning
- 1/2 Cup Water
- 3/4 Cup Milk

Directions:
1. Supply your smoker with wood pellets and follow the start-up procedure. Preheat the grill, with the lid closed, to 225° F. If using a gas or charcoal grill, set it up for low, indirect heat.
2. Peel, halve, and core apples.
3. Season apples with Tennessee Apple Butter then place directly on the grill grate, and smoke for 1 hour.
4. Meanwhile, prepare crêpe batter: combine eggs, milk, water, flour, and 3 tbsp of melted butter in a blender, and blend until smooth.
5. Refrigerate for 30 minutes.
6. Remove apples from grill, cool slightly, then slice thin.
7. Place a cast iron skillet on the grill and melt 3 tbsp butter with brown sugar, cinnamon, cornstarch, apple and lemon juices. Cook for 5 minutes until thick.
8. Add apples and cook for another 3 to 5 minutes, stirring to coat apples in sauce.
9. Remove from grill and set aside.
10. Preheat griddle to medium-low. If using a standard grill, preheat a cast iron skillet on medium-low heat.
11. Melt 1 teaspoon of butter on the griddle.
12. Then add ½ cup of batter, and spread with the bottom of a metal spatula, working quickly, as the batter cooks fast.
13. Cook one minute per side, until edges begin to brown. Remove from griddle, set aside, and repeat with remaining batter.
14. Spoon ¼ cup of apple filling into the center of each crêpe, then quarter-fold into a triangle.
15. Serve warm with additional apple filling, drizzle of warm caramel, and a dusting of cinnamon-sugar.

Cake With Smoked Berry Sauce

Servings: 12
Cooking Time: 90 Minutes

Ingredients:
- 12 Oz Blackberries
- 18 Oz Blueberries, Fresh
- 1/4 Cup Brown Sugar
- 2 Tsp Cinnamon, Ground
- 4 Eggs
- 2 Tbsp Flour
- 1 3/4 Cup Granulated Sugar
- 1 Lemon, Juice & Zest
- 1/2 Cup Unsalted Butter
- 3.4 Ounce Box Vanilla Instant Pudding Mix
- 3/4 Cup Vegetable Oil
- 3/4 Cup Water
- 1 Cup White Wine
- 1 Box Yellow Cake Mix

Directions:
1. Fire up your Grill and set to Smoke mode. If using a gas or charcoal grill, set it up for low, indirect heat. Supply your smoker with wood pellets and follow the start-up procedure. Preheat the grill, with the lid closed, to 450° F.
2. Place blueberries and blackberries on a sheet tray, then transfer to upper shelf of smoking cabinet. Make sure that the sear slide and side dampers are open, then preheat the grill, with the lid closed, to 375° F, to ensure the cabinet maintains temperature between 225° F and 250° F. Smoke for 30 to 45 minutes.

3. Place cast iron skillet on grill grate. Add sugar, lemon juice and zest, and wine to skillet. Stir with a wooden spoon until sugar dissolves, then add berries from smoking cabinet.

4. Simmer berries for 15 minutes, then remove sauce from grill to cool.

5. While berries are smoking, prepare cake pans and batter. Grease and flour 2 - 9-inch round cake pans. Set aside.

6. In a large mixing bowl, combine cake mix, brown sugar, granulated sugar, pudding mix, cinnamon, eggs, water, oil, and white wine. Using a hand mixer, mix on low speed for 1 minute, then slowly increase mixing speed to high, and beat an additional 2 to 3 minutes, or until batter is smooth.

7. Evenly distribute batter among cake pans, then place pans on grill shelf and bake at 350° F, for 25 to 30 minutes, or until a toothpick inserted comes out clean. Remove from grill and set aside to cool slightly.

8. While cake is cooling, prepare glaze. Melt butter with sugar in a sauce pot on the grill. Stir for 3 minutes, then add wine. Remove from grill and set aside.

9. Turn out cake onto a sheet tray lined with parchment. Use a toothpick to poke holes in the cake, then slowly pour hot glaze over cake.

10. Spread half of smoked berry sauce on top of one layer, then place second cake layer on top. Pour additional sauce on top of cake and dust with powdered sugar, if desired. Serve warm, or room temperature.

Chicken Pot Pie

Servings: 6
Cooking Time: 60 Minutes

Ingredients:
- 2 Chicken, Boneless/Skinless
- 1 Cream Of Chicken Soup, Can
- 1 Tsp Curry Powder
- 1/2 Cup Mayo
- 1 1/2 Cups Mixed Frozen Vegetables
- 1 Onion, Sliced
- 2 Frozen Pie Shell, Deep
- 1/2 Cup Sour Cream

Directions:
1. Supply your smoker with wood pellets and follow the start-up procedure. Preheat the grill, with the lid closed, to 425° F.

2. Cut the onion in half and place on the grates of the grill. If you"re using fresh chicken breasts, barbecue the chicken at the same time as the onions. The chicken is fully cooked when the internal temperature reached 170F. While the onion and chicken are cooking, prepare the pie crust by putting one crust in a pie plate. When the chicken and onions are done, shred chicken and chop onion into small pieces and place in the prepared pie plate along with the mixed vegetables.

3. Combine cream of chicken soup, mayo, sour cream, and curry powder in a bowl. Pour into the pie crust with the chicken and mix to combine. Wet the sides of the bottom crust with a small amount of water and top with the second pie crust. Push gently along the sides of the crust to seal the two pie crusts together.

4. Place in the and bake for 40 minutes, or until the crust is golden brown. Serve hot.

Garlic Lemon Pepper Chicken Wings

Servings: 4
Cooking Time: 30 Minutes

Ingredients:
- 1/4 Cup Black Peppercorns, Ground
- 4 Pounds Chicken, Wing
- 2 Tsp Coriander, Ground
- 2 Tsp Garlic Powder
- 2-3 Tbsp Lemon, Zest
- 1 Tsp Salt, Kosher
- 3 Tsp Dried Thyme, Fresh Sprigs

Directions:
1. Supply your smoker with wood pellets and follow the start-up procedure. Preheat the grill, with the lid closed, to 400° F.

2. In a bowl, begin to mix the ground pepper and zest of the lemon together, then add the rest of the ingredients.

3. Place the wings in a bowl and toss with a little olive oil, add a few tablespoons of the seasoning, toss with your hands, then repeat until the wings are well seasoned to your liking.

4. Place the wings on the grill, and cook them for about 15 minutes, then flip and grill for another 15 minutes.

5. Continue to flip the wings, until they are done and crispy. Remove the wings from the grill, and serve.

Garlic Cheese Pull Apart Bread

Servings: 2
Cooking Time: 20 Minutes

Ingredients:
- 1 Loaf Bread, Sourdough Round
- 2 1/2 Tbsp Butter, Salted
- 8 Oz Fontina Cheese
- 1 Grated Garlic, Roasted
- 1/4 Cup Parsley, Minced Fresh
- 1 Tsp Red Flakes Pepper
- 1 Pinch Salt

Directions:
1. Start your Grill on "smoke" with the lid open until a fire is established in the burn pot (3-7 minutes). Supply your smoker

with wood pellets and follow the start-up procedure. Preheat the grill, with the lid closed, to 300° F.

2. In a small bowl, add the soft butter, grated garlic, red pepper flakes, sea salt, and ¼ cup of the chopped parsley, and whisk together. With a bread serrated knife, cut 1-inch slices into the bread, not cutting all the way through the bottom of the load. With a butter knife, spread a thin layer of the butter mixture on each slice of the bread. Take the serrated knife again, and cut across the loaf to form 1 inch squares. Next, slice the cheese into small thin slices, then stuff one slice into each bread opening. Place the bread on a baking sheet, and cover tightly with aluminum foil. Place on the grill for about 10 minutes, remove the foil, and grill for a few more minutes until the top is nicely golden and the cheese is oozing. Remove from the grill, sprinkle with fresh parsley leaves, then serve.

Anzac Coconut Biscuits

Servings: 4
Cooking Time: 30 Minutes

Ingredients:
- This recipe makes a dozen biscuits.
- 1 cup rolled oats
- 3/4 cup raw sugar
- 3/4 cup desiccated coconut
- 1 cup plain flour, sifted
- 125 g butter, melted
- 2 tablespoons Golden Syrup
- 1/2 tsp bicarb soda
- 3 tablespoons boiling water

Directions:
1. Combine and mix thoroughly sifted flour, oats, sugar and coconut in a large bowl.
2. Melt the butter and Golden Syrup over low heat.
3. Add boiling water to the bicarb soda, once dissolved add into the butter/syrup mix, it will bubble/fizz up a bit.
4. Add the liquid into the dry ingredients and mix throughly.
5. Rolls the mix into golf ball size balls and layout on grease proof paper on baking tray and flatten the tops just slightly.
6. Space the balls with about 3 fingers between each ball as they will flatten to about triple the diameter as they cook.
7. Supply your smoker with wood pellets and follow the start-up procedure. Preheat the grill, with the lid closed, to 350° F. Cook for 25-30 minutes until golden brown.
8. Rest on cooling rack until at room temperature then store in air-tight container.

Grilled Apple Pie

Servings: 4
Cooking Time: 40 Minutes

Ingredients:
- 5 Whole Apples
- 1/4 Cup sugar
- 1 Tablespoon cornstarch
- 1 Whole refrigerated pie crust
- 1/4 Cup Peach, preserves

Directions:
1. Supply your smoker with wood pellets and follow the start-up procedure. Preheat the grill, with the lid closed, to 375° F. In a medium bowl, mix the apples, sugar, and cornstarch; set aside.
2. Unroll pie crust. Place in ungreased pie pan. With the back of a spoon, spread preserves evenly on crust. Arrange the apple slices in an even layer in the pie pan. Slightly fold crust over filling.
3. Place a baking sheet upside down on the grill grate to make an elevated surface. Put the pan with pie on top so it is elevated off grill. (This will help prevent the bottom from overcooking.) Cook the pie for 30 to 40 minutes or until crust is golden brown, the filling is bubbly. Grill: 375 °F
4. Remove from grill; cool 10 minutes before serving. Enjoy!
*Cook times will vary depending on set and ambient temperatures.

Traeger Baked Focaccia

Servings: 4
Cooking Time: 40 Minutes

Ingredients:
- 2 1/2 Cup all-purpose flour
- 1 Cup warm water (110°F to 115°F)
- 1 Tablespoon instant yeast
- 1 Teaspoon sugar
- 1 Teaspoon salt
- 3 Tablespoon olive oil, plus more as needed
- 1 Tablespoon fresh herbs such as thyme, rosemary and sage
- 2 Tablespoon freshly grated Parmesan, optional
- flaky sea salt

Directions:
1. Place the flour, water, yeast, sugar, salt and oil in the bowl of a stand mixer and mix for 60 seconds. You may also use a food processor by adding the flour, sugar, salt and yeast to the bowl and process while streaming in the warm water followed by the olive oil. Process until combined and a ball forms.
2. Gently form the sticky dough into a ball, if needed, and place in a well-oiled 12 inch cast iron skillet. Drizzle the top of the dough with more olive oil. Cover with plastic wrap and a kitchen towel and let rise in a warm spot for 45 to 60 minutes.
3. After the dough has risen, press the dough to the edges of the pan and cover it again. Let rise for 15 minutes.
4. Supply your smoker with wood pellets and follow the start-up procedure. Preheat the grill, with the lid closed, to 375° F.

5. Uncover the dough and press it again to the edges of the pan using your fingertips to create divots.
6. Drizzle with olive oil, then sprinkle with herbs, Parmesan and flaky salt.
7. Bake it on the Traeger for 30 to 40 minutes, or until golden brown and cooked through. Allow it to cool slightly before removing from cast iron and slicing. Enjoy! Grill: 375 °F

Blueberry Bread Pudding

Servings: 4
Cooking Time: 60 Minutes

Ingredients:
- 5 eggs
- 3 Cup sugar
- 2 1/2 Cup milk
- 1 1/2 Teaspoon vanilla
- 1 Teaspoon cinnamon
- 1 Pinch salt
- 5 Cup Bread
- 3 Cup blueberries

Directions:
1. Beat the eggs in a large mixing bowl. Whisk in the sugar, milk, vanilla, cinnamon, and salt.
2. In another large bowl, combine the bread and 2 cups (200 g) of the blueberries.
3. Pour the egg mixture over the bread-blueberry mixture and let sit for 30 minutes. Meanwhile, place muffin liners in a muffin tin.
4. Supply your smoker with wood pellets and follow the start-up procedure. Preheat the grill, with the lid open.
5. Spoon the bread-blueberry mixture into the prepared cups; evenly top each with the remaining cup of blueberries, pressing them gently into the pudding with the back of a spoon.
6. Dust the top with sugar.
7. Arrange the pan directly on the grill grate and smoke for 30 minutes. Grill:180°F
8. Increase the temperature to 350F (180 C), and bake until the pudding is set and golden brown on top, about 25 minutes. Grill:350°F
9. Let cool slightly, then sift powdered sugar on top. Serve warm with sweetened whipped cream or vanilla ice cream, if desired.

Vanilla Chocolate Bacon Cupcakes

Servings: 12
Cooking Time: 120 Minutes

Ingredients:
- 1 Lb Bacon
- 1 1/2 Tsp Baking Powder
- 1 1/2 Tsp Baking Soda
- 1 Cup Cocoa, Powder
- 2 Egg
- 1 3/4 Cups Flour
- 1 Cup Milk, Whole
- 1/2 Cup Oil
- 1 Tsp Salt
- 2 Cups Sugar
- 2 Tsp Vanilla

Directions:
1. Supply your smoker with wood pellets and follow the start-up procedure. Preheat the grill, with the lid closed, to 250° F.
2. Once your grill is preheated, place bacon strips on the grates. Smoke for 1hr-1 ½ hours or until desired crispiness is achieved.
3. Remove the bacon from the grill and set aside.
4. Increase set the temperature to 350°F and preheat.
5. Mix the rest of the ingredients in a bowl with an electric mixer until it is nice and smooth.
6. Pour the mixture into a cupcake tin.
7. Transfer the tin to your grill and bake for about 20 - 25 minutes.
8. Allow the cupcakes to cool on a wire rack. Once cooled, top with your favorite premade icing and a half of strip of the bacon. Serve and enjoy!

Dark Chocolate Brownies With Bacon-salted Caramel

Servings: 8
Cooking Time: 40 Minutes

Ingredients:
- 8 Strips bacon
- 1/2 Cup kosher salt
- 1 Whole Brownie Mix
- 1 Jar caramel sauce

Directions:
1. For the bacon salt: Cook a few strips of bacon (6 to 8) until very crisp: 350 degrees for about 25 minutes should do it. Let cool, then pulse in a food processor until finely chopped. Mix with 1/2 cup kosher salt. Store in the refrigerator until ready to use.
2. Supply your smoker with wood pellets and follow the start-up procedure. Preheat the grill, with the lid closed, to 350° F.
3. Mix the brownies according to package directions and pour into a greased pan. Drizzle approximately 2 tablespoons of the caramel sauce over the brownie batter. Sprinkle with approximately 1 teaspoon of the bacon salt. Place directly on the grill grate of your preheated Traeger.
4. Bake the brownies for 20-25 minutes, until the batter has started to set up. Remove from the grill and drizzle with 2 more tablespoons of caramel sauce and sprinkle with more bacon salt.

Return to the grill for 20-25 more minutes, or until a toothpick inserted in the middle of the brownies comes out clean.
5. If you like extra caramel, drizzle another layer of caramel on the hot brownies and sprinkle with a final bit of bacon salt. Allow the brownies to cool completely before cutting them into squares. Clean your knife in between each slice to prevent the brownies from sticking to the knife. Enjoy!

Baked Irish Creme Cake

Servings: 4
Cooking Time: 60 Minutes

Ingredients:
- 1 Cup Pecans, pieces
- 1 Yellow Cake Mix, Boxed
- 1 Vanilla Pudding Mix, Instant Package (3.4oz)
- 4 Large eggs
- 1/2 Cup water
- 1/2 Cup vegetable oil
- 1 Cup Irish Cream Liquor
- 1/2 Cup butter
- 1 Cup sugar

Directions:
1. Grease and flour a 10" (25 cm) Bundt pan. Sprinkle pecans along the bottom.
2. In a large bowl, with a mixer, combine yellow cake mix, pudding mix, eggs, water, oil, and Irish Cream liquor. Pour batter over nuts in the pan.
3. Supply your smoker with wood pellets and follow the start-up procedure. Preheat the grill, with the lid closed, to 325° F.
4. Place Bundt pan on the Traeger and bake for 1 hour, or until a toothpick comes out clean. Remove from heat, cool for 10 minutes. Grill: 325 °F
5. While the cake is cooling, combine the butter, water and sugar and bring to a boil. Boil for 5 minutes, stirring constantly. Remove from heat and add Irish cream liquor.
6. Use a bamboo skewer to poke holes in the cooled cake. Spoon glaze over the cake. Allow cake to absorb the glaze. Enjoy!

S'mores Dip Skillet

Servings: 4-6
Cooking Time: 8 Minutes

Ingredients:
- 2 tablespoons salted butter, melted
- ¼ cup milk
- 12 ounces semisweet chocolate chips
- 16 ounces Jet-Puffed marshmallows
- Graham crackers and apple wedges, for serving

Directions:
1. Supply your smoker with wood pellets and follow the start-up procedure. Preheat, with the lid closed, to 450°F.
2. Place a cast iron skillet on the preheated grill grate and pour in the melted butter and milk, stirring for about 1 minute.
3. Once the mixture starts to heat, top with the chocolate chips in an even layer and arrange the marshmallows standing up to cover all of the chocolate.
4. Close the lid and smoke for 5 to 7 minutes, or until the marshmallows are lightly toasted.
5. Remove from the heat and serve immediately with graham crackers and apple wedges for dipping.

Cast Iron Pineapple Upside Down Cake

Servings: 6
Cooking Time: 40 Minutes

Ingredients:
- 1/4 Cup butter, melted
- 1 Cup brown sugar
- 20 Ounce Pineapple, sliced
- 6 Ounce maraschino cherries
- 1 Whole Yellow Cake Mix, Boxed
- vegetable oil
- eggs

Directions:
1. Supply your smoker with wood pellets and follow the start-up procedure. Preheat the grill, with the lid closed, to 350° F.
2. Pour melted butter into a 12-inch cast iron pan. Sprinkle brown sugar on top of the butter. Arrange pineapple slices on brown sugar, squeezing in as many slices as possible. Place a cherry in center of each pineapple slice; press gently into brown sugar.
3. Make cake batter as directed on box, substituting pineapple juice mixture for as much of the water as possible, and adding in required oil and eggs. Pour batter into cast iron dish, over pineapple and cherries.
4. Place the cast iron pan on the grill grate and cook for 20 minutes. Rotate the pan a half turn to ensure it cooks evenly. Cook for an additional 20 minutes, or until toothpick inserted in center comes out clean.
5. Immediately run knife around side of pan to loosen cake. Place heatproof serving plate upside down onto pan; turn plate and pan over.
6. Leave pan over cake 5 minutes so brown sugar topping can drizzle over cake. Cool 30 minutes. Enjoy!

Baked Cheesy Parmesan Grits

Servings: 4
Cooking Time: 60 Minutes

Ingredients:
- 4 Cup chicken stock
- 3 Tablespoon butter
- 3/4 Teaspoon salt
- 1 Cup quick grits
- 1 Cup shredded cheddar cheese
- pepper
- 1/2 Cup Monterey Jack cheese, shredded
- 1/2 Cup whole milk
- 2 Large eggs

Directions:
1. Supply your smoker with wood pellets and follow the start-up procedure. Preheat the grill, with the lid closed, to 350° F.
2. Butter an 8" baking dish or a 10" cast iron pan.
3. Bring the chicken stock, butter, and salt to boil in medium saucepan. Gradually whisk in grits.
4. Reduce heat to medium and cook until mixture thickens slightly, stirring often about 8 minutes. Remove from heat.
5. Add cheeses and stir until melted. Season with pepper and salt to taste.
6. Whisk together milk and eggs in small bowl. Gradually whisk mixture into grits.
7. Pour the cheese grits into the buttered cast iron pan. Bake until grits feel firm to touch, about 1 hour. Grill: 350 °F
8. Remove from grill and let stand 10 minutes before serving. Enjoy!

Eyeball Cookies

Servings: 20
Cooking Time: 35 Minutes

Ingredients:
- 2 Packages Candy Eyeballs
- Green, Blue And Purple Food Coloring
- 1 Box Of Yellow Gluten Free Cake Mix
- 1/2 Cup (Optional) Granulated Sugar
- 2 Large Eggs
- 1/3 Cup Powdered Sugar
- 1 Teaspoon Pure Vanilla Extract
- 6 Tablespoon Melted Vegan Butter (Unsalted)

Directions:
1. Supply your smoker with wood pellets and follow the start-up procedure. Preheat the grill, with the lid closed, to 350° F.
2. Line two large baking sheets with parchment paper. In a large bowl, combine cake mix, melted butter, eggs (or egg substitute), powdered sugar, sugar (optional), and vanilla and stir until combined. (substitute 2 flax eggs for Vegan – 1 tbsp flax seed meal and 5 tbsp water per egg).
3. Divide dough between 3 bowls and dye each bowl a different color.(We used green, blue and purple).
4. Roll dough into tablespoon-sized balls.
5. Place about 2" apart on the baking sheet and grill until tops have cracked and the tops look set, 8 to 10 minutes. – Turn half way through baking, after 4-5 minutes.
6. Immediately, while the cookies are still warm, stick candy eyeballs all over the cookies.
7. Let cool completely before serving.

Smoked Lemon Cheesecake

Servings: 16
Cooking Time: 130 Minutes

Ingredients:
- For the crust
- Vegetable oil, for oiling the pan
- 12 ounces gingersnaps (about 36) or chocolate icebox cookies (about 36)
- 3 tablespoons light brown sugar
- 8 tablespoons (1 stick) unsalted butter, melted
- For the filling
- 4 packages (8 ounces each) cream cheese, at room temperature
- 1 cup firmly packed light brown sugar
- 2 teaspoons pure vanilla extract
- 2 teaspoons finely grated lemon zest
- 1 tablespoon fresh lemon juice
- 2 tablespoons (1/4 stick) unsalted butter, melted
- 5 large eggs
- Burnt Sugar Sauce (recipes follows, optional)

Directions:
1. Supply your smoker with wood pellets and follow the start-up procedure. Preheat the grill, with the lid closed, to 400° F. Lightly oil the springform pan with vegetable oil and wrap a sheet of aluminum foil around the outside.
2. Make the crust: Break the cookies into pieces and grind with the brown sugar to a fine powder in a food processor. You'll want about 1 3/4 cups of crumbs. Add the melted butter and run the processor in short bursts to obtain a crumbly dough. Press the mixture evenly across the bottom and halfway up the sides of the springform pan. Indirect-grill or bake the crust until lightly browned, 5 to 8 minutes. Transfer the pan to a wire rack and let cool.
3. Make the filling: Wipe out the food processor bowl. Add the cream cheese, brown sugar, vanilla, lemon zest, lemon juice, and butter, and process until smooth. Work in the eggs one by one, processing until smooth after each addition. (You can also use a

stand mixer, beating the cream cheese mixture until smooth and beating in the eggs one at a time.) Pour the filling into the crust. Gently tap the pan on the countertop a few times to knock out any air bubbles.

4. Supply your smoker with wood pellets and follow the start-up procedure. Preheat the grill, with the lid closed, to 225 °F-250 °F.

5. Place the cheesecake in the smoker. Smoke until the top is bronzed with smoke and the filling is set, 1 1/2 to 2 hours. To test for doneness, gently poke the side of the pan—the filling will jiggle, not ripple. Alternatively, insert a slender metal skewer in the center of the cake; it should come out clean.

6. Transfer the cheesecake in its pan to a wire rack to cool to room temperature. Refrigerate until serving; the cheesecake can be made up to 8 hours ahead. Run a slender knife around the inside of the springform pan. Unclasp and remove the ring. (You'll serve the cheesecake off the bottom of the pan.) Let the cheesecake warm slightly at room temperature before serving.

7. If serving with the sauce, pour some of it over the cheesecake and the rest into a pitcher. Cut into wedges and pass the remaining sauce.

Pound Cake

Servings: 8
Cooking Time: 60 Minutes

Ingredients:
- 1 1/2 Cup butter
- 8 Ounce cream cheese
- 3 Cup sugar
- 6 eggs
- 3 Teaspoon Bourbon Vanilla
- 1 Tablespoon lemon zest
- fresh strawberries
- whipped cream

Directions:
1. In a large bowl, cream the butter, cream cheese, and sugar. Add eggs one at a time, whipping in between. Add vanilla and lemon zest, whip.
2. Pour batter into greased loaf pans, about halfway full to allow cake to rise.
3. Supply your smoker with wood pellets and follow the start-up procedure. Preheat the grill, with the lid closed, to 325° F.
4. Place loaf pans on grill and cook for 1 hour - 1 hour and 15 minutes. Check the cake at 45 minutes, if golden brown, cover loosely with foil and continue to cook until a toothpick inserted comes out clean. Grill: 325 °F
5. Cool loaf in pan for 10 minutes before removing to a wire rack.
6. Cut into 1 inch slices and serve with fresh sliced strawberries, top with smoked whip cream.

Grilled Bourbon Pecan Pie

Servings: 6
Cooking Time: 45 Minutes

Ingredients:
- 2 Tbsp Bourbon
- 1/2 Cup Brown Sugar
- 1/3 Cup Unsalted Butter, Melted
- 1/2 Cup Light, 1/2 Cup Dark Corn Syrup
- 3 Egg
- 1/4 Tsp Hickory Honey Smoked Salt
- Decoration Pecan
- 1 1/4 Cup Chopped Pecans, Coarsely Broken
- 1 Prepared Or Homemade Pie Shell, Deep
- 1/2 Cup Sugar
- 1 Tsp Vanilla Extract

Directions:
1. Supply your smoker with wood pellets and follow the start-up procedure. Preheat the grill, with the lid closed, to 375° F. Meanwhile, prepare your pie crust in a 9 cast iron skillet or heat proof pie plate.
2. In a large bowl, beat the eggs until smooth. Add the brown sugar and white sugar and mix until smooth. Add the light corn syrup, dark corn syrup, vanilla, bourbon, melted butter, and Hickory Honey Salt. Mix until smooth. Stir in your chopped pecans and pour into the pie crust. Top with the whole pecans, if desired.
3. Grill covered for 35-45 minutes, until the pie is just set around the edges but still has a slight jiggle in the center.
4. Allow the pie to cool completely before slicing. Enjoy!

Crème Brûlée

Servings: 2
Cooking Time: 45minutes

Ingredients:
- 1 Quart heavy whipping cream
- 1 Pieces Vanilla Bean, split and scraped
- 6 Large egg yolk
- 1 Cup sugar

Directions:
1. Supply your smoker with wood pellets and follow the start-up procedure. Preheat the grill, with the lid closed, to 325° F.
2. Pour the cream into a saucepan over medium-high heat, add the vanilla bean and the scraped seeds. Bring to a boil. Remove from the heat and allow to steep (about 15 minutes). Remove the vanilla bean from saucepan and discard.
3. In a bowl, whisk together egg yolks and 1/2 cup (100 g) of the sugar until the mix starts to lighten in color. Add the cream a little at a time, stirring continually.

4. Pour the mixture into 6 (8 oz) ramekins and place the ramekins into a large roasting pan. Pour hot water into the pan so that it comes halfway up the sides of the ramekins.
5. Place water bath pan on the grill and bake until the Crème Brûlées still jiggle in the center, about 40 to 45 minutes. Grill: 325 °F
6. Remove the ramekins from the roasting pan and refrigerate for at least 2 hours and up to 2 days.
7. To serve, let the Crème Brûlée come to temperature (about 20 minutes) before torching the tops.
8. Sprinkle the remaining 1/2 cup (100 g) sugar equally on top of each ramekin. Using a torch in a circular motion, melt the sugar until it caramelizes and forms a crispy top.
9. Allow the Crème Brûlée to sit for a few minutes before serving. Enjoy!

Chocolate Peanut Cookies

Servings: 4
Cooking Time: 12 Minutes

Ingredients:
- 1/2 Tsp Baking Soda
- 1/2 Cup Brown Sugar
- 1/2 Cup + 1 Tbsp Butter, Unsalted
- 1/3 Cup Cocoa Powder, Dark And Unsweetened
- 2 Eggs, Beaten
- 1 1/2 Cups Flour, All-Purpose
- 1/3 Cup Miniature Chocolate Chips
- 2 Cups Peanut Butter Chips, Divided
- 1/4 Tsp Sea Salt
- 1/2 Cup Sugar, Granulated
- 1 Tsp Vanilla Extract

Directions:
1. Supply your smoker with wood pellets and follow the start-up procedure. Preheat the grill, with the lid closed, to medium-low heat. If using a gas or charcoal grill, preheat a cast iron skillet.
2. In a mixing bowl, whisk together the flour, cocoa powder, baking soda, and salt. Set aside.
3. Set a metal saucepan on the griddle, then add ½ cup of butter to melt. Whisk in the sugars and vanilla extract and cook for 2 minutes. Remove the pan from the griddle, and transfer contents to a large mixing bowl.
4. Slowly pour the beaten eggs into the sugar mixture, whisking constantly to temper the eggs.
5. Add the dry mixture to the wet ingredients until just combined. Fold in 1 cup of peanut butter chips and chocolate chips. Refrigerate mixture for 15 to 30 minutes.
6. Remove the dough from the refrigerator, then add an additional cup of peanut butter chips.
7. Portion dough into 16 to 18 cookie balls.
8. Melt 1 tablespoon of butter on the griddle, then transfer the cookie balls to the griddle. Press down gently on the cookies, then cook for 10 to 12 minutes, flipping halfway.
9. Transfer cookies to a cooling rack for 5 minutes before enjoying.

Bacon Chocolate Chip Cookies

Servings: 2
Cooking Time: 10-12 Minutes

Ingredients:
- 2¾ cups all-purpose flour
- 1½ teaspoons baking soda
- ½ teaspoon salt
- 12 tablespoons (1½ sticks) unsalted butter, softened
- 1 cup light brown sugar
- 1 cup granulated sugar
- 2 eggs, at room temperature
- 2½ teaspoons apple cider vinegar
- 1 teaspoon vanilla extract
- 2 cups semisweet chocolate chips
- 8 slices bacon, cooked and crumbled

Directions:
1. In a large bowl, combine the flour, baking soda, and salt, and mix well.
2. In a separate large bowl, using an electric mixer on medium speed, cream the butter and sugars. Reduce the speed to low and mix in the eggs, vinegar, and vanilla.
3. With the mixer speed still on low, slowly incorporate the dry ingredients, chocolate chips, and bacon pieces.
4. Supply your smoker with wood pellets and follow the start-up procedure. Preheat, with the lid closed, to 375°F.
5. Line a large baking sheet with parchment paper.
6. Drop rounded teaspoonfuls of cookie batter onto the prepared baking sheet and place on the grill grate. Close the lid and smoke for 10 to 12 minutes, or until the cookies are browned around the edges.

Pineapple Cake

Servings: 4
Cooking Time: 30 Minutes

Ingredients:
- 2/3 cup of vegetable oil (olive oil works great, not virgin)
- 3 eggs
- 1/3 cup brown sugar (not too sweet)
- 3/4 cup self raising plain flour
- 1/4 cup wholemeal self raising flour
- 1/3 cup saltanas
- 1/3 cup diced canned pineapple (drained)
- 1/3 cup diced raw walnuts

- 2 large carrots grated
- Icing Ingredients
- 250 grams cream cheese
- 35 grams icing sugar (not too sweet)
- Whole lemon or orange zest

Directions:
1. Mix all ingredients in a large bowl.
2. Place into 6" greased baking tray or un-greased silicone tray.
3. Supply your smoker with wood pellets and follow the start-up procedure. Preheat the grill, with the lid closed, to 190 °F. Cook for 25-30min until golden brown and no dough when probed.
4. Let cool on rack (not directly on plate or board) then apply icing.
5. Whip icing ingredients and place in fridge until ready to coat the cake.

Chocolate Almond Cake

Servings: 8
Cooking Time: 50 Minutes

Ingredients:
- 7 oz good quality dark chocolate; melted
- 5 eggs; separated
- Pinch salt
- 6.5 oz caster sugar
- 7 oz butter; cubed at room temperature
- 7 oz ground almonds
- 1 oz cocoa powder
- 1 tsp. baking powder
- Icing sugar; for dusting

Directions:
1. Supply your smoker with wood pellets and follow the start-up procedure. Preheat the grill, with the lid closed, to 347 °F.
2. Beat together the butter and sugar until light and fluffy. Then beat in the yolks, one at a time.
3. Gently fold in the almonds.
4. Add the melted chocolate and mix well.
5. Beat the egg whites with a pinch of salt in a separate bowl until stiff.
6. Sift the baking powder and cocoa powder into the cake mix and fold in gently, then fold in the egg whites.
7. Pour the mix into an 8.5" round spring form cake tin (greased and lined), smooth over, and bake in the center of the grill for about 50 minutes. If the top starts to dry out after 25-30 minutes, cover with foil.

Cornbread Chicken Stuffing

Servings: 6 - 8
Cooking Time: 95 Minutes

Ingredients:
- 2 Tbsp Butter
- 1 Cup Chicken Stock
- 6 Cups Cornbread, Cubed
- ½ Cup Dried Cranberries
- 1 Egg
- ½ Cup Heavy Whipping Cream
- 1 Lb. Italian Sausage
- 1 Diced Onion
- 1 ½ Tsp Pulled Pork Rub
- 2 Tbsp Sage, Fresh
- ½ Tsp Fresh Thyme

Directions:
1. Supply your smoker with wood pellets and follow the start-up procedure. Preheat the grill, with the lid closed, to 250° F. If using a gas or charcoal grill, set the temp to low heat.
2. Portion sausage into quarter-size pieces and place on mesh grate. Place grate on the grill and cook for 1 hour. Sausage pieces will have a smoky deep brown color. Move the mesh tray of sausage to the side of the grill with indirect heat.
3. Open the Flame Broiler Plate and increase the temperature to 350°F. Place a large cast iron skillet on the grill, over direct flame. Add butter and onions and cook until the onions caramelize lightly, stirring often. Add the sage and thyme and stir to combine.
4. Gently fold in the dried cranberries and cubed cornbread, then add sausage directly from mesh grate.
5. In a small mixing bowl, whisk together the heavy cream, chicken stock, egg, and Pulled Pork Rub. Pour mixture over the cornbread stuffing mix.
6. Cover grill and cook 30 minutes or until heated through and crispy on top.

PORK RECIPES

Fast Ribs

Servings: 5
Cooking Time: 240 Minutes

Ingredients:
- 1 Rack Baby Back Rib
- 1 Bottle Sweet Rib Rub

Directions:
1. Remove the ribs from their packaging and pat dry. Flip to back of ribs and score the membrane with a knife, then peel off the membrane.
2. Generously sprinkle the ribs with Sweet Rib Rub on both sides of the ribs and rub.
3. Supply your smoker with wood pellets and follow the start-up procedure. Preheat the grill, with the lid open, to 250° F. Once the smoker is ready, add the ribs and smoke for 4 hours, or until the ribs are tender and the meat is pulling away from the bone.
4. Serve and enjoy!

Grilled Lasagna With Cold-smoked Mozzarella

Servings: 8-12
Cooking Time: 70 Minutes

Ingredients:
- 15 Oz. Ricotta Cheese
- 3 Cups Cold-Smoked Mozzarella, Grated Divided
- 2 Eggs
- 6 Garlic Cloves, Chopped
- 1 Tsp Garlic Powder
- 1 Cup Grated Parmesan Cheese, Divided
- 1 Lb. Italian Sausage
- 1 Tbsp Italian Seasoning
- 1 Pkg. "No-Bake" Lasagna Noodles
- 48 Oz. Marinara Sauce
- 1 Lb. Mozzarella Block
- 1 Tbsp Olive Oil
- 1 Tbsp Chopped Oregano
- ¼ Cup Italian Parsley, Chopped
- 1 Yellow Onion, Chopped

Directions:
1. In a glass bowl, mix together the eggs, Italian seasoning, garlic powder, ricotta cheese, ½ cup parmesan cheese, and 1 cup of smoked mozzarella, and 2 tablespoons of parsley. Cover and refrigerate for 1 hour.
2. Supply your smoker with wood pellets and follow the start-up procedure. Preheat the grill, with the lid open, to 400° F. If using a gas or charcoal grill, set it up for medium-high heat. Place a cast iron skillet on the grill grates and allow to preheat.
3. Heat olive oil in skillet, then add Italian sausage and cook for 5 minutes, then add in onion and garlic, and cook an additional 3 minutes. Remove from heat and stir in 1 tablespoon of parsley and dried oregano. Set aside and reduce grill temperature to 350° F.
4. To assemble, begin by covering the bottom of a 9x13 pan with 1 cup of sauce. For the first layer, place a single layer of uncooked noodles over the sauce, followed by ⅓ of the ricotta cheese mixture, half of the Italian sausage, 1 cup of mozzarella cheese, and 1 cup of sauce. Repeat for layer two with a single layer of uncooked lasagna noodles, ⅓ of the ricotta cheese mixture, and 1 ½ cups of sauce. Repeat for layer three with a layer of uncooked lasagna noodles, remaining ricotta mixture, remaining Italian sausage, 1 cup of sauce. For the final layer, add a layer of uncooked lasagna noodles, remaining sauce, and remaining 1 cup mozzarella plus ½ cup parmesan.
5. Transfer lasagna to grill and cook, covered with foil, for 35 minutes. Remove foil and continue cooking for 10 minutes, sprinkle with additional parmesan and parsley, if desired. Remove from grill and let stand 15 minutes before serving.

Baked Honey Glazed Ham

Servings: 8
Cooking Time: 120 Minutes

Ingredients:
- 1 (6-8 lb) Snake River Farms Kurobuta Half Bone-In Ham
- 20 whole cloves
- 1 Stick butter, softened
- 1/4 Cup dark corn syrup
- 1 Cup honey, room temperature

Directions:
1. Supply your smoker with wood pellets and follow the start-up procedure. Preheat the grill, with the lid closed, to 325° F.
2. Score ham. Smear the entire ham with softened butter and stud with the whole cloves and place ham in foil-lined pan.
3. Combine the dark corn syrup and honey. Warm to combine if needed. Pour 3/4 of the glaze over ham, and bake for 1-1/2 to 2 hours on the grill or until the ham reaches 140°F. Grill: 325 °F Probe: 140 °F
4. Baste ham every 20 minutes with remaining honey glaze. Grill: 325 °F Probe: 140 °F
5. Remove from grill and let rest a few minutes.
6. Slice and serve. Enjoy!

Hawaiian Pulled Pork

Servings: 8-10
Cooking Time: 640 Minutes

Ingredients:
- 2 Cups Aloe Leaf Juice
- 1 Tsp Coriander, Ground
- 2 Tsp Cracked Pepper
- 1 Tsp Cumin
- Dash Of Salt
- 4-6 Garlic, Cloves
- 1 (3-Inch) Ginger, Fresh
- 1-2 Limes
- 4 Cups No Sodium Added Chicken Bone Broth
- ¼ Cup Olive Oil
- 4 Tsp Paprika
- 6-8 Lbs Pork Shoulder/Butt
- 1/2 Sweet Onion
- 2 Packets Truvia To Sweeten Above Aloe Juice
- 2 Tbs Or 2 Tbs Swerve Brown Sugar Truvia – Honey Substitute

Directions:
1. Supply your smoker with wood pellets and follow the start-up procedure. Preheat the grill, with the lid closed, to 300° F. Make sure your flame broiler is closed, you want to use indirect heat for this recipe.
2. Add all spices into a bowl (salt, paprika, cumin, coriander, pepper, onion powder if needed). Set bowl aside.
3. Grate the ginger into a separate bowl (wet ingredients bowl).
4. Mince or smash the garlic cloves into the same bowl.
5. Dice onion and add it to the ginger and garlic (if no onion sub onion powder).
6. Juice 1-2 limes and add to the "wet" ingredients bowl.
7. Add 4 cups chicken bone broth.
8. Add two cups aloe leaf juice w/lemon and add two packets Truvia to sweeten.
9. Add 1-2 tbsp Truvia honey substitute. Mix and set bowl aside.
10. Add the oil to your Cast Iron and coat the bottom and sides. Place the pork in the cast iron roasting pan.
11. Take your dry rub and coat the pork.
12. Pour the wet ingredients around the pork, into the Cast Iron Roasting Pan.
13. Cover the roasting pan with the lid and set it on your grill.
14. Check the pork every couple hours (basting if you prefer). When internal temperature reaches 195°F (after around 6 – 8 hours of cook time), it should easily start to pull apart. Don't pull apart the whole shoulder yet.
15. Remove the Roasting Pan from the grill and set aside to allow it to rest for 1 hour. Remove the lid to help speed cooling.
16. Once cooled, shred the pork into a separate bowl, removing the fat as you go.
17. If you want to add some of the marinade to the pork for additional flavor, make sure you skim the fat off the top first and discard.
18. Viola! Pair with fresh grilled veggies, delicious fruit or make tacos or salads! So many options for this type of protein.

Chinese Alcoholic Bbq Pork Tenderloin

Servings: 4
Cooking Time: 30 Minutes

Ingredients:
- 14 Cup Bbq Sauce
- 2 Garlic Cloves, Minced
- 14 Cup Hoisin Sauce
- 2 Lbs Pork Tenderloin, Trimmed With Silver Skins Removed
- 1 Tbsp Sugar, Granulated
- 1 Tsp Sweet Rib Rub Seasoning
- 14 Cup Tamari
- 14 Cup White Wine

Directions:
1. In a glass measuring cup, whisk together the hoisin sauce, tamari, wine, garlic, sugar, and Sweet Rib Rub.
2. Place pork tenderloin in a resealable bag, then pour the marinade over the pork and allow to marinate in the refrigerator for 4 to 6 hours.
3. Supply your smoker with wood pellets and follow the start-up procedure. Preheat the grill, with the lid open, to 400° F. If using a gas or charcoal grill, preheat to medium-high heat.
4. Remove the pork from the marinade, then pour the marinade into a grill-safe pan.
5. Place the marinade on the grill and bring to a boil for 3 minutes. Add the BBQ sauce and simmer for 2 minutes. Remove from the grill, and set aside.
6. Place the pork on the grill and cook for 18 to 20 minutes, until an internal temperature of 145° F. Flip and baste the pork with the sauce every 3 to 5 minutes.
7. Remove the pork from the grill and allow it to rest on a cutting board for 10 minutes, prior to serving warm with additional sauce.

Traeger Smoked Sausage

Servings: 4
Cooking Time: 120 Minutes

Ingredients:
- 3 Pound ground pork
- 1/2 Tablespoon ground mustard
- 1 Tablespoon onion powder

- 1 Tablespoon garlic powder
- 1/2 Teaspoon pink curing salt
- 1 Tablespoon salt
- 4 Teaspoon black pepper
- 1/2 Cup ice water
- Hog casings, soaked and rinsed in cold water

Directions:
1. In a medium bowl, combine the meat and seasonings, mix well.
2. Add ice water to meat and mix with hands working quickly until everything is incorporated.
3. Place mixture in a sausage stuffer and follow manufacturers Directions:for operating. Use caution not to overstuff or the casing might burst.
4. Once all the meat is stuffed, determine your desired link length and pinch and twist a couple of times or tie it off. Repeat for each link.
5. Supply your smoker with wood pellets and follow the start-up procedure. Preheat the grill, with the lid closed, to 225° F.
6. Place links directly on the grill grate and cook for 1 to 2 hours or until the internal temperature registers 155°F. Let sausage rest a few minutes before slicing. Enjoy! Grill: 225 °F Probe: 155 °F

Bbq Pulled Pork With Sweet & Heat Bbq Sauce

Servings: 4
Cooking Time: 540 Minutes

Ingredients:
- 10 Pound Bone-In Pork Butt
- 2 Tablespoon Pork & Poultry Rub
- 1 1/2 Cup apple juice
- 4 Tablespoon brown sugar
- 1 Tablespoon salt
- 1 To Taste salt
- 1 To Taste Pork & Poultry Rub
- 1 As Needed Sweet & Heat BBQ Sauce

Directions:
1. Trim pork butt of all excess fat leaving 1/4" of the fat cap attached. Combine 2 Tbsp Pork and Poultry rub, apple juice, brown sugar, and salt in a small bowl stirring until most of the sugar and salt are dissolved. Inject the pork butt every square inch or so with the apple juice mixture. Season the exterior of the pork butt with remaining rub.
2. Supply your smoker with wood pellets and follow the start-up procedure. Preheat the grill, with the lid closed, to 225° F.
3. Place pork butt directly on the grill grate and cook for about 6 hours or until the internal temperature reaches 160°F. Grill: 225 °F Probe: 160 °F
4. Wrap the pork butt in two layers of foil and pour in 1/2 cup of apple juice. Secure tin foil tightly to contain the apple juice. Increase temperature to 275°F and return to grill in a pan large enough to hold the pork butt in case of leaks. Cook an additional 3 hours or until internal temperature reaches 205°F. Grill: 275 °F Probe: 205 °F
5. Remove from the grill and discard the bone. Shred the pork removing any excess fat or tendons. Season with additional Pork and Poultry Rub and salt if needed.
6. Add Sweet & Heat BBQ sauce and serve. Enjoy!

Bacon Onion Ring

Servings: 6
Cooking Time: 60 Minutes

Ingredients:
- 16 Slices bacon
- 2 Whole Vidalia onion, sliced
- 1 Tablespoon Chili Garlic Sauce
- 1 Tablespoon yellow mustard
- 1 Teaspoon honey

Directions:
1. Wrap a piece of bacon around an individual onion ring; continue until bacon is gone. Some onion slices may be larger and require 2 pieces of bacon to complete a ring.
2. Place a skewer through the bacon-wrapped onion slice, to keep bacon from unraveling while cooking.
3. Supply your smoker with wood pellets and follow the start-up procedure. Preheat the grill, with the lid closed, to 400° F.
4. Meanwhile, mix chili garlic sauce and yellow mustard in a small bowl until incorporated; add honey.
5. Place skewers on the grill grate and cook for approximately 90 minutes, flipping after 45 minutes. Enjoy! Grill: 400 °F

St. Louis Bbq Ribs

Servings: 4
Cooking Time: 240 Minutes

Ingredients:
- 2 Rack St. Louis-style ribs
- 1/4 Cup Pork & Poultry Rub
- 1 Cup apple juice
- 1 Bottle Sweet & Heat BBQ Sauce

Directions:
1. Trim ribs and peel off membrane from the back of ribs. Apply an even coat of rub to the front and back of ribs. Let sit for 20 minutes and up to 4 hours if refrigerated.
2. Supply your smoker with wood pellets and follow the start-up procedure. Preheat the grill, with the lid closed, to 225° F.

3. Place ribs bone side down on grill grate. Put apple juice in a spray bottle and evenly spray ribs. Grill: 225 °F
4. After 3 hours, remove ribs from grill and wrap them in aluminum foil. Leave an opening at one end, pour in remainder of apple juice (about 6 oz) into the foil and wrap tightly.
5. Place ribs back on grill, meat side down and smoke for an additional 3 hours. Grill: 225 °F Probe: 203 °F
6. After 1 hour, start checking the internal temperature of ribs. Ribs are done when the internal temperature reaches 203°F. Grill: 225 °F
7. When ribs are done, remove from the foil and brush a light layer of sauce on the front and back on the ribs.
8. Return to the grill and cook an additional 10 minutes to set the sauce. Grill: 225 °F
9. After sauce has set, take ribs off the grill and let rest for 10 minutes. To serve, slice ribs in between the bones. Enjoy!

Pig On A Stick With Buffalo Glaze

Servings: 12
Cooking Time: 75 Minutes

Ingredients:
- 4lb (1.8kg) pork shanks, each about 4 to 6oz (110 to 170g), trimmed and thawed if frozen
- 1½ cups sugar-free dark-colored soda, sugar-free root beer, or no-sugar-added apple juice
- for the brine (optional)
- 1 gallon (3.8 liters) distilled water
- ¾ cup kosher salt
- 5 tsp pink curing salt #1
- for the glaze (optional)
- ½ cup unsalted butter
- 1 cup hot sauce
- 2 tsp granulated garlic
- 1 tsp Worcestershire sauce

Directions:
1. In a stockpot on the stovetop over medium-high heat, make the brine by combining the ingredients and bringing the mixture to a boil. Stir until the salts dissolve. Remove the pot from the stovetop and let the brine cool to room temperature.
2. Add the pork shanks to the brine. Cover and refrigerate for 2 days.
3. Supply your smoker with wood pellets and follow the start-up procedure. Preheat the grill, with the lid closed, to 180° F.
4. Drain the pork shanks and discard the brine. (If you didn't brine the pork shanks, season them on all sides with your favorite barbecue rub.) Place the pork on the grate and smoke for 3 hours. Transfer the shanks to an aluminum roasting pan.
5. Raise the temperature to 275°F (135°C).
6. Add the soda to the pan and cover tightly with aluminum foil. Place the pan on the grate and braise the meat until it's tender but still attached to the bone, about 2 to 3 hours. Be careful when removing the foil because steam will escape. Remove the pan from the grill and set aside.
7. Raise the temperature to 325°F (163°C).
8. In a saucepan on the stovetop over medium heat, make the buffalo glaze by melting the butter. Stir in the remaining ingredients. Let the sauce simmer for 5 minutes to allow the flavors to blend.
9. Dip the pork shanks into the glaze and then transfer them to an aluminum foil roasting pan. Cover tightly with aluminum foil. Place the pan on the grate and cook the shanks until hot, about 30 minutes.
10. Remove the pan from the grill. Serve the pork with plenty of napkins.

Apple & Bourbon Glazed Ham

Servings: 6
Cooking Time: 60 Minutes

Ingredients:
- 1 Large ham
- 1 Cup apple jelly
- 2 Tablespoon Dijon mustard
- 2 Tablespoon bourbon
- 2 Teaspoon fresh lemon juice
- 1/2 Teaspoon ground cloves
- 2 Cup apple juice or cider

Directions:
1. Supply your smoker with wood pellets and follow the start-up procedure. Preheat the grill, with the lid closed, to 325° F.
2. When the grill is hot, place ham directly on the grill grate. Cook for 30 minutes. Grill: 325 °F
3. Meanwhile, in a small saucepan over medium-low heat, melt the apple jelly. Whisk in the apple juice, mustard, bourbon, lemon juice and ground cloves, then remove from the heat and set aside.
4. After 30 minutes, glaze ham with the apple bourbon mixture. Continue cooking for another 30 minutes or until a thermometer that is inserted into the thickest part of the meat reaches an internal temperature of 135°F. Grill: 325 °F Probe: 135 °F
5. Remove ham from grill and allow to rest for 20 minutes before serving. Warm remaining sauce and serve with ham if desired. Enjoy!

Amazing Bacon Cheese Fries

Servings: 2
Cooking Time: 25 Minutes

Ingredients:
- 2 Bacon, Strip

- 1/2 Cup Colby Jack Cheese, Shredded
- 1/2 Package Fries, Frozen
- 1/2 Cup Monterey Jack Cheese, Shredded

Directions:

1. Supply your smoker with wood pellets and follow the start-up procedure. Preheat the grill, with the lid open, to 350° F.
2. Place the bacon on the bacon rack and place on the grill. Cook until crispy, about 15 minutes.
3. Once slightly cooled, crumble the strips into small pieces and set it aside.
4. Grill the frozen French fries based on the package instructions, cooking on a pan in the instead of the oven.
5. Once fries are golden brown, sprinkle cheese and bacon on top of the fries, and return the pan to the grill and barbecue at 450°F for 1 minute. Remove from grill and enjoy!

Baked Sage & Sausage Stuffing

Servings: 4
Cooking Time: 45 Minutes

Ingredients:

- 1 Pound Sage-Flavored Sausage, Such as Bob Evans Or Jimmy Dean
- 1/2 Cup onion, diced
- 1/2 Cup celery, diced
- 14 Ounce (14 oz) package herb seasoned stuffing
- 1/2 Cup dried sweetened cranberries
- 2 Cup low sodium chicken broth
- 6 Tablespoon butter
- butter

Directions:

1. Brown the sausage in a large frying pan, breaking up the sausage with a wooden spoon.
2. Add the onion and celery and cook until softened. Drain any excess fat. Transfer to a large mixing bowl. Add the stuffing mix and cranberries, if using.
3. Warm the chicken broth over medium-low heat; add butter and cook until melted. Toss with the bread/sausage mixture and mix lightly.
4. Butter a 3-qt casserole or baking dish. Do not compress the mixture or it will be dense.
5. Supply your smoker with wood pellets and follow the start-up procedure. Preheat the grill, with the lid closed, to 350° F.
6. Bake the stuffing, covered, for 35 to 45 minutes; uncover during the last 20 minutes of cooking if you prefer a crunchier texture. Grill: 350 °F
7. Remove from grill and serve. Enjoy!

Pretzel Bun With Pulled Pork

Servings: 4
Cooking Time: 300 Minutes

Ingredients:

- ⅓ Cup Apple Cider Vinegar
- 1 ½ Cups Bbq Sauce, Divided
- 1 Qt. Chicken Stock
- ⅓ Cup Ketchup
- 3 Tbsp Pulled Pork Rub, Divided
- 1, 4 Lb. Pork Shoulder, Bone In
- 4 Pretzel Buns

Directions:

1. Supply your smoker with wood pellets and follow the start-up procedure. Preheat the grill, with the lid open, to 400° F. If using a gas or charcoal grill, set it up for medium-high heat. In a bowl, combine the apple cider vinegar, chicken stock, ketchup, and 1 tablespoon of Pulled Pork Rub. Whisk well to combine and set aside.
2. Season the pork shoulder with the remaining 2 tablespoons of Pulled Pork Seasoning on all sides of the pork shoulder, then place on the grill and sear on all sides until golden brown, about 10 minutes.
3. Remove the pork shoulder from the grill and place in the disposable aluminum pan. Pour the sauce over the pork shoulder. It should come about 1/3 to ½ way up the side of the pork shoulder. Cover the top of the pan tightly with aluminum foil.
4. Reduce the temperature of your grill to 250°F. Place the foil pan on the grill and cook for 4 to 5 hours, or until the pork is tender and falling off the bone.
5. Remove the pork from the grill and allow to rest for 15 minutes. Drain the liquid from the pan, reserving about a cup, then shred the pork and cover with the reserved liquid. Set 3 ½ to 4 cups of pulled pork aside for sandwiches, and save the remaining for future use.
6. While pork is resting, place 1 cup of BBQ sauce in a skillet and heat to simmer. Toss in reserved shredded pork. Divide pork among 4 pretzel buns, spoon additional BBQ sauce over the top and dig in!

Bbq Brown Sugar Bacon Bites

Servings: 2
Cooking Time: 25 Minutes

Ingredients:

- 1/2 Cup brown sugar
- 1 Tablespoon Fennel, ground
- 2 Teaspoon kosher salt
- 1 Teaspoon ground black pepper
- 1 Pound Pork Belly, diced

Directions:

1. Fold a 12" x 36" piece of aluminum foil in half and crimp the edges so there is a rim. Using a fork, poke holes in the bottom of

the foil. This way some of the bacon fat will be rendered out and the bacon bites will crisp.
2. Supply your smoker with wood pellets and follow the start-up procedure. Preheat the grill, with the lid closed, to 350° F.
3. In a large bowl, combine the brown sugar, ground fennel, salt, and black pepper. Stir to combine.
4. Place the diced pork belly into the mixture and toss until well-coated. Transfer the pork pieces to the foil.
5. Place on the grill and bake until the pieces are crispy, glazed, and bubbly, about 20-30 minutes. Enjoy!

Pulled Pork Stew

Servings: 4
Cooking Time: 120 Minutes

Ingredients:
- 16 Ounce salsa verde
- 15 Ounce black beans, drained and rinsed
- 15 Ounce fire roasted red peppers, drained and rinsed
- 1 Pound pulled pork
- 1 Teaspoon ground cumin
- 2 Cup chicken stock
- salt and pepper
- Avocado, Sliced

Directions:
1. Supply your smoker with wood pellets and follow the start-up procedure. Preheat the grill, with the lid closed, to 375° F.
2. Stir in salsa verde, black beans, fire-roasted tomatoes, shredded pork, cumin and chicken broth. Season with salt and pepper to taste.
3. Cook on Traeger for 1 hour stirring every 20 minutes. After 1 hour, cover Dutch oven with lid and cook an additional hour.
4. Top stew with fresh herbs, avocado and sour cream. Serve hot, enjoy!

Grilled Prosciutto Wrapped Asparagus

Servings: 6
Cooking Time: 15 Minutes

Ingredients:
- 2 Bunch asparagus
- 4 Ounce prosciutto
- olive oil
- salt and pepper
- 1 Medium lemon, zested
- 2 Tablespoon balsamic vinegar, divided
- 3 Tablespoon toasted pine nuts, for serving

Directions:
1. Supply your smoker with wood pellets and follow the start-up procedure. Preheat the grill, with the lid closed, to 400° F.
2. Rinse the asparagus and pat dry with a paper towel. Cut the bottom third off of the asparagus stalks and discard.
3. Wrap a piece of prosciutto around 4 to 5 stalks, and place on a baking sheet. Drizzle the asparagus with olive oil, then sprinkle with salt, pepper and lemon zest.
4. Place the baking sheet on the grill and cook. After 5 minutes, shake the pan to turn the asparagus once, then drizzle with 1 tablespoon balsamic vinegar. Grill: 400 °F
5. Place back on the grill and cook until the prosciutto is crispy and the asparagus is cooked through, about 5 to 8 minutes. Grill: 400 °F
6. Place the asparagus on the serving tray and sprinkle with the pine nuts and drizzle with remaining balsamic. Enjoy!

Smoked Chili Con Queso By Doug Scheiding

Servings: 8
Cooking Time: 45 Minutes

Ingredients:
- 1 Pound hot pork sausage
- 1 (2 lb) block Velveeta cheese
- 1 Pound smoked Gouda cheese
- 1 (10 oz) can RO*TEL Original Diced Tomatoes and Green Chilies
- 1 (10 oz) can RO*TEL Fire Roasted Diced Tomatoes and Green Chilies
- 1 (10 oz) can cream of mushroom soup
- 4 Tablespoon Coffee Rub
- 1/2 Cup chopped cilantro

Directions:
1. Heat a medium cast iron skillet over medium heat and fully cook pork sausage, breaking into small chunks as you go. Remove the sausage and drain and discard the fat.
2. Supply your smoker with wood pellets and follow the start-up procedure. Preheat the grill, with the lid closed, to 350° F.
3. Use a 4 to 5 quart cast iron Dutch oven or other oven safe dish. Divide the block of Velveeta into 5 to 6 large pieces and cut the smoked Gouda into small 1 inch cubes. Add the canned ingredients including the liquid. Add the sausage and Traeger Coffee Rub last. Grill: 350 °F
4. Smoke the queso for 45 minutes on the Traeger, stirring 3 to 4 times. Grill: 350 °F
5. Add most of the cilantro the last 5 minutes of smoking. Sprinkle remaining cilantro on the top before serving. Enjoy!

Apple-smoked Bacon

Servings: 4-6
Cooking Time: 30 Minutes

Ingredients:
- 1 (1-pound) package thick-sliced bacon

Directions:
1. Supply your smoker with wood pellets and follow the start-up procedure. Preheat the grill, with the lid closed, to 275°F.
2. Supply your smoker with wood pellets and follow the start-up procedure. Preheat the grill, with the lid closed, to 275°F.

Delicious Pulled Pork Poutine

Servings: 4
Cooking Time: 240 Minutes

Ingredients:
- 2 Tbsp Apple Cider Vinegar
- 1/2 Cup Bbq Sauce
- 1 1/2 Cups Beef Stock
- 2 Tbsp Butter
- For Assembly, Cheese Curds
- 2 Cups Chicken Stock
- 2 Tbsp Flour
- For Assembly, French Fries
- 3 Garlic Cloves, Minced
- 1 Tbsp Olive Oil
- 2 1/2 Lbs Pork Shoulder Roast, Bone-In
- To Taste, Pulled Pork Rub
- For Assembly, Sliced Scallions
- 1/2 Yellow Onion, Minced
- 1/2 Yellow Onion, Sliced

Directions:
1. Supply your smoker with wood pellets and follow the start-up procedure. Preheat the grill, with the lid open, to 225° F. If using a gas or charcoal grill, set it up for low, indirect heat.
2. Season the pork shoulder with a pork rub, then transfer to the grill grate, fat side up. Smoke the pork shoulder for 2 ½ hours.
3. Add chicken stock, vinegar, and sliced onion to a Dutch oven. Transfer the smoked pork shoulder to the Dutch oven, then cover and increase the grill temperature to 325° F. Braise the pork shoulder for 1 ½ hours, until tender.
4. When tender, remove the pork from the grill and rest for 20 minutes, then shred.
5. While the pork is resting, prepare the gravy: set a cast iron skillet on the grill. Heat the butter and olive oil in the skillet, then sauté the onion and garlic for 2 minutes, stirring often. Stir in the flour and cook for 1 minute. Slowly add the beef stock, and stir until thickened. Add bbq sauce and simmer for 3 minutes. Remove from the grill and set aside for assembly.
6. Assemble the poutine: spread out a layer of French fries, then layer gravy, pulled pork, cheese curds, additional gravy, and scallions. Serve warm.

Anytime Pork Roast

Servings: 6
Cooking Time: 360 Minutes

Ingredients:
- 6 (4-6 lb) pork roast
- Pork & Poultry Rub
- 1/4 Cup apple juice

Directions:
1. Supply your smoker with wood pellets and follow the start-up procedure. Preheat the grill, with the lid closed, to 180° F.
2. Sprinkle pork roast with Traeger Pork & Poultry Rub on all sides. Place roast in an aluminum foil pan and pour apple juice on top. Place roast in the grill and smoke the for 1 hour. Grill: 180 °F
3. Remove roast from grill and increase Traeger temperature to 275°F and preheat, lid closed 15 minutes. Grill: 275 °F
4. Cook roast for an additional 2 hours, uncovered. After two hours, wrap pan with aluminum foil and return to grill to cook for an additional 3 hours or until the internal temperature reaches 205°F. Grill: 275 °F Probe: 205 °F
5. Allow to rest for 10 minutes before serving. Serve with roasted onions, potatoes, carrots and apples. Enjoy!

Crown Roast Of Pork

Servings: 4
Cooking Time: 60 Minutes

Ingredients:
- 1 Whole Crown Roast of Pork, 12-14 ribs
- 1/4 Cup Pork & Poultry Rub
- 1 Cup apple juice
- 1 Cup Apricot BBQ Sauce

Directions:
1. Supply your smoker with wood pellets and follow the start-up procedure. Preheat the grill, with the lid closed, to 375° F.
2. Season the pork roast liberally with Traeger Pork and Poultry Rub. Let sit at room temperature for 30 minutes. Wrap each tip of the crown roast in a small piece of aluminum foil. This will protect the bones during the cook and prevent them from turning black.
3. Place the roast directly on the grill grate and cook for about 90 minutes spraying with apple juice every 30 minutes or so.
4. When the roast reaches an internal temperature of 125 degrees F, remove the aluminum foil from the bones and return to the grill.
5. Spray again with apple juice and continue to cook until the internal temperature reaches 135 degrees F in the thickest part of

the roast. In the last ten minutes, baste the roast with the Apricot BBQ Sauce to let the glaze set.
6. Remove from the grill, tent with foil, and let it rest 15-20 minutes before slicing. Enjoy!

Smoked Bologna

Servings: 4
Cooking Time: 240 Minutes

Ingredients:
- 1 Pound bologna log
- 1/4 Cup brown sugar
- 1 Tablespoon yellow mustard
- 1 Teaspoon soy sauce
- Worcestershire sauce

Directions:
1. Score the bologna log being careful not to cut too deep.
2. Mix brown sugar, mustard, soy sauce and Worcestershire sauce together.
3. Once mixed, rub it all over the bologna.
4. Supply your smoker with wood pellets and follow the start-up procedure. Preheat the grill, with the lid closed, to 225° F.
5. Smoke bologna for 3 to 4 hours. Grill: 225 °F
6. Remove from grill and let cool.
7. Slice and serve with sandwiches. Enjoy!

Smoked Pork Loin

Servings: 6
Cooking Time: 180 Minutes

Ingredients:
- 1 Pork, Loins
- Rub

Directions:
1. Season pork loin with Traeger Rub.
2. Supply your smoker with wood pellets and follow the start-up procedure. Preheat the grill, with the lid closed, to 180° F.
3. Place pork loin on the grill grates, on a diagonal, and smoke for 3 to 4 hours. Grill: 180 °F
4. Increase grill temperature to 350°F and cook for 20 to 30 minutes. Grill: 350 °F
5. Remove from grill, cut into 1-1/2" steaks. Serve. Enjoy!

Turkey Stuffing Bacon Balls

Servings: 8
Cooking Time: 25 Minutes

Ingredients:
- 1 Can Cranberry Sauce, Whole Berry (16oz) Can
- 1 jalapeño, diced
- 3 Cup Your Favorite Stuffing, Prepared According to the Package Directions, or Homemade
- 1 Cup Shredded Cooked Turkey
- 6 Slices bacon

Directions:
1. In a small saucepan, combine cranberry sauce and jalapenos. Bring to a boil over medium high heat then reduce the heat to a simmer. Cook for 4-5 minutes then remove from the heat and allow to cool.
2. Supply your smoker with wood pellets and follow the start-up procedure. Preheat the grill, with the lid closed, to 375° F.
3. Start by filling the palm of your hand with approximately 1/4 cup of the stuffing. Use your thumb to create an indentation. Fill the indentation with a heaping tablespoon of the shredded turkey and then close the stuffing all around to form into a ball.
4. Wrap the ball of stuffing with a half a piece of bacon and hold in place with a toothpick, if necessary. Repeat until all of the bombs are made.
5. When ready to cook, place the stuffing balls directly on the grill grate and cook for 25-30 minutes, turning once. The bacon should be crisp. Grill: 375 °F
6. Serve with cranberry jalapeno jelly. Enjoy!

Dry Rub Grilled Ribs

Servings: 4
Cooking Time: 300 Minutes

Ingredients:
- 1 Rack Baby Back Rib
- 1 Tablespoon Olive Oil
- Sweet Heat Rub

Directions:
1. Supply your smoker with wood pellets and follow the start-up procedure. Preheat the grill, with the lid open, to 225° F.
2. Remove the membrane from the back of the ribs. Rub the ribs down with olive oil, then generously coat both sides with Sweet Heat Rub. For deeper flavor penetration, gently pat the spices into the meat and let sit in the refrigerator for at least an hour.
3. Smoke the ribs for about 5 hours or until the temperature is between 180°F and 195°F, and the meat is dark, glossy and easily tears apart.
4. When the ribs are finished, remove from the grill and let them rest for 5 minutes before serving.

Grilled Sweet Pork Tenderloin

Servings: 4
Cooking Time: 20 Minutes

Ingredients:
- 2 Tablespoons Brown Sugar
- 2 Tablespoons Olive Oil
- 2 Tablespoons Tennessee Apple Butter Seasoning
- 1 Pork Tenderloin, Trimmed With Silver Skins Removed

Directions:

1. In a small bowl, combine the olive oil, brown sugar, and Tennessee Apple Butter seasoning until well combined. Generously rub the pork tenderloin with the mixture. Allow the pork tenderloin to marinade for 1 hour.
2. Supply your smoker with wood pellets and follow the start-up procedure. Preheat the grill, with the lid open, to 350° F.
3. Grill the tenderloin for 5-7 minutes on each side, flipping the tenderloin only once and cooking until the internal temperature reaches 140-145°F.
4. Remove the tenderloin from the grill and allow to rest 10 minutes before slicing and serving.

Korean Pulled Pork Lettuce Wraps

Servings: 8
Cooking Time: 480 Minutes

Ingredients:
- 1 bone-in pork shoulder, about 6lb (2.7kg)
- 1 cup low-carb beer or sugar-free light-colored soda
- for the sauce
- 1½ cups low-carb barbecue sauce
- ¼ cup low-carb beer or sugar-free light- or dark-colored soda
- 3 tbsp gochujang
- 3 tbsp light soy sauce
- 1 tbsp rice wine vinegar
- 1 tbsp toasted Asian sesame oil
- 1 tsp gochugaru
- for the rub
- 3 tbsp coarse salt
- 3 tbsp gochugaru
- 3 tbsp granulated light brown sugar or low-carb substitute
- 2 tsp granulated garlic
- 2 tsp onion powder
- 1 tsp ground ginger

Directions:

1. Supply your smoker with wood pellets and follow the start-up procedure. Preheat the grill, with the lid closed, to 250° F.
2. In a small bowl, make the barbecue sauce by whisking together the ingredients. Cover and refrigerate until ready to serve.
3. In a small bowl, make the rub by combining the ingredients. Rinse the meat with cold running water and pat dry with paper towels. Sprinkle the rub evenly over the surface, using your fingertips to pat it on.
4. Place the pork shoulder on the grate and smoke until the internal temperature reaches 165°F (74°C), about 4 to 5 hours. Transfer the meat to an aluminum foil roasting pan. Add the beer and then cover the pan tightly with heavy-duty aluminum foil. Continue to cook until the internal temperature reaches 200°F (93°C), about 3 hours more. (Keep the probe from touching bone or it will give you a false reading.) When the pork is tender enough to pull, the meat will release easily from the bone.
5. Transfer the pork shoulder to a cutting board. Drain the accumulated juices into a separate container and reserve. While the pork is still hot, pull out the bone and separate the meat into chunks. Using meat claws, forks, or your fingers, pull the meat into shreds, discarding any lumps of fat or undesirable bits. Return the meat to the pan. Stir in some of the reserved cooking juices if desired. You want the pork to be moist but not soupy.
6. Wrap the hot pork in lettuce leaves. Top with thinly sliced garlic, thinly sliced crosswise jalapeños, toasted sesame seeds, pickled ginger, and barbecue sauce. You can also serve the pork the American way: piled high on sesame seed buns.

Jalapeno Cheddar Smoked Sausages

Servings: 6
Cooking Time: 180 Minutes

Ingredients:
- hog casings
- 2 Pound ground pork
- 5 Medium jalapeños, seeded and diced small
- 1/2 Cup shredded sharp cheddar cheese
- 1/2 Tablespoon kosher salt
- 1 Teaspoon black pepper
- 1 Teaspoon granulated garlic
- 1 Teaspoon onion powder

Directions:

1. Soak your hog casings in water according to package directions. While casings are soaking, make your sausage.
2. Place all ingredients in the bowl of a food processor and pulse to combine. Be careful not to overwork, the meat should be a little tacky and all spices fully incorporated.
3. Place sausage mixture in your sausage stuffer and proceed to stuff the casing according to manufacturer's directions. Be sure to stuff the length of the casing, then create the links afterwards. Use caution not to overstuff or they will burst when you go to create the links.
4. Hang the sausages and allow to air dry at room temperature for an hour or so, then transfer to the refrigerator to dry overnight.

5. Supply your smoker with wood pellets and follow the start-up procedure. Preheat the grill, with the lid closed, to 180° F.
6. Place the sausages directly on the grill grate and smoke for 2 to 3 hours, or until they reach an internal temperature of 155°F. Enjoy! Grill: 180 °F Probe: 155 °F

Brats In Beer

Servings: 4
Cooking Time: 60 Minutes

Ingredients:
- 4 Can (12 oz) cans beer
- 2 Large onions, peeled and sliced into rings
- 2 Tablespoon butter
- 10 uncooked bratwurst
- 10 hot dog buns
- mustard, for serving

Directions:
1. Pour beer into a large saucepan. Add onions and butter. Bring to a simmer on the stovetop.
2. Supply your smoker with wood pellets and follow the start-up procedure. Preheat the grill, with the lid closed, to 350° F.
3. Put a deep disposable aluminum foil pan on one side of the Traeger. Carefully pour the beer and onions from the saucepan into the pan on the grill.
4. Arrange the brats on the other side of the grill grate. Grill the brats until cooked through, turning frequently with tongs, about 20 to 25 minutes. Grill: 350 °F
5. Transfer the brats to the beer mixture and cover the pan tightly with aluminum foil.
6. Let the brats simmer until the onions are tender, 45 minutes to an hour. Grill: 350 °F
7. Butter the cut sides of the buns and toast on the grill.
8. To serve, lift a brat out of the mixture and put it on a bun. Top it with onions and mustard. Enjoy!

Smoked Pork Tenderloin

Servings: 4
Cooking Time: 180 Minutes

Ingredients:
- 1/2 Cup apple juice
- 3 Tablespoon honey
- 3 Tablespoon Pork & Poultry Rub
- 1/4 Cup brown sugar
- 2 Tablespoon thyme leaves
- 1/2 Tablespoon black pepper
- 2 (1-1/2 lb) pork tenderloins, silverskin removed

Directions:
1. For the Marinade: In a large bowl, add the apple juice, honey (warmed), Traeger Pork & Poultry rub, brown sugar, thyme leaves and black pepper. Whisk to combine.
2. Add pork loins to the bowl with the marinade. Turn pork to coat and cover bowl with plastic wrap.
3. Transfer to the refrigerator and marinate for 2 to 3 hours.
4. Supply your smoker with wood pellets and follow the start-up procedure. Preheat the grill, with the lid closed, to 225° F.
5. Place the tenderloins directly on the grill grate and smoke until the internal temperature registers 145°F, about 2-1/2 to 3 hours. Grill: 225 °F Probe: 145 °F
6. Remove from grill and let rest 5 minutes before slicing. Enjoy!

Honey Glazed Pork Chops

Servings: 6
Cooking Time: 16 Minutes

Ingredients:
- 4-6 Pork Chop
- 1/2 Cup of Honey
- 4 Tablespoons Soy Sauce
- 2 Tablespoons Olive Oil
- 2 Garlic Cloves, pressed
- Salt & Pepper

Directions:
1. Supply your smoker with wood pellets and follow the start-up procedure. Preheat the grill, with the lid closed, to 350° F.
2. Mix together the honey, soy sauce, and garlic in a small dish.
3. Brush the olive oil over the pork chops and sprinkle with salt and pepper.
4. Place the pork chops on the grill and brush the honey mixture over the top side.
5. When you flip the pork chops over, brush the second side with the honey mixture.
6. Grill for about 8 minutes on each side or until a thermometer inserted reads 170 degrees. Brush a final layer of the honey glaze over the pork chops before serving. Enjoy!

Smoked Traeger Pulled Pork

Servings: 8
Cooking Time: 540 Minutes

Ingredients:
- 1 (6-9 lb) bone-in pork shoulder
- Pork & Poultry Rub
- 2 Cup apple cider
- 'Que BBQ Sauce

Directions:
1. Supply your smoker with wood pellets and follow the start-up procedure. Preheat the grill, with the lid closed, to 250° F.

2. While the Traeger comes to temperature, trim excess fat off pork butt.
3. Generously season with Traeger Pork & Poultry Rub on all sides and let sit for 20 minutes.
4. Place the pork butt fat side up directly on the grill grate and cook until the internal temperature reaches 160°F, about 3 to 5 hours. Grill: 250 °F Probe: 160 °F
5. Remove the pork butt from the grill.
6. On a large baking sheet, stack 4 large pieces of aluminum foil on top of each other, ensuring they are wide enough to wrap the pork butt entirely on all sides. If not, overlap the foil pieces to create a wider base. Place the pork butt in the center on the foil, then bring up the sides of the foil a little bit before pouring the apple cider on top of the pork butt. Wrap the foil tightly around the pork, ensuring the cider does not escape.
7. Place the foil-wrapped pork butt back on the grill fat side up and cook until the internal temperature reaches 204°F, in the thickest part of the meat, about 3 to 4 hours longer depending on the size of the pork butt. Grill: 250 °F Probe: 204 °F
8. Remove from the grill. Allow the pork to rest for 45 minutes in the foil packet.
9. Remove the pork from the foil and pour off any excess liquid into a fat separator.
10. Place the pork in a large dish and shred the meat, removing and discarding the bone and any excess fat. Add separated liquid back into pork and season to taste with additional Traeger Big Game Rub. Optionally, add Traeger 'Que BBQ Sauce or your favorite BBQ sauce to taste.

Roasted Pork With Balsamic Strawberry Sauce

Servings: 2
Cooking Time: 35 Minutes

Ingredients:
- 2 Pound pork tenderloin
- salt and pepper
- 2 Tablespoon dried rosemary
- 2 Tablespoon extra-virgin olive oil
- 12 Large fresh strawberries
- 1 Cup balsamic vinegar
- 4 Tablespoon sugar

Directions:
1. Supply your smoker with wood pellets and follow the start-up procedure. Preheat the grill, with the lid closed, to 350° F.
2. Rinse pork and pat dry. Sprinkle both sides with salt, pepper, and rosemary.
3. In a large Dutch oven skillet, heat oil on High until almost smoking. Add the tenderloin and sear on each side until the skin is golden brown, about 2 minutes per side.
4. Set the skillet in the Traeger and cook until pork is no longer pink and internal temperature reaches 150°F, about 20 minutes. Grill: 350 °F Probe: 150 °F
5. Remove from grill and let the pork rest for 5-10 minutes.
6. Add strawberries to the skillet over the stove on medium heat and quickly sear on both sides for less than a minute. Remove berries from the pan.
7. Add balsamic vinegar to the same pan and scrape the browned bits from the bottom.
8. Bring to a boil and then reduce heat to medium low. Add the sugar, stirring frequently. Sauce is ready when it has reduced by half and texture is thick.
9. Slice the pork and place the seared strawberries on top. Serve with a drizzle of the balsamic vinegar sauce. Enjoy!

Southern Sugar-glazed Ham

Servings: 12-15
Cooking Time: 300 Minutes

Ingredients:
- 1 (12- to 15-pound) whole bone-in ham, fully cooked
- ¼ cup yellow mustard
- 1 cup pineapple juice
- ½ cup packed light brown sugar
- 1 teaspoon ground cinnamon
- ½ teaspoon ground cloves

Directions:
1. Supply your smoker with wood pellets and follow the start-up procedure. Preheat, with the lid closed, to 275°F.
2. Trim off the excess fat and skin from the ham, leaving a ¼-inch layer of fat. Put the ham in an aluminum foil–lined roasting pan.
3. On your kitchen stove top, in a medium saucepan over low heat, combine the mustard, pineapple juice, brown sugar, cinnamon, and cloves and simmer for 15 minutes, or until thick and reduced by about half.
4. Baste the ham with half of the pineapple–brown sugar syrup, reserving the rest for basting later in the cook.
5. Place the roasting pan on the grill, close the lid, and smoke for 4 hours.
6. Baste the ham with the remaining pineapple–brown sugar syrup and continue smoking with the lid closed for another hour, or until a meat thermometer inserted in the thickest part of the ham reads 140°F.
7. Remove the ham from the grill, tent with foil, and let rest for 20 minutes before carving.

Pulled Pork Shoulder And Chicken

Servings: 6 - 8
Cooking Time: 300 Minutes

Ingredients:
- 1/3 Cup Apple Cider Vinegar
- 4 Cups Chicken Broth
- 1/3 Cup Ketchup
- 2 Tbsp Pulled Pork Seasoning
- 4 Lbs. Pork Shoulder, Bone In

Directions:
1. Supply your smoker with wood pellets and follow the start-up procedure. Preheat the grill, with the lid open, to 350° F. In a bowl, combine the chicken broth, ketchup, apple cider vinegar, and 1 tablespoon of Pulled Pork Seasoning. Whisk well to combine and set aside.
2. Generously season the pork shoulder with the remaining 3 tablespoons of Pulled Pork Seasoning on all sides of the pork shoulder, then place on the grill and sear on all sides until golden brown, about 10 minutes.
3. Remove the pork shoulder from the grill and place in the disposable aluminum pan. Pour the chicken broth mixture over the pork shoulder. It should come about 1/3 to ½ way up the side of the pork shoulder. Cover the top of the pan tightly with aluminum foil.
4. Reduce the temperature of your grill to 250°F. Place the foil pan on the grill and grill for four to five hours, or until the pork is tender and falling off the bone.
5. Remove the pork from the grill and allow to cool slightly. Drain the liquid from the pan, reserving about a cup, then shred the pork and cover with the reserved liquid. Serve and enjoy!

Bbq Pork Belly

Servings: 6
Cooking Time: 180 Minutes

Ingredients:
- 1 (3 lb) pork belly, skin removed
- 4 Tablespoon salt
- 1/2 Teaspoon black pepper
- Pork & Poultry Rub

Directions:
1. Supply your smoker with wood pellets and follow the start-up procedure. Preheat the grill, with the lid closed, to 275° F.
2. Meanwhile, season pork belly on both sides with salt, pepper and Traeger Pork & Poultry Rub. Place pork belly directly on the grill grate and cook for 3 to 3-1/2 hours or until the internal temperature reaches 200°F. Grill: 275 °F Probe: 200 °F
3. Remove from grill and let rest 10 to 15 minutes before slicing.
4. Serve in tacos, mac and cheese, nachos or your favorite dish. Enjoy!

Roasted Ham With Apricot Sauce

Servings: 8
Cooking Time: 120 Minutes

Ingredients:
- 1 (8-10 lb) Snake River Farms Kurobuta Whole Bone-In Ham
- 1 Bottle Apricot BBQ Sauce
- 1/4 Cup horseradish
- 2 Tablespoon Dijon mustard

Directions:
1. Supply your smoker with wood pellets and follow the start-up procedure. Preheat the grill, with the lid closed, to 325° F.
2. Place ham in a large roasting pan lined with aluminum foil. Place pan on grill and cook for 90 minutes. Grill: 325 °F
3. For the Glaze: In a saucepan over medium heat, combine the Traeger Apricot BBQ Sauce, horseradish and mustard. Set aside and keep warm.
4. After 90 minutes, brush the ham with the glaze. Continue to cook for another 30 minutes or until a thermometer inserted into the thickest part of the ham reaches an internal temperatures of 135°F. Grill: 325 °F Probe: 135 °F
5. Remove ham from grill and rest for 20 minutes before slicing.
6. Serve with remaining glaze if desired. Enjoy!

Braised Pork Carnitas

Servings: 6
Cooking Time: 180 Minutes

Ingredients:
- 2 Tbsp Bacon Fat Or Olive Oil
- 1 Cup Chicken Stock
- Cilantro, Chopped
- Corn Tortillas
- 3 Jalapeno Pepper, Minced
- 1 Lime, Wedges
- 2 Tbsp Pulled Pork Rub
- 3 Lbs Pork Shoulder, Boneless, Cut Into 1 ½ To 2 Inch Cubes
- Queso Fresco, Crumbled
- Red Onion, Minced

Directions:
1. Supply your smoker with wood pellets and follow the start-up procedure. Preheat the grill, with the lid open, to 300° F. If using a gas or charcoal grill, set it up for medium-low heat.
2. Season cubed pork shoulder with Pulled Pork Rub, then transfer to a cast iron Dutch oven, and add chicken stock. Transfer

to center of grill with sear slide open. Bring mixture to a boil, then cover and close the sear slide. Simmer pork for 2 ½ hours, until tender.
3. Remove the lid and open the sear slide. Bring to boil and reduce liquid by half, about 15 minutes. Remove from grill and set aside.
4. Heat 1 tablespoon of bacon fat in the skillet, then use a slotted spoon to transfer the pork to the skillet. Fry pork in fat, stirring occasionally, for 8 to 10 minutes, until pork crisps up. Remove from grill.
5. Serve pork carnitas warm in fresh corn tortillas, with cilantro, red onion, jalapeño, queso fresco, and fresh lime.

Apple Bacon Smoked Ham

Servings: 8-12
Cooking Time: 120 Minutes

Ingredients:
- 1 1/2 Cup Apple Cider
- 3 Tablespoon Apple Cider Vinegar
- 2 Apples
- 1 Lb. Bacon
- 2 Tablespoon Butter, Unsalted
- 2 Tablespoon Cornstarch
- 3 Tablespoon Dijon Mustard
- Smoke Infused Applewood Bacon Rub
- 1/2 Cup Pure Maple Syrup
- 1 Large Bone In Spiral Cut Smoked Ham
- 2 Tablespoon Yellow Mustard

Directions:
1. Supply your smoker with wood pellets and follow the start-up procedure. Preheat the grill, with the lid open, to 250° F.
2. Smoke the bacon directly on the grates for 25 minutes, flipping at the 15-minute mark. Thinly slice the apples while the bacon cooks. Once the bacon is done, set your temperature down to 225 degrees F.
3. Put the spiral-sliced ham into an aluminum foil roasting pan. Start by adding apple into the first slice and every other slice after that. Fill in all other slices with the bacon strips. Season with Smoke Infused Applewood Bacon Rub. Add any extra apple cider to the bottom of the pan for added flavor.
4. Place ham in the grill for 60 minutes.
5. Meanwhile, in a saucepan, whisk together apple cider, maple syrup, apple cider vinegar, Dijon mustard, yellow mustard, cornstarch and Smoke Infused Applewood Bacon Rub. Bring to a boil. Reduce to a simmer, stirring often, until the sauce has thickened and reduced (approximately 15-20 minutes). Stir in the butter until it has completely melted. Glaze should thicken more as it stands.

6. After 60 minutes, add carrots into the roasting pan and glaze the entire ham. Glaze again every 30 minutes until done.
7. Remove ham from grill and allow to rest covered with foil for 20 minutes before serving.
8. Serve with remaining warmed up sauce if desired.

Baked Candied Bacon Cinnamon Rolls

Servings: 6
Cooking Time: 35 Minutes

Ingredients:
- 12 Slices Bacon, sliced
- 1/3 Cup brown sugar
- pre-made cinnamon rolls
- 2 Ounce cream cheese

Directions:
1. Supply your smoker with wood pellets and follow the start-up procedure. Preheat the grill, with the lid closed, to 350° F.
2. Dredge 8 of the slices of bacon in brown sugar, making sure to cover both sides of the bacon.
3. Place the brown sugared bacon slices along with the other slices of bacon on a cooling rack placed on top of a large baking sheet.
4. Cook the bacon on the Traeger for 15-20 minutes or until the fat renders but bacon is still pliable. Turn the Traeger down to 325°F.
5. Open and unroll the cinnamon rolls. While bacon is still warm, place 1 slice of the brown sugared bacon on top of 1 of the unrolled rolls and roll back up. Repeat for all the rolls.
6. Place cinnamon rolls in an 8" x 8" baking dish or cake pan that has been sprayed with nonstick cooking spray. Cook the cinnamon rolls at 325°F for 10 to 15 minutes or until golden. Rotate the pan a half turn halfway through cooking time. Grill: 325 °F
7. Meanwhile, take the provided cream cheese frosting and mix in the softened cream cheese. Crumble the cooked bacon and add into the cream cheese frosting.
8. Spread frosting over warm cinnamon rolls. Serve warm, enjoy!

Grilled Pork Loin

Servings: 4
Cooking Time: 30 Minutes

Ingredients:
- 2 Tablespoons Balsamic Vinegar
- 2 Cups Fresh Washed And Dried Blackberries
- ¼ Cup Seedless Blackberry Preserve
- ½ Teaspoon Dijon Mustard
- Pinch Of Kosher Salt
- 1 Tablespoon Olive Oil
- 1 Pound Silver Skin And Extra Fat Removed Pork Loin

- 2 Tablespoons Sweet Rib Rub
- 1 Tablespoon Worcestershire Sauce

Directions:
1. Place your pork loin on a flat work surface. Trim the pork loin if necessary. Rub the tenderloin all over with olive oil until it is fully coated. Once the pork loin is completely coated, generously season all over with Sweet Rib Rub until every part of the pork loin is coated. Allow the pork tenderloin to rest at room temperature for 30 minutes.
2. While the pork loin rests, make the blackberry sauce. In a small bowl, place a metal strainer on top combine the fresh blackberries, seedless blackberry preserves, balsamic vinegar, Worcestershire sauce, Dijon mustard, and Sweet Rib Rub. Mix well and set aside.
3. Supply your smoker with wood pellets and follow the start-up procedure. Preheat the grill, with the lid open, to 350° F. If you're using a gas or charcoal grill, set it up for medium heat. Insert a temperature probe into the thickest part of the pork loin and smoke at 225°F for 4-5 hours, flipping once, until the pork loin is golden brown and charred in some spots, and reaches an internal temperature of 145°-165°F. Remove the pork loin from the grill and allow it to rest for 5 minutes.
4. Slice the pork loin thinly and serve with the blackberry sauce.

Baked Maple And Brown Sugar Bacon

Servings: 4
Cooking Time: 60 Minutes

Ingredients:
- 1 Pound cold bacon
- 1/2 Cup pure maple syrup, warmed
- 1/2 Cup brown sugar, plus more as needed

Directions:
1. Supply your smoker with wood pellets and follow the start-up procedure. Preheat the grill, with the lid closed, to 300° F.
2. Line a rimmed baking sheet with foil and place a wire rack on top. Lay bacon strips in a single layer on the wire rack.
3. Using a pastry brush, brush each strip of bacon on both sides with the warmed maple syrup, then sprinkle brown sugar evenly on both sides.
4. Put the baking sheet in the grill and cook bacon for 60-75 minutes, or until bacon browns and appears to be crisping. Grill: 300 °F
5. Allow the bacon to cool slightly before eating. Enjoy!

Traeger Pork Chops

Servings: 2
Cooking Time: 30 Minutes

Ingredients:
- 2 (1-1/2 inch thick) pork chops
- Blackened Saskatchewan Rub
- kosher or sea salt

Directions:
1. Rub salt and Traeger Blackened Saskatchewan Rub into pork chops.
2. Supply your smoker with wood pellets and follow the start-up procedure. Preheat the grill, with the lid closed, to 450° F.
3. Place pork chops directly on grill grate and cook for 30 minutes flipping once halfway through. Grill: 450 °F
4. Remove from grill and let rest 5 minutes. Enjoy!

Smoked Porchetta With Italian Salsa Verde

Servings: 8-12
Cooking Time: 180 Minutes

Ingredients:
- 3 Tablespoon dried fennel seed
- 2 Tablespoon red pepper flakes
- 2 Tablespoon sage, minced
- 1 Tablespoon rosemary, minced
- 3 Clove garlic, minced
- As Needed lemon zest
- As Needed orange zest
- To Taste salt and pepper
- 6 Pound Pork Belly, skin on
- As Needed salt and pepper
- 1 Whole shallot, thinly sliced
- 6 Tablespoon parsley, minced
- 2 Tablespoon freshly minced chives
- 1 Tablespoon Oregano, fresh
- 3 Tablespoon white wine vinegar
- 1/2 Teaspoon kosher salt
- 3/4 Cup olive oil
- 1/2 Teaspoon Dijon mustard
- As Needed fresh lemon juice

Directions:
1. Prepare herb mixture: In a medium bowl, mix together fennel seeds, red pepper flakes, sage, rosemary, garlic, citrus zest, salt and pepper.
2. Place pork belly skin side up on a clean work surface and score in a crosshatch pattern. Flip the pork belly over and season flesh side with salt, pepper and half of the herb mixture.
3. Place trimmed pork loin in the center of the belly and rub with remaining herb mixture. Season with salt and pepper.
4. Roll the pork belly around the loin to form a cylindrical shape and tie tightly with kitchen twine at 1" intervals.
5. Season the outside with salt and pepper and transfer to refrigerator, uncovered and let air dry overnight.
6. When ready to cook, start the smoker grill and set to Smoke.

7. Fit a rimmed baking sheet with a rack and place the pork on the rack seam side down.
8. Place the pan directly on the grill grate and smoke for 1 hour.
9. Increase the grill temperature to 325 degrees F and roast until the internal temperature of the meat reaches 135 degrees, about 2 1/2 hours. If the exterior begins to burn before the desired internal temperature is reached, tent with foil.
10. Remove from grill and let stand 30 minutes before slicing.
11. To make the Italian salsa verde: Combine shallot, parsley, chives, vinegar, oregano and salt in a medium bowl. Whisk in olive oil then stir in mustard and lemon juice.
12. Drizzle slices with Italian salsa verde and enjoy!

Smoked Curry Ketchup Pork Ribs

Servings: 4
Cooking Time: 205 Minutes

Ingredients:
- 1 Tsp Chili Powder
- 1 Tbsp Curry Powder
- 1/2 Tsp Ground Mustard
- 2 Tsp Honey
- To Taste, Kansas City Barbecue Rub Seasoning
- 1 Cup Ketchup
- 2 Pork Back Rib Racks, Membrane Removed
- 2 Tsp Smoked Paprika
- 2 Tsp Worcestershire Sauce

Directions:
1. Supply your smoker with wood pellets and follow the start-up procedure. Preheat the grill, with the lid open, to 225° F. If using a gas or charcoal grill, set it up for low, indirect heat.
2. Place rib racks on a sheet tray, then season both sides with Kansas City Barbeque Rub. Transfer ribs to the grill and smoke for 1 hour.
3. Meanwhile, prepare the curry ketchup: In a mixing bowl, add ketchup, curry powder, smoked paprika, chili powder, ground mustard, Worcestershire, and honey and whisk to incorporate. Set aside.
4. Rotate the rib racks and increase temperature to 250 F. Cook for another hour, then remove the ribs from the grill and place on butcher paper. Brush ribs with sauce then wrap with paper.
5. Return ribs to the grill. Cook for one more hour, until tender.
6. Remove ribs from the grill, cut open the butcher paper, and baste with remaining curry ketchup. Place racks back on the grill, increase the temperature to 275 F, then cook for an additional 15 minutes. Remove ribs from the grill, cut open the butcher paper, and baste with remaining curry ketchup. Place racks back on the grill, increase the temperature to 275 F, then cook for an additional 15 minutes.
7. Remove ribs from the grill, rest for 10 minutes, then slice and serve warm.

Pulled Pork Taquitos With Sour Cream

Servings: 4
Cooking Time: 300 Minutes

Ingredients:
- ⅓ Cup Apple Cider Vinegar
- ½ Cup, Plus Extra For Dipping Bbq Sauce
- 4 Cups Chicken Broth
- 1 Teaspoon Chili Powder
- ⅓ Cup Mustard
- 2 Tbsp Olive Oil
- 6 Tbsp Pulled Pork Rub
- 4 Lb. Pork Shoulder, Bone In
- 1 ½ Cup Sharp Cheddar Cheese, Shredded
- ¼ Cup Sour Cream
- 10 Flour Tortillas

Directions:
1. Supply your smoker with wood pellets and follow the start-up procedure. Preheat the grill, with the lid open, to 400° F. If using a gas or charcoal grill, set the temp to medium heat. In a bowl, combine the chicken broth, mustard, apple cider vinegar, and 1 tablespoon of Pulled Pork Seasoning. Whisk well to combine and set aside.
2. Generously season the pork shoulder with the remaining 3 tablespoons of Pulled Pork Seasoning on all sides of the pork shoulder, then place on the grill and sear on all sides until golden brown, about 10 minutes.
3. Remove the pork shoulder from the grill and place in the disposable aluminum pan. Pour the chicken broth mixture over the pork shoulder. It should come about 1/3 to ½ way up the side of the pork shoulder. Cover the top of the pan tightly with aluminum foil.
4. Reduce the temperature of your grill to 250°F. Place the foil pan on the grill and grill for four to five hours, or until the pork is tender and falling off the bone.
5. Remove the pork from the grill and allow to cool slightly. Place on a cutting board and shred with meat claws, reserving about 2.5 cups. Fire up grill to 425°F.
6. In a mixing bowl, combine sour cream, BBQ sauce, and chili powder. Stir in cheddar cheese and pork until well combined.
7. Lay each tortilla flat on your work surface and scoop about ¼ cup of pork mixture in the center, lengthwise. Roll up tightly and place seam side down on baking sheet. Repeat with all tortillas, then brush tops lightly with olive oil.
8. Transfer baking sheet to grill and cook for 15-20 minutes at 400°F , or until cheese has melted and tortilla edges have turned a golden brown. Serve with extra BBQ sauce for dipping and enjoy!

Home-cured Picnic Ham With Mustard Caviar

Servings: 8
Cooking Time: 420 Minutes

Ingredients:
- 1 pork shoulder roast, about 5lb (2.3kg) total
- 1 cup distilled water, apple cider, or apple juice, plus more
- Mustard Caviar
- for the brine
- 1 cup kosher salt
- 5 tsp pink curing salt #1
- 1 cup light brown sugar or turbinado sugar or low-carb substitute
- ¼ cup molasses or honey
- 1 gallon (3.8 liters) distilled water, divided, plus more

Directions:
1. Trim any excess fat from the pork shoulder, leaving at least ¼ inch. Use a sharp knife to score the skin of the ham in the classic diamond pattern, making the cuts about 1 inch (2.5cm) apart, but don't penetrate the meat. (If you purchased a shoulder without skin, skip this step.)
2. In a stockpot on the stovetop over medium-high heat, make the brine by combining the salts, brown sugar, molasses, and water. Bring the mixture to a boil. Whisk to dissolve the salts and sugar. Remove the stockpot from the stovetop and let the brine cool to room temperature.
3. Submerge the pork shoulder in the brine. If it floats, place a resealable bag of ice on top. Refrigerate for 3 days.
4. Place the ham in a clean container and cover with cold water. Let the ham soak for 30 minutes. Drain and pat dry with paper towels.
5. Supply your smoker with wood pellets and follow the start-up procedure. Preheat the grill, with the lid closed, to 225° F.
6. Place the ham on the grate and grill until the internal temperature in the thickest part of the meat reaches 160°F (71°C), about 4 to 5 hours. Remove the ham from the grill. Let the ham come to room temperature. Cover and refrigerate for up to 3 days. This helps establish the ham's smokiness.
7. Preheat the grill to 325°F (163°C).
8. Transfer the ham to an aluminum foil roasting pan and add the water to the bottom of the pan. Place the pan on the grate and roast the ham until the skin is nicely browned and the internal temperature reaches 145°F (63°C), about 1½ to 2 hours.
9. Remove the ham from the grill and let rest for 10 minutes. Carve the ham and serve with the mustard caviar.

Spiced Pork Belly

Servings: 4
Cooking Time: 130 Minutes

Ingredients:
- 2lb (1kg) skinless pork belly
- for the rub
- 2 tbsp fine kosher salt
- 2 tbsp granulated white or light brown sugar or low-carb substitute
- 2 tsp freshly ground black pepper
- 2 tsp ground mustard
- 2 tsp Chinese five-spice powder

Directions:
1. In a small bowl, make the rub by combining the ingredients. Mix well. Lightly season the pork belly on all sides with the rub. Cover and refrigerate overnight.
2. Supply your smoker with wood pellets and follow the start-up procedure. Preheat the grill, with the lid closed, to 450° F.
3. Place the pork belly on the grate and roast for 30 minutes, turning once. Lower the temperature to 275°F (135°C). Roast the pork until tender and the internal temperature reaches 185°F (85°C), about 1 to 1½ hours more.
4. Remove the pork belly from the grill and let cool completely. Wrap tightly in plastic wrap and refrigerate until firm and well chilled.
5. Preheat the grill to 450°F (232°C).
6. Cut the pork belly into slices, slabs, or cubes. Place the pork on the grate and grill until the edges crisp, about 8 to 10 minutes, turning as needed.
7. Remove the pork from the grill and serve immediately.

Grilled Lemon Pepper Pork Tenderloin

Servings: 4
Cooking Time: 20 Minutes

Ingredients:
- 2 lemons, zested
- 1 Clove garlic, minced
- 1 Teaspoon freshly minced parsley
- 1 Teaspoon lemon juice
- 1/4 Teaspoon black pepper
- 1/2 Teaspoon kosher salt
- 2 Tablespoon olive oil
- 1 (2 lb) pork tenderloin

Directions:
1. In a small bowl, whisk together everything except the tenderloin.
2. Trim all silverskin and excess fat from the tenderloin.
3. Place pork in a large resealable bag. Pour the marinade over the tenderloin and zip closed. Transfer to the refrigerator and marinate for at least 2 hours but no more than 8.
4. Supply your smoker with wood pellets and follow the start-up procedure. Preheat the grill, with the lid closed, to 375° F.

5. Remove the tenderloin from the bag and discard the marinade.

6. When the grill is hot, place tenderloin directly on the grill grate and cook 15 to 20 minutes, flipping once halfway through until the internal temperature reaches 145°F. Grill: 375 °F Probe: 145 °F

7. Remove from the heat and let rest 5 to 10 minutes before slicing. Enjoy!

Grilled Raspberry Chipotle Pork Ribs

Servings: 4
Cooking Time: 180 Minutes

Ingredients:
- Baby Back Rib
- Original Bbq Sauce
- Raspberry Chipotle Spice Rub

Directions:
1. Begin by gently rinsing off your ribs in cool water. Pat dry and remove the flavor blocker (thin membrane on the underside of the ribs) to allow the seasoning to permeate right into the meat.
2. Generously season your ribs with Raspberry Chipotle seasoning and place in the refrigerator for an hour for flavor to set in.
3. Supply your smoker with wood pellets and follow the start-up procedure. Preheat the grill, with the lid open, to 250° F. Place your seasoned rack of ribs on the grill and let cook for 2 hours. Next, lather on a thick coating of Original BBQ Sauce, turn up the grill to 300°F and let your ribs roast for another hour. Remove, cut and serve for a meal that will surely make its way into the weekly rotation.

Smoked Apple Pork Belly

Servings: 12
Cooking Time: 370 Minutes

Ingredients:
- 4 Pounds Slab Pork Belly (Uncured)
- 2 Cups Apple Juice (Divided Use)
- ½ Cup BBQ Sauce
- ¼ Cup Signature Sweet Rub

Directions:
1. Supply your smoker with wood pellets and follow the start-up procedure. Preheat the grill, with the lid closed, to 250° F.
2. Score the top layer of fat on the pork belly in 1 inch squares. Don't cut too deep, just barely into the muscle. Season liberally with the Sweet Rub on all sides.
3. Place the seasoned pork belly on the grill and smoke until the internal temperature reaches 165 degrees F (about 6 hours). Spritz with the apple juice every hour while it is cooking.

4. Once the belly reaches 165 degrees F, remove from the grill and wrap in heavy duty tinfoil with 1/2 cup of the apple juice. Seal the edges of the foil completely and return to the grill until the internal temperature reaches 200 degrees F.

5. Carefully remove the belly from the foil and drizzle with the apple juices from the foil. Return the pork belly to the grill and brush with BBQ sauce. Cook on the grill for 10 more minutes.

6. Remove the finished pork belly from the grill and let it rest for 10-15 more minutes before serving.

Spiced Grilled Pork Chops

Servings: 4
Cooking Time: 30 Minutes

Ingredients:
- 3 Tbsp Black Peppercorns, Ground
- 1 Tbsp Coriander, Seed
- 1/4 Cup Cumin
- 1 - 2 Tsp Dry Rub
- 1 Tsp Olive Oil
- 4 Pork, Chop Bone-In
- 1 1/2 Tsp Salt
- 2 Tbsp Sugar

Directions:
1. Supply your smoker with wood pellets and follow the start-up procedure. Preheat the grill, with the lid open, to 450° F.
2. Combine the cumin seeds, whole black peppercorns, and coriander seeds in a cast iron skillet. Stir over medium heat for about 8 minutes until toasted. Let them cool slightly. Finely grind toasted spices in a blender and transfer to a small bowl, then mix in sugar and salt.
3. Rub the spices into the pork chops on both sides. Place cast iron skillet inside the grill. Once hot, add the olive oil to the skillet and coat the bottom. Sprinkle the pork chops with salt, and then add to the skillet. Make sure that each pork chop has enough space in between one another. Cook the chops for about 30 minutes. Once pork chops are fully cooked, turn off the grill, remove skillet, plate and enjoy!

Prosciutto Wrapped Dates With Marcona Almonds

Servings: 8
Cooking Time: 5 Minutes

Ingredients:
- 24 Whole medjool dates
- 1 Small container Marcona salted almonds
- 8 Ounce prosciutto
- 2 Tablespoon olive oil
- 2 limes, washed and dried for zesting

- honey, for serving
- flake salt, for serving

Directions:
1. Supply your smoker with wood pellets and follow the start-up procedure. Preheat the grill, with the lid closed, to 400° F.
2. Place a large cast iron pan into the grill to preheat. Using a small paring knife, cut a slit lengthwise across the top of each date. Remove the pit. Replace pits with 1 to 2 Marcona almonds, then press the dates back together with your fingers to seal.
3. Cut the prosciutto into 24 pieces lengthwise. To wrap each date, place one at the bottom of a strip of prosciutto, then roll the prosciutto around the date to cover, leaving a little bit of the date showing on each end.
4. Add 2 Tablespoons olive oil to the preheated cast iron pan. Place the dates in the pan and cook, searing the prosciutto on all sides, turning as needed, about 3 to 5 minutes total. When the prosciutto is crispy, carefully remove the pan from the grill.
5. Zest the limes over the pan so the citrus zest is absorbed into the olive oil and onto the dates. Place the dates on a serving platter. Sprinkle with flake salt, an additional drizzle of olive oil, honey and serve. Enjoy!

Smoked Porchetta

Servings: 6
Cooking Time: 360 Minutes

Ingredients:
- 1 Tbs Ancho Chili Powder
- 1/2 Cup Brown Sugar
- 3 Tbs Grilling Seasoning
- 1 Tbs Chopped Italian Parsley
- 1/2 Cup Maple Syrup
- 1 Tsp Dry Oregano
- 1 Tbs Chopped Oregano, Leaves
- 1/2 Pork, Belly (Skinless)
- 1 Whole Pork, Tenderloins
- 6 Slices Prosciutto, Sliced
- 1 Tbs Chopped Rosemary, Fresh
- 1 Tbs Chopped Sage, Leaves
- 1/2 Cup Sugar, Cure

Directions:
1. Sprinkle Sugar Cure on each side and rub in. (You can cure pork belly without using Sodium Nitrite (in the cure mix) but it is much safer if you use it, so I definitely recommend it).
2. In a small bowl, mix brown sugar, maple syrup, ancho chili powder and oregano, and whisk. Slather on both sides of each pork belly piece.
3. Place pork bag (if you can find a 2 gallon or larger one) or container and refrigerate Rotate and flip each 24 hours.
4. After 3 days remove pork belly and rinse each piece thoroughly.
5. If you do not rinse well the porchetta (or bacon) will be too salty due to the sugar cure.
6. Lay pork belly skin side down on a large cutting board.
7. Lightly score the meat side with diamond cuts to allow the seasoning to penetrate.
8. Lightly sprinkle with grilling seasoning, then coat well with the herb mix.
9. Lay out the prosciutto, then lay the pork tenderloin on the pork belly.
10. Lightly sprinkle tenderloin with seasoning, and wrap the pork belly tightly around it.
11. Use cooking twine to tie up tightly.
12. Season the exterior of the pork belly lightly but evenly with grilling seasoning.
13. Supply your smoker with wood pellets and follow the start-up procedure. Preheat the grill, with the lid open, to 250° F.
14. Smoke for 6 hours, or until internal temperature reaches around 175°F.
15. Remove and allow to rest for 20 minutes. Once it cools, then slice thinly and sear in a hot skillet.
16. Let it cool again for about 10 minutes before serving.

Traeger Pulled Pork Sandwiches

Servings: 8
Cooking Time: 660 Minutes

Ingredients:
- 1 (5-7 lb) bone-in pork shoulder
- Pork & Poultry Rub
- 2 Cup apple juice, in food-grade spray bottle
- BBQ Sauce
- 10 hamburger buns
- coleslaw, for serving

Directions:
1. Generously season pork roast on all sides with Traeger Pork & Poultry rub.
2. Supply your smoker with wood pellets and follow the start-up procedure. Preheat the grill, with the lid closed, to 225° F.
3. Put the roast on the grill grate, fat-side up and smoke for 3 hours. Spray the roast with apple juice every hour after the first hour. Grill: 225 °F
4. After 3 hours, transfer pork to a disposable aluminum foil pan large enough to hold the roast. Increase the grill temperature to 250°F, and continue to cook for 6 to 8 additional hours, or until an instant-read meat thermometer inserted in the thickest part, but not touching bone, registers 203°F. If the pork starts to brown too much, cover it loosely with aluminum foil. Grill: 250 °F Probe: 203 °F

5. Carefully transfer the pork roast to a cutting board and let it rest for 20 minutes. Pour the juices from the bottom of the pan into a gravy separator. Discard any fat that has floated to the top.

6. With your hands (preferably protected from the heat with lined, heavy-duty rubber gloves) pull the pork into chunks. Discard the bone and any lumps of fat, including the cap. Pull each chunk into shreds and transfer to a large mixing bowl.

7. Season with additional rub and moisten with the reserved pork juice. Add your favorite Traeger BBQ sauce to the pulled pork and mix well.

8. Pile the pork mixture on the hamburger buns and serve with coleslaw. Enjoy!

Balsamic Brussels Sprouts With Bacon

Servings: 8
Cooking Time: 25 Minutes

Ingredients:

- 6 Strips thick-cut bacon
- 2 Pound Brussels sprouts, trimmed and halved
- 1 Small onion, diced
- 2 Tablespoon olive oil or vegetable oil
- freshly ground black pepper
- salt
- 1/2 Cup chicken stock
- 1 Tablespoon balsamic vinegar

Directions:

1. Supply your smoker with wood pellets and follow the start-up procedure. Preheat the grill, with the lid closed, to 450° F.
2. Place the bacon strips directly on the grill grate and cook for 20 minutes. Grill: 450 °F
3. Line a large baking sheet with foil for easy cleanup. Place the onion and sprouts cut-side down on the baking sheet, drizzle with oil and season with salt and pepper.
4. Place the baking sheet directly on the grill grate next to the bacon and roast until they turn a light golden brown, about 8 to 10 minutes. Grill: 450 °F
5. Add the cooked bacon, pour chicken stock and balsamic vinegar over the sprouts, mix and continue to cook until the liquid has thickened. Remove from heat. Enjoy!

Grilled Sugar Snap Peas And Smoked Bacon

Servings: 4
Cooking Time: 20 Minutes

Ingredients:

- 2 Pound Sugar Snap Peas, ends trimmed
- 2 Tablespoon extra-virgin olive oil
- 1 To Taste salt and pepper
- 1 Pound bacon
- 2 Tablespoon butter
- 2 Medium shallot, thinly sliced
- 1 Clove garlic, minced
- 1/4 Cup bourbon
- 2 Tablespoon maple syrup

Directions:

1. Supply your smoker with wood pellets and follow the start-up procedure. Preheat the grill, with the lid closed, to 350° F.
2. In a medium bowl, toss peas with olive oil and season with salt and pepper to taste.
3. Place a grill mat or tray on the grill grate to prevent peas from falling through the grates.
4. Place peas on grill mat and cook for 10 minutes until lightly browned and tender but still bright green. Grill: 350 °F
5. Place bacon slices on the grill next to peas and cook for 15-20 minutes or until fat is rendered and slightly crisp. Grill: 350 °F
6. While the bacon and peas cook, heat butter in a pan over medium-high heat.
7. Add shallot and garlic and sauté until tender and cooked through. Deglaze with bourbon and cook until reduced by half. Add maple syrup and salt and pepper to taste. Set aside.
8. Remove bacon from grill and chop into 1/2-inch pieces.
9. Toss the bacon pieces with the grilled sugar snap peas and maple bourbon mixture. Enjoy!

Delicious Smoked Bone-in Pork Chops

Servings: 4
Cooking Time: 90 Minutes

Ingredients:

- 1/2 Cup Apple Cider Vinegar
- 4 Pork Butt Roast, Bone-In
- 2 Tbsp Salt
- 1 Tbsp Sugar
- 4 Tablespoons Tennessee Apple Butter Seasoning
- 1/4 Cup Vinegar, Red Wine
- 1/4 Cup Water

Directions:

1. Supply your smoker with wood pellets and follow the start-up procedure. Preheat the grill, with the lid closed, to 250° F.
2. In a large mixing bowl, combine the sugar, red wine vinegar, salt, 2 tablespoons of Tennessee Apple Butter and water to create a brine for the pork chops. Whisk the brine well until the sugar, salt and Tennessee Apple Butter have dissolved.
3. Generously rub the pork chops on all sides with olive oil and season on all sides with the Tennessee Apple Butter. Make sure the meat is coated on all sides.
4. Place the pork chops in the smoker, insert a temperature probe into the thickest part of one of the pork chops, and smoke until the internal temperature reaches 145°F, or about 1 hour 30

minutes. The pork chops should have developed a good color and be juicy, but no longer be pink in the center.
5. Remove the pork chops from the smoker and allow them to rest for 5-10 minutes under tented aluminum foil, then slice along the grain and serve.

Old-fashioned Roasted Glazed Ham

Servings: 8
Cooking Time: 60 Minutes

Ingredients:
- 1 (10 lb) fully cooked bone-in spiral cut ham
- 1 Cup pineapple juice
- 1/2 Cup brown sugar
- 1 cinnamon stick
- 14 whole cloves
- 1 Whole Pineapple, fresh
- 10 Cherries, fresh, sweet

Directions:
1. Supply your smoker with wood pellets and follow the start-up procedure. Preheat the grill, with the lid closed, to 325° F.
2. Rinse ham under cold water and pat dry with paper towel.
3. In a saucepan combine pineapple juice, brown sugar, cinnamon stick and four cloves. Bring to a boil. Reduce heat to medium low and simmer for about 15 minutes or until pineapple juice is reduced by half, thick and syrupy.
4. Brush half of the glaze onto the ham and into the folds of the cut slices. Reserve the other half of the glaze for later.
5. Cut pineapple in desired sized pieces, about 2 inch squares, then place on ham with a cherry and a clove to pin in place, repeating all over ham.
6. Put ham in a deep baking dish with fat side up. Place on the Traeger and cook for about 1-¼ hours. Grill: 325 °F
7. Carefully remove from Traeger and brush remaining glaze onto ham.
8. Return ham to Traeger and continue cooking for another 15 to 20 minutes, until internal temperature of ham reaches 160°F. Grill: 325 °F Probe: 160 °F
9. Allow ham to rest for 15 – 20 minutes before serving. Enjoy!

Smoked Chorizo & Arugula Pesto

Servings: 4
Cooking Time: 20 Minutes

Ingredients:
- 4 Cup Arugula, fresh
- 1 Clove garlic
- 1/2 Cup Parmesan cheese, grated
- 1/2 Cup pine nuts
- 1/4 Cup extra-virgin olive oil
- 1/4 Cup grapeseed oil
- sea salt
- freshly ground black pepper
- water

Directions:
1. To make the pesto, add arugula, garlic, cheese, and nuts to the bowl of a food processor or blender, and puree. As the processor is running, drizzle in the oil. Season the mixture with salt and pepper, to taste. If the pesto is too thick, thin it out with water.
2. Supply your smoker with wood pellets and follow the start-up procedure. Preheat the grill, with the lid closed, to 375° F.
3. Smoke the sausages whole for 20 minutes, or until it reaches an internal temperature of 170°F. Grill: 375 °F Probe: 170 °F
4. Let rest for 10 minutes, then cut the sausage links into large 1-1/2" chunks. Transfer the sausage to a platter and serve with dollops of the arugula pesto. Enjoy!

Mini Sausage Rolls

Servings: 4
Cooking Time: 25 Minutes

Ingredients:
- 3/4 Cup dry mustard
- 3/4 Cup distilled white vinegar
- 1/2 Cup honey
- 4 egg yolk, beaten
- 2 Pound Sausage, Uncooked
- ground sage
- 1 Small onion, diced small
- 17 1/2 Ounce frozen puff pastry

Directions:
1. Make the mustard: Combine the mustard and vinegar in a small mixing bowl. Cover with plastic wrap and let sit overnight at room temperature to develop the flavors. Transfer the mustard mixture to a small heavy saucepan and add the honey and egg yolks. Cook over low heat, whisking constantly, until thickened, about 7 minutes. Cool, then refrigerate until serving time.
2. In a medium mixing bowl, thoroughly combine the sausage and onion. On a lightly floured work surface, roll each sheet of thawed puff pastry - there are two to a package - into an 11 by 10-1/2 inch rectangle.
3. Using a pizza cutter or knife, cut each rectangle widthwise into three strips, each 3-1/2 inches wide. Wet your hands and mold some of the sausage into a tube-like shape. Lay it down the center of one of the puff pastry strips.
4. Wrap the pastry around the sausage and seal the seams with a bit of beaten egg. Repeat with the remaining sausage and puff pastry. Put all the rolls seam side down on your work surface and brush the tops lightly with the egg.

5. Cut the rolls into pieces about 1-1/2 inches long and transfer to a rimmed baking sheet lined with parchment paper. Leave about an inch between each roll. Supply your smoker with wood pellets and follow the start-up procedure. Preheat the grill, with the lid closed, to 350° F.
6. Bake the sausage rolls for about 25 minutes, or until the sausage is cooked through and the pastry is golden brown. Serve hot with the honey mustard. Grill: 350 °F

Everything Pigs In A Blanket

Servings: 4
Cooking Time: 15 Minutes

Ingredients:
- 2 Tablespoon poppy seeds
- 1 Tablespoon dried minced onion
- 2 Teaspoon garlic, minced
- 2 Tablespoon sesame seeds
- 1 Teaspoon salt
- 8 Ounce (8 oz) Can Pillsbury Original Crescent Rolls
- 1/4 Cup Dijon mustard
- 1 Large egg, beaten

Directions:
1. Supply your smoker with wood pellets and follow the start-up procedure. Preheat the grill, with the lid closed, to 350° F.
2. Mix together poppy seeds, dried minced onion, dried minced garlic, salt and sesame seeds. Set aside.
3. Cut each triangle of crescent roll dough into thirds lengthwise, making 3 small strips from each roll.
4. Brush the dough strips lightly with Dijon mustard. Put the mini hot dogs on 1 end of the dough and roll up.
5. Arrange them, seam side down, on a greased baking pan. Brush with egg wash and sprinkle with seasoning mixture.
6. Bake in Traeger until golden brown, about 12 to 15 minutes.
7. Serve with mustard or dipping sauce of your choice. Enjoy!

Bbq Pulled Pork Hash

Servings: 4
Cooking Time: 30 Minutes

Ingredients:
- 1/2 Cup carrots, peeled and cut into 1 inch pieces
- 1/2 Cup beets
- 1/2 Cup small new potatoes
- 1/2 Cup asparagus
- 1 Tablespoon olive oil
- leftover pulled pork
- 3 egg

Directions:
1. Supply your smoker with wood pellets and follow the start-up procedure. Preheat the grill, with the lid closed, to 375° F.
2. Chop all vegetables into even pieces, about 1/2 inch cubes. Pre heat a cast iron pan over Medium-High heat.
3. Add a Tablespoon of olive oil then the carrots, new potatoes, and beets. Season with salt and pepper to taste and sauté stirring every few minutes until vegetables are cooked through (about 8 to 10 minutes).
4. Add the asparagus and cook an additional 2 minutes. Add a layer of pulled pork over vegetables. Crack 3 eggs over that being careful not to break the yokes.
5. Place into preheated Traeger and cook for about 10 minutes or until eggs are just set. Remove from grill and serve immediately with your favorite hot sauce. Enjoy! Grill: 375 °F

Smoked Baby Back Ribs

Servings: 4
Cooking Time: 180 Minutes

Ingredients:
- 3 Rack baby back ribs
- kosher salt
- cracked black pepper

Directions:
1. Peel membrane from back side of the ribs and season both sides with salt and pepper.
2. Supply your smoker with wood pellets and follow the start-up procedure. Preheat the grill, with the lid closed, to 225° F.
3. Cook meat side up for two hours. Flip ribs so the meat side is down and cook for an additional hour. Enjoy! Grill: 225 °F

St Louis Style Bbq Ribs With Texas Spicy Bbq Sauce

Servings: 8
Cooking Time: 300 Minutes

Ingredients:
- 3 Rack St. Louis-style ribs, membrane removed
- 4 Tablespoon Rub
- 6 Tablespoon butter
- 1 1/2 Cup brown sugar
- 1 1/2 Cup agave
- 1 1/2 Cup Texas Spicy BBQ Sauce

Directions:
1. Supply your smoker with wood pellets and follow the start-up procedure. Preheat the grill, with the lid closed, to 250° F.
2. Season ribs with Traeger rub and place directly on grill grate rib side down or in a Traeger rib rack with the bone resting on the rack. Cook for 3 hours. Grill: 250 °F

3. Stack 2 pieces of tin foil on the table large enough to cover one rack of ribs. In the center of the foil place 3 tablespoons butter, 1/2 cup brown sugar, and 1/2 cup agave. Place the rib rack meat side down on top of the brown sugar mixture and wrap tightly. Repeat with remaining 2 racks.
4. Place all ribs directly on the grill grate meat side down and cook an additional 1-1/2 to 2 hours or until internal temperature reaches 203°F. Grill: 250 °F Probe: 203 °F
5. Remove ribs from the grill and cover each rack with 1/2 cup Texas Spicy BBQ sauce.
6. Rewrap and return to grill an additional 10 minutes allowing sauce to thicken. Grill: 250 °F
7. Remove ribs from the grill, slice and enjoy!

Sweet Smoked Country Ribs

Servings: 12-15
Cooking Time: 240 Minutes

Ingredients:
- 2 pounds country-style ribs
- 1 batch Sweet Brown Sugar Rub
- 2 tablespoons light brown sugar
- 1 cup Pepsi or other cola
- ¼ cup The Ultimate BBQ Sauce

Directions:
1. Supply your smoker with wood pellets and follow the start-up procedure. Preheat the grill, with the lid closed, to 180°F.
2. Sprinkle the ribs with the rub and use your hands to work the rub into the meat.
3. Place the ribs directly on the grill grate and smoke for 3 hours.
4. Remove the ribs from the grill and place them on enough aluminum foil to wrap them completely. Dust the brown sugar over the ribs.
5. Increase the grill's temperature to 300°F.
6. Fold in three sides of the foil around the ribs and add the cola. Fold in the last side, completely enclosing the ribs and liquid. Return the ribs to the grill and cook for 45 minutes.
7. Remove the ribs from the foil and place them on the grill grate. Baste all sides of the ribs with barbecue sauce. Cook for 15 minutes more to caramelize the sauce.
8. Remove the ribs from the grill and serve immediately.

Texas Grilled Ribs

Servings: 4
Cooking Time: 240 Minutes

Ingredients:
- 1 Cup Apple Cider Vinegar
- 1 Rack Baby Back Rib
- 2 Tablespoons Whole Grain Mustard
- 2 Tablespoons Olive Oil
- 1 Bottle Sweet Heat Rub
- 1 Tablespoons Worcestershire Sauce

Directions:
1. Remove the ribs from their packaging and pat dry.
2. Flip to back of ribs and score the membrane with a knife, then peel off the membrane.
3. Rub the ribs with the olive oil, followed by a generous amount of Sweet Heat Rub & Grill, on both sides.
4. In a small bowl, mix together the mustard, apple cider vinegar, and Worcestershire. Set aside.
5. Supply your smoker with wood pellets and follow the start-up procedure. Preheat the grill, with the lid open, to 225° F. Add the ribs and smoke for 3 hours.
6. Transfer the ribs onto a foil lined sheet pan and brush both sides with the apple cider vinegar mixture. Wrap the ribs tightly in foil and place back on the smoker for 2 more hours.
7. Carefully remove the ribs from the foil and brush with more of the apple cider vinegar mixture. Place the ribs back on the smoker grates and smoke for 1 additional hour.
8. Remove from the smoker and let rest for 5 minutes before serving.

Whiskey- & Cider-brined Pork Shoulder

Servings: 8
Cooking Time: 540 Minutes

Ingredients:
- 1 bone-in pork shoulder, about 5 to 7lb (2.3 to 3.2kg)
- fresh coarsely ground black pepper
- granulated garlic
- 1 cup apple juice or apple cider
- low-carb barbecue sauce, warmed
- hamburger buns (optional)
- for the brine
- 1 gallon (3.8 liters) cold distilled water
- 1 cup coarse salt
- 1¼ cup whiskey, divided
- ½ cup light brown sugar or low-carb substitute

Directions:
1. In a large saucepot on the stovetop over medium-high heat, make the brine by bringing the water, salt, 1 cup of whiskey, and brown sugar to a boil. Stir with a long-handled wooden spoon until the salt and sugar dissolve. Let the brine cool to room temperature. Cover and cool completely in the refrigerator.
2. Submerge the pork in the brine. If it floats, place a resealable bag of ice on top. Refrigerate for 24 hours.
3. Supply your smoker with wood pellets and follow the start-up procedure. Preheat the grill, with the lid closed, to 250° F.
4. Remove the pork shoulder from the brine and pat dry with paper towels. (Discard the brine.) Season the pork with pepper

and granulated garlic. Place the pork on the grate and smoke until the internal temperature reaches 165°F (74°C), about 5 hours.

5. Transfer the pork to an aluminum foil roasting pan and add the apple juice and the remaining ¼ cup of whiskey. Cover tightly with aluminum foil. Place the pan on the grate and cook the pork until the bone releases easily from the meat and the internal temperature reaches 200°F (93°C), about 3 hours more. (Be careful when lifting a corner of the foil to check on the roast because steam will escape.)

6. Remove the pan from the grill and let the pork rest for 20 minutes. Reserve the juices.

7. Wearing heatproof gloves, pull the pork into chunks. Discard the bone or any large lumps of fat. Pull the meat into shreds and transfer to a clean aluminum foil roasting pan. Moisten with the barbecue sauce or serve the sauce on the side. Stir in some of the drippings—not too much because you don't want the pork to be swimming in its juices. Serve on buns (if using).

Kodiak Cakes Candied Bacon Crumble Brownies

Servings: 6
Cooking Time: 45 Minutes

Ingredients:
- 1 Box Big Bear Brownie Mix, Kodiak Cakes
- 2 eggs
- 1 Stick butter, melted
- 2 Tablespoon coconut oil
- 2 Tablespoon water
- 2 Cup cooked bacon
- 1/2 Cup Almonds, chopped
- 1/2 Cup sugar

Directions:
1. Supply your smoker with wood pellets and follow the start-up procedure. Preheat the grill, with the lid closed, to 300° F.
2. Spray an 8" baking pan with non-stick spray.
3. Empty Kodiak Cake brownie mix into a medium-size mixing bowl. Add eggs, melted butter, coconut oil, and water. Gently mix, being careful not to overmix. Pour into prepared pan.
4. Place brownies in center of grill grate; bake for 45 minutes. Grill: 300 °F
5. While the brownies are baking, begin assembling bacon crumble. Add honey or sugar to a medium-size saucepan, over high heat. Add bacon and almonds. Stir for 2-3 minutes, or until sugar has dissolved. Remove from heat and let cool.
6. Remove brownies from grill and cool completely. Sprinkle candied bacon crumble over the top of brownies. Enjoy!

Bacon Weave Smoked Country Sausage

Servings: 4
Cooking Time: 120 Minutes

Ingredients:
- Pound Sausage, Uncooked
- Pork & Poultry Rub
- 8 Slices bacon

Directions:
1. Using your hands, form sausage into a loaf-shape. Season lightly with Traeger Pork and Poultry Shake.
2. Supply your smoker with wood pellets and follow the start-up procedure. Preheat the grill, with the lid closed, to 180° F.
3. Put the sausage loaf directly on the grill grate and smoke for 1-1/2 hours.
4. While sausage is smoking, assemble the bacon weave on a piece of wax paper. First, lay out 4 pieces of bacon so they are touching each other on the wax paper. Next, lay the 5th piece of bacon so it crosses the others. Tuck every other slice under the 5th piece of bacon. Find the two pieces of bacon that were under the 5th piece of bacon and fold them back on top of themselves.
5. Lay down the 6th piece of bacon and unfold the two that were laid back. Continue folding the bacon back that was most recently under the last piece of bacon, two pieces at a time, laying the next piece of bacon on top until your weave is complete. Set aside. After your sausage has smoked for 1-1/2 hours, take it off the grill and increase the heat of your Traeger, lid closed to 350°F and preheat. Grill: 350 °F
6. While the grill is heating, wrap your sausage loaf in the bacon weave. Lay the middle of the weave directly on top of the sausage loaf and press the bacon all around the sausage.
7. Flip the sausage and bacon over to finish the weave on the bottom of the sausage. Alternate the bacon ends across the bottom and tuck the ends around each other.
8. Put your sausage back on the grill and cook for 25-30 minutes until the internal temperature of the sausage reaches 160°F. Enjoy! Probe: 160 °F

Cajun Double-smoked Ham

Servings: 12-15
Cooking Time: 300 Minutes

Ingredients:
- 1 (5- or 6-pound) bone-in smoked ham
- 1 batch Cajun Rub
- 3 tablespoons honey

Directions:
1. Supply your smoker with wood pellets and follow the start-up procedure. Preheat the grill, with the lid closed, to 225°F.
2. Generously season the ham with the rub and place it either in a pan or directly on the grill grate. Smoke it for 1 hour.
3. Drizzle the honey over the ham and continue to smoke it until the ham's internal temperature reaches 145°F.
4. Remove the ham from the grill and let it rest for 5 to 10 minutes, before thinly slicing and serving.

Grilled Stuffed Pork Chops

Servings: 4
Cooking Time: 45 Minutes

Ingredients:
- 4 Whole Pork, Loins
- 2 Cup Herb-Seasoned or Cornbread Stuffing Mix
- Apples, chopped
- onion, chopped
- Celery, Chopped
- chopped sage
- Pork & Poultry Rub or salt and pepper

Directions:
1. Cut a deep pocket in the side of each chop with a small sharp knife, cutting toward the bone but not all the way through.
2. Prepare the stuffing mix according to the package directions, adding your own touches if desired (try adding in chopped onion, a stalk of chopped celery, a finely diced apple, a few leaves of chopped sage and about 4 oz browned sausage).
3. Generously stuff each pork chop pocket with the mixture. Season both sides of the chops with Traeger Pork and Poultry Rub.
4. Supply your smoker with wood pellets and follow the start-up procedure. Preheat the grill, with the lid closed, to 325° F.
5. Arrange the chops directly on the grill grate. Bake for 45 to 50 minutes, or until the chops reach an internal temperature of 160 degrees F. There is no need to turn the chops.
6. Let the pork rest for 2 to 3 minutes before transferring to a platter or plates. Enjoy!

Bourbon Chile Glazed Ham

Servings: 8 – 10
Cooking Time: 90 Minutes

Ingredients:
- ¼ Cup Apple Cider Vinegar
- 2 Cups Bourbon
- 1 Cup Brown Sugar
- 2 Canned Chipotle Chiles In Adobo Sauce
- 2 Cups Chicken Stock
- 2 Dried Ancho Chiles
- 1 Dried Arbol Chile
- 2 Dried Guajillo Chiles
- 2 Tbsp Extra Virgin Olive Oil
- 4 Fresh Garlic, Roughly Chopped
- 4 Cloves Roasted Garlic
- Salt
- 2 Shallots, Roughly Chopped
- 1 Spiral Cut Ham

Directions:
1. Supply your smoker with wood pellets and follow the start-up procedure. Preheat the grill, with the lid open, to 450° F.
2. In a large, heavy-bottomed skillet, heat the oil over medium-high heat. Add the shallots and cook for 5 minutes, or until softened.
3. Add the roasted and fresh garlic and cook, stirring occasionally, for 3 to 4 minutes, until the garlic is browned.
4. Remove the skillet from the heat and add the bourbon.
5. Return the skillet to medium-high heat, add the vinegar, and cook until the liquid is reduced by one third, about 10 minutes.
6. Add the ancho, guajillo, árbol, and chipotle chiles and the brown sugar, then add the chicken stock and continue to cook until the mixture reduces by two thirds, about 15 minutes.
7. Strain the reduction through a fine-mesh strainer into a bowl, then pour it into a small saucepan.
8. Return to the heat over medium and reduce until the glaze coats the back off a spoon. Taste and add salt if needed.

Bacon Wrapped Asparagus

Servings: 4
Cooking Time: 20 Minutes

Ingredients:
- 1 Bunch asparagus
- 1 Tablespoon olive oil
- 1/2 Teaspoon garlic powder
- 1/2 Teaspoon onion powder
- salt and pepper
- 1 Pound Bacon, sliced

Directions:
1. Coat the Asparagus evenly with olive oil, then sprinkle the asparagus evenly with, garlic powder, onion powder, salt and pepper. Individually wrap each asparagus with 1 piece of thin cut bacon.
2. Supply your smoker with wood pellets and follow the start-up procedure. Preheat the grill, with the lid closed, to 450° F.
3. Place the wrapped asparagus on the grill and roast for 15-20 minutes, or until the bacon is crispy. Enjoy!

Smoked Rack Of Pork

Servings: 6
Cooking Time: 360 Minutes

Ingredients:
- 4 Bay Leaves
- 2 Jalapeno Peppers
- 1 Six Bone Rack Of Pork
- 1 Cup Salt
- Salt & Freshly Ground Black Pepper
- 2 Tbsp Smokey Apple Chipotle Rub
- 10 Thyme, Fresh Sprigs

- 1 Gallon Water

Directions:

1. To make the rack of pork: Combine the salt, water, bay, thyme and jalapeño in a large stock pot and bring to a boil, let boil for 10 minutes until salt is dissolved.
2. Remove from heat and let cool completely, add pork to the brine and brine overnight. Remove from the brine and rinse. Pat dry and season with Apple Chipotle seasoning and salt and pepper.
3. Supply your smoker with wood pellets and follow the start-up procedure. Preheat the grill, with the lid open, to 140° F. Place the rack of pork on the smoker with a probe inserted and cook for about 5 to 6 hours.
4. Turn the heat up to 450°F and open the heat shield.
5. Sear the pork on all sides, once seared move to a cutting board and tent with foil, rest for 20 minutes then slice in between each bone and serve.
6. To make the pickled fennel: Place the fennel in a bowl. In a small saucepan over medium low heat, add the pickling spice and toast for about 2 minutes or until fragrant.
7. Add the cider vinegar and bring to a boil over high heat. Add the sugar, salt and water and bring to a boil.
8. Cook for 10 minutes over medium high heat to meld the flavors. Strain over the fennel and set aside to cool. Once cool cover and place in the fridge until ready to use.
9. To make the caramelized sweet potato puree: In a large pan add the olive oil over high heat until the oil is shimmering, add the sweet potatoes and cook browning on all sides.
10. Once the sweet potatoes are caramelized add 1 cup of the water and cook until it has evaporated and repeat the process with the remaining water.
11. In a saucepan add the milk and the cream and warm over low heat. Once the sweet potatoes are tender add them to a blender with the milk mixture and blend until smooth but be careful not to over process and turn the potatoes into glue.
12. To make the mustard gravy: Add the olive oil to a large pan over medium high heat, once shimmering, add the shallots and cook until translucent but not browned.
13. Add the bourbon and cooked until almost entirely reduced. Add the heavy cream and the mustard and cook for about 8 to 10 minutes stirring often until the sauce thickens and coats the back of a spoon.
14. Stir in the parsley and season with salt and pepper.
15. To make the fried shallots: Place the shallots in a small bowl and cover them with the milk, let soak in the milk for at least 1 hour.
16. Drain the shallots and transfer them to a large Ziplock bag, add the flour, salt and pepper. Seal the bag and shake well to coat all the shallots in the flour. Remove from the bag shaking off the excess flour.
17. Heat the oil to 350°F in a deep pot. Fry the shallots until golden brown then remove them to a plate lined with paper towels. Season with salt.
18. To put it all together and plate: Spread the puree in a circle in the middle of the plate, place a small handful of the pickled fennel on one side of the puree, Place the pork leaning on the fennel, Spoon over the sauce and top with the fried shallots and the micro arugula.

Smoked Bacon Roses

Servings: 2
Cooking Time: 60 Minutes

Ingredients:
- 1 Pack Bacon, Thick Cut
- 1 Dozen Roses, Fake

Directions:

1. Supply your smoker with wood pellets and follow the start-up procedure. Preheat the grill, with the lid open, to 225° F.
2. Roll each piece of bacon tightly, starting on the thicker side of the strip. Take a toothpick and skewer the middle of the bottom of the bacon roll to keep the bacon from unraveling. With a second toothpick, skewer the bacon roll so that the two toothpicks form an "X" at the bottom of the roll of bacon. Do this to every piece of bacon.
3. Place the bacon rolls directly on the grates of your preheated Grill and smoke for an hour, checking on them every 20 minutes.
4. While the bacon is smoking, rip the petals of the fake roses off of the steams.
5. Once the bacon is fully cooked, remove the toothpicks and pierce the bacon in the head of the steam (where the fake flowers once were). If the bacon isn't staying, you can break a toothpick in half and stick it in the tip of the steam, press firmly and try piercing the bacon again.
6. Place in a nice vase with some babies breath and gift to your Valentine.

Smoked Pork Tomato Tamales

Servings: 6-8
Cooking Time: 60 Minutes

Ingredients:
- 1 Boneless, Netted Pork Roast
- 1 Cup, Fresh Cilantro, Chopped
- 3 Cloves Garlic, Peeled
- 20 Dried Cornhusks
- 1 Tbsp Lime Juice
- ¼ Cup Olive Oil
- 1 Onion, Quartered
- 4 - 6 Cups Prepared Masa Harina Tamale Dough
- 3 – 4 Serrano Peppers, Deseeded

- 1 Tbsp Sweet Heat Rub
- 1 Lb. Tomatillos, Husked And Washed

Directions:

1. Began by soaking the corn husks in a pan filled with water. Soak for 2 – 4 hours, or if needed, overnight.
2. Unwrap the tomatillos from their shell and place all of them into a grill basket followed by a few Serranos, deseeded, garlic cloves and 1 onion cut into quarters.
3. Supply your smoker with wood pellets and follow the start-up procedure. Preheat the grill, with the lid open, to 400° F. If you're using a gas or charcoal grill, set it up for medium low heat, and use smoke chips to fill your grill with smoke for 15 minutes. Place the grill basket filled with your vegetables and roast them over an open flame on your smoker until vegetables have become charred.
4. Place tomatillos, peppers, garlic and onions in a bowl, cover with plastic wrap, and let stand until cool enough to handle, 10 to 15 minutes.
5. Season the pork roast generously with Sweet Heat Rub and grill at 350°F for 1 hour until the roast has a nice crust on the outside.
6. While the pork roast is cooking, add a handful of cilantro, charred vegetables, 1 tbsp of Sweet Heat Rub, 1 tbsp lime juice, and ¼ cup of olive oil to a food processor. Pulse in food processor until mixture is consistent. Set aside
7. After the pork roast has been grilled for an hour, turn heat down to 275°F. Put roast in pan with about a cup of water, cover with aluminum foil and cook for another 4 hours or until the roast can be shredded. Pour chile verde sauce over shredded pork and toss to combine.
8. To being assembling tamales, place a corn husk on a work surface. Place 2-3 tablespoons of tamale dough on larger end of husk and spread into a rectangle, about ¼" thick, leaving a small border along the edge. Place large tablespoon of chili and pork filling on top of dough. Fold over sides of husk so dough surrounds filling, then fold bottom of husk up and secure closed by tying a thin strip of husk around tamale.
9. To cook tamales, place them in a large metal colander over a large stockpot filled with water. Cover and let steam for 1 hour. After the tamales have been steamed, take them off and grill them at 350°F for about 10-20 minutes until corn husks have charred marks.

Bbq Pork Chops

Servings: 4
Cooking Time: 30 Minutes

Ingredients:

- 4 8-To-10-Ounce Bone-In Pork Loin Chops, Trimmed Of Excess Fat
- 1/2 Cup Brown Sugar
- 2 Garlic Clove, Minced
- 2 Tbsp Honey
- 1 Cup Ketchup
- 1/4 Cup Molasses
- Sweet Rib Rub Seasoning
- 2 Tbsp Worcestershire Sauce

Directions:

1. First, place pork chops onto sheet pan lined with butcher paper. Season generously with Sweet Rib Rub, making sure to coat all sides of the chops. Set aside while you make the glaze.
2. In a medium sized mixing bowl, combine the ketchup, brown sugar, molasses, honey, garlic, Worcestershire, and 1 tbsp Sweet Rib Rub. Mix well, add 1 shot of bourbon, mix again until sauce becomes smooth. Transfer sauce into an oven proof sauce pan.
3. Supply your smoker with wood pellets and follow the start-up procedure. Preheat the grill, with the lid open, to 375° F. If you're using a gas or charcoal grill, set it up for medium direct heat.
4. Grill the pork chops for 10-15 minutes per side. Place the saucepan on the grill and allow the sauce to come to a boil. Glaze the chops on both sides and let the glaze caramelize onto the chops.
5. Grill the pork chops until they are lightly charred and reach an internal temperature of 145°F - 165°F. Remove the pork chops from the grill and allow them to rest for 5 minutes.
6. Once the pork chops have finished resting, glaze them again if you choose to. Serve immediately.

Cuban Onion Pork Sandwich

Servings: 4
Cooking Time: 270 Minutes

Ingredients:

- 1 Tbsp Butter
- 3 Cups Chicken Stock
- 4 Ciabatta Bread Or Torta Rolls, Halved
- 1/4 Cup Dijon Mustard
- 4 Dill Pickle, Slice
- 1 Lb Ham Or Prosciutto
- 1/4 Cup Mayonnaise
- Pulled Pork Rub
- 3 1/2 Lbs Pork Shoulder
- 8 Oz Swiss Cheese, Sliced
- 1 Tbsp Vegetable Oil
- 1 White Onion, Sliced

Directions:

1. Supply your smoker with wood pellets and follow the start-up procedure. Preheat the grill, with the lid open, to 250° F. If using a gas or charcoal grill, set it up for low, indirect heat.

2. Generously season pork shoulder with Pulled Pork Rub, then transfer to the grill grate. Smoke for 1 hour, then flip pork and smoke for an additional hour.
3. Place onion and chicken stock in a deep cast iron skillet, or metal grill pan. Transfer the pork to the skillet, then cover with a shallow cast iron skillet, or aluminum foil. Braise for 2 hours, then increase grill temperature to 300° F, and braise for 1 more hour.
4. Remove the cover then pull pork with tongs while still on the grill. The stock will have reduced, so be sure and toss the pork in the reduced, seasoned stock and onions. Remove from the grill and set aside.
5. Preheat the griddle to medium-low flame. If using a different grill, preheat a clean cast iron skillet on medium low heat.
6. Heat butter and oil on the griddle, then toast rolls, pressing down by hand or with a metal spatula. Combine mustard and mayonnaise, then spread onto both sides of rolls. Set aside.
7. Divide pork into 4 portions, and place on the griddle, along with the sliced ham. Cook for 2 to 3 minutes, rotating ham and pork. Layer pork, ham, cheese, and pickles. Cover for 1 minute to allow cheese to melt. Return rolls to the griddle, cut each portion of filling in half, then stack 2 per prepared rolls. Press each sandwich down with the bottom of a metal spatula. Carefully flip, and press down again.
8. Remove sandwiches from the griddle and serve warm.

Sweet And Spicy Pork Roast

Servings: 2
Cooking Time: 60 Minutes

Ingredients:
- 2 Pound Pork, Loins
- 2/3 habanero peppers, seeded
- 2/3 Can coconut milk
- 1/3 Teaspoon Chinese five-spice powder
- 2/3 Tablespoon paprika
- 2/3 Teaspoon curry powder
- 2/3 Tablespoon lime juice
- 2/3 Tablespoon garlic, minced
- 2/3 Teaspoon freshly grated ginger

Directions:
1. Mix all ingredients, except pork, in a bowl. Rub the mixture onto your pork and let it sit overnight.
2. Supply your smoker with wood pellets and follow the start-up procedure. Preheat the grill, with the lid closed, to 300° F.
3. Place pork on hot grill. Cook for 1 to 1-1/2 hours, or until it reaches an internal temperature of 145-150°F for medium-rare to medium. Enjoy! Grill: 300 °F Probe: 150 °F

Bbq Pork Belly Burnt Ends

Servings: 8
Cooking Time: 240 Minutes

Ingredients:
- 1 (5-7 lb) skinless pork belly, cut into 1 inch cubes
- Meat Church Honey Hog, Honey Hog Hot or The Gospel Rub
- 1 Cup apple juice, for spritzing
- 1 1/2 Cup Apricot BBQ Sauce
- 1/2 Cup clover honey

Directions:
1. Supply your smoker with wood pellets and follow the start-up procedure. Preheat the grill, with the lid closed, to 275° F.
2. Thoroughly coat all sides of the pork belly cubes with your choice of Meat Church Honey Hog, Honey Hog Hot or The Gospel Rub. I prefer a spicier rub because I finish these with a sweet sauce.
3. Allow the rub to adhere on all sides for at least 15 minutes. Place the pork belly in the Traeger fat-side down. I prefer to do this on a wire rack.
4. Cook the pork belly for 3 hours, spritzing with apple juice every 45 minutes or whenever it starts to look dry. Grill: 275 °F
5. Pull the belly when the meat reaches an internal temperature of 190°F to 195°F. Some people pull the belly a lot earlier, but I want it really tender. Grill: 275 °F Probe: 190 °F
6. Place the cubes in the half-size aluminum pan. Season and toss the cubes with more Meat Church rub.
7. Cover the cubes with Traeger Apricot BBQ Sauce. Drizzle clover honey across the top. Finally, toss the cubes thoroughly to ensure they are completely covered.
8. Return the pan (uncovered) to the Traeger and cook for another hour or until all liquid has reduced and caramelized. Grill: 275 °F
9. Allow them to cool for 15 minutes before serving. Enjoy!

Smoked Pig Shots

Servings: 8
Cooking Time: 45 Minutes

Ingredients:
- 1 (8 oz) block cream cheese, softened
- 2 Large green chile peppers, diced
- 1 Cup shredded cheese
- 1 Tablespoon chile powder
- 2 Tablespoon Meat Church Honey Hog BBQ Rub
- 1 Pound Sausage, Smoked
- 1 Pound thick-cut bacon

Directions:
1. Supply your smoker with wood pellets and follow the start-up procedure. Preheat the grill, with the lid closed, to 350° F.
2. Mix cream cheese, chiles, shredded cheese, chili powder and Honey Hog BBQ Rub thoroughly in a mixing bowl. Set aside.

3. Slice sausage into 1/2 inch slices. Cut bacon strips in half. Wrap bacon around the sausage, creating a bowl and secure with a toothpick.
4. Fill the bowl with the cream cheese mixture. Top with more Honey Hog BBQ Rub.
5. Place the pig shots on the Traeger until the bacon is crispy and golden brown, about 45 to 60 minutes. Grill: 350 °F
6. Remove the pig shots from the grill and cool for 10 minutes, the cream cheese may still be hot. Enjoy!

Bbq Sweet & Smoky Ribs

Servings: 6
Cooking Time: 300 Minutes

Ingredients:
- 2 Rack Pork, Spare Ribs Trimmed
- 6 Cup apple juice
- 2 Tablespoon Big Game Rub
- 2 Cup 'Que BBQ Sauce
- 1/4 Cup brown sugar

Directions:
1. If your butcher has not already done so, remove the thin papery membrane from the bone-side of the ribs by working the tip of a butter knife underneath the membrane over a middle bone. Use paper towels to get a firm grip, then tear the membrane off.
2. Lay the ribs in a baking dish. Pour the apple juice over ribs, using as much apple juice as needed to submerge the meaty side of the ribs. Turn to coat.
3. Cover and refrigerate ribs for 4 to 6 hours or overnight. Remove the ribs from the apple juice; reserve juice.
4. Sprinkle ribs on all sides with Traeger Big Game Rub.
5. Supply your smoker with wood pellets and follow the start-up procedure. Preheat the grill, with the lid closed, to 225° F.
6. Transfer the apple juice to a saucepan and place in a corner of the grill, the juice will keep the cooking environment moist.
7. Arrange the ribs bone side down, directly on the grill grate. Cook for 4 to 5 hours, or until a skewer or paring knife inserted between the bones goes in easily.
8. Check the internal temperature of the ribs, the desired temperature is 202°F. If not at temperature, cook for an additional 30 minutes or until temperature is reached.
9. Meanwhile, combine the BBQ sauce and brown sugar in a small saucepan. Generously brush the ribs on all sides with the BBQ sauce the last hour of cooking
10. Using a sharp knife, cut the slabs into individual ribs. Serve. Enjoy!

Hickory Smoked Pork Shoulder

Servings: 7
Cooking Time: 420 Minutes

Ingredients:
- 1 Cup Apple Cider Vinegar
- 2 Tbsp Hickory Bacon Seasoning
- 5 - 6 Lbs Pork Shoulder, Bone In
- 1 Tbsp Sugar

Directions:
1. Supply your smoker with wood pellets and follow the start-up procedure. Preheat the grill, with the lid open, to 225° F. If you're using a gas or charcoal, set up your grill for low, indirect heat.
2. Rinse the pork shoulder (aka pork butt) under cold running water and make sure to pat dry the entire surface, including any small cracks and crevices.
3. Place the pork shoulder in the aluminum pan, fat side up, and sprinkle a liberal amount of Hickory Bacon seasoning over the top. You want to be very generous with the outer layer of seasoning here, making sure to coat the meat from end to end.
4. In a large bowl, pour the 1 cup of apple cider vinegar, the 2 tablespoons of Hickory Bacon, and 1 tablespoon of sugar. Mix until the sugars are completely dissolved.
5. Fill your marinade injector with the marinade and inject it deep into the meat. For even flavor, inject the marinade all over the pork shoulder at one-inch intervals. Pressing the syringe slowly will help avoid the marinade squirting out.
6. Tightly wrap aluminum foil over the top of the pan, set it on your grill, and close the lid.
7. Smoke the pork shoulder for 6-8 hours, or until the meat is tender and the internal temperature is 195°F to 200°F.
8. Remove from the grill and let it rest on a cutting board for 20-30 minutes with the aluminum foil loosely tented over the top.
9. When you're ready to serve, shred the pork shoulder, discarding any large pieces of fat.

Lip-smackin' Pork Loin

Servings: 8
Cooking Time: 180 Minutes

Ingredients:
- ¼ cup finely ground coffee
- ¼ cup paprika
- ¼ cup garlic powder
- 2 tablespoons chili powder
- 1 tablespoon packed light brown sugar
- 1 tablespoon ground allspice
- 1 tablespoon ground coriander
- 1 tablespoon freshly ground black pepper
- 2 teaspoons ground mustard
- 1½ teaspoons celery seeds
- 1 (1½- to 2-pound) pork loin roast

Directions:

1. Supply your smoker with wood pellets and follow the start-up procedure. Preheat, with the lid closed, to 250°F.
2. In a small bowl, combine the ground coffee, paprika, garlic powder, chili powder, brown sugar, allspice, coriander, pepper, mustard, and celery seeds to create a rub, and generously apply it to the pork loin roast.
3. Place the pork loin on the grill, fat-side up, close the lid, and roast for 3 hours, or until a meat thermometer inserted in the thickest part of the meat reads 160°F.
4. Let the pork rest for 5 minutes before slicing and serving.

Simple Smoked Baby Backs

Servings: 4-8
Cooking Time: 360 Minutes

Ingredients:
- 2 (2- or 3-pound) racks baby back ribs
- 2 tablespoons yellow mustard
- 1 batch Pork Rub

Directions:
1. Supply your smoker with wood pellets and follow the start-up procedure. Preheat the grill, with the lid closed, to 225°F.
2. Remove the membrane from the backside of the ribs. This can be done by cutting just through the membrane in an X pattern and working a paper towel between the membrane and the ribs to pull it off.
3. Coat the ribs on both sides with mustard and season them with the rub. Using your hands, work the rub into the meat.
4. Place the ribs directly on the grill grate and smoke until their internal temperature reaches between 190°F and 200°F.
5. Remove the racks from the grill and cut into individual ribs. Serve immediately.

Beer Pork Belly Chili Con Carne

Servings: 4
Cooking Time: 120 Minutes

Ingredients:
- Avocado, Diced
- 2 Bay Leaves
- 1 Lbs Beef Stew Meat
- 12 Oz Beef Stock
- 12 Oz Beer, Bottle
- 15 Oz Black Beans, Rinsed And Drained
- 3 Tbsp Chili Powder
- Cilantro, Chopped
- 1 Tsp Coriander, Ground
- 2 Tsp Cumin, Ground
- 1 Tbsp Flour
- 4 Garlic Cloves, Minced
- 2 Tsp Mexican Oregano, Dried
- 2 Tbsp Olive Oil
- 2 Oz Pancetta, Diced
- Pork Belly, Cut Into 1 Inch Chunks
- 2 Red Onion, Chopped
- Rice, Cooked
- To Taste, Salt & Pepper
- Scallion, Sliced Thin
- 1/4 Cup Tomato Purée

Directions:
1. Supply your smoker with wood pellets and follow the start-up procedure. Preheat the grill, with the lid open, to 425° F. If using a gas or charcoal grill, set it up for medium-high heat. Place Dutch oven on grill and allow to preheat.
2. Heat the olive oil in the Dutch oven, then sauté the pancetta until crisp. Add the onions and sauté for 3 minutes, then add the garlic and sauté 1 minute, until fragrant. Remove mixture with a slotted spoon and set aside.
3. Add the pork belly and beef to the pot to brown, then add the chili powder, cumin, oregano, and coriander. Add the flour and cook for 2 minutes, stirring constantly.
4. Add the beer, beef stock, and tomato purée. Stir well, then return the pancetta mixture to the pot. Add the black beans and bay leaves, then season with salt and pepper.
5. Bring chili to a simmer, then reduce temperature to 325°F and simmer, uncovered, for 2 hours, stirring occasionally, until meat is tender, and sauce has thickened.
6. Remove the chili from the grill, then serve warm with cooked rice, avocado, fresh cilantro, and scallions.

Championship Ribs With Kansas City Style

Servings: 4
Cooking Time: 210 Minutes

Ingredients:
- Apple Juice
- 2 Racks Baby Back Rib
- 2 Cups Brown Sugar
- 24 Oz Dijon Mustard
- 4 Tbsp Sweet Rib Rub
- Spray Bottle

Directions:
1. Pour Dijon Mustard into a mixing bowl. Mix in brown sugar until mustard taste diminishes and a sweet taste takes over.
2. Generally, you will use a half bag of brown sugar for 2 bottles and the whole bag for 4 bottles. The key is for the tangy mustard taste to turn sweet.
3. When this mix is brushed on the ribs the mix of pork flavor and this glaze will produce a sweet and sassy result. The easiest way to mix is with an electric mixer but a whisk will do nicely. This will become very thick and sticky.

4. Supply your smoker with wood pellets and follow the start-up procedure. Preheat the grill, with the lid open, to 275° F.
5. Place ribs, back side down, on the cooking grid. Note: If you are doing multiple slabs, I suggest you use a rib rack. Most Rib Racks will hold 6 slabs. This will allow ribs to cook evenly. The rib rack allows for more slabs since ribs will sit in rack on their edge. Try to put meatier side up.
6. Spray ribs thoroughly with apple juice every 30-40 minutes. Apple Juice not only helps to keep meat moist and juicy while cooking, the acidity also helps to break down the muscles, thus tenderizing as well. I have had people tell me they prefer Pineapple juice or a mixture of apple and pineapple. Personally, I can't tell the difference, but you can experiment for yourself if you want to. The result will be same.
7. Note: How to tell when ribs are done? It is hard to measure temp of a rib with a meat thermometer due to the meat between the bones being so tight. You can get a false reading if the thermometer is touching a bone. Take your tongs and pick up slab in the middle. If the rib folds over and is limp and the meat just begins to pull away from the bone, they are done.
8. Remove ribs from grill and place in a pan (long enough for ribs to fit)
9. Glaze both sides of ribs with a light coat of the sassy glaze. This is a flavor enhancer, not a cover up. Just a light coat is plenty. If you really like the glaze there will generally always be some left over, and you can add to your desire while on the plate.
10. Wrap ribs in foil and let stand for 15 minutes
11. Serve (you can serve in slab form and let each guest cut his own or I like to cut ribs and serve as single bones.
12. Enjoy!

Unique Carolina Mustard Ribs

Servings: 4
Cooking Time: 300 Minutes

Ingredients:
- 1 Rack St. Louis Style Ribs
- 2 Cups Apple Juice
- 1/4 Cup Cider Vinegar
- 1/4 Cup Dark Brown Sugar
- 1/4 Cup Honey
- 1 Tablespoon Hot Sauce
- 2 Tablespoons Ketchup
- 7 Tablespoon Sweet Rib Rub
- 1 Tablespoon Worcestershire Sauce
- 2 Cups, Prepared Yellow Mustard

Directions:
1. Make the sauce for the ribs. In a large mixing bowl, combine 1 cup of the yellow mustard, cider vinegar, dark brown sugar, honey, ketchup, Worcestershire sauce, hot sauce, and 1 tablespoon of the Sweet Rib Rub. Mix well to combine and set in the refrigerator until ready to use.
2. Make the ribs. Using a paper towel, peel the membrane off of the backs of the rib racks and discard. Generously coat the ribs in a thin coat of mustard, and sprinkle all over with Sweet Rib Rub.
3. Supply your smoker with wood pellets and follow the start-up procedure. Preheat the grill, with the lid closed, to 275° F. If you're using a gas or charcoal grill set it up for low, indirect heat. Place the ribs meaty-side up and grill for 2-3 hours. Once the ribs have grilled for 2-3 hours, fill a spray bottle with 2 cups of apple juice and spray the ribs to keep them moist. Continue to grill the ribs, spraying every 45 minutes, until the meat bends slightly at the ends when lifted and is a deep mahogany color, about another 2-3 hours.
4. Remove the ribs from the grill and brush with mustard sauce, then slice and serve immediately.

Bbq Pork Shoulder Roast With Sugar Lips Glaze

Servings: 8
Cooking Time: 540 Minutes

Ingredients:
- 1 (8-10 lb) bone-in pork butt
- 1/4 Cup Pork & Poultry Rub, divided
- 1 1/2 Cup apple juice, divided
- 4 Tablespoon brown sugar
- 1 Tablespoon salt
- 1/2 Cup apple juice
- Sugar Lips Glaze

Directions:
1. Trim pork butt of all excess fat leaving 1/4 inch of the fat cap attached.
2. Combine 2 tablespoons Traeger Pork & Poultry Rub, 1 cup apple juice, brown sugar and salt in a small bowl stirring until most of the sugar and salt are dissolved. Inject the pork butt every square inch or so with the apple juice mixture.
3. Season the exterior of the pork butt with remaining Traeger Pork & Poultry Rub.
4. Supply your smoker with wood pellets and follow the start-up procedure. Preheat the grill, with the lid closed, to 250° F.
5. Place pork butt directly on the grill grate and cook for about 6 hours or until the internal temperature reaches 160°F. Grill: 250 °F Probe: 160 °F
6. Wrap the pork butt in two layers of foil and pour in 1/2 cup of apple juice. Secure tin foil tightly to contain the apple juice.
7. Increase Traeger temperature to 275°F and return wrapped pork butt to grill in a pan large enough to hold the pork butt in case it leaks. Cook an additional 3 hours or until internal temperature reaches 195°F. Grill: 275 °F Probe: 195 °F
8. Remove from the grill and allow to rest 10 to 15 minutes. Slice the pork butt around the bone and top with Traeger Sugar Lips BBQ Sauce. Serve with your favorite sides. Enjoy!

SEAFOOD RECIPES

Cajun-blackened Shrimp

Servings: 4
Cooking Time: 20 Minutes

Ingredients:
- 1 pound peeled and deveined shrimp, with tails on
- 1 batch Cajun Rub
- 8 tablespoons (1 stick) butter
- ¼ cup Worcestershire sauce

Directions:
1. Supply your smoker with wood pellets and follow the start-up procedure. Preheat the grill, with the lid closed, to 450°F and place a cast-iron skillet on the grill grate. Wait about 10 minutes after your grill has reached temperature, allowing the skillet to get hot.
2. Meanwhile, season the shrimp all over with the rub.
3. When the skillet is hot, place the butter in it to melt. Once the butter melts, stir in the Worcestershire sauce.
4. Add the shrimp and gently stir to coat. Smoke-braise the shrimp for about 10 minutes per side, until opaque and cooked through. Remove the shrimp from the grill and serve immediately.

Bacon Wrapped Shrimp

Servings: 6
Cooking Time: 20 Minutes

Ingredients:
- 1 1/2 Pound Jumbo Shrimp, Peeled And Deveined
- 10 Strips Bacon
- Cheesy Grits, For Serving
- 1/4 Cup extra-virgin olive oil
- 2 Tablespoon lemon juice
- 1 Teaspoon Fresh Chopped Parsley
- 1 Tablespoon lemon zest
- 1 Teaspoon garlic, minced
- 1 Teaspoon salt
- 1/2 Teaspoon black pepper

Directions:
1. Rinse the shrimp under cold running water and dry thoroughly on paper towels.
2. Transfer to a re-sealable plastic bag or a bowl.
3. For the marinade: Combine the olive oil, lemon juice, lemon zest, garlic, salt, pepper, and parsley in a small jar with a tight-fitting lid and shake vigorously until combined.
4. Pour over the shrimp and refrigerate for 30 minutes to 1 hour.
5. Supply your smoker with wood pellets and follow the start-up procedure. Preheat the grill, with the lid closed, to 400° F.
6. Lay the bacon strips diagonally on the grill grate and grill for 10 to 12 minutes, or until the bacon is partially cooked but still very pliable.
7. Cut each strip in half width-wise. Leave the grill on.
8. Drain the shrimp, discarding the marinade. Wrap a strip of bacon around the body of each shrimp, securing with a toothpick. Grill for 4 minutes per side, turning once. Enjoy! Grill: 400 °F
9. Wrap a strip of bacon around the body of each shrimp, securing with a toothpick.
10. Grill for 4 minutes per side, turning once. Serve over cheesy grits, if desired. Enjoy!

Simple Glazed Salmon Fillets

Servings: 2
Cooking Time: 25 Minutes

Ingredients:
- 4 (6-8 oz) center-cut salmon fillets, skin on
- Fin & Feather Rub
- 1/2 Cup mayonnaise
- 2 Tablespoon Dijon mustard
- 1 Tablespoon fresh lemon juice
- 1 Tablespoon fresh chopped tarragon or dill
- lemon wedges

Directions:
1. Season the fillets with the Traeger Fin & Feather Rub.
2. Make the Glaze: Combine the mayonnaise and mustard in a small bowl. Stir in the lemon juice and dill or tarragon.
3. Spread the flesh-side of the fillets with the glaze.
4. Supply your smoker with wood pellets and follow the start-up procedure. Preheat the grill, with the lid closed, to 350° F.
5. Arrange the salmon fillets on the grill grate, skin-side down. Grill for 25 to 30 minutes, or until the salmon is opaque and flakes easily with a fork. Grill: 350 °F
6. Transfer to a platter or plates, garnish with sliced lemons and chopped dill and serve immediately. Enjoy!

Lemon Herb Grilled Salmon

Servings: 4
Cooking Time: 25 Minutes

Ingredients:
- 1 1/2 pounds salmon with skin
- 1/2 tablespoon lemon zest
- 1 tablespoon lemon juice
- 1 tablespoon unsalted butter
- 1/2 teaspoon sea salt
- 1/2 teaspoon ground black pepper

- 2 teaspoons freshly chopped dill
- 1 teaspoon freshly chopped parsley
- lemon slices for the garnish

Directions:
1. Supply your smoker with wood pellets and follow the start-up procedure. Preheat the grill, with the lid closed, to 325° F.
2. In a small bowl, combine the lemon zest, lemon juice, softened unsalted butter, dill, parsley, sea salt, and ground black pepper.
3. Generously slather the top of the salmon fillet with the mixture and top with a slice of lemon. You may allow marinating for about 10 minutes or so to absorb the mixture.
4. Place the salmon fillets on the hot grill grate, skin-side facing down.
5. Cook the salmon for 20 to 25 minutes, until it reaches an internal temperature of 145 °F and flakes easily, or until the salmon is cooked to your preferred taste.
6. Serve with lemon slices. Enjoy!

Lobster Tail

Servings: 2
Cooking Time: 25 Minutes

Ingredients:
- 2 lobster tails
- Salt
- Freshly ground black pepper
- 1 batch Lemon Butter Mop for Seafood

Directions:
1. Supply your smoker with wood pellets and follow the start-up procedure. Preheat the grill, with the lid closed, to 375°F.
2. Using kitchen shears, slit the top of the lobster shells, through the center, nearly to the tail. Once cut, expose as much meat as you can through the cut shell.
3. Season the lobster tails all over with salt and pepper.
4. Place the tails directly on the grill grate and grill until their internal temperature reaches 145°F. Remove the lobster from the grill and serve with the mop on the side for dipping.

Salmon Cakes With Homemade Tartar Sauce

Servings: 4
Cooking Time: 15 Minutes

Ingredients:
- 1 1/2 Cups Breadcrumb, Dry
- 1/2 Tablespoon Capers, Diced
- 1/4 Cup Dill Pickle Relish
- 2 Eggs
- 1 1/4 Cup Mayonnaise, Divided
- 1 Tablespoon Mustard, Grainy
- 1/2 Tablespoon Olive Oil
- 1/2 Red Pepper, Diced Finely
- 1/2 Tablespoon Sweet Rib Rub
- 1 Cup Cooked Salmon, Flaked

Directions:
1. In a large bowl, mix together the salmon, eggs, ¼ cup mayonnaise, breadcrumbs, red bell pepper, Sweet Rib Rub, and mustard. Allow the mixture to sit for 15 minutes to hydrate the breadcrumbs.
2. Supply your smoker with wood pellets and follow the start-up procedure. Preheat the grill, with the lid closed, to 350° F.
3. In a small bowl, mix together the remaining mayonnaise, dill pickle relish, and diced capers. Set aside.
4. Place the baking sheet on the grill to preheat. Once the baking sheet is hot, drizzle the olive oil over the pan and drop rounded tablespoons of the salmon mixture onto the sheet pan. Press the mixture down into a flat patty with a spatula. Allow to grill for 3 to 5 minutes, then flip and grill for 1 to 2 more minutes. Remove from the grill and serve with the reserved tartar sauce.

Smoked Salt Cured Lox

Servings: 8
Cooking Time: 30 Minutes

Ingredients:
- 1 Cup kosher salt
- 1 Cup sugar
- 1 Tablespoon cracked black pepper
- 1 Whole lemon zest
- 1 Whole orange zest
- 1 Whole Packaged Dill, roughly chopped including stems
- 2 Pound salmon fillet, skin on

Directions:
1. Mix together salt, sugar, black pepper, lemon zest, orange zest, and dill.
2. Slice salmon in half. Coat all flesh of salmon completely with salt sugar mixture. Sandwich the 2 pieces together, flesh to flesh and completely cover with salt sugar mixture.
3. Wrap tightly with plastic wrap and place into a gallon zip top bag. Squeeze out as much air as possible. Place wrapped salmon into a baking dish and place something heavy on top like a pot filled with water or a brick wrapped in foil. Place into the refrigerator for 10 hours. After 10 hours, flip over and put the weight back on top. Refrigerate for another 10 hours.
4. Remove from refrigerator, unwrap and rinse of remaining salt with cold water. Pat dry and leave on counter for 1 hour.
5. Supply your smoker with wood pellets and follow the start-up procedure. Preheat the grill, with the lid closed, to 180° F.
6. Place salmon onto a baking pan. Fill another baking pan with ice and place baking pan with salmon over ice.

7. Place onto grill and smoke for 30 minutes. Remove from grill and slice thin. Grill: 180 °F
8. Serve with bagels, cream cheese, capers, dill, lemon wedges, sliced tomatoes, and red onion. Enjoy!

Grilled Tuna Steaks With Lemon & Caper Butter

Servings: 4
Cooking Time: 8 Minutes

Ingredients:
- 4 tuna steaks, each about 8oz (225g) and 1 inch (2.5cm) thick
- extra virgin olive oil
- coarse salt
- freshly ground black pepper
- for the butter
- 6 tbsp unsalted butter, chilled, divided
- 1 garlic clove, peeled and minced
- 3 tbsp brined capers, drained and coarsely chopped
- 1 tbsp freshly squeezed lemon juice, plus more
- 1 tsp lemon zest
- 1 tbsp minced fresh chives or flat-leaf parsley

Directions:
1. Supply your smoker with wood pellets and follow the start-up procedure. Preheat the grill, with the lid closed, to 450° F.
2. In a small saucepan on the stovetop over medium-low heat, begin making the butter by melting 1 tablespoon of butter. (Cut the remaining butter into ½-inch (1.25cm) cubes and keep them cold.) Add the garlic and capers. Cook until the garlic is softened, about 3 minutes. Stir in the lemon juice and zest. Remove the saucepan from the heat and set aside.
3. Lightly brush the tuna steaks with olive oil. Season with salt and pepper. Place the steaks on the grate and grill until seared, about 3 to 4 minutes per side. (The tuna will be quite rare in the center, almost like sashimi. If you prefer your tuna more well done, add 4 to 6 minutes to the grilling time.)
4. Transfer the steaks to a platter and let rest for 5 minutes.
5. Reheat the butter and caper mixture over low heat. Whisk in the chilled butter one or two cubes at a time until the sauce has emulsified. Stir in the chives. Ladle the sauce over the tuna. Serve immediately.

Grilled Albacore Tuna With Potato-tomato Casserole

Servings: 8
Cooking Time: 20 Minutes

Ingredients:
- 6 Tuna Steaks, 6oz
- 1 Whole lemon zest
- 1 chile de árbol, thinly sliced
- 1 Tablespoon thyme
- 1 Tablespoon fresh parsley

Directions:
1. To make the fish: Season the fish with the lemon zest, chile, thyme, and parsley. Cover and refrigerate at least 4 hours.
2. Remove fish from the refrigerator 30 minutes before cooking to come to room temperature.
3. Season the fish with salt and pepper on both sides. Grill 2-3 minutes per side (next to the cast iron with the casserole) rotating it once or twice. The tuna should be well seared but still rare.

Shrimp Cabbage Tacos With Lime Cream

Servings: 4
Cooking Time: 10 Minutes

Ingredients:
- 1/4 Cabbage, Shredded
- 2 Tsp Cilantro, Chopped
- Corn Tortillas
- 1/2 Lime, Wedges
- 1/4 Cup Mayonnaise
- Blackened Sriracha Rub
- 1/4 Red Bell Pepper, Chopped
- 1 Lb Shrimp, Peeled & Deveined
- 1/4 Cup Sour Cream
- 2 Tsp Vegetable Oil
- 1/2 White Onion, Chopped

Directions:
1. Place shrimp In a medium bowl. Season with Blackened Sriracha Rub, then drizzle with vegetable oil. Toss by hand to coat well then set aside.
2. In a small mixing bowl, stir together mayonnaise, sour cream, and fresh lime juice. Season to taste with Blackened Sriracha. Set aside.
3. In a small mixing bowl, combine jalapeño, onion, red bell pepper, and cilantro. Set aside.
4. Supply your smoker with wood pellets and follow the start-up procedure. Preheat the grill, with the lid closed, till over medium heat. If using a grill, preheat a cast iron skillet over medium-heat.
5. Place tortillas on the griddle to warm each side, then turn off the burner below.
6. Transfer shrimp to the hot griddle, and cook for 4 to 6 minutes, tossing occasionally, until opaque. For spicier shrimp, season with additional Blackened Sriracha.
7. Assemble tacos: shredded cabbage, shrimp, pepper mixture, then drizzle with sauce. Serve warm with fresh lime wedges.

Smoked Honey Salmon

Servings: 2
Cooking Time: 25 Minutes

Ingredients:
- 1 lb. salmon fillets
- 1/2 tsp. pepper
- 1/4 tsp. salt
- 2 tbsp. sriracha
- 2 tsp. honey
- 2 tsp. chili sauce
- 1 tsp. lime juice
- 1/2 tsp. fish sauce

Directions:
1. Supply your smoker with wood pellets and follow the start-up procedure. Preheat the grill, with the lid closed, to 350° F.
2. Sprinkle the salmon with salt and pepper.
3. In a bowl, whisk together the sriracha, honey, chili sauce, lime juice, and fish sauce.
4. Once the grill is hot, place the salmon on the grill and leave for 15 minutes.
5. After 15 minutes, brush the salmon with the sriracha chili sauce and keep cooking for 5-10minutes. The salmon should be firm to the touch and crispy on the edges.
6. Serve hot!

Whole Vermillion Red Snapper

Servings: 6
Cooking Time: 20 Minutes

Ingredients:
- 1 Whole Vermillion Red Snapper, scaled & gutted
- 4 Clove garlic, chopped
- 1 Whole lemon, thinly sliced
- 2 Sprig rosemary sprigs
- sea salt and freshly ground black pepper

Directions:
1. Supply your smoker with wood pellets and follow the start-up procedure. Preheat the grill, with the lid closed, to High heat.
2. Stuff the cavity of the fish with chopped garlic. Sprinkle the fish with sea salt, pepper, rosemary, and lemon.
3. Grill fish directly on the grill grate. Cook for 20-25 minutes. Serve. Enjoy!

Cold-smoked Salmon Gravlax

Servings: 6
Cooking Time: 30 Minutes

Ingredients:
- 1 Cup kosher salt
- 1 Cup sugar
- 1 Tablespoon freshly ground black pepper
- 2 Pound Sushi-Grad Salmon Fillet, Skin-on, Pin Bones Removed
- 2 Bunch Dill Weed, fresh
- capers, drained
- red onion, sliced
- cream cheese
- lemons

Directions:
1. In a bowl stir together the salt, sugar and black pepper until thoroughly combined. On a work surface, turn salmon skin side up and sprinkle about half of salt mixture all over and rub in.
2. Arrange half the dill on the bottom of a baking dish large enough to hold the salmon. Set salmon skin side down on bed of dill.
3. Rub remaining salt mixture all over top and sides of salmon, then top with remaining dill. Cover with plastic, then top with a weight on a smaller baking dish or a plate with cans of beans on top, then place in refrigerator and allow to cure for 2 days.
4. Remove salmon from refrigerator, rinse under cold water and pat dry with paper towels. Allow to sit at room temperature on the counter for 1 hour
5. Supply your smoker with wood pellets and follow the start-up procedure. Preheat the grill, with the lid closed, to 180° F. Place salmon onto a baking pan. Fill another baking pan with ice and place baking pan with salmon over ice. Place onto grill and smoke for 30 minutes.
6. Remove from grill and slice thin. Serve with capers, red onion, dill, cream cheese, and lemon. Enjoy!

Roasted Halibut With Spring Vegetables

Servings: 4
Cooking Time: 20 Minutes

Ingredients:
- 4 thick-cut halibut fillets
- 2 Tablespoon Fin & Feather Rub
- Butcher Paper
- 1 Pound Carrots, Peeled and Cut into 3/4" Inch Slices
- 1 Pound asparagus, ends trimmed
- 1/2 Pound Oyster Mushrooms
- 2 Tablespoon butter
- salt and pepper
- 1/2 Cup white wine

Directions:
1. Season the halibut fillets with Traeger Fin and Feather Rub.
2. To build the packets: Start with four sheets of parchment paper about twenty inches long. Fold in half, then open it back up.
3. Divide the carrots, asparagus, and mushrooms between the four pieces of parchment and top each with a little bit of butter.

Season with salt and pepper. Place a halibut fillet on top of the vegetables in each packet.

4. Next, fold the paper over so the two ends meet, enclosing the food. Beginning at either end of the center crease, make small, overlapping diagonal folds around the filling, sealing the packet tight. Before finishing the final fold, pour a little bit of wine in each packet then seal completely.

5. Supply your smoker with wood pellets and follow the start-up procedure. Preheat the grill, with the lid closed, to 500° F.

6. Place all four packets on a sheet tray and place in the grill. Cook for 7-10 minutes or until the internal temperature of the fish reaches 145°F. Remove from the grill and place packet on a serving dish. Grill: 500 °F Probe: 145 °F

7. Using a knife or scissors, cut open each packet and fold the edges back. Finish with a little bit of lemon juice if desired. Enjoy!

Mango Rice Wine Thai Shrimp

Servings: 4
Cooking Time: 15 Minutes

Ingredients:
- 2 Tablespoons Brown Sugar
- 2 Tablespoons Mango Magic Seasoning
- 1 Pinch (Optional) Red Pepper Flakes
- 1/2 Tablespoons Rice Wine Vinegar
- 1 Pound Raw Tail-On, Thaw And Deveined Shrimp, Uncooked
- 2 Tablespoons Soy Sauce
- 1 Teaspoon Sriracha Hot Sauce
- 1/2 Cup Sweet Chili Sauce

Directions:
1. Supply your smoker with wood pellets and follow the start-up procedure. Preheat the grill, with the lid closed, to 425° F. Rinse shrimp off in sink with cold water. Place in bowl and put in all of the ingredients listed above. Let marinade for 2 - 4 hours.
2. Thread several shrimp onto a skewer, so that they are all just touching each other. Repeat with other skewers and remaining shrimp.
3. Grill shrimp for 2 - 3 minutes on each side, or until pink and opaque all the way through. Remove from grill and serve immediately.

Kimi's Simple Grilled Fresh Fish

Servings: 2
Cooking Time: 45 Minutes

Ingredients:
- 1 Cup soy sauce
- 1/3 Cup extra-virgin olive oil
- 1 Tablespoon garlic, minced
- 2 lemons, juiced
- fresh basil
- 4 Pound Fresh Fish, cut into portion-sized pieces

Directions:
1. Mix all ingredients to create sauce and cover fish in marinade for 45 minutes.
2. Supply your smoker with wood pellets and follow the start-up procedure. Preheat the grill, with the lid closed, to 140° F. Grill the marinated fish on the grill until it reaches an internal temperature of 140-145°F. Serve immediately, enjoy! Grill: 350 °F Probe: 145 °F

Grilled Whole Steelhead Fillet

Servings: 6
Cooking Time: 30 Minutes

Ingredients:
- (2-1/2 to 3 lb) steelhead or salmon fillet, skin-on
- 2 Tablespoon Montana Mex Sweet Seasoning
- 1 Teaspoon Montana Mex Jalapeño Seasoning Blend
- 1 Teaspoon Montana Mex Mild Chile Seasoning Blend
- 2 Tablespoon Montana Mex Avocado Oil
- 2 Tablespoon freshly grated ginger
- 1 lemon, thinly sliced

Directions:
1. Coat fillet evenly with all three dry seasonings, avocado oil, grated ginger and thinly sliced lemon.
2. Supply your smoker with wood pellets and follow the start-up procedure. Preheat the grill, with the lid closed, to 380° F.
3. Place the fish skin-side down on the grill grate and cook for 20 minutes. Grill: 380 °F
4. Remove fillet from grill and let rest for 5 minutes. Enjoy!

Bacon Wrapped Scallops

Servings: 8
Cooking Time: 20 Minutes

Ingredients:
- 24 jumbo deep sea diver scallops, dry-packed
- 1/2 Cup butter
- salt
- freshly ground black pepper
- 1 Clove garlic, minced
- 12 Slices thin-cut bacon, cut in half crosswise
- lemon wedges, for serving

Directions:
1. Remove the small, crescent-shaped muscle from the side of each scallop, if still attached. Dry the scallops thoroughly on paper towels, then transfer to a medium bowl.

2. Melt butter in a small saucepan, add garlic and cook for 1 minute. Let cool slightly then pour over the scallops. Season with salt and pepper and gently toss to coat.
3. Wrap a piece of bacon around each scallop and secure with a toothpick.
4. Supply your smoker with wood pellets and follow the start-up procedure. Preheat the grill, with the lid closed, to 400° F.
5. Arrange the scallops directly on the grill grate. Grill for 15 to 20 minutes, or until the scallop is opaque and the bacon has begun to crisp. If desired, you can turn the scallops on their side, bacon-side down, turning occasionally to crisp the bacon. Do not overcook. Grill: 400 °F
6. Transfer the scallops to a platter and serve with lemon wedges.

Grilled Lemon Shrimp Scampi

Servings: 4
Cooking Time: 6 Minutes

Ingredients:
- 1 ½ pounds medium shrimp, peeled and deveined
- ¼ cup olive oil
- ¼ cup lemon juice
- 3 tablespoons chopped fresh parsley
- 1 tablespoon minced garlic
- ground black pepper to taste
- ¼ teaspoon crushed red pepper flakes to taste

Directions:
1. In a large, non-reactive bowl, stir together the olive oil, lemon juice, parsley, garlic, and black pepper. Season with crushed red pepper, if desired. Add shrimp, and toss to coat. Marinate in the refrigerator for 30 minutes.
2. Supply your smoker with wood pellets and follow the start-up procedure. Preheat the grill, with the lid closed, to high heat.
3. Thread shrimp onto skewers, piercing once near the tail and once near the head. Discard any remaining marinade.
4. Lightly oil grill grate. Place the shrimp skewers on the grill grates.
5. Grill for 2 to 3 minutes per side, or until opaque.

Grilled Crab Legs With Herb Butter

Servings: 2
Cooking Time: 15 Minutes

Ingredients:
- 12 Tablespoon butter
- 3 Tablespoon Fresh Herbs (Parsley, Chives, Tarragon), finely chopped
- 4 Pound King Crab Legs or Dungeness Crab Leg Clusters
- 3 Whole Lemons, cut into wedges

Directions:
1. Supply your smoker with wood pellets and follow the start-up procedure. Preheat the grill, with the lid closed, to 375° F.
2. Place the butter, garlic, herbs, and a pinch of salt into a small cast iron sauce pan. Place on grill for 5 minutes to melt. Remove from grill and stir. Grill: 375 °F
3. If using king crab legs, split down the center and pour herb butter over meat reserving a quarter for serving. If using crab clusters, toss clusters with herb butter in a large mixing bowl reserving a quarter for serving.
4. Place crab legs directly on the grill grate, meat side up. Grill for 5 to 10 minutes or until hot and beginning to develop a little char on the shell. Grill: 375 °F
5. Serve crab legs with lemon wedges and reserved herb butter. Enjoy!

Mezcal Shrimp With Salsa De Molcajete

Servings: 4
Cooking Time: 14 Minutes

Ingredients:
- 18 to 24 jumbo shrimp, about 1½lb (680g) total, peeled and deveined
- ⅓ cup mezcal
- juice of ½ lime
- 2 tbsp extra virgin olive oil
- 2 tsp coarse salt
- 1 tsp ground cumin
- lime wedges
- for the salsa
- 2 Roma tomatoes
- 2 tomatillos, husked and washed
- 2 garlic cloves, peeled and impaled on a toothpick
- 1 jalapeño or serrano pepper
- 1 small white onion, halved
- ½ tsp coarse salt, plus more
- juice of ½ lime
- ¼ cup loosely packed fresh cilantro leaves

Directions:
1. Supply your smoker with wood pellets and follow the start-up procedure. Preheat the grill, with the lid closed, to 450° F.
2. In a large bowl, combine the shrimp, mezcal, lime juice, olive oil, salt, and ground cumin. Toss with your hands to mix thoroughly. Set aside for 15 minutes and then toss once more.
3. Begin to make the salsa by placing the tomatoes, tomatillos, garlic, jalapeño, and onion on the grate. Grill until they begin to char, about 3 minutes for the garlic and about 6 to 8 minutes for the other vegetables, turning as needed. Transfer the vegetables to a rimmed sheet pan. Remove the skewers from the garlic. Let

everything cool. Coarsely chop the vegetables and leave them in separate piles.

4. Place the garlic in the molcajete and add the salt. Mash the garlic to a purée using the temolote. Add the onion and grind it into the garlic paste. Stir in the jalapeño (deseeded for a milder salsa), tomatoes, and tomatillos. Stir in the lime juice and cilantro leaves. Taste, adding salt. (If you don't own a molcajete or temolote, prepare the salsa using a small food processor.)

5. Drain the shrimp and discard the marinade. Thread the shrimp on wood or bamboo skewers. Place the shrimp on the grate and grill until they're white and opaque, about 4 to 6 minutes, tossing with tongs.

6. Transfer the shrimp to a platter. Serve with the salsa and lime wedges.

Spicy Lime Shrimp

Servings: 4
Cooking Time: 10 Minutes

Ingredients:
- 2 Tsp Chili Paste
- 1/2 Tsp Cumin
- 2 Cloves Garlic, Minced
- 1 Large Lime, Juiced
- 1/4 Tsp Paprika, Powder
- 1/4 Tsp Red Flakes Pepper
- 1/2 Tsp Salt

Directions:
1. In a bowl, whisk together the lime juice, olive oil, garlic, chili powder, cumin, paprika, salt, pepper, and red pepper flakes.
2. Then pour it into a resealable bag, add the shrimp, toss the coat, let it marinate for 30 minutes.
3. Supply your smoker with wood pellets and follow the start-up procedure. Preheat the grill, with the lid closed, to 400° F.
4. Next place the shrimp on skewers, place on the grill, and grill each side for about two minutes until it's done. One finished, remove the shrimp from the grill and enjoy!

Tequila & Lime Shrimp With Smoked Tomato Sauce

Servings: 4
Cooking Time: 6 Minutes

Ingredients:
- 24 to 28 jumbo shrimp, about 2lb (1kg) total, peeled and deveined
- 1 lime, quartered
- Smoked Tomato Sauce
- for the marinade
- ½ cup tequila or mezcal
- juice and zest of 1 lime
- 2 garlic cloves, peeled and roughly chopped
- ½ cup freshly squeezed orange juice
- ¼ cup extra virgin olive oil
- 2 tsp agave, light brown sugar, or low-carb substitute
- 2 tsp Mexican hot sauce, plus more
- 1½ tsp coarse salt
- 1 tsp baking soda
- 1 tsp chili powder
- ½ tsp ground cumin

Directions:
1. In a medium bowl, make the marinade by whisking together the ingredients. Whisk until the salt dissolves. Taste for seasoning, adding more hot sauce if desired.
2. Place the shrimp in a resealable plastic bag and pour the marinade over them, turning the bag several times to coat thoroughly. Refrigerate for 30 minutes.
3. Supply your smoker with wood pellets and follow the start-up procedure. Preheat the grill, with the lid closed, to 450° F.
4. Drain the shrimp and discard the marinade. Pat the shrimp dry with paper towels. Thread the shrimp on 4 bamboo skewers (preferably flat ones). Make sure all the shrimp face the same direction. Finish each skewer with a lime wedge.
5. Place the skewers on the grate and grill until the shrimp are white and opaque, about 2 to 3 minutes per side, turning once. (Don't overcook.)
6. Remove the shrimp from the grill. Serve immediately with the warm tomato sauce.

Smoked Lobster Scampi

Servings: 2
Cooking Time: 30 Minutes

Ingredients:
- 1 Lobster Tail
- 1 Handful Pasta, Angel Hair
- 2 Tablespoon butter
- 1 Teaspoon garlic, minced
- 1/2 Teaspoon lemon juice
- 2 Teaspoon Parmesan cheese, grated
- 2 Tablespoon Sun Dried Tomato Pesto
- fresh parsley

Directions:
1. Supply your smoker with wood pellets and follow the start-up procedure. Preheat the grill, with the lid closed, to 180° F.
2. Use kitchen shears to cut along the top of the lobster on both sides to expose the meat. Place the lobster directly on the grill for 20-25 minutes, depending on the size of the lobster. Grill: 180 °F
3. While lobster smokes, cook pasta according to packaged directions.

4. After 20-25 minutes, take lobster off the grill and remove the meat from the tail. Cut meat into chunks.
5. While the pasta is boiling, melt butter over medium high heat. Once butter starts to brown, add the garlic and lobster chunks. Toss in pan a few times then add lemon and parmesan. Set aside.
6. When pasta has finished, place 1 tbsp of the sun dried tomato pesto on the bottom of a bowl or plate. Top with pasta, then finish with the lobster scampi. Garnish with parsley. Enjoy!

Swordfish With Sicilian Olive Oil Sauce

Servings: 4
Cooking Time: 10 Minutes

Ingredients:
- 1/2 Cup extra-virgin olive oil, plus 2 tablespoons for oiling the fish
- 1 Whole lemon, juiced
- 2 Clove garlic, minced
- 3 Tablespoon finely chopped fresh parsley
- 1 Tablespoon finely chopped fresh oregano or 1 teaspoon dried oregano
- 1 Tablespoon brined capers, drained (optional)
- 4 (6 to 8 oz) swordfish, halibut, tuna or salmon steaks, 1 inch thick
- salt and pepper

Directions:
1. Put 1/2 cup of olive oil in a small saucepan and warm over low heat.
2. Whisk in lemon juice and 2 tablespoons hot water. Stir in garlic, parsley, oregano, capers (if using), and salt and pepper to taste (go easy on the salt if you're using capers). Keep warm.
3. Supply your smoker with wood pellets and follow the start-up procedure. Preheat the grill, with the lid closed, to 400° F.
4. Brush the fish steaks with 2 tablespoons of olive oil and season with salt and pepper. Grill: 400 °F
5. Arrange on the grill grate and grill until the fish is opaque and flakes easily when pressed with a fork, about 18 minutes. (If you prefer your tuna or salmon on the rare side, cook them for less time.) Grill: 400 °F
6. Transfer the fish steaks to a platter or plates and drizzle with the warm olive oil sauce.
7. Serve the remaining sauce on the side. Enjoy!

Spiced Smoked Swordfish

Servings: 4
Cooking Time: 60 Minutes

Ingredients:
- 4 swordfish fillets (about 4 ounces each)
- For the brine:
- 1 gallon water
- ½ cup kosher salt
- ½ cup brown sugar
- For the rub:
- 1 tablespoon olive oil
- 1 tablespoon kosher salt
- 1 tablespoon coarse ground black pepper
- 1 tablespoon garlic powder
- 1 tablespoon onion powder

Directions:
1. Make the brine by mixing the water, salt, and sugar in a large pot and stir. Add swordfish fillets to the bowl and refrigerate overnight in the mixture.
2. Supply your smoker with wood pellets and follow the start-up procedure. Preheat the grill, with the lid closed, to 225° F.
3. Remove the fillets from the brine, rinse, and blot dry.
4. Brush a coat of olive oil on each fillet and mix salt, pepper, garlic powder, and onion powder in a small bowl for the rub. Apply the rub liberally to each fillet.
5. Put the fillets skin-side down on the smoker and cook for about 1 hour or until the internal temperature in the thickest part of the fillets reaches 145 °F.
6. Enjoy.

Grilled Pepper Lobster Tails

Servings: 3
Cooking Time: 10 Minutes

Ingredients:
- Tt Black Pepper
- 3/4 Stick Butter, Room Temp
- 2 Tablespoons Chives, Chopped
- 1 Clove Garlic, Minced
- Lemon, Sliced
- 3 (7-Ounce) Lobster, Tail
- Tt Salt, Kosher

Directions:
1. Start your Grill on "SMOKE" with the lid open until a fire is established in the burn pot (3-7 minutes).
2. Supply your smoker with wood pellets and follow the start-up procedure. Preheat the grill, with the lid closed, to 350° F.
3. Blend butter, chives, minced garlic, and black pepper in a small bowl. Cover with plastic wrap and set aside.
4. Butterfly the tails down the middle of the softer underside of the shell. Don't cut entirely through the center of the meat. Brush the tails with olive oil and season with salt, to your liking.
5. Grill lobsters cut side down about 5 minutes until the shells are bright red in color. Flip the tails over and top with a generous tablespoon of herb butter. Grill for another 4 minutes, or until the lobster meat is an opaque white color.
6. Remove from the grill and serve with more herb butter and lemon wedges.

Lime Mahi Mahi Fillets

Servings: 4
Cooking Time: 8 Minutes

Ingredients:
- 3/4 cup extra-virgin olive oil
- 1 clove garlic, minced
- 1/8 teaspoon ground black pepper
- 1/2 teaspoon cayenne pepper
- 2 tablespoons dill weed.
- 1 pinch salt
- 2 tablespoons lime juice
- 1/8 teaspoon grated lime peel
- 2 (4 ounce) mahi mahi fillets

Directions:
1. Supply your smoker with wood pellets and follow the start-up procedure. Preheat the grill, with the lid closed, to 325° F.
2. Lightly oil the grate.
3. Combine in a bowl the extra-virgin olive oil, minced garlic, black pepper, cayenne pepper, salt, lime juice, and grated lime zest.
4. Wisk to prepare the marinade.
5. Place the mahi mahi fillets in the marinade and turn to coat.
6. Allow to marinate at least 15 minutes.
7. Cook on preheated grill until fish flakes easily with a fork and is lightly browned (Typically 3 to 4 minutes per side).
8. Garnish with the twists of lime zest to serve.

Florentine Shrimp Al Cartoccio

Servings: 4
Cooking Time: 13 Minutes

Ingredients:
- 6 tbsp unsalted butter, melted
- ½ cup heavy whipping cream
- ½ cup grated Parmesan cheese
- 2 garlic cloves, peeled and minced
- 1 cup thinly sliced button mushrooms, cleaned and destemmed
- 1 cup baby spinach leaves
- 2 tbsp chopped sun-dried, oil-packed tomatoes
- ½ tsp dried oregano
- ½ tsp dried basil
- ½ tsp crushed red pepper flakes, plus more
- ½ tsp coarse salt
- ½ tsp freshly ground black pepper
- 20 to 24 jumbo shrimp, about 1lb (450g) total, peeled and deveined
- sprigs of fresh rosemary, basil, thyme, or oregano

Directions:
1. Supply your smoker with wood pellets and follow the start-up procedure. Preheat the grill, with the lid closed, to 400° F.
2. In a large bowl, combine the butter and whipping cream. Stir in the Parmesan, garlic, mushrooms, spinach, tomatoes, oregano, basil, red pepper flakes, and salt and pepper. Add the shrimp and stir gently to coat.
3. Place four 12-inch (30.5cm) sheets of wide heavy-duty aluminum foil on a workspace and pull up the sides. Divide the shrimp mixture evenly between the sheets of foil. Roll and crimp the top and sides of the foil to create sealed packages.
4. Place the packets seam side up on the grate and grill until the shrimp are cooked through, about 10 to 13 minutes. (You can carefully open one package to check on the shrimp.)
5. Transfer the packets to plates. Carefully open the packets to avoid any steam. Scatter fresh herbs over the shrimp before serving.

Cedar Smoked Garlic Salmon

Servings: 6
Cooking Time: 60 Minutes

Ingredients:
- 1 Tsp Black Pepper
- 3 Cedar Plank, Untreated
- 1 Tsp Garlic, Minced
- 1/3 Cup Olive Oil
- 1 Tsp Onion, Salt
- 1 Tsp Parsley, Minced Fresh
- 1 1/2 Tbsp Rice Vinegar
- 2 Salmon, Fillets (Skin Removed)
- 1 Tsp Sesame Oil
- 1/3 Cup Soy Sauce

Directions:
1. Soak the cedar planks in warm water for an hour or more.
2. In a bowl, mix together the olive oil, rice vinegar, sesame oil, soy sauce, and minced garlic.
3. Add in the salmon and let it marinate for about 30 minutes.
4. Start your grill on smoke with the lid open until a fire is established in the burn pot (3-7 minutes).
5. Supply your smoker with wood pellets and follow the start-up procedure. Preheat the grill, with the lid closed, to 225° F.
6. Place the planks on the grate. Once the boards start to smoke and crackle a little, it's ready for the fish.
7. Remove the fish from the marinade, season it with the onion powder, parsley and black pepper, then discard the marinade.
8. Place the salmon on the planks and grill until it reaches 140°F internal temperature (start checking temp after the salmon has been on the grill for 30 minutes).
9. Remove from the grill, let it rest for 10 minutes, then serve.

Lemon Lobster Rolls

Servings: 4
Cooking Time: 35 Minutes

Ingredients:
- 1/2 Cup Butter
- 4 Hot Dog Bun(S)
- 1 Lemon, Whole
- 4 Lobster, Tail
- 1/4 Cup Mayo
- Pepper

Directions:
1. Supply your smoker with wood pellets and follow the start-up procedure. Preheat the grill, with the lid closed, to 300° F.
2. Using kitchen shears, cut the shell of the tail and crack in half so that the meat is exposed. Pour in butter and season with pepper. Place the tails meat side up on the grill and cook until the shell has turned red and the meat is white, about 35 minutes.
3. Remove from the grill and separate the shell from the meat. Place the meat in a bowl with mayo, lemon juice and rind and season with pepper. Stir to combine and evenly distribute into the hot dog buns.

Grilled Shrimp Brochette

Servings: 6
Cooking Time: 20 Minutes

Ingredients:
- 1 Pound extra-large shrimp, peeled and deveined
- 6 Whole fresh jalapeños
- 8 Ounce block Monterey Jack cheese
- 1 Pound bacon
- 2 Tablespoon Meat Church The Gospel All-Purpose Rub
- oil

Directions:
1. Fillet shrimp open slightly and set aside. Core the jalapeños and cut them into small slivers. Slice the cheese into similar-sized slivers as the peppers. Cut the bacon slices in half.
2. Place one slice of jalapeño and one slice of cheese inside each shrimp. Wrap stuffed shrimp in a half piece of bacon and secure with a toothpick.
3. After you have constructed all of the shrimp, season lightly with Meat Church The Gospel All-Purpose Rub.
4. Supply your smoker with wood pellets and follow the start-up procedure. Preheat the grill, with the lid closed, to 425° F.
5. Lightly oil the grill grate then place shrimp directly on the grate. Cook for about 20 minutes, turning at least once halfway through. Shrimp should turn pink and bacon will begin to crisp up. Grill: 425 °F

6. Remove from the grill and let rest for at least 10 minutes. Enjoy!

Sweet Smoked Salmon Jerky

Servings: 6
Cooking Time: 300 Minutes

Ingredients:
- 2 Quart water
- 3/4 Cup kosher salt
- 1 Cup Morton Tender Quick Home Meat Cure, optional
- 4 Cup dark brown sugar
- 2 Cup maple syrup, divided
- 1 (2-3 lb) wild caught salmon fillet, skinned and pin bones removed

Directions:
1. In a large nonreactive bowl, combine 2 quarts water, salt, curing salt (if using), brown sugar and 1 cup of the maple syrup. Stir with a long-handled spoon to dissolve the salts and sugar.
2. With a sharp, serrated knife, slice the salmon into 1/2 inch thick slices with the short side parallel to you on the cutting board. In other words, make your cuts from the head end to the tail end. (This is considerably easier if the fish is frozen.) Cut each strip crosswise into 4 or 5 inch lengths.
3. Immerse the strips in the brine, weighing down with a plate or a bag of ice. Cover with plastic wrap and refrigerate for 12 hours.
4. Supply your smoker with wood pellets and follow the start-up procedure. Preheat the grill, with the lid closed, to 180° F.
5. Drain the salmon strips and discard the brine. Arrange the salmon strips in a single layer directly on the grill grate. Smoke for several hours (5 to 6), or until the jerky is dry but not rock-hard. You want it to yield when you bite into it. Halfway through the smoking time, mix the remaining cup of maple syrup with 1/4 cup of warm water and brush the salmon strips on all sides with the mixture. Grill: 180 °F
6. Transfer to a resealable bag while the jerky is still warm. Let the jerky rest for an hour at room temperature. Squeeze any air from the bag, and refrigerate the jerky. Enjoy!

Garlic Blackened Salmon

Servings: 4
Cooking Time: 10 Minutes

Ingredients:
- 1 Tablespoon, Optional Cayenne Pepper
- 2 Cloves Garlic, Minced
- 2 Tablespoons Olive Oil
- 4 Tablespoons Sweet Rib Rub
- 2 Pound Salmon, Fillet, Scaled And Deboned

Directions:
1. Supply your smoker with wood pellets and follow the start-up procedure. Preheat the grill, with the lid closed, to 350° F.
2. Remove the skin from the salmon and discard. Brush the salmon on both sides with olive oil, then rub the salmon fillet with the minced garlic, cayenne pepper and Sweet Rib Rub.
3. Grill the salmon for 5 minutes on one side. Flip the salmon and then grill for another 5 minutes, or until the salmon reaches an internal temperature of 145°F. Remove from the grill and serve.

Spicy Shrimp Skewers

Servings: 4
Cooking Time: 6 Minutes

Ingredients:
- 2 Pound shrimp, peeled and deveined
- 6 Thai chiles
- 6 Clove garlic
- 2 Tablespoon Winemaker's Napa Valley Rub
- 1 1/2 Teaspoon sugar
- 1 1/2 Tablespoon white vinegar
- 3 Tablespoon olive oil

Directions:
1. If using bamboo skewers, place them in cold water to soak for 1 hour before grilling.
2. Place shrimp in a bowl and set aside. Combine all remaining ingredients in a blender and blend until a coarse-textured paste is reached. Note: if a milder flavor is preferred, feel free to adjust amount of chiles to taste.
3. Add chile-garlic mixture to the shrimp and place in fridge to marinate for at least 30 minutes.
4. Remove from fridge and thread shrimp onto bamboo or metal skewers.
5. Supply your smoker with wood pellets and follow the start-up procedure. Preheat the grill, with the lid closed, to 450° F.
6. Place shrimp on grill and cook for 2 to 3 minutes per side or until shrimp are pink and firm to touch. Enjoy! Grill: 450 °F

Garlic Pepper Shrimp Pesto Bruschetta

Servings: 12
Cooking Time: 15 Minutes

Ingredients:
- 12 Slices Bread, Baguette
- 1/2 Tsp Chili Pepper Flakes
- 1/2 Tsp Garlic Powder
- 4 Cloves Garlic, Minced
- 2 Tbsp Olive Oil
- 1/2 Tsp Paprika, Smoked
- 1/4 Tsp Parsley, Leaves
- Pepper
- Pesto
- Salt
- 12 Shrimp, Jumbo

Directions:
1. Supply your smoker with wood pellets and follow the start-up procedure. Preheat the grill, with the lid closed, to 350° F. Place the baguette slices on a baking sheet lined with foil. Stir together the olive oil, and minced garlic, then brush both sides of the baguette slices with the mix. Place the pan inside the grill, and bake for about 10-15 minutes.
2. In a skillet, add a splash of olive oil, shrimp, chili powder, garlic powder, smoked paprika, salt pepper, and grill on medium-high heat for about 5 minutes (until the shrimp is pink). Be sure to stir often. Once pink, remove pan from heat. Once the baguettes are toasted, let them cool for 5 minutes, then spread a layer of pesto onto each one, then top with a shrimp, and serve.

Mexican Mahi Mahi With Baja Cabbage Slaw

Servings: 4
Cooking Time: 10 Minutes

Ingredients:
- 1½lb (680g) skinless mahi mahi, cod, or other firm white fish fillets
- coarse salt
- freshly ground black pepper
- chili powder
- lime wedges
- for the slaw
- 2 cups finely shredded green cabbage
- 2 cups finely shredded purple cabbage
- 4 tbsp reduced-fat mayo
- 2 tsp hot sauce, plus more
- 2 tsp freshly squeezed lime juice
- ½ tsp coarse salt
- for the marinade
- ¼ cup freshly squeezed orange juice
- ¼ cup freshly squeezed lime juice
- 2 tbsp extra virgin olive oil

Directions:
1. In a medium bowl, make the slaw by combining the ingredients. Stir well. Transfer to a serving bowl. Cover and refrigerate until ready to serve.
2. Place the fish fillets in a baking dish and pour the orange and lime juices and olive oil over them. Turn the fillets to coat thoroughly. Cover and refrigerate for 15 to 20 minutes.
3. Supply your smoker with wood pellets and follow the start-up procedure. Preheat the grill, with the lid closed, to 450° F.
4. Drain the fish and pat dry with paper towels. (Discard the marinade.) Season the fillets on both sides with salt and pepper

and chili powder. Place the fillets on the grate and grill until golden brown, about 4 to 5 minutes per side, turning with a thin-bladed spatula.

5. Transfer the fish to a platter. Serve with the slaw and lime wedges.

Citrus-smoked Trout

Servings: 6
Cooking Time: 120 Minutes

Ingredients:
- 6 to 8 skin-on rainbow trout, cleaned and scaled
- 1 gallon orange juice
- ½ cup packed light brown sugar
- ¼ cup salt
- 1 tablespoon freshly ground black pepper
- Nonstick spray, oil, or butter, for greasing
- 1 tablespoon chopped fresh parsley
- 1 lemon, sliced

Directions:
1. Fillet the fish and pat dry with paper towels.
2. Pour the orange juice into a large container with a lid and stir in the brown sugar, salt, and pepper.
3. Place the trout in the brine, cover, and refrigerate for 1 hour.
4. Cover the grill grate with heavy-duty aluminum foil. Poke holes in the foil and spray with cooking spray (see Tip).
5. Supply your smoker with wood pellets and follow the start-up procedure. Preheat, with the lid closed, to 225°F.
6. Remove the trout from the brine and pat dry. Arrange the fish on the foil-covered grill grate, close the lid, and smoke for 1 hour 30 minutes to 2 hours, or until flaky.
7. Remove the fish from the heat. Serve garnished with the fresh parsley and lemon slices.

Vodka Brined Smoked Wild Salmon

Servings: 4
Cooking Time: 60 Minutes

Ingredients:
- 1 Cup brown sugar
- 1 Tablespoon black pepper
- 1/2 Cup coarse salt
- 1 Cup vodka
- 1 (1-1/2 to 2 lb) wild caught salmon
- 1 lemon wedges
- capers

Directions:
1. In a small bowl, whisk together brown sugar, pepper, salt and vodka.
2. Place the salmon in a large resealable bag. Pour in marinade and massage into the salmon. Refrigerate for 2 to 4 hours.
3. Remove from bag, rinse and dry with paper towels.
4. Supply your smoker with wood pellets and follow the start-up procedure. Preheat the grill, with the lid closed, to 180° F.
5. Smoke the salmon, skin-side down for 30 minutes.
6. Increase grill temperature to 225°F and continue to cook salmon for an additional 45 to 60 minutes or until the internal temperature in the thickest part of the fish reaches 140°F or the fish flakes easily when pressed with a finger or fork. Grill: 225 °F Probe: 140 °F
7. Serve with lemons and capers. Enjoy!

Sweet Mandarin Salmon

Servings: 2
Cooking Time: 10 Minutes

Ingredients:
- 1 Whole lime juice
- 1 Teaspoon sesame oil
- 1 1/2 Cup Mandarin Orange Sauce
- 1 1/2 Tablespoon soy sauce
- 2 Tablespoon cilantro, finely chopped
- Freshly cracked black pepper
- 1 Whole (4 oz) wild salmon fillets

Directions:
1. Supply your smoker with wood pellets and follow the start-up procedure. Preheat the grill, with the lid closed, to 375° F.
2. For the glaze, combine Mandarin orange sauce, lime juice, sesame oil, soy sauce, cilantro and fresh cracked black pepper. Mix together.
3. Cut the salmon into 4 fillets. Brush with glaze and place directly on the grill grate, skin side down.
4. Cook until salmon reaches an internal temperature of 155 degrees F (about 15-20 minutes). Half way through cook time, brush salmon again with the glaze.
5. Remove the salmon from the grill and serve with remaining glaze if desired. Enjoy!

Grilled Lobster Tails With Smoked Paprika Butter

Servings: 4
Cooking Time: 10-12 Minutes

Ingredients:
- 4 lobster tails, each about 8 to 10oz (225 to 285g), thawed if frozen
- 3 lemons, 1 quartered lengthwise, 2 halved through their equators
- for the butter

- 1¼ cup unsalted butter, at room temperature
- 2 garlic cloves, peeled and finely minced
- 3 tbsp chopped fresh parsley
- 2 tbsp chopped fresh chives
- 1 tbsp freshly squeezed lemon juice
- 2 tsp finely chopped lemon zest
- 2 tsp smoked paprika
- 1 tsp coarse salt

Directions:
1. Supply your smoker with wood pellets and follow the start-up procedure. Preheat the grill, with the lid closed, to 450° F.
2. In a medium bowl, make the paprika butter by combining the ingredients. Beat with a wooden spoon until well blended.
3. Use a sharp, heavy knife or sturdy kitchen shears to cut lengthwise through the top shell of each lobster tail in a straight line toward the tail fin. Gently loosen the meat from the bottom shell and sides. Lift the meat through the slit you just made so the meat sits on top of the shell. Slip a lemon quarter underneath the meat (between the meat and the bottom shell) to keep it elevated. Spread 1 tablespoon of paprika butter on top of each lobster. Melt the remaining butter and keep it warm.
4. Place the lobster tails flesh side up and lemon halves cut sides down on the grate. Grill the lobsters until the flesh is white and opaque and the internal temperature of the lobster meat reaches 135 to 140°F (57 to 60°C), about 10 to 12 minutes, basting at least once with some of the melted butter. (Don't overcook or the lobster will become unpleasantly rubbery.)
5. Transfer the lobsters and the lemon halves to a platter. Divide the remaining melted butter between 4 ramekins before serving.

Garlic Blackened Catfish

Servings: 4
Cooking Time: 10 Minutes

Ingredients:
- ½ Cup Cajun Seasoning
- ¼ Tsp Cayenne Pepper
- 1 Tsp Granulated Garlic
- 1 Tsp Ground Thyme
- 1 Tsp Onion Powder
- 1 Tsp Ground Oregano
- 1 Tsp Pepper
- 4 (5-Oz.) Skinless Catfish Fillets
- 1 Tbsp Smoked Paprika
- 1 Stick Unsalted Butter

Directions:
1. In a small bowl, combine the Cajun seasoning, smoked paprika, onion powder, granulated garlic, ground oregano, ground thyme, pepper and cayenne pepper.
2. Sprinkle fish with salt and let rest for 20 minutes.
3. Supply your smoker with wood pellets and follow the start-up procedure. Preheat the grill, with the lid closed, to 450° F. If you're using a gas or charcoal grill, set it up for medium-high heat. Place cast iron skillet on the grill and let it preheat.
4. While grill is preheating, sprinkle catfish fillets with seasoning mixture, pressing gently to adhere. Add half the butter to preheated cast iron skillet and swirl to coat, add more butter if needed. Place fillets in hot skillet and cook 3-5 minutes or until a dark crust has been formed. Flip and cook an additional 3-5 minutes or until the fish flakes apart when pressed gently with your finger.
5. Remove fish from grill and sprinkle evenly with fresh parsley. Serve with lemon wedges and enjoy!

Cider Hot-smoked Salmon

Servings: 4
Cooking Time: 60 Minutes

Ingredients:
- 1 1/2 Pound Wild Caught Salmon Fillet, skinned, pin bones removed
- 12 Ounce apple juice or cider
- 4 Pieces juniper berries
- 1 Pieces Star Anise, Broken
- 1 Pieces bay leaf, coarsely crumbled
- 1/2 Cup kosher salt
- 1/4 Cup brown sugar
- 2 Teaspoon Blackened Saskatchewan Rub
- 1 Teaspoon coarse ground black pepper, divided

Directions:
1. Rinse the salmon fillet under cold running water and check for pin bones by running a finger over the fleshy part of the fillet. If you feel a bone, remove it with kitchen tweezers or a needle-nose pliers.
2. In a sturdy resealable plastic bag, combine the cider, crushed juniper berries, star anise, and bay leaf. Add the salmon fillet and put the bag in a bowl or pan in the refrigerator. Let sit for at least 8 hours, or overnight.
3. Remove the salmon from the bag and discard the cider mixture. Dry the salmon well on paper towels. Make the cure: In a small mixing bowl, combine the kosher salt, brown sugar, and Traeger rub.
4. Pour half into a shallow plate, or baking dish. Put the salmon fillet, skin-side down, on top of the cure. Generously sprinkle the top with the remaining cure, cover with plastic wrap, and refrigerate for 1 to 1-1/2 hours. Any longer, and the fish will get too salty.
5. Remove the salmon from the cure and pat dry with paper towels. Sprinkle the black pepper on top of the fillet.

6. Supply your smoker with wood pellets and follow the start-up procedure. Preheat the grill, with the lid closed, to 200° F.
7. Lay the salmon skin-side down on the grill grate. Cook for 1 hour, or until the internal temperature in the thickest part of the fish reaches 150 or the fish flakes easily when pressed with a finger or fork. Grill: 200 °F Probe: 150 °F
8. Let cool slightly. Turn the fillet over and remove the skin; it should come off in one piece.
9. If not serving immediately, let the salmon cool completely, then wrap in plastic wrap and refrigerate for up to 2 days. Transfer to a platter and serve with some or all of the suggested accompaniments. Enjoy!

Baked Steelhead

Servings: 4
Cooking Time: 20 Minutes

Ingredients:

- 1 steelhead fillet
- 16-oz bottle Italian dressing
- 3 Tablespoon unsalted butter
- Blackened Saskatchewan Rub
- 1/2 shallot, minced
- 2 Clove garlic, minced
- 1 lemon

Directions:

1. Supply your smoker with wood pellets and follow the start-up procedure. Preheat the grill, with the lid closed, to 350° F.
2. Put butter in a small cast iron pan and place inside Traeger while preheating to soften. Pour Italian dressing over fillet to evenly coat.
3. Shake Traeger Blackened Saskatchewan rub evenly in a thin layer to cover dressing. Mince shallot and garlic.
4. Remove butter from pre-heated grill, careful as the cast iron will be hot. Stir in shallots and garlic.
5. Spread a nice thick layer of mixture on the top-middle of the fillet. Cut lemon into thin slices and place on top of butter mix.
6. Place steelhead on the grill and cook for 20 to 30 minutes, until fish is flaky, being careful not to over cook.
7. Remove fillet from the grill. Enjoy!

Thai-style Swordfish Steaks With Peanut Sauce

Servings: 4
Cooking Time: 8 Minutes

Ingredients:

- 4 center-cut swordfish steaks, each about 6oz (170g) and 1 inch (2.5cm) thick
- Peanut Sauce
- lime wedges
- for the marinade
- 1/2 cup light Thai-style unsweetened coconut milk
- 2 garlic cloves, peeled and smashed with a chef's knife
- juice and zest of 1 lime
- 1-inch (2.5cm) piece of fresh ginger, peeled and roughly chopped
- 1/2 Thai bird's eye chili pepper or serrano pepper, deseeded and thinly sliced, plus more
- 2 tbsp fresh cilantro leaves, coarsely chopped
- 1 tbsp Asian fish sauce
- 1 tbsp light soy sauce or liquid aminos
- 1 tbsp light brown sugar or low-carb substitute
- 1 tsp ground coriander
- 1/2 tsp ground turmeric

Directions:

1. In a medium bowl, make the marinade by whisking together the ingredients. Whisk until the brown sugar dissolves.
2. Place the swordfish steaks in a single layer in a nonreactive baking dish and pour the marinade over them, turning the steaks to coat thoroughly. Refrigerate for 1 hour.
3. Supply your smoker with wood pellets and follow the start-up procedure. Preheat the grill, with the lid closed, to 450° F.
4. Remove the swordfish from the marinade and scrape off any solids. (Discard the marinade.) Place the steaks on the grate and grill until the fish easily flakes when pressed with a fork, about 3 to 4 minutes per side, turning with a thin-bladed spatula.
5. Transfer the swordfish steaks to a platter. Serve with the peanut sauce and lime wedges.

Smoked Cedar Plank Salmon

Servings: 4
Cooking Time: 20 Minutes

Ingredients:

- 1/4 Cup Brown Sugar
- 1/2 Tablespoon Olive Oil
- Competition Smoked Seasoning
- 4 Salmon Fillets, Skin Off

Directions:

1. Soak the untreated cedar plank in water for 24 hours before grilling. When ready to grill, remove and wipe down.
2. Supply your smoker with wood pellets and follow the start-up procedure. Preheat the grill, with the lid closed, to 350° F.
3. In a small bowl, mix the brown sugar, oil, and Lemon Pepper, Garlic, and Herb seasoning. Rub generously over the salmon fillets.
4. Place the plank over indirect heat, then lay the salmon on the plank and grill for 15-20 minutes, or until the salmon is cooked through and flakes easily with a fork. Remove from the heat and serve immediately.

Smoke-roasted Halibut With Mixed Herb Vinaigrette

Servings: 4
Cooking Time: 12 Minutes

Ingredients:

- 4 halibut fillets, each about 6 to 8oz (170 to 225g)
- for the vinaigrette
- 2 tbsp white wine vinegar or sherry vinegar, plus more
- ¼ tsp coarse salt, plus more
- ¼ tsp freshly ground black pepper, plus more
- ½ cup extra virgin olive oil
- 2 tbsp minced fresh herbs, such as dill, flat-leaf parsley, or oregano
- for serving
- 4 cups loosely packed baby arugula, spinach, or other mixed greens
- 1 lemon, cut lengthwise into 4 wedges

Directions:

1. Supply your smoker with wood pellets and follow the start-up procedure. Preheat the grill, with the lid closed, to 400° F.
2. In a small bowl, make the vinaigrette by whisking together the vinegar, and salt and pepper. Whisk until the salt dissolves. Continue to whisk while slowly adding the olive oil. Whisk until the vinaigrette is emulsified. Stir in the herbs. Taste, adding vinegar or salt and pepper to taste. Pour 1/3 of the vinaigrette into a separate container. Reserve the remainder.
3. Place the fillets on a rimmed sheet pan. Lightly brush both sides with the smaller portion of vinaigrette. (Dividing the vinaigrette into two containers prevents cross-contamination.) Lightly season with salt and pepper.
4. Place the fillets on the grate at an angle to the bars. Grill until the edges begin to look opaque, about 4 to 6 minutes. Gently turn and grill until the fish is cooked through, about 4 to 6 minutes more. (A fillet will break into clean flakes when pressed with a fork when it's done.)
5. Remove the fish from the grill. Place the greens in a large bowl and toss them with 2 to 3 tablespoons of the reserved vinaigrette (you want the greens lightly coated) and divide between 4 plates. Place a fillet on the greens on each plate. Drizzle a bit more of the vinaigrette over the top. Serve with lemon wedges.

Grilled Tilapia With Blistered Cherry Tomatoes

Servings: 4
Cooking Time: 15 Minutes

Ingredients:

- 1½lb (680g) tilapia fillets or other mild white fish fillets
- chopped fresh curly or flat-leaf parsley
- for the marinade
- ½ cup extra virgin olive oil
- 1 garlic clove, peeled and smashed with a chef's knife
- 3 tbsp freshly squeezed lemon juice
- 1 tsp smoked paprika
- ½ tsp coarse salt
- ¼ tsp freshly ground black pepper
- for the tomatoes
- 2 tbsp extra virgin olive oil
- 2 pints (1 liter) cherry tomatoes (red, yellow, or heirloom varieties)
- coarse salt
- freshly ground black pepper

Directions:

1. Place a cast iron skillet on the grate. Supply your smoker with wood pellets and follow the start-up procedure. Preheat the grill, with the lid closed, to 400° F.
2. In a jar with a tight-fitting lid, make the marinade by combining the ingredients. Shake the jar vigorously to emulsify the ingredients.
3. Place the fillets in a single layer in a nonreactive baking dish. Pour half the marinade over them and turn the fillets to thoroughly coat. Cover with plastic wrap and refrigerate for 15 minutes. (Refrigerate no more than 30 minutes or the acid in the marinade will begin to cook the fish.)
4. Place the olive oil in the skillet. Add the tomatoes and season with salt and pepper. Stir to coat. Cook the tomatoes until they begin to blister and collapse, about 5 minutes, stirring once or twice. Remove the skillet from the grill and transfer the tomatoes to a bowl.
5. Carefully lift each fish fillet from the marinade and let the excess drip off. Place the fillets on the grate at a slight angle to the bars. Lightly season with salt and pepper. Grill until the fish flakes easily when pressed with a fork, about 4 to 5 minutes per side, turning carefully with a thin-bladed spatula.
6. Transfer the fillets to a warmed platter. Top with some of the tomatoes. (Place the remaining tomatoes in a serving bowl.) Scatter the parsley around the platter. Drizzle some of the remaining marinade over the top. Serve immediately.

Coconut Shrimp Jalapeño Poppers

Servings: 6
Cooking Time: 55 Minutes

Ingredients:

- 8 Whole shrimp, peeled and deveined
- 1/2 Teaspoon Chicken Rub, plus more as needed
- olive oil
- 6 Whole jalapeños
- 8 Ounce cream cheese, softened

- 2 Tablespoon fresh chopped cilantro
- 1/2 Cup unsweetened coconut flakes
- 12 Slices bacon

Directions:
1. Supply your smoker with wood pellets and follow the start-up procedure. Preheat the grill, with the lid closed, to 425° F.
2. Rinse and season the shrimp with the Traeger Chicken Rub.
3. Drizzle the shrimp with olive oil and cook on the Traeger for about 5 minutes per side, or until the shrimp is opaque. Grill: 425 °F
4. Remove the shrimp and let cool.
5. Reduce Traeger temperature to 350°F. Grill: 350 °F
6. Meanwhile, get those poppers going. Cut the jalapeños in half then remove the stems and seeds.
7. Chop the shrimp. Mix together the softened cream cheese, chopped shrimp, 1/2 teaspoon Traeger Chicken Rub and 2 tablespoons chopped cilantro.
8. Load a generous amount of the filling in each pepper half. Top with a sprinkle of coconut.
9. Wrap each stuffed pepper with a slice of bacon and place on a foil-lined baking sheet.
10. Cook the peppers on the Traeger for about 45 minutes, or until the bacon fat has rendered and the cream cheese is golden. Enjoy! Grill: 350 °F

Oysters Margarita

Servings: 4
Cooking Time: 10minutes

Ingredients:
- 24 fresh oysters in the shell
- 4oz (120ml) freshly squeezed lime juice
- 2oz (60ml) tequila
- 2oz (60ml) orange liqueur, such as triple sec
- 6 tbsp cold butter, cut into 24 cubes
- crunchy salt, such as margarita rimming salt
- lime wedges
- hot sauce (optional)

Directions:
1. Supply your smoker with wood pellets and follow the start-up procedure. Preheat the grill, with the lid closed, to 450° F.
2. Carefully shuck each oyster to remove the top shell. Run your shucking knife under the oyster to release it from the bottom shell, but don't spill the juices. Discard the top shells, but keep the oysters in the bottom shells. Balance each oyster on a wire rack placed on a rimmed sheet pan.
3. Place 1 teaspoon of lime juice, ½ teaspoon of tequila, ½ teaspoon of orange liqueur, and 1 cube of butter on each oyster.
4. Place the pan on the grate and smoke until the butter has melted and the juices are bubbling, about 8 to 10 minutes. (The oysters should be just barely cooked.)
5. Remove the pan from the grill. Sprinkle a pinch of salt on each oyster. Serve immediately with lime wedges and hot sauce (if using).

Alder Smoked Scallops With Citrus & Garlic Butter Sauce

Servings: 4
Cooking Time: 35 Minutes

Ingredients:
- 2 Pound large dry sea scallops
- kosher salt
- freshly ground black pepper
- 8 Tablespoon salted butter, melted
- 1 Clove garlic, minced
- 1 Small orange
- 1/4 Teaspoon Worcestershire sauce
- 1 1/2 Teaspoon fresh chopped parsley or tarragon
- flat-leaf parsley, for serving

Directions:
1. Wash the scallops under cold running water and thoroughly pat dry on paper towels. Remove any tags of abductor muscle tissue you find on the sides of the scallops.
2. Arrange the scallops on a baking sheet fitted with a cooling rack, and season with salt and pepper.
3. Supply your smoker with wood pellets and follow the start-up procedure. Preheat the grill, with the lid closed, to 165° F.
4. Place the baking sheet with the scallops on the grill grate and smoke for 20 minutes.
5. While your scallops are smoking, make your sauce. Melt the butter in a small saucepan over medium-low heat. Add a pinch of salt, garlic, Worcestershire sauce, zest and juice from half of the orange, and parsley. Simmer for 5 minutes. Keep warm.
6. Remove the baking sheet with the scallops from the grill and set aside. Increase the temperature to 400°F and preheat, lid closed. Optional: Place an oyster bed or oyster pan in the grill to preheat. These heavy iron pans are a great way to sear the scallops. Grill: 400 °F
7. Return the baking sheet with the scallops to the grill, brush with the butter sauce, reserving some for serving. Roast until just opaque and tender, 10 to 15 minutes. The time will depend on how thick the scallops are. Do not overcook. If you are using an oyster pan, brush each compartment lightly with olive oil to prevent sticking. Spoon butter sauce on each of the scallops, reserving some for serving.
8. Serve the scallops hot with a little more orange zest, fresh parsley and the the warm citrus and garlic butter sauce. Enjoy!

Barbecued Scallops

Servings: 4
Cooking Time: 10 Minutes

Ingredients:
- 1 pound large scallops
- 2 tablespoons olive oil
- 1 batch Dill Seafood Rub

Directions:
1. Supply your smoker with wood pellets and follow the start-up procedure. Preheat the grill, with the lid closed, to 375°F.
2. Coat the scallops all over with olive oil and season all sides with the rub.
3. Place the scallops directly on the grill grate and grill for 5 minutes per side. Remove the scallops from the grill and serve immediately.

Baked Whole Fish In Sea Salt

Servings: 4
Cooking Time: 30 Minutes

Ingredients:
- 3 Pound Whole Branzino, (1.5 each)
- 10 Sprig thyme sprigs
- 1 Medium lemon, thinly sliced
- 5 Cup sea salt
- 10 Whole egg white
- olive oil
- 1 Whole lemon juice

Directions:
1. Supply your smoker with wood pellets and follow the start-up procedure. Preheat the grill, with the lid closed, to High heat.
2. Clip the fins and remove the gills from the fish. Stuff cavity with thyme and lemon slices. Whip the egg whites to soft peaks and fold in the sea salt.
3. Place directly on the grill grate and bake for 30 minutes or until a thermometer poked through the salt crust and into the flesh of the fish registers an internal temperature of 135-140 degrees F. Remove fish from the grill and let stand 10 minutes.
4. Using a wooden spoon, strike the crust to crack it open and brush remaining salt from the surface of the fish.
5. Remove the skin and drizzle fish with good olive oil and a squeeze of lemon. Enjoy!

Traeger Smoked Salmon

Servings: 6
Cooking Time: 240 Minutes

Ingredients:
- 1 (2-1/2 to 3 lb) salmon fillet
- 1/2 Cup kosher salt
- 1 Cup brown sugar, firmly packed
- 1 Tablespoon ground black pepper

Directions:
1. Remove all pin bones from salmon.
2. In a small bowl, combine salt, sugar and black pepper. Lay a large piece of plastic wrap on a flat surface that is at least 6 inches longer than the fillet. Spread 1/2 of the mixture on top of the plastic and lay the fillet skin side down on top of the cure. Top with the other 1/2 of the cure spreading it evenly over the top of the fillet. Fold up the edges of the plastic and wrap tightly.
3. Place the wrapped salmon fillet in the bottom of a flat, rectangle baking dish or hotel pan. Place another identical pan on top of the fillet. Place a couple of cans or something heavy inside the top pan to weigh it down making sure the weight is distributed evenly.
4. Transfer the weighted salmon to the refrigerator and cure for 4 to 6 hours.
5. Remove the salmon from the plastic wrap and rinse the cure thoroughly (not rinsing thoroughly will result in a salty finished product). Place skin side down on a wire rack atop a sheet tray and pat dry. Place the sheet tray in the refrigerator and allow the salmon to dry overnight. This allows a tacky film called a pellicle to form on the surface of the salmon. The pellicle helps smoke adhere to the fish.
6. Supply your smoker with wood pellets and follow the start-up procedure. Preheat the grill, with the lid closed, to 180° F.
7. Place the salmon skin side down directly on the grill grate and smoke for 3 to 4 hours or until the internal temperature of the fish registers 140°F. Enjoy warm or chilled. Grill: 180 °F Probe: 140 °F

Grilled Artichoke Cheese Salmon

Servings: 12
Cooking Time: 270 Minutes

Ingredients:
- 28 Oz Artichoke Hearts, Whole, Canned
- 1/2 Cup Breadcrumbs
- 1/2 Cup Brown Sugar
- 8 Oz Cream Cheese
- 1 Tbsp Garlic Powder
- 1 Cup Italian Cheese Blend, Shredded
- 1/4 Cup Kosher Salt
- 1 Cup Mayonnaise
- 2 Tsp Olive Oil
- 1 Tbsp Onion Powder
- 1/2 Cup Parmesan Cheese
- 2 Tbsp Parsley, Chopped
- Blackened Sriracha Rub
- 1 1/4 Lbs Salmon, Fillet, Scaled And Deboned

- Sour Cream
- 1/2 Tsp White Pepper, Ground

Directions:
1. In a small mixing bowl, whisk together the brown sugar, salt, garlic powder, onion powder, and white pepper. This will make twice the cure needed, so be sure and place the remaining half in a resealable plastic bag and save for smoking fish at a later date.
2. Lay a sheet of plastic wrap on a sheet tray and sprinkle a thin layer of the cure on it. Place the salmon skin-side down on top of the cure, then sprinkle a couple tablespoons of cure on top. Gently press the cure on top of the salmon flesh, then wrap in plastic wrap.
3. Refrigerate for 8 hours, or overnight.
4. Remove salmon from the refrigerator and wash off the cure in the sink, under cold water.
5. Blot salmon with a paper towel, then set salmon skin side on a wire rack. Dry at room temperature for two hours, or until a yellowish shimmer appears on the salmon.
6. Supply your smoker with wood pellets and follow the start-up procedure. Preheat the grill, with the lid closed, to 250° F. If using a gas, charcoal or other grill, set it to low, indirect heat.
7. Place the salmon in the upper cabinet. Smoke for 2 hours, then increase the grill temperature to 350° F to maintain a cabinet temperature of 225°F and smoke another 1 to 2 hours, until salmon reaches an internal temperature of 145° F.
8. Remove salmon from the cabinet and set aside to rest for 15 minutes, then flake apart. Reserve ½ cup to top dip after grilling.
9. While the salmon is resting, drain the artichokes, then skewer onto metal skewers (if using wooden skewers, make sure to soak in water for 1 hour prior to grilling, or you can use a grill basket as well).
10. Season with Blackened Sriracha, then set on the grill. Grill for 2 to 3 minutes, until lightly browned.
11. Remove from the grill, cool slightly, then roughly chop. Set aside.
12. In a mixing bowl, combine shredded Italian cheese, grated parmesan, breadcrumbs and parsley. Set aside.
13. Place cream cheese, mayonnaise, and sour cream in a cast iron skillet. Stir frequently, with a wooden spoon, for about 5 minutes, until the mixture is smooth.
14. Carefully fold in flaked salmon and grilled artichoke hearts, then spread breadcrumb mixture over dip.
15. Drizzle with olive oil, then close the grill lid and bake for 25 to 30 minutes, until dip begins to bubble around the edges, and cheese begins to caramelize on top.
16. Remove dip from the grill, top with reserved salmon and a pinch of parsley. Serve warm with bagel chips, crackers, or crusty bread.

Traeger Jerk Shrimp

Servings: 8
Cooking Time: 10 Minutes

Ingredients:
- 1 Tablespoon brown sugar
- 1 Tablespoon smoked paprika
- 1 Teaspoon garlic powder
- 1/4 Teaspoon Thyme, ground
- 1/4 Teaspoon ground cayenne pepper
- 1 Teaspoon sea salt
- 1 lime zest
- 2 Pound shrimp in shell
- 3 Tablespoon olive oil

Directions:
1. Combine spices, salt, and lime zest in a small bowl and mix. Place shrimp into a large bowl, then drizzle in the olive oil, Add the spice mixture and toss to combine, making sure every shrimp is kissed with deliciousness.
2. Supply your smoker with wood pellets and follow the start-up procedure. Preheat the grill, with the lid closed, to 450° F.
3. Arrange the shrimp on the grill and cook for 2 – 3 minutes per side, until firm, opaque, and cooked through. Grill: 450 °F
4. Serve with lime wedges, fresh cilantro, mint, and Caribbean Hot Pepper Sauce. Enjoy!

Wood-fired Halibut

Servings: 4
Cooking Time: 20 Minutes

Ingredients:
- 1 pound halibut fillet
- 1 batch Dill Seafood Rub

Directions:
1. Supply your smoker with wood pellets and follow the start-up procedure. Preheat the grill, with the lid closed, to 325°F.
2. Sprinkle the halibut fillet on all sides with the rub. Using your hands, work the rub into the meat.
3. Place the halibut directly on the grill grate and grill until its internal temperature reaches 145°F. Remove the halibut from the grill and serve immediately.

Smoked Fish Chowder

Servings: 4
Cooking Time: 60 Minutes

Ingredients:
- 12 Ounce (1-1/2 to 2 lb) skin-on salmon fillet, preferably wild-caught
- Fin & Feather Rub
- 2 Corn Husks

- 3 Slices Bacon, sliced
- 4 Can Cream of Potato Soup, Condensed
- 3 Cup whole milk
- 8 Ounce cream cheese
- 3 green onions, thinly sliced
- 2 Teaspoon hot sauce

Directions:
1. Supply your smoker with wood pellets and follow the start-up procedure. Preheat the grill, with the lid closed, to 180° F.
2. Sprinkle Traeger Fin & Feather rub as needed on salmon. Arrange the salmon skin-side down on the grill grate. Smoke for 30 minutes. Grill: 180 °F
3. Increase the grill temperature to 350°F. Grill: 350 °F
4. Cook the salmon for 30 minutes, or until the fish flakes easily with a fork. (The exact time will depend on the thickness of the fillet.) There is no need to turn the fish. Using a large thin spatula, transfer the salmon to a wire rack to cool. Remove the skin. (The salmon can be made a day ahead, wrapped in plastic wrap and refrigerated.) Break into flakes and set aside.
5. Arrange the corn and bacon strips on the grill grate. (The salmon will be roasting while you do this.) Roast the corn and the bacon until the corn is cooked through and browned in spots, turning as needed, and the bacon is crisp, about 15 minutes.
6. In the meantime, bring the cream of potato soup and the milk to a simmer over medium heat in a large saucepan or Dutch oven on the stovetop. Gradually stir in the cream cheese and whisk to blend. Chop the bacon into bits and slice the corn off the cobs using long strokes of a chef's knife.
7. Add to the soup along with the green onions. Stir in the salmon. Heat gently for 5 to 10 minutes. Add the hot sauce to taste. If the chowder is too thick, add more milk. Serve at once. Enjoy!

Seared Bluefin Tuna Steaks

Servings: 2
Cooking Time: 5 Minutes

Ingredients:
- 3 Whole Tuna, steak
- olive oil
- salt and pepper
- soy sauce
- Sriracha

Directions:
1. Lightly baste both sides of tuna steaks in olive oil; sprinkle sea salt and ground pepper on each side.
2. Supply your smoker with wood pellets and follow the start-up procedure. Preheat the grill, with the lid closed, to High heat.
3. Grill tuna steaks on each side for 2 to 2-1/2 minutes.
4. Remove tuna from grill and allow to cool slightly.

5. Cut into 1/2 - 3/4" pieces. Serve with a mixture of Soy Sauce and Sriracha. Enjoy!"

Barbecued Shrimp

Servings: 4
Cooking Time: 10 Minutes

Ingredients:
- 1 pound peeled and deveined shrimp, with tails on
- 2 tablespoons olive oil
- 1 batch Dill Seafood Rub

Directions:
1. Soak wooden skewers in water for 30 minutes.
2. Supply your smoker with wood pellets and follow the start-up procedure. Preheat the grill, with the lid closed, to 375°F.
3. Thread 4 or 5 shrimp per skewer.
4. Coat the shrimp all over with olive oil and season each side of the skewers with the rub.
5. Place the skewers directly on the grill grate and grill the shrimp for 5 minutes per side. Remove the skewers from the grill and serve immediately.

Planked Trout With Fennel, Bacon & Orange

Servings: 4
Cooking Time: 40minutes

Ingredients:
- 4 whole trout, each about 14 to 16oz (400 to 450g), cleaned and gutted, fins removed
- coarse salt
- freshly ground black pepper
- for the filling
- 1 large navel orange
- 4 slices of thick-cut bacon, diced
- 1 large fennel bulb, trimmed, halved, decored, and diced, green fronds reserved
- 4oz (110g) baby spinach, about 6 cups
- coarse salt
- freshly ground black pepper

Directions:
1. Supply your smoker with wood pellets and follow the start-up procedure. Preheat the grill, with the lid closed, to 450° F. Place 4 cedar planks on the grate and allow them to singe slightly on both sides. Remove them from the grill and place them on a heatproof surface to cool.
2. Lower the temperature to 300°F (149°C).
3. Slice 4 thin rounds from the center of the orange and then slice each in half for 8 pieces total. Zest the remainder of the orange and set aside.

4. In a cold skillet on the stovetop over medium heat, sauté the bacon, until the fat has rendered and the bacon is golden brown, about 6 to 8 minutes, stirring frequently. Use a slotted spoon to transfer the bacon to paper towels to drain. Add the fennel to the fat in the skillet and cook until tender crisp, about 5 minutes. Add the spinach and stir until it wilts, about 1 to 2 minutes. Squeeze the juice of one of the reserved orange ends over the mixture. Add the drained bacon. Season with salt and pepper and then stir. Remove the skillet from the stovetop and set aside.

5. Rinse each trout inside and out under cold running water and pat dry with paper towels. Place three 12-inch (30.5cm) pieces of butcher's twine on each plank and place a trout on top. Season the inside of each fish with salt and pepper. Place two half-rounds of orange in each belly, rind side facing out. Top with some of the filling. Tie the trout with the butcher's twine and trim any ends. Repeat with the remaining trout.

6. Place the planks on the grate and cook the trout until they're cooked through, about 30 to 40 minutes.

7. Remove the planks from the grill and remove the twine. Top each trout with a few curls of orange zest and some reserved fennel fronds. Serve the trout on the planks.

Oysters In The Shell

Servings: 4
Cooking Time: 20 Minutes

Ingredients:
- 8 medium oysters, unopened, in the shell, rinsed and scrubbed
- 1 batch Lemon Butter Mop for Seafood

Directions:
1. Supply your smoker with wood pellets and follow the start-up procedure. Preheat the grill, with the lid closed, to 375°F.
2. Place the unopened oysters directly on the grill grate and grill for about 20 minutes, or until the oysters are done and their shells open.
3. Discard any oysters that do not open. Shuck the remaining oysters, transfer them to a bowl, and add the mop. Serve immediately.

Teriyaki Smoked Honey Tilapia

Servings: 4
Cooking Time: 120 Minutes

Ingredients:
- 4 tilapia fillets
- 1 cup teriyaki sauce
- 2/3 cup honey
- 1 tbsp sriracha sauce
- Green onions (optional)

Directions:
1. In a large bowl, make the marinade by mixing together the teriyaki sauce, honey, and sriracha. Make sure honey is dissolved and well blended.
2. Place the tilapia fillets in the marinade. Turn the fillets so they are completely coated. Cover with a plastic wrap and marinate in the fridge for about 2 hours.
3. Supply your smoker with wood pellets and follow the start-up procedure. Preheat the grill, with the lid closed, to 275°F.
4. Remove the tilapia fillets from the marinade and transfer them to the grill. Smoke the fillets until they reach an internal temperature of 145°F, about 2 hours.
5. Sprinkle with green onions if desired.

Bbq Roasted Salmon

Servings: 4
Cooking Time: 15 Minutes

Ingredients:
- 1/3 Cup honey
- 3 Tablespoon Mustard, whole-grain
- 1 Cup ketchup
- 1/2 Cup dark brown sugar
- 1 Teaspoon Cider Vinegar
- 1/2 Teaspoon Thyme Leaves, finely chopped
- 1/8 Teaspoon Jacobsen Salt Co. Pure Kosher Sea Salt
- 1/8 Teaspoon freshly ground black pepper
- 4 Whole Salmon Fillets, 6oz each, skin-on

Directions:
1. Combine all sauce ingredients in a large bowl, preferably one day prior to making the salmon.
2. Rub salmon fillets on both sides with sauce. Reserve any extra, unused sauce.
3. Supply your smoker with wood pellets and follow the start-up procedure. Preheat the grill, with the lid closed, to 350°F.
4. Place fillets on grill, skin-side down, and cook for 15 minutes. Grill: 350 °F
5. Let the fish rest for about 3-5 minutes. Serve with extra sauce. Enjoy!

Honey Balsamic Salmon

Servings: 2
Cooking Time: 25 Minutes

Ingredients:
- 1 Medium salmon fillet
- Fin & Feather Rub
- 1/2 Cup balsamic vinegar
- 1 Tablespoon minced garlic
- 2 Tablespoon honey

Directions:
1. Season the fillet with the Traeger Fin & Feather Rub.
2. Make the glaze: Combine the vinegar, garlic and honey in a small saucepan. Simmer over medium heat until reduced by half. Usually 10 to 15 minutes. The glaze will be properly reduced when it coats the back of a spoon. Using a basting brush, coat the fillet with the glaze.
3. Supply your smoker with wood pellets and follow the start-up procedure. Preheat the grill, with the lid closed, to 350° F.
4. Arrange the salmon fillet on the grill grate. Grill for 25 to 30 minutes, or until the salmon is opaque and flakes easily with a fork. Grill: 350 °F
5. Transfer to a platter or plates and serve immediately. If desired, heat any remaining glaze to a boil and drizzle over top of the salmon. Enjoy!

Smoked Sugar Halibut

Servings: 8
Cooking Time: 120 Minutes

Ingredients:
- 1/4 cup granulated sugar
- 1/4 cup brown sugar
- 1/2 cup kosher salt
- 1 tsp ground coriander
- 2 lbs fresh halibut

Directions:
1. In a small bowl, mix the sugars, salt, and coriander together. Season the halibut on all sides.
2. Wrap the halibut in plastic wrap, place on a rimmed sheet pan, and brine in the fridge for 3 hours.
3. Remove the plastic wrap and rinse the fish. Pat it dry. Set it on a drying rack over a sheet pan for 1-2 hours in the fridge.
4. Supply your smoker with wood pellets and follow the start-up procedure. Preheat the grill, with the lid closed, to 200° F. Smoke the fish for 2 hours or until its internal temperature reaches 140 °F.
5. Serve your preferred sauce with the fish.

Cured Cold-smoked Lox

Servings: 6
Cooking Time: 360 Minutes

Ingredients:
- ¼ cup salt
- ¼ cup sugar
- 1 tablespoon freshly ground black pepper
- 1 bunch dill, chopped
- 1 pound sashimi-grade salmon, skin removed
- 1 avocado, sliced
- 8 bagels
- 4 ounces cream cheese
- 1 bunch alfalfa sprouts
- 1 (3.5-ounce) jar capers

Directions:
1. In a small bowl, combine the salt, sugar, pepper, and fresh dill to make the curing mixture. Set aside.
2. On a smooth surface, lay out a large piece of plastic wrap and spread half of the curing salt mixture in the middle, spreading it out to about the size of the salmon.
3. Place the salmon on top of the curing salt.
4. Top the fish with the remaining curing salt, covering it completely. Wrap the salmon, leaving the ends open to drain.
5. Place the wrapped fish in a rimmed baking pan or dish lined with paper towels to soak up liquid.
6. Place a weight on the salmon evenly, such as a pan with a couple of heavy jars of pickles on top.
7. Put the salmon pan with weights in the refrigerator. Place something (a dishtowel, for example) under the back of the pan in order to slightly tip it down so the liquid drains away from the fish.
8. Leave the salmon to cure in the refrigerator for 24 hours.
9. Place the wood pellets in the smoker, but do not follow the start-up procedure and do not preheat.
10. Remove the salmon from the refrigerator, unwrap it, rinse it off, and pat dry.
11. Put the salmon in the smoker while still cold from the refrigerator to slow down the cooking process. You'll need to use a cold-smoker attachment or enlist the help of a smoker tube to hold the temperature at 80°F and maintain that for 6 hours to absorb smoke and complete the cold-smoking process.
12. Remove the salmon from the smoker, place it in a sealed plastic bag, and refrigerate for 24 hours. The salmon will be translucent all the way through.
13. Thinly slice the lox and serve with sliced avocado, bagels, cream cheese, alfalfa sprouts, and capers.

Delicious Smoked Trout

Servings: 8
Cooking Time: 120 Minutes

Ingredients:
- 6 rainbow trout fillets
- Brine:
- 2 Tablespoons kosher salt
- 2 Tablespoons brown sugar
- 4 cups cool water

Directions:
1. For the brine, dissolve the kosher salt and brown sugar in water.
2. Place the trout fillets in the brine, skin side up, and brine the fillets for 15 minutes.

3. Supply your smoker with wood pellets and follow the start-up procedure. Preheat the grill, with the lid closed, to 180° F.
4. Remove the trout from the brine and transfer it to the grill grates.
5. Smoke the trout for 1.5 to 2 hours with the lid closed, depending on the thickness of your fillets.
6. Smoke until the trout reaches an internal temperature of 145 °F, or until the trout flakes easily.
7. Remove the trout from the smoker and serve warm, or let it cool completely and serve chilled with your favorite accouterments.

Lemon Shrimp Scampi

Servings: 3
Cooking Time: 10 Minutes

Ingredients:
- 2 Tsp Blackened Sriracha Rub Seasoning
- 1/2 Cup Butter, Cubed, Divided
- 1/2 Tsp Chili Pepper Flakes
- 3 Garlic Cloves, Minced
- To Taste, Lemon Wedges, For Serving
- 1 Lemon, Juice & Zest
- Linguine, Cooked
- 3 Tbsp Parsley, Chopped
- 1 1/2 Lbs Shrimp, Peeled & Deveined
- Toasted Baguette, For Serving

Directions:
1. Supply your smoker with wood pellets and follow the start-up procedure. Preheat the grill, with the lid closed, to medium-high heat. If using a gas or charcoal grill, set it up for medium-high heat.
2. Add half of the butter to the griddle, then sauté the garlic, Blackened Sriracha, and chili flakes for 1 minute, until fragrant.
3. Add the shrimp, turning occasionally for 2 minutes, until opaque.
4. Add the remaining butter, parsley, lemon zest and juice. Toss the shrimp to coat in lemon butter, then remove from the griddle, and transfer to a serving bowl.
5. Serve immediately, with fresh lemon wedges, and toasted baguette. Serve over linguine, spaghetti or zucchini noodles, if desired.

Smoky Crab Dip

Servings: 6
Cooking Time: 20 Minutes

Ingredients:
- 1/3 Cup mayonnaise
- 3 Ounce sour cream
- 1 Teaspoon smoked paprika
- 1/4 Teaspoon cayenne pepper
- 1 1/2 Pound Crab meat, lump
- salt and pepper
- scallions, chopped
- butter crackers

Directions:
1. Supply your smoker with wood pellets and follow the start-up procedure. Preheat the grill, with the lid closed, to 350° F.
2. Meanwhile, in a large bowl gently stir together all of the ingredients except the crackers, garnish scallions and the crab meat until thoroughly combined. Gently fold in the crab meat, being careful not to break it up too much.
3. Season to taste and transfer to an oven-safe serving dish.
4. Bake for 20 to 25 minutes, until bubbly and golden on top. Grill: 350 °F
5. Garnish with the additional chopped scallions and serve warm with butter crackers. Enjoy!

Peper Fish Tacos

Servings: 12
Cooking Time: 10 Minutes

Ingredients:
- 1 Tsp Black Pepper
- 1/4 Tsp Cayenne Pepper
- 1 1/2 Lbs Cod Fish
- 1/2 Tsp Cumin
- 1 Tsp Garlic Powder
- 1 Tsp Oregano
- 1 1/2 Tsp Paprika, Smoked
- 1/2 Tsp Salt

Directions:
1. Supply your smoker with wood pellets and follow the start-up procedure. Preheat the grill, with the lid closed, to 350° F.
2. Mix together paprika, garlic powder, oregano, cumin, cayenne, salt and pepper. Sprinkle over cod.
3. Place the cod on your preheated for about 5 minutes per side. Toast tortillas over heat, if desired.
4. Break the cod into pieces, smash the avocado, slice the tomatoes in half and place evenly among the tortillas. Top with red onion, lettuce, jalapenos, sour cream, and cilantro. Spritz with lime juice and enjoy!

Grilled Blackened Saskatchewan Salmon

Servings: 4
Cooking Time: 30 Minutes

Ingredients:
- 1 salmon fillets
- zesty Italian dressing
- Blackened Saskatchewan Rub

- lemon wedges

Directions:
1. Brush salmon with Italian dressing and season with Traeger Blackened Saskatchewan Rub.
2. Supply your smoker with wood pellets and follow the start-up procedure. Preheat the grill, with the lid closed, to 325° F.
3. Place salmon on the grill and cook for 20 to 30 minutes, until it reaches an internal temperature of 145°F and flakes easily. Remove salmon from grill. Serve with lemon wedges. Enjoy! Grill: 325 °F Probe: 145 °F

Seared Ahi Tuna Steak With Soy Sauce

Servings: 2
Cooking Time: 60 Minutes

Ingredients:
- 1/2 Cup Gluten Free Soy Sauce
- 1 Large Sushi Grade Ahi Tuna Steak, Patted Dry
- 1/4 Cup Lime Juice
- 2 Tablespoons Rice Wine Vinegar
- 2 Tablespoons Sesame Oil, Divided
- 2 Tablespoons Sriracha Sauce
- 4 Tablespoons Sweet Heat Rub
- 2 Cups Water

Directions:
1. Supply your smoker with wood pellets and follow the start-up procedure. Preheat the grill, with the lid closed, to 400° F. If using gas or charcoal, set it up for high heat over direct heat.
2. In the glass baking dish, pour in the water, soy sauce, lime juice, rice wine vinegar, 1 tablespoon sesame oil, sriracha sauce, and mirin. Whisk the marinade together with the whisk until everything is well combine. Place the ahi steak into the marinade and place the glass baking dish with the ahi steak in the refrigerator for 30 minutes. After 30 minutes, flip the ahi steak over so that the ahi has the chance to fully marinate on all sides, and allow to marinate for 30 more minutes.
3. After the tuna steak has finished marinating, drain off the marinade and pat the steak dry with paper towels on all sides. Pour the Sweet Heat Rub onto the plate and rub the remaining tablespoon of sesame oil generously on all sides of the tuna steak, and then gently place the tuna steak into the seasoning on the plate, turning on all sides to coat evenly.
4. Insert a temperature probe into the thickest part of the ahi steak and place the steak on the hottest part of the grill. Grill the ahi tuna steak for 45 seconds on each side, or just until the outside is opaque and has grill marks. Flip the steak and allow it to grill for another 45 seconds until the outside is just cooked through. The ahi tuna steak's internal temperature should be just at 115°F.
5. Remove the steak from the grill once it reaches 115°F, and immediately slice and serve. The inside of the steak should still be cool and ruby pink.

Honey-soy Garlic Salmon

Servings: 4
Cooking Time: 6 Minutes

Ingredients:
- 1 Tsp Chili Paste
- Chives, Chopped
- 2 Grate Garlic, Cloves
- 2 Tbsp Minced Ginger, Fresh
- 1 Tsp Honey
- 2 Tbsp Lemon, Juice
- 4 Salmon, Fillets (Skin Removed)
- 1 Tsp Sesame Oil
- 2 Tbsp Soy Sauce, Low Sodium

Directions:
1. Supply your smoker with wood pellets and follow the start-up procedure. Preheat the grill, with the lid closed, to 400° F.
2. Take the salmon and place it in a large resealable plastic bag, and then top with all remaining ingredients, except the chives. Seal the plastic bag and toss evenly to coat the salmon. Marinade in the refrigerator for 20 minutes.
3. After the salmon has been marinading for 20 minutes, place salmon on a flat pan or right on the grates and grill for about 3 minutes, and then flip and grill on the second side for about 3 minutes. Turn off the Grill, remove the pan from grill, plate, garnish with chives, and enjoy!

Grilled Salmon Steaks With Dill Sauce

Servings: 4
Cooking Time: 8 Minutes

Ingredients:
- 4 salmon steaks, each about 6 to 8oz (170 to 225g) and 1 inch (2.5cm) thick
- extra virgin olive oil
- coarse salt
- freshly ground rainbow peppercorns or freshly ground black pepper
- lemon wedges
- for the sauce
- 1 cup reduced-fat mayo
- ⅓ cup light sour cream
- ¼ cup chopped fresh dill
- 2 tbsp freshly squeezed lemon juice
- coarse salt
- freshly ground black pepper
- sprigs of fresh dill

Directions:
1. Supply your smoker with wood pellets and follow the start-up procedure. Preheat the grill, with the lid closed, to 450° F.
2. In a small bowl, make the dill sauce by combining the mayo, sour cream, dill, and lemon juice. Mix until smooth. Season with salt and pepper to taste. Transfer to a serving bowl. Scatter the dill sprigs over the top. Cover and refrigerate until ready to serve.
3. Brush the salmon with olive oil and season with salt and pepper. Place the salmon on the grate at an angle to the bars. Grill until grill marks begin to appear, about 4 minutes. Use a thin-bladed spatula to turn the salmon. Grill until the internal temperature reaches 140°F (60°C), about 4 minutes more.
4. Transfer the salmon to a platter. Serve immediately with the lemon wedges and dill sauce.

Smoked Trout

Servings: 6
Cooking Time: 120 Minutes

Ingredients:
- 8 rainbow trout fillets
- 1 Gallon water
- 1/4 Cup salt
- 1/2 Cup brown sugar
- 1 Tablespoon black pepper
- 2 Tablespoon soy sauce

Directions:
1. Clean the fresh fish and butterfly them.
2. For the Brine: Combine one gallon water, brown sugar, soy sauce, salt and pepper and stir until salt and sugar are dissolved. Brine the trout in the refrigerator for 60 minutes.
3. Supply your smoker with wood pellets and follow the start-up procedure. Preheat the grill, with the lid closed, to 225° F.
4. Remove the fish from the brine and pat dry. Place fish directly on grill grate for 1-1/2 to 2 hours, depending on the thickness of the trout. Fish is done when it turns opaque and starts to flake. Serve hot or cold. Enjoy! Grill: 225 °F
5. Fish is done when it turns opaque and starts to flake. Serve hot or cold. Enjoy!

Grilled Trout With Citrus & Basil

Servings: 4
Cooking Time: 10 Minutes

Ingredients:
- 6 Whole Trout
- 2 Teaspoon Blackened Saskatchewan Rub
- 10 Sprig fresh basil
- 2 Lemons, cut in half
- extra-virgin olive oil

Directions:
1. Supply your smoker with wood pellets and follow the start-up procedure. Preheat the grill, with the lid closed, to 450° F.
2. Season the center cavity of the trout with the Traeger Blackened Saskatchewan. Place two sprigs of Basil in each cavity, then add 4 lemon halves.
3. Next tie the fish closed using the Butchers twine, and then rub with olive oil.
4. Place the trout on the hot grill and cook 5 minutes on each side. Enjoy! Grill: 450 °F

Bbq Oysters

Servings: 4
Cooking Time: 6 Minutes

Ingredients:
- 1 Pound unsalted butter, softened
- 1 Tablespoon Meat Church Holy Gospel BBQ Rub
- 1 Bunch green onions, chopped
- 2 Clove garlic, minced
- 12 oysters
- 1/4 Cup seasoned breadcrumbs
- 8 Ounce shredded pepper jack cheese
- Sweet & Heat BBQ Sauce
- 1/2 Bunch green onions, minced

Directions:
1. Supply your smoker with wood pellets and follow the start-up procedure. Preheat the grill, with the lid closed, to 375° F.
2. For the compound butter: Combine butter, garlic, onion and Meat Church Rub thoroughly.
3. Lay the butter on parchment paper or plastic wrap. Roll it up to form a log and tie each end with butcher's twine. Place in the freezer for an hour to solidify. You can use this butter on any grilled meat to enhance the flavor. You can also use a high-quality butter to replace the compound butter.
4. Shuck the oysters, keeping all of the juice in the shell. Sprinkle the oysters with breadcrumbs and place directly on the Traeger. Cook them for 5 minutes. You will be looking for the edge of the oyster to start to curl slightly.
5. After 5 minutes, place a spoonful of compound butter in the oysters. After the butter melts, add a pinch of pepper jack cheese.
6. Remove the oysters after 6 minutes on the grill total. Top oysters with a squirt of Traeger Sweet & Heat BBQ Sauce and a few chopped onions. Allow to cool for 5 minutes, then enjoy!

Smoked Mango Shrimp

Servings: 4
Cooking Time: 5 Minutes

Ingredients:
- 2 Tablespoon Olive Oil

- 1 Pound Raw Tail-On, Thawed And Deveined Shrimp, Uncooked

Directions:
1. Supply your smoker with wood pellets and follow the start-up procedure. Preheat the grill, with the lid closed, to 425° F. Rinse shrimp off in sink with cold water. Place in bowl and season generously with Mango Magic seasoning and olive oil. Toss well in bowl.
2. Thread several shrimp onto a skewer, so that they are all just touching each other. Repeat with other skewers and remaining shrimp.
3. Grill shrimp for 2 - 3 minutes on each side, or until pink and opaque all the way through. Remove from grill and serve immediately.

Pacific Northwest Salmon

Servings: 4
Cooking Time: 75 Minutes

Ingredients:
- 1 (2-pound) half salmon fillet
- 1 batch Dill Seafood Rub
- 2 tablespoons butter, cut into 3 or 4 slices

Directions:
1. Supply your smoker with wood pellets and follow the start-up procedure. Preheat the grill, with the lid closed, to 180°F.
2. Season the salmon all over with the rub. Using your hands, work the rub into the flesh.
3. Place the salmon directly on the grill grate, skin-side down, and smoke for 1 hour.
4. Place the butter slices on the salmon, equally spaced. Increase the grill's temperature to 300°F and continue to cook until the salmon's internal temperature reaches 145°F. Remove the salmon from the grill and serve immediately.

Traeger Crab Legs

Servings: 4
Cooking Time: 30 Minutes

Ingredients:
- 3 Pound crab legs, thawed and halved
- 1 Cup butter, melted
- 2 Tablespoon fresh lemon juice
- 2 Clove garlic, minced
- 1 Tablespoon Fin & Feather Rub or Old Bay Seasoning, plus more to taste
- lemon wedges
- Italian Parsley, chopped

Directions:
1. If the crab legs are too long to fit in the roasting pan, break them down at the joints by twisting, or use a heavy knife or cleaver. Split the shells open lengthwise. Transfer to the roasting pan.
2. Combine the butter, lemon juice and garlic; whisk to mix. Pour mixture over the crab legs, turning the legs to coat. Sprinkle the Traeger Fin & Feather Rub or Old Bay Seasoning over the legs.
3. Supply your smoker with wood pellets and follow the start-up procedure. Preheat the grill, with the lid closed, to 350° F.
4. Cook the crab legs, basting once or twice with the butter sauce from the bottom of the pan, for 20 to 30 minutes (depending on the size of the crab legs) or until warmed through. Grill: 350 °F
5. Transfer the crab legs to a large platter and divide the sauce and accumulated juices between 4 dipping bowls. Enjoy!

Prosciutto-wrapped Scallops

Servings: 4
Cooking Time: 10 Minutes

Ingredients:
- 1½lb (680g) jumbo sea or diver scallops (size U-10)
- 8 to 10 thin slices of prosciutto, each halved lengthwise
- coarse salt
- freshly ground black pepper
- for the butter
- 8oz (225g) unsalted butter
- 2 tsp minced fresh curly or flat-leaf parsley
- 1½ tsp finely grated orange zest
- 1 tbsp freshly squeezed orange juice
- 1 tsp finely grated lemon zest
- 1 tsp finely grated lime zest
- ½ tsp coarse salt

Directions:
1. Supply your smoker with wood pellets and follow the start-up procedure. Preheat the grill, with the lid closed, to 450° F.
2. In a small saucepan on the stovetop over medium-low heat, make the citrus butter by melting the butter. Add the remaining ingredients and simmer for 3 to 5 minutes to blend the flavors. Keep warm.
3. Rinse the scallops under cold running water and dry with paper towels. Place each scallop on its side at the end of a piece of prosciutto and wrap the prosciutto around the scallop. Secure with a toothpick. Season the exposed sides of the scallop with salt and pepper.
4. Place the scallops exposed sides down on the grate and grill until the edges of the prosciutto begin to frizzle and the scallop is warm inside, about 3 to 5 minutes per side.
5. Transfer the scallops to a platter. Brush with some of the warm citrus butter before serving. Serve the remaining butter on the side.

Traeger Baked Rainbow Trout

Servings: 2
Cooking Time: 20 Minutes

Ingredients:
- 2 Tablespoon olive oil, divided
- 2 Whole rainbow trout, gutted and cleaned, heads and tails still on
- 1/2 Teaspoon fresh dill
- 1/2 Teaspoon fresh thyme
- 1 Teaspoon Jacobsen Salt Co. Pure Kosher Sea Salt
- 1/2 Large onion, sliced
- 1 Large lemon, thinly sliced
- 1 Teaspoon freshly ground black pepper

Directions:
1. Supply your smoker with wood pellets and follow the start-up procedure. Preheat the grill, with the lid closed, to 400° F.
2. Grease a 9x13 inch baking dish with 1 tablespoon olive oil.
3. Place trout in the prepared baking dish and coat fish with remaining olive oil. Season the inside and outside of fish with dill, thyme and salt. Stuff each fish with onion and lemon slices then grind pepper over the top. Place 1 lemon slice on each fish.
4. Bake in the Traeger for 10 minutes. Add 2 tablespoons hot water to the baking dish. Continue baking until fish flakes easily with a fork, about 10 more minutes. Enjoy! Grill: 400 °F

Garlic Bacon Wrapped Shrimp

Servings: 4
Cooking Time: 11 Minutes

Ingredients:
- 8 Bacon, Strip
- 1/4 Cup Butter Style Shortening (Melted)
- 1 Clove Garlic, Minced
- 1 Tsp Lemon, Juice
- Pepper
- Salt
- 16 (Peeled And Veined) Shrimp, Jumbo

Directions:
1. Supply your smoker with wood pellets and follow the start-up procedure. Preheat the grill, with the lid closed, to 450° F.
2. Take one slice of bacon, and wrap it around each piece of shrimp, and lock it in place with a wooden toothpick.
3. Place the shortening into a mixing bowl and whisk in the garlic and lemon juice. Brush each shrimp with the sauce on both sides.
4. Place on the grill, and barbecue for 11 minutes.
5. Turn the grill off, remove the shrimp, serve and enjoy!

Moules Marinières With Garlic Butter Sauce

Servings: 4
Cooking Time: 12 Minutes

Ingredients:
- 3lb (1.4kg) fresh mussels, scrubbed under cold running water and debearded
- lemon wedges
- crusty bread (optional)
- for the sauce
- 6 tbsp unsalted butter
- 3 garlic cloves, peeled and minced
- 1 cup dry white wine or hard cider
- 1 tbsp freshly squeezed lemon juice
- 2 tsp hot sauce, plus more
- coarse salt
- freshly ground black pepper
- 2 tbsp chopped fresh curly parsley or tarragon

Directions:
1. Supply your smoker with wood pellets and follow the start-up procedure. Preheat the grill, with the lid closed, to 450° F.
2. In a small saucepan on the stovetop over medium-low heat, make the sauce by melting the butter. Add the garlic and sauté for 1 to 2 minutes. Add the wine, lemon juice, and hot sauce. Season with salt and pepper to taste. Simmer for 5 minutes. Remove the saucepan from the heat and stir in the parsley. Keep warm.
3. Discard any mussels that are cracked or don't snap shut when tapped. Place the mussels in a large aluminum foil roasting pan and cover tightly with heavy-duty aluminum foil.
4. Place the pan on the grate and steam the mussels until the shells open, about 10 to 12 minutes. Remove the pan from the grill and use long-handled tongs to remove the foil from the pan. (Be careful of escaping steam.) Use the tongs to discard any mussels that don't open.
5. Pour the reserved garlic butter sauce over the mussels. Serve from the pan or transfer the mussels to a shallow serving bowl. Serve immediately with lemon wedges, additional hot sauce, and crusty bread (if using) to sop up the juices.

Charleston Crab Cakes With Remoulade

Servings: 4
Cooking Time: 45 Minutes

Ingredients:
- 1¼ cups mayonnaise
- ¼ cup yellow mustard
- 2 tablespoons sweet pickle relish, with its juices
- 1 tablespoon smoked paprika
- 2 teaspoons Cajun seasoning
- 2 teaspoons prepared horseradish
- 1 teaspoon hot sauce

- 1 garlic clove, finely minced
- 2 pounds fresh lump crabmeat, picked clean
- 20 butter crackers (such as Ritz brand), crushed
- 2 tablespoons Dijon mustard
- 1 cup mayonnaise
- 2 tablespoons freshly squeezed lemon juice
- 1 tablespoon salted butter, melted
- 1 tablespoon Worcestershire sauce
- 1 tablespoon Old Bay seasoning
- 2 teaspoons chopped fresh parsley
- 1 teaspoon ground mustard
- 2 eggs, beaten
- ¼ cup extra-virgin olive oil, divided

Directions:
1. For the remoulade:
2. In a small bowl, combine the mayonnaise, mustard, pickle relish, paprika, Cajun seasoning, horseradish, hot sauce, and garlic.
3. Refrigerate until ready to serve.
4. For the crab cakes:
5. Supply your smoker with wood pellets and follow the start-up procedure. Preheat, with the lid closed, to 375°F.
6. Spread the crabmeat on a foil-lined baking sheet and place over indirect heat on the grill, with the lid closed, for 30 minutes.
7. Remove from the heat and let cool for 15 minutes.
8. While the crab cools, combine the crushed crackers, Dijon mustard, mayonnaise, lemon juice, melted butter, Worcestershire sauce, Old Bay, parsley, ground mustard, and eggs until well incorporated.
9. Fold in the smoked crabmeat, then shape the mixture into 8 (1-inch-thick) crab cakes.
10. In a large skillet or cast-iron pan on the grill, heat 2 tablespoons of olive oil. Add half of the crab cakes, close the lid, and smoke for 4 to 5 minutes on each side, or until crispy and golden brown.
11. Remove the crab cakes from the pan and transfer to a wire rack to drain. Pat them to remove any excess oil.
12. Repeat steps 6 and 7 with the remaining oil and crab cakes.
13. Serve the crab cakes with the remoulade.

Grilled Salmon

Servings: 4
Cooking Time: 25 Minutes

Ingredients:
- 1 (2-pound) half salmon fillet
- 3 tablespoons mayonnaise
- 1 batch Dill Seafood Rub

Directions:
1. Supply your smoker with wood pellets and follow the start-up procedure. Preheat the grill, with the lid closed, to 325°F.
2. Using your hands, rub the salmon fillet all over with the mayonnaise and sprinkle it with the rub.
3. Place the salmon directly on the grill grate, skin-side down, and grill until its internal temperature reaches 145°F. Remove the salmon from the grill and serve immediately.

Grilled Garlic Lobster Tails

Servings: 2
Cooking Time: 11 Minutes

Ingredients:
- 4 Lobster Tails (8 oz Each)
- 3 Sticks Unsalted Butter
- 4 Cloves Garlic Minced
- ½ Cup Fresh Parsley Chopped
- Juice of 1 Lemon
- 2 Tablespoons Fresh Lemon Zest
- 2 Teaspoons Crushed Red Pepper
- ¼ Cup Olive Oil
- 1 TBS Kosher Salt
- 1 TBS Cracked Black Pepper

Directions:
1. Supply your smoker with wood pellets and follow the start-up procedure. Preheat the grill, with the lid closed, to 375° F.
2. Split lobster tails in half lengthwise and season with salt, pepper, and olive oil.
3. Place butter in an aluminum pan and put the pan on the hot side of the grill to melt the butter.
4. Add garlic, parsley, lemon zest, lemon juice, and red pepper to butter and simmer for 5 minutes.
5. Place lobster tails meat side down on the grill and cook for 6 minutes. Baste the shell side with the butter mixture.
6. Dunk each tail in the butter mixture and then transfer to the grill, shell side down. Baste meat again with butter mixture.
7. Cook for an additional 5 minutes or until the lobster meat turns opaque and shells are bright pink.
8. Serve with remaining butter mixture, fresh parsley, and lemon wedges.

Spicy Crab Poppers

Servings: 8
Cooking Time: 30 Minutes

Ingredients:
- 18 Whole jalapeño
- 8 Ounce cream cheese, softened
- 1 Cup Canned Corn, drained
- 1/2 Cup Crab meat, lump
- 1 1/4 Teaspoon Old Bay Seasoning
- 2 Scallions, minced

Directions:
1. Cut each jalapeño in half lengthwise through the stem and remove the ribs and seeds.
2. Filling: In a mixing bowl, combine the cream cheese, corn, crab meat, scallions, and Old Bay Seasoning and stir until blended. Stir in the scallions. Spoon the filling into the jalapeño halves, mounding it slightly.
3. Arrange the poppers on a baking sheet covered with foil or parchment paper.
4. Supply your smoker with wood pellets and follow the start-up procedure. Preheat the grill, with the lid closed, to 350° F.
5. Roast the jalapeños for 25 to 30 minutes, or until the peppers have softened and the filling is hot and bubbling.
6. Let cool slightly before serving. Enjoy!

Flavour Fire Spiced Shrimp

Servings: 2
Cooking Time: 8 Minutes

Ingredients:
- 1 pound of extra large raw whole wild shrimp
- 1 tablespoon vegetable oil
- 1 tablespoon chili powder
- 1 teaspoon garlic powder
- 1/2 teaspoon onion powder
- 1/2 teaspoon cayenne pepper
- 1/4 teaspoon paprika
- 1/4 teaspoon dried oregano
- Pinch of Kosher salt

Directions:
1. Supply your smoker with wood pellets and follow the start-up procedure. Preheat the grill, with the lid closed, to High heat.
2. While grill is preheating, remove the shrimp shells, leaving the heads.
3. Butterfly shrimp by using a knife to cut each shrimp down the middle, from the head down to the tail.
4. Remove the vein, rinse off the shrimp and lightly dry off with paper towels.
5. Place the shrimp in a large bowl, sprinkle with all the seasonings and the oil.
6. Mix together, ensuring the mixture evenly covers each shrimp.
7. Using a skewer, impale the whole body of a shrimp, from head to tail. (Wrap them in aluminum foil if using wooden skewers).
8. Place the whole shrimp on the grill and cook for 3-4 minutes on each side (Or until shells turns pink and the shrimp is opaque).
9. Serve with your favorite sauce or condiment.

VEGETABLES RECIPES

Roasted Hasselback Potatoes By Doug Scheiding

Servings: 6
Cooking Time: 120 Minutes

Ingredients:
- 6 Large russet potatoes
- 1 Pound bacon
- 1/2 Cup butter
- salt
- black pepper
- 1 Cup cheddar cheese
- 3 Whole scallions

Directions:
1. To cut potatoes, place two wooden spoons on either side of the potato (this prevents your knife from going all the way through). Slice potato into thin chips leaving about 1/4" attached on the bottom.
2. Freeze bacon slices for about 30 minutes then cut into small pieces about the size of a stamp. Place these in the cracks between every other slice.
3. Place the potato in a large cast iron skillet. Top the potato with slices of hard butter (you can also place thin slivers of cold butter between the potato slices with the bacon if desired). Season with salt and pepper.
4. Supply your smoker with wood pellets and follow the start-up procedure. Preheat the grill, with the lid closed, to 350° F.
5. Place the cast iron directly on the grill grate and cook for two hours. Top potatoes with more butter and baste with melted butter every 30 minutes.
6. In the last 10 minutes of cooking, sprinkle with cheddar and return to grill to melt.
7. To finish, top with chives or scallions. Enjoy!

Roasted Mashed Potatoes

Servings: 8
Cooking Time: 40 Minutes

Ingredients:
- 5 Pound Yukon Gold potatoes
- 1 1/2 Stick butter, softened
- 1 1/2 Cup heavy whipping cream, room temperature
- kosher salt
- white pepper

Directions:
1. Supply your smoker with wood pellets and follow the start-up procedure. Preheat the grill, with the lid closed, to 300° F.
2. Peel and cut potatoes into 1/2 inch cubes. Place the potatoes in a shallow baking dish with 1/2 cup water and cover. Bake until tender, about 40 minutes. Grill: 300 °F
3. In a medium saucepan, combine cream and butter. Cook over medium heat until butter is melted.
4. Remove potatoes from the grill and drain water.
5. Transfer potatoes to a bowl and mash using a potato masher. Gradually add in cream and butter mixture and mix using the masher. Be careful not to overwork or the potatoes will becomes gluey. Season with salt and pepper to taste. Enjoy!

Broccoli-cauliflower Salad

Servings: 4
Cooking Time: 25 Minutes

Ingredients:
- 1½ cups mayonnaise
- ½ cup sour cream
- ¼ cup sugar
- 1 bunch broccoli, cut into small pieces
- 1 head cauliflower, cut into small pieces
- 1 small red onion, chopped
- 6 slices bacon, cooked and crumbled (precooked bacon works well)
- 1 cup shredded Cheddar cheese

Directions:
1. In a small bowl, whisk together the mayonnaise, sour cream, and sugar to make a dressing.
2. In a large bowl, combine the broccoli, cauliflower, onion, bacon, and Cheddar cheese.
3. Pour the dressing over the vegetable mixture and toss well to coat.
4. Serve the salad chilled.

Roasted Potato Poutine

Servings: 6
Cooking Time: 40 Minutes

Ingredients:
- 4 Large russet potatoes
- Tablespoon olive oil or vegetable oil
- Prime Rib Rub
- Cup chicken or beef gravy (homemade or jarred)
- 1 1/2 Cup white or yellow cheddar cheese curds
- freshly ground black pepper
- 2 Tablespoon scallions

Directions:

1. Supply your smoker with wood pellets and follow the start-up procedure. Preheat the grill, with the lid closed, to 500° F.
2. Scrub the potatoes and slice into fries, wedges or preferred shape.
3. Put potatoes into a large mixing bowl and coat with oil. Season generously with Traeger Prime Rib rub.
4. Tip the potatoes onto a rimmed baking sheet and spread in a single layer, cut sides down.
5. Roast for 20 minutes, then using a spatula, turn the potatoes to the other cut side. Continue to roast until the potatoes are tender and golden brown, about 15 to 20 minutes more.
6. While potatoes cook, warm the gravy on the stovetop or in a heat-proof saucepan on your Traeger.
7. To assemble the poutine, arrange the potatoes in a large shallow bowl or on a serving platter. Distribute the cheese curds on top. Pour the hot gravy evenly over the potatoes and cheese curds.
8. Season with black pepper and garnish with thinly sliced scallions. Serve immediately. Enjoy!

Salt Crusted Baked Potatoes

Servings: 4
Cooking Time: 60 Minutes

Ingredients:
- 6 russet potatoes, scrubbed and dried
- 3 Tablespoon canola oil
- 1 Tablespoon kosher salt
- butter
- sour cream
- Chives, fresh
- Bacon Bits
- cheddar cheese

Directions:
1. In a large bowl, coat the potatoes in canola oil and sprinkle heavily with salt.
2. Supply your smoker with wood pellets and follow the start-up procedure. Preheat the grill, with the lid closed, to 450° F.
3. Place the potatoes directly on the grill grate and bake for 30-40 minutes, or until soft in the middle when pricked with a fork. Serve loaded with your favorite toppings. Enjoy! Grill: 450 °F

Grilled Street Corn

Servings: 6
Cooking Time: 10 Minutes

Ingredients:
- 6 ears corn, husked
- 1 As Needed extra-virgin olive oil
- 1/4 Cup mayonnaise
- 1 Tablespoon ancho or guajillo chile powder
- 1/2 Cup chopped cilantro, plus more for serving
- 1 lime, zested and juiced
- salt
- 1/2 Cup Cotija cheese
- 1 As Needed cilantro, finely chopped

Directions:
1. Supply your smoker with wood pellets and follow the start-up procedure. Preheat the grill, with the lid closed, to 450° F.
2. Brush corn with oil and place on grill, turning occasionally.
3. While corn is on the grill, mix mayonnaise with chile powder, cilantro, lime juice and zest in a bowl. Season with salt.
4. After about 10 minutes corn should be cooked through and slightly charred on the outside. Remove from grill.
5. Top corn with chile mayonnaise then sprinkle on the Cotija cheese and chopped cilantro. Enjoy!

Roasted Asparagus

Servings: 4
Cooking Time: 30 Minutes

Ingredients:
- 1 Bunch asparagus
- 2 Tablespoon olive oil, plus more as needed
- Veggie Rub

Directions:
1. Coat asparagus with olive oil and Veggie Rub, stirring to coat all pieces.
2. Supply your smoker with wood pellets and follow the start-up procedure. Preheat the grill, with the lid closed, to 350° F.
3. Place asparagus directly on the grill grate for 15-20 minutes.
4. Remove from grill and enjoy!

Twice-smoked Potatoes

Servings: 16
Cooking Time: 95 Minutes

Ingredients:
- 8 Idaho, Russet, or Yukon Gold potatoes
- 1 (12-ounce) can evaporated milk, heated
- 1 cup (2 sticks) butter, melted
- ½ cup sour cream, at room temperature
- 1 cup grated Parmesan cheese
- ½ pound bacon, cooked and crumbled
- ¼ cup chopped scallions
- Salt
- Freshly ground black pepper
- 1 cup shredded Cheddar cheese

Directions:
1. Supply your smoker with wood pellets and follow the start-up procedure. Preheat, with the lid closed, to 400°F.

2. Poke the potatoes all over with a fork. Arrange them directly on the grill grate, close the lid, and smoke for 1 hour and 15 minutes, or until cooked through and they have some give when pinched.
3. Let the potatoes cool for 10 minutes, then cut in half lengthwise.
4. Into a medium bowl, scoop out the potato flesh, leaving ¼ inch in the shells; place the shells on a baking sheet.
5. Using an electric mixer on medium speed, beat the potatoes, milk, butter, and sour cream until smooth.
6. Stir in the Parmesan cheese, bacon, and scallions, and season with salt and pepper.
7. Generously stuff each shell with the potato mixture and top with Cheddar cheese.
8. Place the baking sheet on the grill grate, close the lid, and smoke for 20 minutes, or until the cheese is melted.

Bacon Wrapped Corn On The Cob

Servings: 4
Cooking Time: 21 Minutes

Ingredients:
- 4 Whole Corn, ears
- 8 Slices bacon
- 1 Teaspoon freshly ground black pepper
- 1 Teaspoon chili powder
- 1 To Taste Parmesan cheese, grated

Directions:
1. Peel back the corn husks, remove silk strings and rinse corn under cold water.
2. Wrap 2 pieces of bacon around each ear of corn, securing with toothpicks.
3. Dust each ear of corn with some chili powder and cracked black pepper.
4. Supply your smoker with wood pellets and follow the start-up procedure. Preheat the grill, with the lid closed, to 375° F.
5. Place the ears of corn directly on the Traeger and grill for approximately 20 minutes or until the bacon is cooked crisp. Grill: 375 °F
6. Take the corn off the Traeger. Carefully remove the toothpicks and season with a little more chili powder and a grating of parmesan cheese, if desired. Serve & enjoy!

Grilled Asparagus And Hollandaise Sauce

Servings: 4
Cooking Time: 10 Minutes

Ingredients:
- 1 Pound asparagus
- 2 Teaspoon red pepper flakes
- 2 Tablespoon olive oil
- salt and pepper
- 4 egg yolk
- 1 Tablespoon lemon juice
- 1/2 Cup butter, melted
- cayenne pepper
- salt

Directions:
1. Supply your smoker with wood pellets and follow the start-up procedure. Preheat the grill, with the lid closed, to 375° F.
2. In a large bowl, mix asparagus with olive oil, red pepper flakes and salt. Arrange asparagus on a cooking sheet and take to the grill. Cook for approximately 10 to 15 minutes. Grill: 375 °F
3. In an aluminum bowl, whisk the egg yolks well. Add the lemon juice and whisk until creamy.
4. Place bowl over a double boiler, over low heat, making sure that it does not touches the water.
5. While whisking, add the melted butter slowly. Whisk until it doubles the volume. Take off the heat, still whisking and add the cayenne pepper and salt.
6. Arrange asparagus over a serving plater. Pour hollandaise sauce over asparagus and serve. Enjoy!

Traeger Smoked Coleslaw

Servings: 8
Cooking Time: 20 Minutes

Ingredients:
- 1 Head purple cabbage, shredded
- 1 Head green cabbage, shredded
- 1 Cup shredded carrots
- 2 scallions, thinly sliced
- 1 1/2 Cup mayonnaise
- 1/8 Cup white wine vinegar
- 1 Teaspoon celery seed
- 1 Teaspoon sugar
- salt and pepper

Directions:
1. Supply your smoker with wood pellets and follow the start-up procedure. Preheat the grill, with the lid closed, to 180° F.
2. Spread cabbage and carrots out on a sheet tray and place directly on the grill grates. Smoke for 20 to 25 minutes or until cabbage picks up desired amount of smoke. Grill: 180 °F
3. Remove from grill and transfer to the refrigerator immediately to cool. While cabbage is cooling, make the dressing.
4. For the dressing, combine all ingredients in a small bowl and mix well.
5. Place smoked cabbage and carrots in a large bowl and pour dressing over them. Stir to coat well.
6. Transfer to a serving dish and sprinkle with scallions. Enjoy!

Grilled Corn On The Cob With Parmesan And Garlic

Servings: 6
Cooking Time: 30 Minutes

Ingredients:
- 4 Tablespoon butter, melted
- 2 Clove garlic, minced
- salt and pepper
- 8 ears fresh corn
- 1/2 Cup shaved Parmesan
- 1 Tablespoon chopped parsley

Directions:
1. Supply your smoker with wood pellets and follow the start-up procedure. Preheat the grill, with the lid closed, to 450° F.
2. Place butter, garlic, salt and pepper in a medium bowl and mix well.
3. Peel back corn husks and remove the silk. Rub corn with half of the garlic butter mixture.
4. Close husks and place directly on the grill grate. Cook for 25 to 30 minutes, turning occasionally until corn is tender. Grill: 450 °F
5. Remove from grill, peel and discard husks. Place corn on serving tray, drizzle with remaining butter and top with Parmesan and parsley.

Smoked Asparagus Soup

Servings: 4
Cooking Time: 40 Minutes

Ingredients:
- Pound Asparagus Spears
- 1 Tablespoon olive oil
- salt and pepper
- 1/2 yellow onion, diced
- 1 Tablespoon butter
- 2 Clove garlic, minced
- 1 1/2 Cup chicken stock
- 1 1/2 Cup cream
- 2 Stalk Raw Asparagus, Shaved

Directions:
1. Supply your smoker with wood pellets and follow the start-up procedure. Preheat the grill, with the lid closed, to 180° F.
2. Drizzle 1 pound of asparagus with olive oil and season with salt and pepper. Place directly on the grill grate and smoke for 20-30 minutes. Taste along the way to assess smoke level pulling earlier if needed. Grill: 180 °F
3. Place 1 Tbsp butter in a saucepan and melt over medium heat. Add onion and garlic and saute for 2-3 minutes or until onion is translucent.
4. Remove asparagus from the grill and cut into 1" pieces. Place asparagus in the pan with the onions and add stock and cream. Bring to a simmer.
5. Remove from heat and puree using a blender or immersion blender until smooth.
6. Season with salt and pepper and serve. Top with fresh shaved asparagus, sprinkle with salt, pepper, and smoked paprika if desired. Enjoy!

Smoked Pico De Gallo

Servings: 4
Cooking Time: 30 Minutes

Ingredients:
- 3 Cup diced Roma tomatoes
- 1 jalapeño, diced
- 1/2 red onion, diced
- 1/2 Bunch cilantro, finely chopped
- 2 lime, juiced
- salt
- olive oil

Directions:
1. Supply your smoker with wood pellets and follow the start-up procedure. Preheat the grill, with the lid closed, to 180° F.
2. Place the diced tomatoes on a small sheet pan spreading them into a thin layer. Place the sheet pan directly on the grill and smoke for 30 minutes. Grill: 180 °F
3. When the tomatoes are finished, toss all ingredients in a medium bowl and finish with lime juice, salt and olive oil to taste. Serve and enjoy!

Traeger Baked Potato Torte

Servings: 6
Cooking Time: 25 Minutes

Ingredients:
- 6 Yukon Gold potatoes, sliced 1/4 inch thick
- 2 Stick butter, melted
- 3 Clove garlic, crushed
- 2 Tablespoon rosemary, chopped
- 1 Cup Parmesan cheese, grated
- salt and pepper

Directions:
1. Supply your smoker with wood pellets and follow the start-up procedure. Preheat the grill, with the lid closed, to 375° F.
2. While the Traeger is heating up, peel and slice the potatoes (make sure to put them in water so they will not oxidize). Melt the butter and combine it with the crushed garlic.
3. Grease a 12" cast iron pan with butter and start to layer the torte. The layers should go as follows, potatoes, butter garlic

mixture, rosemary, parmesan, continue layering to the top of the pan, about 4 to 5 layers.

4. Place the pan in the Traeger and bake for 20 to 25 minutes, or until the potatoes are fully cooked. If the top of the torte starts to darken before it is finished cooking, reduce the heat to 325°F. Serve hot and enjoy! Grill: 375 °F

Smoked Macaroni Salad

Servings: 4
Cooking Time: 20 Minutes

Ingredients:
- 1 Pound macaroni, uncooked
- 1/2 Small red onion, diced
- 1 green bell pepper, diced
- 1/2 Cup shredded carrot
- 1 Cup mayonnaise
- 3 Tablespoon white wine vinegar
- 2 Tablespoon sugar
- salt
- black pepper

Directions:
1. Bring a large stock pot of salted water to a boil over medium heat and cook pasta according to package directions. Make sure to cook to al dente, strain, and rinse under cold water.
2. Supply your smoker with wood pellets and follow the start-up procedure. Preheat the grill, with the lid closed, to 225° F.
3. Spread cooked pasta out on a sheet tray and place sheet tray directly on the grill grate. Smoke for 20 minutes, remove from heat, and transfer directly to the refrigerator to cool. Grill: 225 °F
4. While the pasta is cooling mix the dressing. Place all ingredients in a medium bowl and whisk to combine.
5. When pasta is cool combine chopped veggies, smoked pasta and dressing in a large bowl.
6. Cover with plastic wrap and place in the fridge for 20 minutes before serving. Enjoy!

Roasted Pumpkin Seeds

Servings: 8
Cooking Time: 40 Minutes

Ingredients:
- 1 Whole Pumpkin, seeds
- olive oil or vegetable oil
- Jacobsen Salt Co. Pure Kosher Sea Salt

Directions:
1. As soon as possible after removing the seeds from the pumpkin, rinse pumpkin seeds under cold water in a colander and pick out the pulp and strings.
2. Place the pumpkin seeds in a single layer on an oiled baking sheet, stirring to coat. Supply your smoker with wood pellets and follow the start-up procedure. Preheat the grill, with the lid closed, to 180° F.
3. Place the baking sheet with the seeds on the grill grate, close the lid, and smoke for 20 minutes. Grill: 180 °F
4. Sprinkle your seeds with salt and turn the temperature on your grill up to 325°F. Roast the seeds until toasted, about 20 minutes. Check and stir seeds after the first 10 minutes. Grill: 325 °F
5. Seeds will be brown because they were smoked before being roasted. Enjoy!

Stuffed Jalapenos

Servings: 8
Cooking Time: 60 Minutes

Ingredients:
- 40 Whole jalapeño
- 8 Ounce cream cheese, room temperature
- 1 Cup Sharp Cheddar Grated
- 1 1/2 Teaspoon Pork & Poultry Rub
- 2 Tablespoon sour cream
- 1 Whole (14 oz) cocktail sausages
- 20 Whole Slices of Smoked Bacon, Cut in Half

Directions:
1. Wash and dry the peppers. Cut the stem ends off with a paring knife, and using the same knife or a small metal spoon, carefully scrape the seeds and ribs out of each pepper. Set aside.
2. In a small bowl, combine the cream cheese, grated cheese, Traeger Pork and Poultry Rub, and the sour cream.
3. Transfer the mixture to a sturdy resealable plastic bag and trim 1/2-inch off one of the lower corners with a scissors. Squeeze the cream cheese mixture into each pepper, filling each a little over the halfway point.
4. Stuff one sausage into each pepper. Wrap the outside of each with a piece of bacon, securing with 1 or 2 toothpicks.
5. Arrange the peppers on a foil-lined baking sheet. Supply your smoker with wood pellets and follow the start-up procedure. Preheat the grill, with the lid closed, to 180° F, and smoke the peppers for 1 to 1-1/2 hours.
6. Increase the heat to 350 degrees F and continue to cook for 20 to 30 minutes, or until the bacon begins to render its fat and crisp. Enjoy! Grill: 350 °F

Roasted Olives

Servings: 4
Cooking Time: 45 Minutes

Ingredients:
- 2 Cup mixed olives
- 3 Sprig fresh rosemary
- 2 Clove garlic, minced
- 2 Tablespoon orange zest
- 1/3 Cup extra-virgin olive oil
- 2 Tablespoon orange juice
- 1/2 Teaspoon red pepper flakes

Directions:
1. Combine the olives, rosemary, garlic, orange zest, red pepper flakes, olive oil, and orange juice in a glass oven-safe pie plate or baking dish. Cover with foil.
2. Supply your smoker with wood pellets and follow the start-up procedure. Preheat the grill, with the lid closed, to 300° F.
3. Roast the olives for 45 minutes, stirring once or twice. Serve warm in an attractive bowl. Enjoy! Grill: 300 °F

Grilled Asparagus And Spinach Salad

Servings: 8
Cooking Time: 10 Minutes

Ingredients:
- 4 Fluid Ounce apple cider vinegar
- 8 Fluid Ounce Honey Bourbon BBQ Sauce
- 2 Bunch asparagus, ends trimmed
- 3 Fluid Ounce extra-virgin olive oil
- 2 Ounce Beef Rub
- 24 Ounce Spinach, fresh
- 4 Ounce candied pecans
- 4 Ounce feta cheese

Directions:
1. Combine apple cider vinegar and Traeger Apricot BBQ Sauce to create salad dressing.
2. Supply your smoker with wood pellets and follow the start-up procedure. Preheat the grill, with the lid closed, to High heat.
3. Toss the asparagus with Olive Oil and the Beef Shake. Put asparagus in the Traeger Grilling Basket and move the basket to the grill grate.
4. Grill for about 10 minutes. Remove the asparagus once it is cooked. Grill: 350 °F
5. Place the hot asparagus right on top of the bowl of spinach.
6. Add candied pecans, feta cheese & salad dressing then toss and serve. Enjoy!

Red Potato Grilled Lollipops

Servings: 4
Cooking Time: 25 Minutes

Ingredients:
- 8 Large red bliss potatoes, halved
- 2 Clove garlic, minced
- 2 Sprig rosemary, minced
- 2 Tablespoon olive oil
- 1 Teaspoon salt
- 1/2 Teaspoon black pepper
- 5 Wooden Skewers, soaked in water
- 1/4 Cup Parmesan cheese, grated

Directions:
1. Supply your smoker with wood pellets and follow the start-up procedure. Preheat the grill, with the lid closed, to 450° F.
2. Halve potatoes and poke each several times with a fork.
3. Put the potatoes in a large bowl and toss with the minced garlic, rosemary leaves, a few tablespoons of olive oil, kosher salt, and pepper. Microwave the potatoes for 4 minutes. Gently toss potatoes and microwave for another 3 minutes.
4. Skewer potato halves threading about 4 or 5 potato halves on each skewer. Brush potatoes with olive oil.
5. Place the potato skewers on the Traeger, cut side down, and grill until the sides begin to brown (4-7 minutes).
6. Flip and grill skin side down for another 7-10 minutes.
7. They are done when a sharp knife tip easily penetrates the sides. Remove potatoes from grill and top with grated parmesan cheese. Enjoy!

Baked Breakfast Mini Quiches

Servings: 8
Cooking Time: 15 Minutes

Ingredients:
- cooking spray
- 1 Tablespoon extra-virgin olive oil
- 1/2 yellow onion, diced
- 3 Cup Spinach, fresh
- 10 eggs
- 4 Ounce shredded cheddar, mozzarella or Swiss cheese
- 1/4 Cup fresh basil
- 1 Teaspoon kosher salt
- 1/2 Teaspoon black pepper

Directions:
1. Spray a 12-cup muffin tin generously with cooking spray.
2. In a small skillet over medium heat, warm the oil. Add the onion and cook, stirring frequently, until softened, about 7 minutes. Add the spinach and cook until wilted, about 1 minute longer.
3. Transfer to a cutting board to cool, then chop the mixture so the spinach if broken up a little.

4. Supply your smoker with wood pellets and follow the start-up procedure. Preheat the grill, with the lid closed, to 350° F.

5. In a large bowl, whisk the eggs until frothy. Add the cooled onions and spinach, cheese, basil, 1 tsp salt and 1/2 tsp pepper. Stir to combine. Divide egg mixture evenly among the muffin cups.

6. Place tray on the grill and bake until the eggs have puffed up, are set, and are beginning to brown, about 18 to 20 minutes. Grill: 350 °F

7. Serve immediately, or allow to cool on a wire rack, then refrigerate in an air tight container for up to 4 days. Enjoy!

Butternut Squash

Servings: 4
Cooking Time: 45 Minutes

Ingredients:
- 1 Whole butternut squash
- Veggie Rub
- Blackened Saskatchewan Rub
- olive oil

Directions:
1. Cut squash in half and lightly coat with mixture of olive oil, Traeger Veggie Shake, and Traeger Blackened Saskatchewan.
2. Wrap in foil with 1/2 cup (120mL) of water.
3. Supply your smoker with wood pellets and follow the start-up procedure. Preheat the grill, with the lid closed, to 450° F.
4. Place squash on grill for 45 minutes. Remove from grill and unwrap. Enjoy!

Steak Fries With Horseradish Creme

Servings: 6
Cooking Time: 25 Minutes

Ingredients:
- 5 Potatoes, Baking
- 2 Tablespoon extra-virgin olive oil
- 1 Teaspoon butter
- 3 Clove garlic, crushed
- 1 Teaspoon onion powder
- 2 Teaspoon Jacobsen Salt Co. Pure Kosher Sea Salt
- 1 Teaspoon black pepper

Directions:
1. Wash the potatoes thoroughly, and cut them in eighths, then toss them in the olive oil, butter, crushed garlic, onion powder, salt, and pepper.
2. Supply your smoker with wood pellets and follow the start-up procedure. Preheat the grill, with the lid closed, to 450° F.
3. In order to get great grill marks, line up the wedges on the front of the grill and the back of the grill, turning to get grill marks on all sides.

4. Once they have been seared, move them to the center of the grill and finish cooking about ten more minutes, serve hot with the horseradish mayo. Enjoy!

Baked Winter Squash Au Gratin

Servings: 8
Cooking Time: 45 Minutes

Ingredients:
- 2 Cup heavy cream
- salt and pepper
- 3 Cup shredded Gruyere cheese
- 4 Clove garlic, diced
- 2 Tablespoon butter
- 3 yellow potatoes, peeled and cubed
- 1 butternut squash seeded, peeled and cubed
- 1 acorn squash seeded, peeled and cubed

Directions:
1. Supply your smoker with wood pellets and follow the start-up procedure. Preheat the grill, with the lid closed, to 375° F.
2. In a medium saucepan, cook the cream, stirring constantly, until it comes to a low boil. Add salt, pepper, garlic and shredded Gruyere cheese. Stir until cheese is melted.
3. Grease a 9x13 inch baking dish with 2 tablespoons of butter. In a large mixing bowl, combine potatoes, butternut and acorn squash. Stir in the cheese sauce. Place mixture in the prepared baking dish and place in grill.
4. Cook for 45 minutes or until potatoes and squash are fork tender. Remove from grill and let cool for 10 minutes before serving. Enjoy! Grill: 375 °F

Parmesan Roasted Cauliflower

Servings: 4
Cooking Time: 40 Minutes

Ingredients:
- 1 Head cauliflower, cut into florets
- 1 Medium onion, sliced
- 4 Clove garlic, unpeeled
- 4 Tablespoon olive oil
- salt
- black pepper
- 1 Teaspoon fresh thyme
- 1/2 Cup Parmesan cheese, grated

Directions:
1. Supply your smoker with wood pellets and follow the start-up procedure. Preheat the grill, with the lid closed, to 400° F.
2. On a baking tray, mix together cauliflower, onion, thyme, garlic, olive oil, salt and pepper.

3. Place tray on preheated grill and cook until cauliflower is firm and almost tender (about 25 minutes). Grill: 400 °F
4. Sprinkle cauliflower with Parmesan cheese and continue to cook on the Traeger for another 10 to 15 minutes. Cauliflower should be tender and the Parmesan crisp. Serve immediately, enjoy!

Smoked Parmesan Herb Popcorn

Servings: 2
Cooking Time: 15 Minutes

Ingredients:
- 4 Tablespoon butter
- 2 Teaspoon Italian Seasoning
- 1 Teaspoon garlic powder
- 1 Teaspoon salt
- 1/4 Cup popcorn kernels
- 1/2 Cup Parmesan cheese, grated

Directions:
1. Supply your smoker with wood pellets and follow the start-up procedure. Preheat the grill, with the lid closed, to 250° F.
2. In a small saucepan, melt the butter over medium heat. Add Italian seasoning, garlic powder, and salt and stir to combine. Remove from heat and set aside.
3. Add 1/4 cup of popcorn to a brown paper lunch bag. Fold the top of the bag over twice to close. Place the bag in the microwave and microwave on high for 1 to 2 minutes, or until there are about 5 seconds between pops. Open the bag with care and dump into a large mixing bowl.
4. Pour butter mixture of popcorn in a bowl and toss to combine. Dump popcorn onto a baking sheet and place in grill.
5. Smoke for 10 minutes; remove from grill. Toss with parmesan cheese to serve. Enjoy! Grill: 250 °F

Baked Heirloom Tomato Tart

Servings: 4
Cooking Time: 45 Minutes

Ingredients:
- 1 Whole Puff Pastry Sheet
- 2 Pound heirloom tomatoes, various shapes and sizes
- 1/2 Tablespoon kosher salt
- 1/2 Cup Ricotta Cheese
- 5 Whole eggs
- 1 To Taste salt and pepper
- 1/2 Teaspoon thyme leaves
- 1/2 Teaspoon red pepper flakes
- 4 Sprig thyme

Directions:
1. Supply your smoker with wood pellets and follow the start-up procedure. Preheat the grill, with the lid closed, to 350° F.
2. Place the puff pastry on a parchment lined sheet tray, and make a cut ¾ of the way through the pastry, ½" from the edge.
3. Slice the tomatoes and season with salt. Place on a sheet tray lined with paper towels.
4. In a small bowl combine the ricotta, 4 of the eggs, salt, thyme leaves, red pepper flakes and black pepper. Whisk together until combined. Spread the ricotta mixture over the puff pastry, staying within ½" from the edge.
5. In a small bowl whisk the last egg. Brush the egg wash onto the exposed edges of the pastry.
6. Place the sheet tray directly on the grill grate and bake for 45 minutes, rotating half-way through. Grill: 350 °F
7. When the edges are browned and the moisture from the tomatoes has evaporated, remove from the grill and let cool 5-7 minutes before serving. Enjoy!

Grilled Ratatouille Salad

Servings: 4
Cooking Time: 25 Minutes

Ingredients:
- 1 Whole sweet potatoes
- 1 Whole red onion, diced
- 1 Whole zucchini
- 1 Whole Squash
- 1 Large Tomato, diced
- vegetable oil
- salt and pepper

Directions:
1. Supply your smoker with wood pellets and follow the start-up procedure. Preheat the grill, with the lid closed, to High heat.
2. Slice all vegetables to a ¼ inch thickness.
3. Lightly brush each vegetable with oil and season with Traeger's Veggie Shake or salt and pepper.
4. Place sweet potato, onion, zucchini, and squash on grill grate and grill for 20 minutes or until tender, turn halfway through.
5. Add tomato slices to the grill during the last 5 minutes of cooking time.
6. For presentation, alternate vegetables while layering them vertically. Enjoy!

Roasted Artichokes With Garlic Butter

Servings: 2
Cooking Time: 60 Minutes

Ingredients:
- 2 Large artichokes
- 3 Tablespoon olive oil
- sea salt
- 1 Stick unsalted butter
- 2 Clove garlic, chopped

- 2 Tablespoon chives, parsley, tarragon or cilantro
- 1 lemon

Directions:
1. Supply your smoker with wood pellets and follow the start-up procedure. Preheat the grill, with the lid closed, to 375° F.
2. Meanwhile, break off and discard any small outer leaves on the artichokes. Use a knife to slice off the tops of the artichokes, then using scissors, cut off any thorns on the remaining artichoke leaves. Trim the very bottom of the stem, then peel the tough and fibrous outer layer of the stem. Finally, cut artichokes in half and rinse off.
3. Transfer artichokes to a large mixing bowl, drizzle with olive oil and generously sprinkle with sea salt. Toss to coat the artichokes thoroughly. Grill: 375 °F
4. Add the artichokes to the grill, cut side down, and roast at 375°F until the artichoke bottoms are tender when poked with a fork or knife, about 50 to 60 minutes. Grill: 375 °F
5. When artichokes are almost done, add butter, chopped garlic and a pinch of sea salt to a small sauce pan and melt slowly over medium-low heat. Once the butter melts all the way and starts to bubble slightly, add the herbs.
6. When the artichokes are done, transfer to a butcher paper lined tray with the cut sides up. Drizzle half the garlic butter and squeeze half of the lemon over the artichokes. Add a small sprinkle of sea salt over the artichokes.
7. Serve with a ramekin of the remaining butter for dipping and extra wedges of lemon. Enjoy! Chef Tip: You can also serve with a ramekin of good mayonnaise mixed with a bit of hot sauce.

Chef Curtis' Famous Chimichurri Sauce

Servings: 4
Cooking Time: 5 Minutes

Ingredients:
- 2 Whole lemon, halved
- 2 Medium flat-leaf Italian parsley, washed and chopped with the majority of stems cut off
- 4 Clove garlic, diced
- 1/4 Cup red wine vinegar
- 1/2 Teaspoon black pepper
- 1/4 Cup extra-virgin olive oil
- 1 Teaspoon salt

Directions:
1. Supply your smoker with wood pellets and follow the start-up procedure. Preheat the grill, with the lid closed, to 450° F.
2. Place lemon halves directly on the grill grate and cook for 5 minutes or until grill marks appear. Grill: 450 °F
3. Take lemons off grill and juice. Combine all of the ingredients in a food processor or blender and purée until smooth, or leave slightly chunky for some texture.

4. Add additional olive oil to taste for a milder flavor if preferred. Serve on protein or as a dip. Enjoy!

Roasted Garlic Herb Fries

Servings: 4
Cooking Time: 45 Minutes

Ingredients:
- 4 Whole russet potatoes
- 1 Teaspoon salt
- 2 Tablespoon avocado oil
- 1 Teaspoon fresh chopped rosemary
- 1 Teaspoon fresh chopped thyme
- 2 Clove garlic, minced
- 2 Teaspoon flake salt
- 1 Teaspoon chopped parsley, for garnish

Directions:
1. Supply your smoker with wood pellets and follow the start-up procedure. Preheat the grill, with the lid closed, to 425° F.
2. Chop potatoes into fries, (a mandolin works great for this) and place directly into an ice water bath with 1 teaspoon salt for 15 to 30 minutes.
3. Combine oil, rosemary, thyme and garlic in a big bowl. Remove potatoes from ice water and dry thoroughly with paper towels.
4. Toss potatoes in the oil mixture and place them on 2 to 3 parchment-lined baking sheets in a single layer. Sprinkle the flake salt over the fries.
5. Place baking sheets on the grill and roast for 30 minutes, flip the fries, then cook for an additional 15 minutes until golden and crispy. Dust with parsley. Grill: 425 °F
6. Serve with your favorite dipping sauce, side dish or as a nacho base.

Grilled Zucchini Squash Spears

Servings: 4
Cooking Time: 10 Minutes

Ingredients:
- 4 Medium zucchini
- 2 Tablespoon olive oil
- 1 Tablespoon sherry vinegar
- 2 thyme, leaves pulled
- salt and pepper

Directions:
1. Clean the zucchini and cut the ends off. Cut each in half lengthwise, then each half into thirds.
2. Combine remaining ingredients in a medium Ziplock bag and add the spears. Toss and mix well to coat the zucchini.

3. Supply your smoker with wood pellets and follow the start-up procedure. Preheat the grill, with the lid closed, to 350° F.
4. Remove the spears from the bag and place directly on the grill grate cut side down.
5. Cook for 3-4 minutes per side, until grill marks appear and zucchini is tender. Grill: 350 °F
6. Remove from grill and finish with more thyme leaves if desired. Enjoy!

Potluck Salad With Smoked Cornbread

Servings: 6
Cooking Time: 45 Minutes

Ingredients:
- 1 cup all-purpose flour
- 1 cup yellow cornmeal
- 1 tablespoon sugar
- 2 teaspoons baking powder
- 1 teaspoon salt
- 1 cup milk
- 1 egg, beaten, at room temperature
- 4 tablespoons (½ stick) unsalted butter, melted and cooled
- Nonstick cooking spray or butter, for greasing
- ½ cup milk
- ½ cup sour cream
- 2 tablespoons dry ranch dressing mix
- 1 pound bacon, cooked and crumbled
- 3 tomatoes, chopped
- 1 bell pepper, chopped
- 1 cucumber, seeded and chopped
- 2 stalks celery, chopped (about 1 cup)
- ½ cup chopped scallions

Directions:
1. For the cornbread:
2. In a medium bowl, combine the flour, cornmeal, sugar, baking powder, and salt.
3. In a small bowl, whisk together the milk and egg. Pour in the butter, then slowly fold this mixture into the dry ingredients.
4. Supply your smoker with wood pellets and follow the start-up procedure. Preheat, with the lid closed, to 375°F.
5. Coat a cast iron skillet with cooking spray or butter.
6. Pour the batter into the skillet, place on the grill grate, close the lid, and smoke for 35 to 45 minutes, or until the cornbread is browned and pulls away from the side of the skillet.
7. Remove the cornbread from the grill and let cool, then coarsely crumble.
8. For the salad:
9. In a small bowl, whisk together the milk, sour cream, and ranch dressing mix.
10. In a medium bowl, combine the crumbled bacon, tomatoes, bell pepper, cucumber, celery, and scallions.
11. In a large serving bowl, layer half of the crumbled cornbread, half of the bacon-veggie mixture, and half of the dressing. Toss lightly.
12. Repeat the layering with the remaining cornbread, bacon-veggie mixture, and dressing. Toss again.
13. Refrigerate the salad for at least 1 hour. Serve cold.

Smoked Pickled Green Beans

Servings: 4
Cooking Time: 45 Minutes

Ingredients:
- 1 Pound Green Beans, blanched
- 1/2 Cup salt
- 1/2 Cup sugar
- 1 Tablespoon red pepper flakes
- 2 Cup white wine vinegar
- 2 Cup ice water

Directions:
1. Supply your smoker with wood pellets and follow the start-up procedure. Preheat the grill, with the lid closed, to 180° F.
2. Place the blanched green beans on a mesh grill mat and place mat directly on the grill grate. Smoke the green beans for 30-45 minutes until they've picked up the desired amount of smoke. Remove from grill and set aside until the brine is ready. Grill: 180 °F
3. In a medium sized saucepan, bring all remaining ingredients, except ice water, to a boil over medium high heat on the stove. Simmer for 5-10 minutes then remove from heat and steep 20 minutes more. Pour brine over ice water to cool.
4. Once brine has cooled, pour over the green beans and weigh them down with a few plates to ensure they are completely submerged. Let sit 24 hours before use. Enjoy!

Sweet Potato Marshmallow Casserole

Servings: 6
Cooking Time: 60 Minutes

Ingredients:
- 5 Yams
- 1 1/2 Stick butter
- 1/2 Cup brown sugar
- 1 Teaspoon vanilla
- 1 Teaspoon kosher salt
- 1 Teaspoon cracked black pepper
- 1 Marshmallows, miniature
- 1/4 Unsalted Butter, Softened

Directions:

1. Supply your smoker with wood pellets and follow the start-up procedure. Preheat the grill, with the lid closed, to 375° F.
2. Pierce the skin of the yams with a fork a few times. Place on a baking sheet or foil tin inside the grill and let roast for 50 minutes or until extremely softened. Grill: 375 °F
3. Remove yams from the grill and set aside until cool enough to handle. While the potatoes cool, with a stiff whisk, whip together 1/2 cup softened butter, the brown sugar, vanilla, salt and pepper.
4. Remove and discard skins from sweet potatoes and mash until smooth. Fold in the butter mixture and transfer to a cast iron pan.
5. Place cast iron on the grill and bake for 15-20 minutes. Remove from the grill, top with marshmallows and dot with remaining 1/4 cup butter.
6. Place back in the grill for 15 minutes until warm and the marshmallows are golden. Enjoy! Grill: 375 °F

Roasted Sheet Pan Vegetables

Servings: 4
Cooking Time: 25 Minutes

Ingredients:
- 1 Small head purple cauliflower, stemmed and cut into 2 inch florets
- 1 Small head yellow cauliflower, stemmed and cut into 2 inch florets
- 4 Cup butternut squash
- 2 Cup oyster or shiitake mushrooms, rinsed and sliced
- 3 Tablespoon olive oil
- 2 Teaspoon kosher salt
- freshly ground black pepper
- 1/4 Cup chopped flat-leaf parsley

Directions:
1. Supply your smoker with wood pellets and follow the start-up procedure. Preheat the grill, with the lid closed, to 450° F.
2. In a large mixing bowl, combine all of the vegetables. Drizzle olive oil over the top, along with kosher salt and a generous grinding of black pepper.
3. Using your hands, toss the vegetables until they are evenly coated.
4. Spread out onto 1 or 2 half sheet pans or baking sheets, ensuring there is a little space between the veggies. (If they are too crowded, the vegetables will steam instead of roast and you won't get that crispy texture.)
5. Place the sheet pans on the grill and cook for 15 minutes. Open and stir, then close the lid and continue to cook until the vegetables are brown around the edges, about 5 to 15 minutes longer. Grill: 450 °F

6. Toss with parsley and serve immediately. The vegetables are also delicious at room temperature. Enjoy!

Roasted Sweet Potato Steak Fries

Servings: 4
Cooking Time: 40 Minutes

Ingredients:
- 3 Whole sweet potatoes
- 4 Tablespoon extra-virgin olive oil
- salt and pepper
- 2 Tablespoon fresh chopped rosemary

Directions:
1. Supply your smoker with wood pellets and follow the start-up procedure. Preheat the grill, with the lid closed, to 450° F.
2. Cut sweet potatoes into wedges and toss with olive oil, salt, pepper and rosemary. Spread on a parchment lined baking sheet and put in the grill. Cook for 15 minutes then flip and continue to cook until lightly browned and cooked through, about 40 to 45 minutes total. Grill: 450 °F
3. Serve with your favorite dipping sauce. Enjoy! Grill: 450 °F

Baked Loaded Tater Tots

Servings: 6
Cooking Time: 35 Minutes

Ingredients:
- 2 Pound frozen tater tots
- 1 Can Black Beans
- 1 1/2 Cup leftover chili
- 1 Cup leftover queso
- 1 red onion, finely diced
- 1/2 Cup chopped cilantro
- 1/2 Cup sour cream
- 1 jalapeños, sliced

Directions:
1. Supply your smoker with wood pellets and follow the start-up procedure. Preheat the grill, with the lid closed, to 375° F.
2. Spread frozen tots out on a sheet tray and place directly on the grill grate.
3. Cook for 20 to 25 minutes or until tots are crispy. Grill: 375 °F
4. Top with warmed chili, queso and beans. Place back on the grill for 15 minutes. Grill: 375 °F
5. Remove from grill and top with red onion, cilantro, sour cream and jalapeño. Enjoy!

Smoked Mushrooms

Servings: 4
Cooking Time: 45 Minutes

Ingredients:
- Pound Mushrooms, fresh
- 1/2 Cup apple cider vinegar
- 1/2 Cup soy sauce
- 1 Teaspoon Blackened Saskatchewan Rub

Directions:
1. Clean mushrooms and place in a large Ziploc bag. Add apple cider vinegar, soy sauce and rub.
2. Mix well and allow to marinate in the refrigerator for at least 2 hours.
3. Supply your smoker with wood pellets and follow the start-up procedure. Preheat the grill, with the lid closed, to 350° F.
4. Place cast iron skillet inside grill for 20 minutes to warm up.
5. Add the mushrooms and marinade slowly into the cast iron skillet.
6. Cook uncovered for 15 minutes, then cover the skillet and cook another 30 minutes until mushrooms are tender. Grill: 350 °F
7. Remove skillet from grill and let mushrooms cool down for 5 minutes before serving. Enjoy!

Roasted New Potatoes

Servings: 4
Cooking Time: 25 Minutes

Ingredients:
- 2 Pound small new potatoes
- 3 Tablespoon butter, melted
- 2 Tablespoon olive oil
- 2 Tablespoon whole mustard seeds
- salt and pepper
- 2 Tablespoon freshly minced chives
- 2 Tablespoon freshly minced parsley

Directions:
1. Place potatoes in a colander and rinse with cold water. Dry on paper towels and transfer to a rimmed baking sheet large enough to hold them in a single layer.
2. Drizzle the potatoes with butter and olive oil, then sprinkle them with the mustard seeds. Season with salt and pepper.
3. Supply your smoker with wood pellets and follow the start-up procedure. Preheat the grill, with the lid closed, to 400° F.
4. Place the baking sheet with the potatoes on the grill grate. Roast for about 25 minutes shaking the pan once or twice, until potatoes are tender and the skins are slightly wrinkled. Grill: 400 °F
5. Transfer potatoes to a bowl or platter. Top with fresh chives and parsley. Enjoy!

Grilled Asparagus & Honey-glazed Carrots

Servings: 4
Cooking Time: 35 Minutes

Ingredients:
- 1 Bunch asparagus, woody ends removed
- 1 Pound Carrots, peeled
- 2 Tablespoon olive oil
- sea salt
- 2 Tablespoon honey
- lemon zest

Directions:
1. Rinse all vegetables under cold water. Drizzle asparagus with olive oil and a generous sprinkling of sea salt. Generously drizzle carrots with honey and lightly sprinkle with sea salt.
2. Supply your smoker with wood pellets and follow the start-up procedure. Preheat the grill, with the lid closed, to 350° F.
3. Place carrots on the grill first and cook for 10-15 minutes, then add asparagus and cook both for another 15 to 20 minutes, or until they're done to your liking. Grill: 350 °F
4. Top the asparagus with some fresh lemon zest. Enjoy!

Baked Bacon Green Bean Casserole

Servings: 6
Cooking Time: 50 Minutes

Ingredients:
- 1 1/2 Pound Green Beans, fresh
- 1 Can cream of mushroom soup
- 1/2 Cup milk
- 1/2 Teaspoon Worcestershire sauce
- 1/2 Teaspoon black pepper
- 2/3 Cup French's Original Crispy Fried Onions
- 8 Slices bacon
- 1/4 Cup red bell pepper, diced
- 2/3 French's Original Crispy Fried Onions

Directions:
1. In a mixing bowl, combine beans, soup, milk, Worcestershire sauce, black pepper, 2/3 cup of the onions, 6 of the slices of crumbled bacon, and red bell pepper. Transfer to a 1-1/2 quart casserole dish.
2. Supply your smoker with wood pellets and follow the start-up procedure. Preheat the grill, with the lid closed, to 350° F.
3. Cook casserole until the filling is hot and bubbling, 35 to 40 minutes. Grill: 350 °F
4. Top with remaining onions and the last 2 slices of crumbled bacon and cook for 5 to 10 minutes more, or until the onions are crisp and beginning to brown. Serve, enjoy! Grill: 350 °F

Baked Sweet Potatoes

Servings: 8
Cooking Time: 60 Minutes

Ingredients:
- 1 Cup butter, softened
- 1/4 Cup pure maple syrup
- 1/2 Teaspoon ground cinnamon
- 8 Medium sweet potatoes

Directions:
1. Make the Maple-Cinnamon Butter: In a mixing bowl, combine the butter, maple syrup, and cinnamon and whip with a wooden spoon. (Alternatively, blend the ingredients using a hand-held mixer or a stand mixer.) Transfer to a small bowl, cover, and chill until serving time.
2. Supply your smoker with wood pellets and follow the start-up procedure. Preheat the grill, with the lid closed, to 375° F. Arrange the sweet potatoes on the grill grate and bake until soft, 1 to 1-1/2 hours, depending on the size of the potatoes. Make a slit in the side of each, and squeeze the ends gently to fluff.
3. Serve hot with the Maple-Cinnamon Butter. Enjoy!

Mashed Red Potatoes

Servings: 4
Cooking Time: 40 Minutes

Ingredients:
- 8 Large red potatoes
- salt
- black pepper
- 1/2 Cup heavy cream
- 1/4 Cup butter

Directions:
1. Supply your smoker with wood pellets and follow the start-up procedure. Preheat the grill, with the lid closed, to 180° F.
2. Slice red potatoes in half, lengthwise then cut in half again to make quarters. Season potatoes with salt and pepper.
3. Increase the heat to High and preheat. Once the grill is hot, set potatoes directly on the grill grate. Grill: 450 °F
4. Every 15 minutes flip potatoes to ensure all sides get color. Continue to do this until potatoes are fork tender.
5. When tender, mash potatoes with cream, butter, salt, and pepper to taste. Serve warm, enjoy!

Smoked Jalapeño Poppers

Servings: 4
Cooking Time: 60 Minutes

Ingredients:
- 12 Medium jalapeño
- 6 Slices bacon, cut in half
- 8 Ounce cream cheese
- 2 Tablespoon Pork & Poultry Rub
- 1 Cup grated cheese

Directions:
1. Supply your smoker with wood pellets and follow the start-up procedure. Preheat the grill, with the lid closed, to 180° F. For optimal flavor, use Super Smoke if available.
2. Slice the jalapeños in half lengthwise. Scrape out any seeds and ribs with a small spoon or paring knife. Mix softened cream cheese with Traeger Pork & Poultry rub and grated cheese. Spoon mixture onto each jalapeño half. Wrap with bacon and secure with a toothpick.
3. Place the jalapeños on a rimmed baking sheet. Place on grill and smoke for 30 minutes. Grill: 180 °F
4. Increase the grill temperature to 375°F and cook an additional 30 minutes or until bacon is cooked to desired doneness. Serve warm, enjoy! Grill: 375 °F

Roasted Vegetable Napoleon

Servings: 4
Cooking Time: 30 Minutes

Ingredients:
- 2 Whole sweet potatoes
- 2 Whole zucchini
- 2 Whole Squash
- 1 Whole red onion
- 2 Whole Bell Pepper, Red
- salt and pepper

Directions:
1. Supply your smoker with wood pellets and follow the start-up procedure. Preheat the grill, with the lid closed, to High heat.
2. Salt and pepper all vegetables and grill them on both sides. Begin with the peppers and onions as they will take a little longer to cook. Grill: 450 °F

Portobello Marinated Mushroom

Servings: 2
Cooking Time: 15 Minutes

Ingredients:
- 1 Teaspoon chopped thyme
- 1 Teaspoon rosemary, chopped
- 1 Teaspoon Oregano, chopped
- 3 Tablespoon extra-virgin olive oil
- 1 To Taste Jacobsen Salt Co. Pure Kosher Sea Salt
- 1 To Taste pepper
- 6 Whole Portobello Mushroom
- 2 Whole russet potatoes

Directions:

1. Supply your smoker with wood pellets and follow the start-up procedure. Preheat the grill, with the lid closed, to 450° F.
2. Mix fresh herbs, olive oil, salt, and pepper together in a bowl. Rub over mushrooms. Grill both sides of mushrooms for approximately 2-3 minutes on each side. Grill: 450 °F
3. Clean the potatoes and slice into long strips.
4. Heat the oil on the Traeger in a sauce pan; drop the potatoes in the hot oil and fry for 7-8 minutes. Let the potatoes cool slightly on a sheet pan. Enjoy! Grill: 450 °F

Roasted Jalapeño Poppers

Servings: 2
Cooking Time: 30 Minutes

Ingredients:
- 8 Slices Bacon, Center Cut
- 2 Cup cream cheese
- 2 Ounce Cheese, sharp cheddar
- 1/2 Cup green onions, minced
- 2 Teaspoon fresh squeezed lime juice
- 4 Tablespoon Seeded Tomato, Chopped
- 4 Tablespoon cilantro, chopped
- 1/2 Teaspoon kosher salt
- 2 Small garlic clove, minced
- 12 Whole Jalapeños

Directions:
1. Supply your smoker with wood pellets and follow the start-up procedure. Preheat the grill, with the lid closed, to 350° F.
2. Place 2 bacon slices directly on the grill grate and cook 10-15 minutes until cooked through and crispy flipping halfway through. Remove from grill, but leave the grill on. When cool enough to handle, coarsely chop the bacon and reserve. Grill: 350 °F
3. In the bowl of a stand mixer, combine cream cheese, cheddar cheese, green onions, chopped bacon, lime juice, tomatoes, cilantro, salt and garlic. Mix on medium speed with a paddle until combined. Transfer mixture to a piping bag.
4. Cut the tops off the jalapeños and remove the seeds and ribs with a small paring knife.
5. Pipe the filling into each pepper so that the filling comes up a 1/4" over the top of the pepper. Place the tops back on each pepper.
6. With a rolling pin, flatten out the remaining six slices of bacon until they are 1/8" thick. Cut each slice in half. Wrap 1/2 a bacon slice around each pepper and secure with a toothpick.
7. Place the peppers in the Traeger Jalapeno Popper Tray. Place the tray directly on the grill grate and cook for 30-40 minutes until the peppers are tender, bacon is crispy, and cheese is melted. Enjoy! Grill: 350 °F

Roasted Green Beans With Bacon

Servings: 4
Cooking Time: 20 Minutes

Ingredients:
- 1 1/2 Pound green beans, ends trimmed
- 4 Strips bacon, cut into small pieces
- 4 Tablespoon extra-virgin olive oil
- 2 Clove garlic, minced
- 1 Teaspoon kosher salt

Directions:
1. Supply your smoker with wood pellets and follow the start-up procedure. Preheat the grill, with the lid closed, to 350° F.
2. Toss all ingredients together and spread out evenly on a sheet tray.
3. Place the tray directly on the grill grate and roast until the bacon is crispy and beans are lightly browned, about 20 minutes. Enjoy! Grill: 450 °F

Double-smoked Cheese Potatoes

Servings: 12
Cooking Time: 35 Minutes

Ingredients:
- 4 large baking potatoes (12 to 14 ounces each—preferably organic)
- 1 1/2 tablespoons bacon fat or butter, melted, or extra virgin olive oil
- Coarse salt (sea or kosher) and freshly ground black pepper
- 4 strips artisanal bacon (like Nueske's), cut crosswise into 1/4-inch slivers
- 6 tablespoons (3/4 stick) cold unsalted butter, thinly sliced
- 2 scallions, trimmed, white and green parts finely chopped (about 4 tablespoons)
- 2 cups coarsely grated smoked or regular white cheddar cheese (about 8 ounces)
- 1/2 cup sour cream
- Spanish smoked paprika (pimentón) or sweet paprika, for sprinkling

Directions:
1. Supply your smoker with wood pellets and follow the start-up procedure. Preheat the grill, with the lid closed, to 400° F. Add enough wood for 1 hour of smoking as specified by the manufacturer.
2. Scrub the potatoes on all sides with a vegetable brush. Rinse well under cold running water and blot dry with paper towels. Prick each potato several times with a fork (this keeps the spud from exploding and facilitates the smoke absorption). Brush or rub the potato on all sides with the bacon fat and season generously with salt and pepper.

3. Place the potatoes on the smoker rack. Smoke until the skins are crisp and the potatoes are tender in the center (they'll be easy to pierce with a slender metal skewer), about 1 hour.
4. Meanwhile, place the bacon in a cold skillet and fry over medium heat until browned and crisp, 3 to 4 minutes. Drain off the bacon fat (save the fat for future potatoes).
5. Transfer the potatoes to a cutting board and let cool slightly. Cut each potato in half lengthwise. Using a spoon, scrape out most of the potato flesh, leaving a 1/4-inch-thick shell. (It's easier to scoop the potatoes when warm.) Cut the potato flesh into 1/2-inch dice and place in a bowl.
6. Add the bacon, 4 tablespoons of the butter, the scallions, and cheese to the potato flesh and gently stir to mix. Stir in the sour cream and salt and pepper to taste; the mixture should be highly seasoned. Stir as little and as gently as possible so as to leave some texture to the potatoes.
7. Spoon the potato mixture back into the potato shells, mounding it in the center. Top each potato half with a thin slice of the remaining butter and sprinkle with paprika. The potatoes can be prepared up to 24 hours ahead to this stage, covered, and refrigerated.
8. Just before serving, preheat your smoker to 400 °F. Add enough wood for 30 minutes of smoking. Place the potatoes in a shallow aluminum foil pan and re-smoke them until browned and bubbling, 15 to 20 minutes.

Whole Roasted Cauliflower With Garlic Parmesan Butter

Servings: 4
Cooking Time: 45 Minutes

Ingredients:
- 1 Whole head cauliflower
- 1/4 Cup olive oil
- salt and pepper
- 1/2 Cup butter, melted
- 1/4 Cup shredded Parmesan cheese
- 2 Clove garlic, minced
- 1/2 Tablespoon chopped parsley

Directions:
1. Supply your smoker with wood pellets and follow the start-up procedure. Preheat the grill, with the lid closed, to 450° F.
2. Brush the cauliflower with olive oil and season liberally with salt and pepper.
3. Put cauliflower in a cast iron skillet, place directly on the grill grate and cook for 45 minutes until golden brown and the center is tender.
4. While the cauliflower is cooking, combine the melted butter, parmesan, garlic and parsley in a small bowl.
5. During the last 20 minutes of cooking, baste the cauliflower with the melted butter mixture.
6. Remove the cauliflower from the grill and top with extra parmesan and parsley if desired. Enjoy!

Roasted Jalapeno Cheddar Deviled Eggs

Servings: 6
Cooking Time: 30 Minutes

Ingredients:
- 7 Eggs, hard boiled
- 3 Tablespoon mayonnaise
- 1 Teaspoon brown mustard
- 1 Teaspoon apple cider vinegar
- 1 Dash hot sauce
- 1 jalapeño pepper, seeded and minced
- salt and pepper
- 1/2 Cup shredded cheddar cheese
- paprika

Directions:
1. Supply your smoker with wood pellets and follow the start-up procedure. Preheat the grill, with the lid closed, to 180° F.
2. Place your eggs directly on the grill grate and smoke for 30 minutes.
3. Remove from the grill and allow the eggs to cool. Smoking the eggs will give them a slightly yellowed color, but an intense smoky flavor. If a classic white egg is your preference, then skip this step.
4. Slice the eggs lengthwise and scoop the egg yolks directly into a gallon zip top bag.
5. Add the mayo, mustard, vinegar, hot sauce, roasted jalapeños and salt and pepper to the bag.
6. Zip the bag closed and, using your hands, knead all of the ingredients together in the bag until completely smooth.
7. Squeeze the yolk mixture into one corner of the bag and then cut the corner off. Pipe the yolk mixture into the whites.
8. Sprinkle with the finely shredded cheddar or paprika and chill until you are ready to serve. Enjoy!

Roasted Beet & Bacon Salad

Servings: 4
Cooking Time: 45 Minutes

Ingredients:
- 2 Medium raw beets, peeled and thinly sliced
- 8 Slices bacon
- 1/4 Cup raw pecans or walnuts
- 2 Medium ripe pears, sliced
- 2 Large avocados, diced
- 1 Head red leaf lettuce or baby spinach, torn into bite-size pieces

- 1/4 Cup champagne vinaigrette

Directions:
1. Supply your smoker with wood pellets and follow the start-up procedure. Preheat the grill, with the lid closed, to 400° F.
2. Place beets on a foil-lined baking sheet and top with bacon. Place baking sheet directly on the grill grate (while preheating) and cook for 25 minutes. Grill: 400 °F
3. Toss to coat beets in rendered bacon fat.
4. Spread everything out in a single layer and continue to cook for another 15 minutes, or until beets are tender and bacon is crispy. Grill: 400 °F
5. Add pecans or walnuts and roast for 5 more minutes. Spoon out nuts and place on paper towels to drain and cool.
6. Once bacon is cool to the touch, roughly chop into medium pieces.
7. Place bacon, beets, nuts, pears, avocado and lettuce in a large salad bowl. Drizzle with champagne vinaigrette, toss to coat, and serve. Enjoy!

Grilled Fingerling Potato Salad

Servings: 6
Cooking Time: 15 Minutes

Ingredients:
- 10 Whole scallions
- 2/3 Cup extra-virgin olive oil, divided
- 1 1/2 Pound fingerling potatoes, cut in half lengthwise
- pepper
- 2 Teaspoon kosher salt, divided, plus more as needed
- 2 Tablespoon rice vinegar
- 2 Teaspoon lemon juice
- 1 Small jalapeño, sliced

Directions:
1. Supply your smoker with wood pellets and follow the start-up procedure. Preheat the grill, with the lid closed, to 450° F.
2. Brush the scallions with oil and place on the grill.
3. Cook until lightly charred, about 2 to 3 minutes. Remove and let cool. Grill: 450 °F
4. Once the scallions have cooled, slice and set aside.
5. Brush the fingerling potatoes with oil (reserving 1/3 cup for later use), then salt and pepper. Place cut-side down on the grill until cooked through, about 4 to 5 minutes. Grill: 450 °F
6. In a bowl, whisk the remaining 1/3 cup olive oil, 1 teaspoon salt, rice vinegar and lemon juice. Next mix in the scallions, potatoes and sliced jalapeño.
7. Season with salt and pepper, and serve. Enjoy!

Butter Braised Green Beans

Servings: 6
Cooking Time: 60 Minutes

Ingredients:
- 24 Ounce thin fresh green beans, trimmed or whole frozen green beans, thawed
- 8 Tablespoon butter, melted
- Veggie Rub or coarse salt
- freshly ground black pepper

Directions:
1. Supply your smoker with wood pellets and follow the start-up procedure. Preheat the grill, with the lid closed, to 325° F.
2. Put the green beans in a pile on a rimmed baking sheet and pour the melted butter over them. Using tongs, spread the beans out in the pan and season with Traeger Veggie Rub and black pepper.
3. Roast the beans for about 1 hour, stirring and lifting with tongs every 20 minutes or so. The beans should be very tender, shriveled, and lightly browned in places. Transfer to a serving bowl and serve while hot. Enjoy!

Roasted Pickled Beets

Servings: 8
Cooking Time: 60 Minutes

Ingredients:
- 6 Medium Red Beets, scrubbed and trimmed
- 1 Cup red wine vinegar
- 1/2 Cup sugar
- 10 Whole peppercorns
- 1 Cup water
- 1 1/2 Teaspoon coarse salt
- 8 whole cloves
- 2 Pieces Star Anise, Broken
- 1 cinnamon stick, broken in half

Directions:
1. Make a foil pouch large enough to enclose the beets. Poke a few holes in the top to allow steam to escape.
2. Supply your smoker with wood pellets and follow the start-up procedure. Preheat the grill, with the lid closed, to 350° F.
3. Roast the beets until they are tender, 50 to 60 minutes. Carefully remove the foil and allow the beets to cool until they can be comfortably handled. Grill: 350 °F
4. Slip the skins off with your fingers. (You may wish to wear latex gloves to avoid staining your hands.) Cut the beets into quarters or slices. (Candy cane beets are especially pretty when sliced.)
5. In the meantime, make the brine: Bring the vinegar, sugar, salt, and water to a boil in a small saucepan over high heat.
6. Put the cloves, peppercorns, star anise, and cinnamon in a clean lidded jar, such as a canning jar
7. Add the beets to the jar. Pour the hot brine over the beets. Put the lid on the jar. Cool the beets to room temperature, then refrigerate for 3 to 5 days before serving. Enjoy!

Traeger Grilled Whole Corn

Servings: 4
Cooking Time: 25 Minutes

Ingredients:
- 3 green onions
- 6 Tablespoon butter, softened
- 1 Teaspoon chile powder
- 1 Teaspoon toasted sesame seeds
- 4 ears corn, in husk

Directions:
1. Supply your smoker with wood pellets and follow the start-up procedure. Preheat the grill, with the lid closed, to 325° F.
2. Place green onions directly on the grill grate and cook 15 minutes until lightly charred. Remove from grill and set aside.
3. Sesame-Chile Butter: Take butter out of fridge and let soften. Chop up charred green onions and add to butter along with chile powder and sesame seeds. Mash all ingredients together.
4. Grill corn, rotating occasionally, until husks are blackened (some will flake and fall off) and kernels are tender with some browned and charred spots, about 25 to 35 minutes. Grill: 325 °F
5. Let corn cool slightly, then shuck. Serve with the Sesame-Chile Butter. Enjoy

Baked Sweet Potato Casserole With Marshmallow Fluff

Servings: 6
Cooking Time: 60 Minutes

Ingredients:
- 3 Pound sweet potatoes
- 1/2 Cup milk
- 1 Cup brown sugar
- 3 eggs
- 4 Tablespoon butter
- 1/2 Teaspoon salt
- 3 egg white
- 1 Pinch salt
- 1 Pinch ground cinnamon

Directions:
1. Supply your smoker with wood pellets and follow the start-up procedure. Preheat the grill, with the lid closed, to 375° F.
2. Rinse, dry and pierce the sweet potatoes and place in grill whole. Cook for 45 minutes or until fork tender. Remove from grill and peel. Grill: 375 °F
3. Once peeled, mash the sweet potatoes in a large bowl with the milk, brown sugar, eggs, butter and salt. Place mashed potatoes in a baking dish and cook for 35 minutes. Grill: 375 °F
4. While the potatoes bake, make the fluff. Make a double boiler by bringing a small pot of water to a simmer, then placing the bowl of your stand mixer or another large stainless steel bowl atop the water.
5. Add the 3 egg whites, 2/3 cup brown sugar, a pinch of salt and a pinch of cinnamon to the bowl and whisk continuously until the sugar dissolves and the liquid is warm to the touch.
6. Transfer the bowl from the stovetop to your stand mixer and use the whisk attachment to whip the whites on medium-high speed until it turns glossy with stiff peaks, about 5-8 minutes.
7. Once the casserole has finished baking, use a rubber spatula to cover the sweet potato mixture with the fluff. Use the back of the spatula to create dramatic peaks.
8. Return to the grill for 5-7 minutes, or until the fluff starts to turn golden and the peaks are just shy of burnt. Remove from grill and enjoy!

Tater Tot Bake

Servings: 4
Cooking Time: 15 Minutes

Ingredients:
- 1 Whole frozen tater tots
- salt and pepper
- 1 Cup sour cream
- 1 Cup shredded cheddar cheese, divided
- 1/2 Cup bacon, chopped
- 1/4 Cup green onion, diced

Directions:
1. Supply your smoker with wood pellets and follow the start-up procedure. Preheat the grill, with the lid closed, to 375° F.
2. Line a baking sheet with aluminum foil for easy clean up and spread frozen tater tots onto sheet.
3. Sprinkle with Veggie Shake or salt and pepper to taste.
4. Place the baking sheet on the preheated grill grate and cook the tater tots for 10 minutes.
5. Drizzle sour cream over cooked tater tots.
6. Sprinkle the cheese, bacon bits and green onions on top of the tater tots.
7. Turn heat up to High heat and cook for 5 more minutes until the cheese melts and serve immediately. Enjoy!

Smoked & Loaded Baked Potato

Servings: 4
Cooking Time: 60 Minutes

Ingredients:
- 6 Yukon Gold or russet potatoes
- 8 Slices bacon
- 1/2 Cup butter, melted
- 1 Cup sour cream
- 1 1/2 Cup shredded cheddar cheese, divided
- salt and pepper

- 1 Bunch green onions, thinly sliced

Directions:
1. Supply your smoker with wood pellets and follow the start-up procedure. Preheat the grill, with the lid closed, to 375° F.
2. Poke potatoes with a fork, then place straight onto the grill. Cook for 1 hour. Grill: 375 °F
3. At the same time, cook bacon on a baking sheet on the grill for about 20 minutes; remove, cool and crumble. Grill: 375 °F
4. Once potatoes are done, remove and allow to cool for 15 minutes.
5. Cut each potato lengthwise, creating long halves. Use a small spoon to scoop out about 70% of the potato to make a boat, keeping a thick layer of potato near skin.
6. Place excess potato in a bowl and reserve. Lightly mash extra potato with a fork; add butter, sour cream, 1/2 cup cheese and season with salt and pepper.
7. Take the potato skins and fill with potato mixture, then sprinkle with extra cheese and bacon.
8. Place back on grill for about 10 minutes or until warm and cheese has melted. Garnish with green onions and extra sour cream. Enjoy! Grill: 375 °F

Roasted Tomatoes

Servings: 2
Cooking Time: 180 Minutes

Ingredients:
- 3 Large ripe tomatoes
- 1/2 Tablespoon kosher salt
- 1 Teaspoon coarse ground black pepper
- 1/4 Teaspoon sugar
- 1/4 Teaspoon thyme or basil
- olive oil

Directions:
1. Line a rimmed baking sheet with parchment paper.
2. Supply your smoker with wood pellets and follow the start-up procedure. Preheat the grill, with the lid closed, to 225° F.
3. Remove the stem end from each tomato and cut the tomatoes into 1/2 inch thick slices.
4. Combine the salt, pepper, sugar and thyme or basil in a small bowl and mix.
5. Pour olive oil into the well of a dinner plate.
6. Dip one side of each tomato slice in the olive oil and arrange on the baking sheet. Dust the tomato slices with the seasoning mixture.
7. Arrange the pan directly on the grill grate and roast the tomatoes until the juices stop running and the edges have contracted, about 3 hours. Remove from grill and enjoy!

Braised Creamed Green Beans

Servings: 4
Cooking Time: 25 Minutes

Ingredients:
- 6 Tablespoon butter
- 2 Clove garlic, pressed or minced
- 1 shallot, thinly sliced
- 1 Cup heavy cream
- 1 Pinch ground nutmeg
- salt
- 3 Pound mixed greens such as kale, chard or collards; washed, stems removed and torn into bite sized pieces

Directions:
1. Supply your smoker with wood pellets and follow the start-up procedure. Preheat the grill, with the lid closed, to 325° F.
2. In a saucepan, heat 2 tablespoons of the butter over high heat until it foams. Add the garlic and shallot and cook over medium-low heat, stirring, until softened and golden, about 5 minutes.
3. Add the cream, bring to a simmer and cook until slightly thickened, about 10 minutes.
4. Add the nutmeg and salt to taste. Using a hand blender, purée until smooth.
5. In a cast iron pan, heat the remaining 4 tablespoons butter over high heat until it foams.
6. Add the greens and cook until tender but still bright green, about 5 minutes.
7. Sprinkle with salt and add the cream mixture. Cover and transfer to the grill.
8. Braise greens for 15-20 minutes until the cream is bubbling and greens are tender. Grill: 325 °F
9. Season to taste with nutmeg and salt. Serve hot. Enjoy!

Blt Pasta Salad

Servings: 6
Cooking Time: 45 Minutes

Ingredients:
- 1 pound thick-cut bacon
- 16 ounces bowtie pasta, cooked according to package directions and drained
- 2 tomatoes, chopped
- ½ cup chopped scallions
- ½ cup Italian dressing
- ½ cup ranch dressing
- 1 tablespoon chopped fresh basil
- 1 teaspoon salt
- 1 teaspoon freshly ground black pepper
- 1 teaspoon garlic powder
- 1 head lettuce, cored and torn

Directions:
1. Supply your smoker with wood pellets and follow the start-up procedure. Preheat, with the lid closed, to 225°F.
2. Arrange the bacon slices on the grill grate, close the lid, and cook for 30 to 45 minutes, flipping after 20 minutes, until crisp.
3. Remove the bacon from the grill and chop.
4. In a large bowl, combine the chopped bacon with the cooked pasta, tomatoes, scallions, Italian dressing, ranch dressing, basil, salt, pepper, and garlic powder. Refrigerate until ready to serve.
5. Toss in the lettuce just before serving to keep it from wilting.

Grilled Chili-lime Corn

Servings: 8
Cooking Time: 45 Minutes

Ingredients:
- 12 Corn, ears
- 1 Teaspoon chili powder
- 1/2 Teaspoon onion powder
- 1 Teaspoon Leinenkugel's Summer Shandy Rub
- 2 lime, juiced
- 1 Tablespoon lime zest

Directions:
1. Soak the ears of corn, still in their husk, in water for 4 to 8 hours.
2. Supply your smoker with wood pellets and follow the start-up procedure. Preheat the grill, with the lid closed, to 350° F.
3. Place corn directly on grill grates. Turn corn every 15 minutes for 45 minutes total cooking time. Grill: 350 °F
4. Combine chili powder, onion powder, Summer Shandy rub, lime juice, lime zest and butter in an oven safe dish and place in grill for 10 minutes. Remove corn and butter from the grill.
5. Pull corn husk back, but not off and remove corn silk. Using the corn husk as a handle, brush the corn with the melted chili-lime butter. Enjoy!

Smoked Beet-pickled Eggs

Servings: 4
Cooking Time: 30 Minutes

Ingredients:
- 6 Eggs, hard boiled
- 1 Red Beets, scrubbed and trimmed
- 1 Cup apple cider vinegar
- 1 Cup Beet, juice
- 1/4 Onion, Sliced
- 1/3 Cup granulated sugar
- 3 Cardamom
- 1 star anise

Directions:
1. Supply your smoker with wood pellets and follow the start-up procedure. Preheat the grill, with the lid closed, to 275° F.
2. Place the peeled hard boiled eggs directly on the grill and smoke for 30 minutes. Grill: 275 °F
3. Put the smoked eggs in a quart size glass jar with the cooked/chopped beets in the bottom.
4. In a medium sauce pan, add the vinegar, beet juice, onion, sugar, cardamom and anise.
5. Bring to a boil and cook, uncovered, until sugar has dissolved and the onions are translucent (about 5 minutes).
6. Remove from the heat and let cool for a few minutes.
7. Pour the vinegar and onions mixture over the eggs and beets in the jar, covering the eggs completely.
8. Securely close with the jar lid. Refrigerate up to a month. Enjoy!

Smoked Mashed Potatoes

Servings: 6
Cooking Time: 45 Minutes

Ingredients:
- 2 Pound red bliss potatoes, washed and diced medium
- chicken stock or water
- 1/2 Stick salted butter
- 1 Cup whole milk
- 1/2 Cup sour cream
- 1/2 Cup shredded or grated Parmesan cheese
- kosher salt
- freshly ground black pepper
- 1/2 Cup fresh sliced green onions

Directions:
1. Place the diced red potatoes into a small saucepan or stockpot and cover with chicken stock or water.
2. Bring to a boil and cook on a simmer until fork tender, then cook 4 to 5 minutes past that until soft.
3. Supply your smoker with wood pellets and follow the start-up procedure. Preheat the grill, with the lid closed, to 400° F.
4. In a separate ovenproof pan, such as a cast iron skillet, add butter and milk and place in the Traeger during start up, until melted (approximately 7 to 10 minutes). Grill: 400 °F
5. Carefully remove the butter/milk mixture from the Traeger using heatproof gloves.
6. Drain the potatoes and place into a large bowl. Add the melted butter/milk mixture and slowly mash.
7. Add sour cream, cheese and green onions, then season to taste with salt and pepper.
8. Place into the cast iron skillet, then place the skillet back into the Traeger and cook until the potatoes have a slight crust and are bubbling, about 15 minutes. Grill: 400 °F
9. Carefully remove the mashed potatoes from the Traeger using heatproof gloves. Allow to cool for 5 minutes. Scoop and enjoy!

Carolina Baked Beans

Servings: 12-15
Cooking Time: 180 Minutes

Ingredients:
- 3 (28-ounce) cans baked beans (I like Bush's brand)
- 1 large onion, finely chopped
- 1 cup The Ultimate BBQ Sauce
- ½ cup light brown sugar
- ¼ cup Worcestershire sauce
- 3 tablespoons yellow mustard
- Nonstick cooking spray or butter, for greasing
- 1 large bell pepper, cut into thin rings
- ½ pound thick-cut bacon, partially cooked and cut into quarters

Directions:
1. Supply your smoker with wood pellets and follow the start-up procedure. Preheat, with the lid closed, to 300°F.
2. In a large mixing bowl, stir together the beans, onion, barbecue sauce, brown sugar, Worcestershire sauce, and mustard until well combined
3. Coat a 9-by-13-inch aluminum pan with cooking spray or butter.
4. Pour the beans into the pan and top with the bell pepper rings and bacon pieces, pressing them down slightly into the sauce.
5. Place a layer of heavy-duty foil on the grill grate to catch drips, and place the pan on top of the foil. Close the lid and cook for 2 hours 30 minutes to 3 hours, or until the beans are hot, thick, and bubbly.
6. Let the beans rest for 5 minutes before serving.

Baked Garlic Duchess Potatoes

Servings: 8
Cooking Time: 60 Minutes

Ingredients:
- 12 Medium Potatoes, Yukon gold
- salt
- 5 Large Egg Yolk
- 2 Clove garlic, minced
- 1.24 Cup heavy cream
- 3/4 Cup sour cream
- 10 Tablespoon butter, melted
- black pepper

Directions:
1. Place potatoes in a large pot and fill with water. Season with salt. Bring to a boil over medium-high heat.
2. Reduce heat and simmer until a paring knife easily slides through potatoes, about 25 to 35 minutes. Drain and let cool slightly.
3. Supply your smoker with wood pellets and follow the start-up procedure. Preheat the grill, with the lid closed, to 450° F.
4. Whisk together egg yolks, garlic, cream, sour cream, butter, and pepper in a large bowl. Season with salt.
5. Peel potatoes and push flesh through a ricer or a food mill directly into bowl with egg mixture. Fold in the egg mixture being careful not to overmix.
6. Transfer to a 3-quart baking dish and bake until golden brown and slightly puffed, about 30–40 minutes. Enjoy! Grill: 450 °F

Roasted Fall Vegetables

Servings: 6
Cooking Time: 30 Minutes

Ingredients:
- 1/2 Pound Potatoes, new
- 2 Tablespoon olive oil
- salt and pepper
- 1/2 Pound Butternut Squash, diced
- 1/2 Pound fresh Brussels sprouts
- 1 Pint mushrooms, sliced

Directions:
1. Supply your smoker with wood pellets and follow the start-up procedure. Preheat the grill, with the lid closed, to 200° F.
2. Toss potatoes and squash with olive oil, salt and pepper and spread out on a sheet tray.
3. Place directly on the grill grate and cook for 15 minutes. Add brussels sprouts and mushrooms and toss to coat.
4. Cook another 15-20 minutes until veggies are lightly browned and cooked through.
5. Adjust seasoning as needed. Enjoy!

Skillet Potato Cake

Servings: 4
Cooking Time: 40 Minutes

Ingredients:
- 8 Tablespoon butter, melted
- 2 Pound russet potatoes, peeled and thinly sliced
- 3 Tablespoon kosher salt
- 2 Tablespoon freshly ground black pepper
- thyme

Directions:
1. Supply your smoker with wood pellets and follow the start-up procedure. Preheat the grill, with the lid closed, to 375° F.
2. Brush the bottom of a cast iron skillet with part of the melted butter. Place potato slices vertically around the outer edges then fill in the middle in the same fashion.

3. Pour additional melted butter over the top of the layers and sprinkle with salt and pepper.
4. Place skillet in grill and cook for 35 to 40 minutes or until potatoes are fork tender and golden brown.
5. Garnish with a sprinkle of fresh thyme over the top of the potatoes. Enjoy!

Baked Artichoke Parmesan Mushrooms

Servings: 8
Cooking Time: 30 Minutes

Ingredients:
- 8 Cremini Mushroom Caps
- 6 1/2 Ounce artichoke hearts
- 1/3 Cup Parmesan cheese, grated
- 1/4 Cup mayonnaise
- 1/2 Teaspoon garlic salt
- your favorite hot sauce
- paprika

Directions:
1. Clean the mushrooms with a damp paper towel. Remove the stems and discard or save for another use.
2. Using a small spoon, scoop out the inside (gills, etc.). Combine the artichoke hearts, parmesan, mayonnaise, garlic salt, and hot sauce and mix well.
3. Mound the filling in the mushroom caps. Dust the tops with paprika.
4. Arrange the mushrooms in an oven-safe baking dish.
5. Supply your smoker with wood pellets and follow the start-up procedure. Preheat the grill, with the lid closed, to 350° F.
6. Bake the mushrooms (uncovered) until the filling is bubbling and just beginning to brown, about 25 to 30 minutes. Serve immediately. Grill: 350 °F
7. For a simple variation, stuff the mushrooms with your favorite bulk sausage and bake on your Traeger as directed above. Enjoy!

Grilled Broccoli Rabe

Servings: 4
Cooking Time: 10 Minutes

Ingredients:
- 4 Tablespoon extra-virgin olive oil
- 4 Bunch broccoli rabe or broccolini
- kosher salt
- 1 lemon, halved

Directions:
1. Supply your smoker with wood pellets and follow the start-up procedure. Preheat the grill, with the lid closed, to 450° F.
2. On a platter or in a mixing bowl, drizzle the olive oil over the broccoli rabe. Use your hands to mix thoroughly, coating the vegetables evenly with the oil. Season with sea salt.
3. Place the broccoli rabe in one layer directly on the lowest grill grate. Close the lid and cook for 5 to 10 minutes. You want there to be some color and slight char on the first side. Flip and cook for a few more minutes. Grill: 450 °F
4. Transfer the broccoli rabe to a serving platter and squeeze the juice of half a lemon evenly over the top.
5. Serve with more lemon wedges on the side. Enjoy!

Baked Sweet And Savory Yams By Bennie Kendrick

Servings: 6
Cooking Time: 60 Minutes

Ingredients:
- 3 Medium Yams
- 3 Tablespoon extra-virgin olive oil
- honey
- Goat Cheese
- 1/2 Cup brown sugar
- 1/2 Cup Pecans, pieces

Directions:
1. Supply your smoker with wood pellets and follow the start-up procedure. Preheat the grill, with the lid closed, to 350° F.
2. While Traeger comes to temperature, wash yams and poke a few holes all over. Wrap yams in foil.
3. Bake for 45-60 minutes or until knife tender. You don't want to overcook and get the yams too soft because you want to be able to cut each yam into rounds.
4. Once yams have cooled to the touch, cut each into 1/4" rounds. Lightly coat each round with oil olive and place on sheet tray.
5. Sprinkle each top with brown sugar. Using a teaspoon, place desired amount of goat cheese on each round. Next top with chopped pecans. Finally, drizzle Bee Local honey over each round.
6. Based on how sweet you like your yams, you can add more brown sugar and honey.
7. After complete, place your sheet tray back in the grill and cook, lid closed, for another 20 minutes. Enjoy!

Spicy Asian Brussels Sprouts

Servings: 4
Cooking Time: 10 Minutes

Ingredients:
- 2 Cup fresh Brussels sprouts
- 2 Tablespoon vegetable oil
- 1 Tablespoon Asian BBQ Rub

- 1/4 Cup Thai sweet chile sauce

Directions:
1. Supply your smoker with wood pellets and follow the start-up procedure. Preheat the grill, with the lid closed, to 350° F.
2. Spread the halved brussel sprouts in a single layer on a lined cookie sheet. Drizzle with the oil and toss to coat.
3. Sprinkle the brussel sprouts evenly with an Asian BBQ rub and put the cookie sheet on the grill. Close the lid and cook for 7-8 minutes. Grill: 350 °F
4. Toss the brussels sprouts in the Thai Chili Sauce and return to the grill for an additional 3-4 minutes, or until the sprouts are crisp-tender. Grill: 350 °F
5. Serve immediately. Enjoy!

Grilled Beer Cabbage

Servings: 4
Cooking Time: 50 Minutes

Ingredients:
- 2 Cabbage, head
- 1 Tablespoon extra-virgin olive oil
- 1 Teaspoon salt
- 1 Teaspoon freshly ground black pepper
- 14 Fluid Ounce Guinness Extra Stout

Directions:
1. Clean and core cabbages. Drizzle with olive oil and salt and pepper. Rub into the cabbage.
2. Supply your smoker with wood pellets and follow the start-up procedure. Preheat the grill, with the lid closed, to 180° F.
3. Place cabbages directly on grill grate; smoke for 15 to 20 minutes. Remove from grill and thickly slice cabbage. Grill: 180 °F
4. Place sliced cabbage in cast-iron skillet. Pour beer over cabbage and return to grill.
5. Increase temperature to 375°F and cook for 30 minutes, or until cabbage has reached desired softness. Grill: 375 °F
6. Serve with corned beef. Enjoy!

Baked Stuffed Avocados

Servings: 6
Cooking Time: 15 Minutes

Ingredients:
- 4 avocados, halved and pit removed
- 8 eggs
- 2 Cup shredded cheddar cheese
- 1/4 Cup cherry tomatoes, halved
- 4 Slices Bacon, cooked & chopped
- salt and pepper
- 1 scallion, thinly sliced

Directions:
1. Supply your smoker with wood pellets and follow the start-up procedure. Preheat the grill, with the lid closed, to 450° F.
2. After removing the pit from the avocado, scoop out a little of the flesh to make enough room to fit 1 egg per half.
3. Fill the bottom of a cast iron pan with kosher salt and nestle the avocado halves into the salt, cut side up. The salt helps to keep them in place while cooking, like ice with oysters.
4. Crack one egg into each half, top with shredded cheddar cheese, cherry tomatoes and bacon. Season with salt and pepper to taste.
5. Place the cast iron pan directly on the grill grate and bake the avocados for 12 to 15 minutes until the cheese is melted and the egg is just set. Grill: 450 °F
6. Remove from the grill and let rest 5 to 10 minutes. Top with sliced scallions and enjoy!

Roasted New Potatoes With Compound Butter

Servings: 4
Cooking Time: 45 Minutes

Ingredients:
- 2 Pound Small Red, White or Purple Potatoes (or Combination of All Three)
- 3 Tablespoon olive oil
- salt and pepper
- 2 Stick Butter, unsalted
- 1 Tablespoon shallot, minced
- 3 Tablespoon Finely Chopped Herbs, Such As Tarragon, Parsley, Basil or Combination
- 2 Teaspoon kosher salt

Directions:
1. Supply your smoker with wood pellets and follow the start-up procedure. Preheat the grill, with the lid closed, to 400° F. Cut the potatoes in half and place in a large mixing bowl. Cover with the olive oil, a teaspoon of salt and generous grinding of pepper.
2. Place on a large baking sheet so there is space between the potatoes. Place on the grill and roast for 45 minutes to 1 hour, until crispy skinned. Toss once during cooking. Grill: 400 °F
3. To make the butter: Place it in a medium sized shallow mixing bowl. Use a wooden spoon or strong spatula to break it up and soften it even more. Sprinkle the shallot, herbs, and salt over the butter, then use the spoon to combine the ingredients. Taste, adding more salt or herbs if necessary. Reserve a few tablespoons of the butter to serve on the potatoes.
4. To freeze the butter for future use, place a foot long piece of plastic wrap on the counter. Spread the butter out into a 6" log across the long direction of the plastic wrap towards the bottom. Begin to roll the plastic wrap away from you to roll it into a log, twisting the sides of the plastic wrap like a candy wrapper to secure.

5. Using your hands, shape the log into an even cylinder. Once it's wrapped tightly, place in the freezer. Then when more is needed, simply slice off coins of it to serve over grilled steak, chicken, veggies, or roasted potatoes. The butter holds well in the freezer for up to one month. Enjoy! *Cook times will vary depending on set and ambient temperatures.

Green Bean Casserole

Servings: 6
Cooking Time: 25 Minutes

Ingredients:
- 1/2 Stick butter
- 1 Small onion
- 1/2 Cup sliced button mushrooms
- 4 Can green beans, drained
- 2 Can cream of mushroom soup
- 1 Teaspoon Lawry's Seasoned Salt
- pepper
- 1 Can French's Original Crispy Fried Onions
- 1 Cup grated sharp cheddar cheese

Directions:
1. Supply your smoker with wood pellets and follow the start-up procedure. Preheat the grill, with the lid closed, to 375° F.
2. Melt butter in a cast iron skillet and add onions and mushrooms, stirring occasionally until softened.
3. Add drained green beans and cream of mushroom soup and stir gently to combine.
4. Season with seasoned salt and pepper and sprinkle the top with grated cheddar cheese and fried onions.
5. Bake for 25 minutes. Serve warm, enjoy! Grill: 375 °F

Sicilian Stuffed Mushrooms

Servings: 6
Cooking Time: 25 Minutes

Ingredients:
- 12 Medium Fresh Mushrooms, about 1-1/2 inches in diameter
- 4 Ounce cream cheese, room temperature
- 1/4 Cup Parmesan cheese, grated
- 1/4 Cup shredded mozzarella cheese
- 8 Whole Pimento Stuffed Green Olives, chopped
- 3 Tablespoon Pepperoni, finely diced
- 1 1/2 Tablespoon Sun Dried Tomatoes, drained & minced
- 1/4 Teaspoon freshly ground black pepper

Directions:
1. Dampen a paper towel and wipe the outside of the mushrooms clean. Remove the stem. Using a small spoon, scoop out the inside of the mushroom leaving a shell.
2. Filling: In a small mixing bowl, beat together the cream cheese, Parmesan, and mozzarella. Stir in olives, pepperoni, tomatoes, basil, and pepper.
3. Mound the filling in the mushroom caps. Set each filled cap into the well of a muffin tin.
4. Supply your smoker with wood pellets and follow the start-up procedure. Preheat the grill, with the lid closed, to 350° F.
5. Arrange the muffin tin on the grill grate and bake the mushrooms for 25 to 30 minutes, or until the mushrooms are tender and the filling is beginning to brown.
6. Transfer to a serving plate or platter. Enjoy!

Roasted Tomatoes With Hot Pepper Sauce

Servings: 4
Cooking Time: 60 Minutes

Ingredients:
- 2 Pound fresh Roma tomatoes
- 3 Tablespoon parsley, chopped
- 2 Tablespoon garlic, chopped
- salt and pepper
- 1/2 Cup extra-virgin olive oil
- 1 Pound Spaghetti
- Hot peppers

Directions:
1. Supply your smoker with wood pellets and follow the start-up procedure. Preheat the grill, with the lid closed, to 400° F.
2. Wash tomatoes and cut them in half, lengthwise. Place them in a baking dish cut side up.
3. Sprinkle with chopped parsley, garlic, add salt and black pepper and pour 1/4 cup (100 mL) of olive oil over them.
4. Place on pre-heated grill and bake for 1 1/2 hours. Tomatoes will shrink and the skins will be partly blackened. Grill: 400 °F
5. Remove tomatoes from baking dish and place in a food processor leaving the cooked oil, and puree them.
6. Drop pasta into boiling salted water and cook until tender. Drain and toss immediately with the pureed tomatoes.
7. Add the remaining 1/4 cup (60mL) of raw olive oil and crumbled hot red pepper to taste. Toss and serve. Enjoy!

Christmas Brussel Sprouts

Servings: 6
Cooking Time: 50 Minutes

Ingredients:
- 1/2 Pound thick-cut bacon
- 1 Medium onion, diced
- 2 Pound fresh Brussels sprouts
- 2 Tablespoon olive oil
- salt and pepper

Directions:
1. Supply your smoker with wood pellets and follow the start-up procedure. Preheat the grill, with the lid closed, to 350° F.
2. Place bacon directly on grill grate and cook for 15-20 minutes, or until lightly browned. Remove from grill and set aside on paper towel lined plate.
3. Slice onion in half and then slice into 1⁄4 inch moons and add to large mixing bowl. Slice brussels sprouts in half lengthwise and add to bowl.
4. Cut reserved bacon into 1⁄2 inch pieces and add to bowl. Drizzle with olive oil and sprinkle with salt and pepper. Toss to coat and pour into baking pan.
5. Turn the temperature on grill to 375 and place baking pan on grill. Roast for 30 minutes mixing halfway through cooking. Grill: 375 °F

Smoked Bbq Onion Brussels Sprout

Servings: 4
Cooking Time: 110 Minutes

Ingredients:
- 4 strip bacon
- 1 onion minced
- 2 cloves garlic minced
- 1 lb brussels sprouts stems trimmed and cut in half
- 1 tbsp BBQ Spice Blend
- 1/2 cup Apple Habanero Bar-B-Que Sauce (or other BBQ sauce)

Directions:
1. Supply your smoker with wood pellets and follow the start-up procedure. Preheat the grill, with the lid closed, to High heat. Place a cast iron skillet over the highest heat spot and cook the bacon until crisp.
2. Remove the bacon from pan and drain, reserving the bacon fat in the pan.
3. Reduce the heat on your smoker to 250°F.
4. Add the onions, garlic, and brussels to the pan and toss to coat in the bacon drippings. Sprinkle the BBQ spice blend over top.
5. Cover the lid and allow to smoke for 1 to 1 1/2 hours, until the sprouts are fork tender.
6. For the last 20 minutes of smoking, toss the brussels sprouts in half of the barbecue sauce.
7. Remove the sprouts from the smoker.
8. Chop the bacon and add it and the remaining barbecue sauce to the pan of sprouts, tossing to coat.
9. Serve hot.

Grilled Cabbage Steaks With Warm Bacon Vinaigrette

Servings: 4
Cooking Time: 10 Minutes

Ingredients:
- 3 Strips thick-cut lean bacon, cut into 1/4 inch strips
- 1 Large shallot, minced
- 2 Tablespoon sherry vinegar
- 1 Tablespoon whole grain mustard
- 1 Teaspoon chopped thyme
- 2 Tablespoon olive oil, plus more as needed
- 1 Head green cabbage, cut into 3/4 inch thick slices (about 6 steaks)
- salt and pepper

Directions:
1. Supply your smoker with wood pellets and follow the start-up procedure. Preheat the grill, with the lid closed, to 450° F.
2. For the Vinaigrette: In a large skillet, cook the bacon in 2 tablespoons olive oil over medium-high heat until browned and crisp. Remove bacon from heat and stir in the shallot, vinegar, mustard and thyme then set aside.
3. Brush cabbage steaks with olive oil and season with salt and pepper. Place cabbage steaks directly on grill grate and grill for 5 minutes per side. Grill: 450 °F
4. Remove cabbage steaks from grill and drizzle with bacon vinaigrette. Enjoy!

Baked Kale Chips

Servings: 4
Cooking Time: 20 Minutes

Ingredients:
- 2 Bunch kale, leaves washed and stems removed
- 1 As Needed extra-virgin olive oil
- 1 To Taste sea salt

Directions:
1. Dry the kale leaves well and lay them out on a sheet tray. Drizzle lightly with olive oil and sprinkle with sea salt.
2. Supply your smoker with wood pellets and follow the start-up procedure. Preheat the grill, with the lid closed, to 250° F.
3. Place the sheet tray directly on the grill grate and cook until kale is lightly browned and crispy, about 20 minutes. Enjoy! Grill: 250 °F

Cast Iron Potatoes

Servings: 4
Cooking Time: 60 Minutes

Ingredients:
- 4 Tablespoon butter, cut into cubes
- 2 1/2 Pound potatoes, peeled and cut into 1/8 inch slices
- 1/2 Large sweet onion, thinly sliced
- salt
- black pepper
- 1 1/2 Cup grated mild cheddar or jack cheese
- 2 Cup milk
- paprika

Directions:
1. Butter the inside of a cast iron skillet and layer half the potato slices on the bottom. Top with half the onions. Season with salt and pepper.
2. Sprinkle 1 cup of the cheese over the potatoes and onions and dot with half the butter. Layer the remaining potatoes and onions on top. Dot with remaining butter.
3. Pour the milk into the skillet. Cover the skillet tightly with aluminum foil.
4. Supply your smoker with wood pellets and follow the start-up procedure. Preheat the grill, with the lid closed, to 350° F.
5. Bake for 1 hour, or until the potatoes are very tender. Grill: 350 °F
6. Remove the foil and top with the remaining 1/2 cup of cheese. Bake for 30 minutes more (uncovered) until the cheese is lightly browned. Dust the top with paprika and serve immediately.

Roasted Red Pepper White Bean Dip

Servings: 4
Cooking Time: 40 Minutes

Ingredients:
- 4 Whole garlic
- 4 Tablespoon extra-virgin olive oil
- 2 Bell Pepper, Red
- 3 Tablespoon Dill Weed, fresh
- 3 Tablespoon chopped flat-leaf parsley
- 2 Can cannellini beans, mashed
- 4 Teaspoon lemon juice
- 1 1/2 Teaspoon salt

Directions:
1. Roasting the garlic and red peppers:
2. Supply your smoker with wood pellets and follow the start-up procedure. Preheat the grill, with the lid closed, to 400° F.
3. Peel away the outside layers of the garlic husk. Cut off the top of the garlic bulb, exposing each of the individual cloves. Drizzle olive oil over the top of the head of garlic and rub it in. Wrap the garlic in foil, completely covering it. Put the head of garlic and the two red peppers (washed and dried) on the Traeger.
4. Roast the garlic for 25-30 minutes and the peppers for about 40 minutes. Rotate the peppers a quarter-turn every 10 minutes until the exterior is blistered and blackened. Grill: 400 °F
5. Pull the peppers off the grill and put them in a bowl. Cover the bowl with plastic wrap and leave them for 15 minutes. The steam will loosen the skins so that they slip off like a drumstick covered in barbecue sauce.
6. Peel off the pepper skin. Cut off the stems and scrape out the seeds and they're ready to use.
7. As for the garlic, let it cool and then pull out the individual cloves as needed.
8. The dip:
9. In a blender put the roasted red peppers, 4 cloves of roasted garlic, dill, parsley, drained and rinsed beans, olive oil, lemon juice and salt.
10. Blend until the dip is smooth and creamy. You may need to scrape down the sides of the blender a couple of times. If it's having difficulty blending or looks too thick add more olive oil or lemon juice. (Add more lemon juice if it tastes like it needs more acid or brightness.) Enjoy!

Roasted Do-ahead Mashed Potatoes

Servings: 6
Cooking Time: 50 Minutes

Ingredients:
- 5 Pound Yukon Gold or russet potatoes
- 9 Tablespoon butter
- 8 Ounce cream cheese
- 1/2 Cup milk
- salt and pepper

Directions:
1. Peel the potatoes and cut into chunks that are roughly the same size. Cover with cold water and add a teaspoon of salt. Bring to a boil over high heat, then reduce the heat to medium and simmer the potatoes until they are tender.
2. Drain the potatoes and return them to the pot. Stir over low heat for 2 to 3 minutes to evaporate any excess moisture.
3. Mash the potatoes with a hand-held potato masher. (Alternative, rice the potatoes using a ricer.) Incorporate 8 tbsp butter and cream cheese. Add milk until the potatoes are of a good consistency. Stir in salt and pepper to taste.
4. Butter the inside of a casserole dish. Spread the potatoes out in an even layer in the casserole dish, smoothing the top with a spatula. Cool, cover, and refrigerate if not cooking right away. Before cooking, let the potatoes warm to room temperature (about an hour).
5. Supply your smoker with wood pellets and follow the start-up procedure. Preheat the grill, with the lid closed, to 350° F.
6. Bake the potatoes for 45 to 50 minutes, or until hot through. Grill: 350 °F

POULTRY RECIPES

Bbq Breakfast Sausage

Servings: 4 - 6
Cooking Time: 35 Minutes

Ingredients:
- 1/4 Cup Bbq Sauce
- 1 Tbsp Brown Sugar
- 4 Oz Cheddar Cheese, Cut Into Sticks
- To Taste, Cracked Black Pepper
- 6 Eggs, Scrambled
- 4 Oz Ham, Diced
- 1 Package, Approx 1 Lb Shady Brook Farms Ground Turkey Sausage
- 10 Oz Turkey Bacon

Directions:
1. Supply your smoker with wood pellets and follow the start-up procedure. Preheat the grill, with the lid closed, to 375° F. If using a gas or charcoal grill, set it up for medium-high heat.
2. Lay out a piece of plastic wrap then make a bacon weave using your favorite turkey bacon. Top with the Shady Brooks Farms Turkey Sausage and spread out into an even layer with your fingers.
3. Spoon the scrambled eggs into the center of the sausage, then place half of the cheese sticks in the middle, followed by ham, then remaining cheese.
4. Gently lift up one end of the plastic wrap and begin rolling the "not so fatty." Once the roll is completed, remove the plastic wrap and secure the ends of the bacon together with toothpicks, if needed.
5. Set in a cast iron skillet, sprinkle with brown sugar, and season with cracked pepper. Transfer to the grill and cook for 30 minutes, until an internal temperature of 155°F.
6. Baste with BBQ sauce and cook for an additional 5 minutes until the sauce is set and the internal temperature increased to 165°F.
7. Remove from the grill and rest for 5 minutes before slicing and serving warm.

Duck Breast With Pomegranate Sauce

Servings: 4
Cooking Time: 13 Minutes

Ingredients:
- 4 duck breasts, each about 6oz (170g), skin on
- for the rub
- 2 tsp coarse salt
- 1 tsp ground cumin
- 1 tsp ground coriander
- 1 tsp freshly ground black pepper
- ½ tsp ground cinnamon
- ½ tsp ground fennel
- for the sauce
- 1 shallot, peeled and minced
- 1 cup pomegranate juice
- 1 tbsp sherry vinegar or balsamic vinegar
- 1 tsp cornstarch
- ¼ cup chicken stock or chicken broth
- 1 tbsp chilled unsalted butter, cut into 4 pieces
- ¼ cup fresh pomegranate seeds (optional)
- 1 tbsp minced fresh chives

Directions:
1. Place a cast iron skillet on the grate. Supply your smoker with wood pellets and follow the start-up procedure. Preheat the grill, with the lid closed, to 400° F.
2. In a small bowl, make the rub by combining the ingredients. Use a sharp knife to diagonally score the skin of each duck breast—but don't nick the flesh. Lightly season the scored side of each breast.
3. Place the duck breasts skin side down in the skillet and sear until the skin is crisp and golden brown, about 8 to 10 minutes. Turn the breasts and cook until the internal temperature in the thickest part of a breast reaches 130°F (54°C), about 2 to 3 minutes more. Transfer the breasts to a plate.
4. In a large saucepan on the stovetop over medium heat, make the sauce by heating 1 tablespoon of duck fat from the skillet. (Reserve the remainder for another use.) Add the shallot and sauté until soft, about 2 to 3 minutes.
5. Add the pomegranate juice and bring the mixture to a boil over medium-high heat. Reduce the sauce by half, about 3 to 5 minutes. Add the vinegar and lower the heat to medium low.
6. Whisk together the cornstarch and chicken stock until smooth. Whisk into the sauce and cook until the sauce thickens, about 1 to 2 minutes. Whisk in the butter and stir in the pomegranate seeds (if using).
7. Place the duck breasts on a warm platter. Drizzle the pomegranate sauce over the top. Scatter the chives around the platter before serving.

Buttered Thanksgiving Turkey

Servings: 12-14
Cooking Time: 300 Minutes

Ingredients:
- 1 whole turkey (make sure the turkey is not pre-brined)
- 2 batches Garlic Butter Injectable

- 3 tablespoons olive oil
- 1 batch Chicken Rub
- 2 tablespoons butter

Directions:

1. Supply your smoker with wood pellets and follow the start-up procedure. Preheat the grill, with the lid closed, to 180°F.
2. Inject the turkey throughout with the garlic butter injectable. Coat the turkey with olive oil and season it with the rub. Using your hands, work the rub into the meat and skin.
3. Place the turkey directly on the grill grate and smoke for 3 or 4 hours (for an 8- to 12-pound turkey, cook for 3 hours; for a turkey over 12 pounds, cook for 4 hours), basting it with butter every hour.
4. Increase the grill's temperature to 375°F and continue to cook until the turkey's internal temperature reaches 170°F.
5. Remove the turkey from the grill and let it rest for 10 minutes, before carving and serving.

Savory Smoked Chicken Breasts

Servings: 2
Cooking Time: 30 Minutes

Ingredients:

- 1 lb Boneless Skinless Chicken Breasts
- 2-3 Tbsp BBQ Chicken Rub

Directions:

1. Supply your smoker with wood pellets and follow the start-up procedure. Preheat the grill, with the lid closed, to 250° F.
2. Pound chicken breasts flat, about 1/2" thick. Rub the dry rub all over chicken breasts.
3. Place chicken breasts on the grill grate. Close pellet grill lid and cook at 250 °F for about 30 minutes or until the chicken reaches an internal temperature of 165 °F.
4. Remove from pellet grill and let rest 5-10 minutes.

Traeger Bbq Half Chickens

Servings: 2
Cooking Time: 60 Minutes

Ingredients:

- 1 (3 to 3-1/2 lb) fresh young chicken
- Leinenkugel's Summer Shandy Rub
- Apricot BBQ Sauce

Directions:

1. Place the chicken breast side down, on a cutting board with the neck pointing away from you. Cut along one side of the backbone, staying as close to the bone as possible, from the neck to the tail. Repeat on the other side of the backbone then remove it.
2. Open the chicken and slice through the white cartilage at the tip of the breastbone to pop it open. Cut down either side of the breast bone then use your fingers to pull it out. Flip the chicken over so it is skin side up and cut down the center splitting the chicken in half. Tuck the wings back on each chicken half.
3. Season on both sides with Traeger Leinenkugel's Summer Shandy Rub.
4. Supply your smoker with wood pellets and follow the start-up procedure. Preheat the grill, with the lid closed, to 375° F.
5. Place chicken directly on the grill grate skin side up and cook until the internal temperature reaches 160°F, about 60-90 minutes. Grill: 375 °F Probe: 160 °F
6. Brush the BBQ sauce all over the chicken skin and cook for an additional 10 minutes. Remove from grill and let rest 5 minutes before serving. Enjoy! Grill: 375 °F

Spiced Smoked Chicken Quarters

Servings: 4
Cooking Time: 120 Minutes

Ingredients:

- 4 chicken leg quarters
- For the rub:
- 2 tbsp paprika
- 1 tbsp thyme
- 2 tbsp chili powder
- 2 tbsp cayenne pepper
- 1 tbsp garlic powder
- 1 tbsp onion powder
- 1 tbsp kosher/table salt
- 2 tbsp black pepper
- 1 tbsp olive oil

Directions:

1. Supply your smoker with wood pellets and follow the start-up procedure. Preheat the grill, with the lid closed, to 220° F.
2. Pat down chicken pieces with a paper towel to make them dry. Cut off any excess fat that's visible on the outside of the meat.
3. Apply a thin layer of oil to the chicken skin. In a small bowl, combine all the BBQ rub ingredients thoroughly. Apply BBQ rub generously to your chicken thighs, rubbing in firmly and thoroughly.
4. Transfer chicken quarters to your smoker rack. Close the lid.
5. Cook until the quarters reach an internal temperature of 165°F, about 2 hours.
6. Once cooked, increase the grill temperature to medium heat. Cook for just a few minutes, turning regularly, for a crispy skin.

Chicken Lollipops

Servings: 8
Cooking Time: 60 Minutes

Ingredients:
- 18 Pieces chicken drumsticks
- Cajun Shake
- 1 Stick butter
- 'Que BBQ Sauce
- Louisiana Brand Hot Sauce (Optional)

Directions:
1. To turn regular chicken legs into lollipops, you'll need a sharp knife and a pair of kitchen shears. Start by making a cut all of the way around the leg just below the knuckle, cutting through the skins and tendons using either a sharp knife or a pair of kitchen shears. Push the meat down to the large end and pull/cut the remaining skin and cartilage off the knuckle. You might want to also remove the tiny bone right against the leg. Remove this bone with your fingers or the shears, and trim away the tendons sticking out the top.
2. Season the chicken with the Cajun Shake. Wrap the bones of the drumsticks with a small piece of aluminum foil to keep them from turning too black. Let the chicken sit for an hour in the fridge to allow the flavor to permeate.
3. Supply your smoker with wood pellets and follow the start-up procedure. Preheat the grill, with the lid closed, to 180° F.
4. Place the chicken lollipops on the grill grate and let them smoke for 30 minutes.
5. After you remove the chicken, increase the grill temperature to 350°F and let it preheat, lid closed for 15 minutes. Place the stick of butter in a baking pan or aluminum pan and put it on the grill to allow the butter to melt while the grill is coming to temperature. (The butter doesn't need to cover the chicken. It just keeps the drumstick moist and of course, gives it a little added buttery finish.)
6. Arrange the lollipops in the pan with the bones sticking up straight. Let the chicken cook for about 40 minutes or until the internal temperature registers 165F on an instant-read thermometer. Grill: 350 °F Probe: 165 °F
7. Meanwhile, warm up the barbecue sauce in a small saucepan on the stove over low heat. If you want it to have that Louisiana kick, add in a few squirts of the hot sauce, to your taste. Once it starts to thin, turn down the heat to just keep it warm. If the sauce needs to be thinned, pour in a little bit of the butter used in the pan until it reaches a thickness that is thick enough to adhere to the drumsticks but not gluey.
8. Dip the lollipops into the barbecue sauce so that it is completely covered. You can also brush the barbecue sauce on the bones if you want a uniform look and sheen on the lollipops.
9. Increase the temperature to 450F. Place the chicken directly on the grill grate and cook until the internal temperature registers 175F, about 10 more minutes. Keep an eye on the lollipops to make sure that the glaze doesn't burn. You're looking for that perfect caramelization of the barbecue sauce on the outside with a crisp skin to give a little texture. Grill: 450 °F Probe: 175 °F

Buffalo Chicken

Servings: 6
Cooking Time: 90 Minutes

Ingredients:
- 1 1/2 Tbsp Apple Cider Vinegar
- 3 Tbsp Bleu Cheese, Crumbled
- 1/4 Cup Buffalo Sauce
- 1/2 Cup Butter, Unsalted, Cubed
- 1/4 Tsp Cayenne Pepper
- 3 Celery Stalks, Cut Into Sticks
- 1 Cup Cheddar Jack Cheese, Shredded
- 1 Lb Chicken Breast, Boneless, Skinless
- 3 Oz Cream Cheese, Softened
- 1/8 Tsp Garlic, Granulated
- 2/3 Cup Hot Pepper Sauce
- 12 Jalapeno Peppers
- Mason Jar(S)
- 1/4 Red Bell Pepper, Chopped
- 2 Scallions, Sliced Thin
- Shredded Chicken
- 3 Tbsp Sour Cream
- To Taste, Sweet Heat Rub
- 1/2 Tsp Sweet Heat Rub (For Sauce)
- 1/4 Tsp Worcestershire Sauce

Directions:
1. Supply your smoker with wood pellets and follow the start-up procedure. Preheat the grill, with the lid open, to 200° F. If using a gas or charcoal grill, set it up for low, indirect heat.
2. Season chicken breasts with Sweet Heat, then place on the grill. Smoke for 1 hour, then remove from the grill, and set aside to rest.
3. While the chicken is resting, prepare the Buffalo sauce: Set a small cast iron pan or saucepan on the grill. Open the sear slide and increase the grill temperature to 350° F. Add the hot pepper sauce, apple cider vinegar, Worcestershire sauce, Sweet Heat, cayenne, and granulated garlic to the skillet, and whisk to combine. When the sauce begins to bubble, remove the skillet from the grill and whisk in butter. Transfer the sauce to a mason jar.
4. Shred the chicken with 2 forks in the sauce skillet. Set aside.
5. Prepare the filling: In a mixing bowl, use a hand mixer to blend cream cheese, bleu cheese, Buffalo sauce and sour cream. Fold in scallions, red bell pepper, and shredded chicken.

6. Prepare the peppers: Cut each jalapeño in half, lengthwise. Use a paring knife or teaspoon to scrape out the seeds and membrane, then place in a cast iron skillet (might need to divide between 2 skillets). Stuff the mixture into the jalapeño halves, then top with shredded cheese.
7. Transfer peppers to the grill, with the sear slide closed. Close the lid and cook for 15 to 20 minutes, until peppers begin to soften and cheese has melted.
8. Remove the peppers from the grill, transfer to a serving board or platter, and serve warm with extra Buffalo sauce.

Bbq Chicken Drumsticks

Servings: 4
Cooking Time: 120 Minutes

Ingredients:
- 8 chicken drumsticks
- 2 Tablespoon Chicken Rub
- 1/2 Cup 'Que BBQ Sauce

Directions:
1. Season each drumstick and let rest for 20 minutes.
2. Supply your smoker with wood pellets and follow the start-up procedure. Preheat the grill, with the lid closed, to 275° F.
3. Hang the drumsticks on the leg hanger (alternatively, place directly on the grill grate flipping halfway through) and cook for 1 hour. Grill: 275 °F
4. Remove the drumsticks from the hanger (or grate) and place in a pan. Grill: 275 °F Probe: 190 °F
5. Cover with foil and cook for 45 more minutes or until meat reaches an internal temperature of 190 degrees F. Grill: 275 °F Probe: 190 °F
6. Remove the foil and sauce all drumsticks in the pan.
7. Cook for an additional 15 minutes so sauce can set. Grill: 275 °F
8. Remove from Traeger and let rest for 15 minutes before serving. Enjoy!

Bbq Chicken Breasts

Servings: 6
Cooking Time: 25 Minutes

Ingredients:
- 6 boneless, skinless chicken breast
- 1 1/2 Cup Sweet & Heat BBQ Sauce
- salt and pepper
- 1 Tablespoon chopped parsley, for garnish

Directions:
1. Place chicken breasts and 1 cup of Traeger Sweet & Heat BBQ Sauce in a resealable bag or large bowl, and gently turn to cover chicken evenly in the sauce. Marinate in the refrigerator overnight.
2. Supply your smoker with wood pellets and follow the start-up procedure. Preheat the grill, with the lid closed, to 450° F.
3. Remove chicken from marinade and season with salt and pepper.
4. Place chicken directly on the grill grate and cook for 10 minutes on each side flipping once or until internal temperature reaches 150°F.
5. Brush on remaining 1/2 cup of Traeger Sweet & Heat BBQ Sauce while chicken is still on the grill, and continue to cook 5 to 10 minutes longer or until a finished internal temperature of 165°F.
6. Remove chicken from grill and let rest 5 minutes before serving. Sprinkle with chopped parsley. Enjoy!

Smoked Turkey Jerky

Servings: 6
Cooking Time: 240 Minutes

Ingredients:
- 1/2 Cup soy sauce
- 1/4 Cup water
- 2 Tablespoon honey
- 2 Tablespoon Asian chili garlic sauce
- 2 Tablespoon lime juice
- 1 Tablespoon Morton Tender Quick Home Meat Cure
- 2 Pound (4-5 lb) boneless turkey breast

Directions:
1. In a mixing bowl, combine the soy sauce, water, honey, chili-garlic paste, lime juice, and curing salt, if using. With a sharp knife, slice the turkey into 1/4" thick slices with the grain, which helps it hold together better as it dries. (This is easier if the meat is partially frozen.) Trim any fat, membrane, or connective tissue.
2. Put the turkey slices in a large resealable plastic bag. Pour the marinade mixture over the turkey, and massage the bag so that all the slices get coated with the marinade. Seal the bag and refrigerate for several hours, or overnight.
3. Supply your smoker with wood pellets and follow the start-up procedure. Preheat the grill, with the lid closed, to 180° F.
4. Remove the turkey from the marinade and discard the marinade. Dry the turkey slices between paper towels. Arrange in a single layer directly on the grill grate.
5. Smoke for 2 to 4 hours, or until the jerky is dry but still chewy and somewhat pliant when you bend a piece. Grill: 180 °F
6. Transfer to a resealable plastic bag while the jerky's still warm. Let the jerky rest for an hour at room temperature. Squeeze any air from the bag, and refrigerate the jerky. It will keep for several weeks. Enjoy!

Grilled Honey Chicken Wings

Servings: 4 - 8
Cooking Time: 30 Minutes

Ingredients:
- 2 Chipotles Chopped In Adobo
- 1 Apple Cider Vinegar
- 2 Tablespoons Balsamic Vinegar
- ¼ Cup Brown Sugar
- 2 ½ Lbs Chicken Wings, Trimmed And Patted Dry
- ¼ Cup Honey
- ½ Cup Ketchup
- ¼ Cup Adobo Sauce
- 2 Tablespoons Sweet Rib Rub
- 2 Teaspoons Worcestershire Sauce

Directions:
1. Supply your smoker with wood pellets and follow the start-up procedure. Preheat the grill, with the lid open, to 350° F. If you're using a charcoal or gas grill, set up the grill for medium high heat.
2. In a large bowl, whisk together the apple cider vinegar, ketchup, brown sugar, honey, chopped chipotle peppers with adobo sauce, balsamic vinegar, Worcestershire sauce, and Sweet Rib Rub. Whisk the glaze until it's well combined.
3. Add the wings to the glaze and place the bowl in the refrigerator. Marinade the chicken wings for up to 12 hours. Once the wings have finished marinating, remove the chicken wings from the marinade and place the chicken wings onto the wing rack.
4. Once all the wings have been placed on the wing rack, place the wing rack on the grill. Insert a temperature probe into the thickest part into one of the wings and grill the wings for 5 minutes, and then rotate the rack 180° and grill for another 5 minutes. Remove the wings once they have an internal temperature of 165°F and the juice from the chicken runs clear.
5. Remove the wings from the grill and serve immediately.

Grilled Cheesy Chicken

Servings: 4
Cooking Time: 45 Minutes

Ingredients:
- 4 Aged Chedder Cheese, Sliced
- 32 Oz Chicken Broth
- 1 Tsp Extra-Virgin Olive Oil
- Sweet Heat Rub And Grill
- 4 Plump Chicken, Boneless/Skinless

Directions:
1. Supply your smoker with wood pellets and follow the start-up procedure. Preheat the grill, with the lid open, to 350° F.
2. Remove the chicken from the brine. Pat the breasts dry and lightly brush olive oil on both sides of the chicken. Take your knife and slice diagonally across the top of each breast. Sprinkle a lit amount of Sweet Heat Rub and Grill on each side.
3. Barbecue your chicken breasts for 30 minutes. Next, place a slice of cheddar cheese on top of each breast.
4. Heat for another 5-10 minutes or until the cheese has fully melted into the incisions you made earlier. Remove and serve for a tender chicken breast with a spicy kick and hot cheesy center. You'll receive too much credit for a recipe this easy.

Cranberry Turkey Breast

Servings: 6
Cooking Time: 90 Minutes

Ingredients:
- 1 Bay Leaf
- 1/2 Tsp Black Pepper
- 3 Tbsp Butter, Divided
- 1 Celery Rib, Chopped
- To Taste, Cracked Black Pepper
- 4 Oz Cremini Mushrooms
- 1/2 Cup Dried Cranberries
- 2 Garlic Cloves, Minced
- 1 Package, Approx 2Lbs Honeysuckle White Turkey Breast, Boneless
- 1/2 Cup Marsala Wine
- 1 Tbsp Olive Oil
- 1 Rosemary Sprigs
- 1/2 Tsp Rubbed Sage
- 1/2 Tsp Salt
- To Taste, Sea Salt
- 6 Oz Stuffing Mix
- 1 1/4 Cup Turkey Stock, Divided
- 1 Yellow Onion, Chopped

Directions:
1. Supply your smoker with wood pellets and follow the start-up procedure. Preheat the grill, with the lid closed, to 325° F. If using a gas or charcoal grill, set it up for medium-low heat.
2. Melt the butter 1 tablespoon of butter and olive oil in a large skillet over medium heat. Add the onions and celery and cook, stirring frequently, until soft, 3 minutes.
3. Add the garlic and mushrooms and continue to cook for 5 minutes, until the mushrooms are slightly browned.
4. Deglaze with marsala wine, using a wooden spoon to scrape up any browned bits from the bottom of the pan.
5. Add the dried cranberries, black pepper, sage, and salt and simmer for 2 minutes, then remove from the heat.
6. Fold the stuffing into the vegetable mixture, then slowly pour over turkey stock, until stuffing is moistened.
7. Place the Honeysuckle White® Turkey Breast on a large cutting board, skin-side down, then butterfly it. Season with salt

and pepper, then spoon over ⅓ of the stuffing, leaving an inch border.
8. Roll the turkey breast, starting at the side with less skin. Use butcher's twine to truss the turkey breast and secure the stuffing. Place in a cast iron skillet, top remaining butter, season with salt and pepper. Place a sprig of rosemary on top, add remaining ¼ cup of stock around the turkey, along with 1 bay leaf. Transfer to the grill.
9. Cook the turkey for 1 to 1 ½ hours, until an internal temperature of 165°F is reached.
10. Remove stuffed turkey breast from the grill, rest for 15 minutes, then slice and serve warm, with remaining stuffing.

Roasted Rosemary Orange Chicken

Servings: 4
Cooking Time: 45 Minutes

Ingredients:
- 1 (3-4 lb) chicken, backbone removed
- 1/4 Cup olive oil
- 2 oranges, juiced
- 1 orange, zested
- 2 Teaspoon Dijon mustard
- 3 Tablespoon chopped rosemary leaves
- 2 Teaspoon kosher salt

Directions:
1. Rinse the chicken and pat dry with paper towels.
2. For the Marinade: In a medium bowl, combine olive oil, juice from the oranges (about 1/4 cup of freshly squeezed juice), orange zest, Dijon mustard, rosemary and salt. Whisk to combine.
3. Place the chicken in a shallow baking dish large enough for chicken to be fully opened in one piece. Pour marinade over the chicken ensuring it is covered with the marinade.
4. Cover with plastic wrap and refrigerate for a minimum of 2 hours or up to overnight, turning once during the process.
5. Supply your smoker with wood pellets and follow the start-up procedure. Preheat the grill, with the lid closed, to 350° F.
6. Remove the chicken from the marinade and place on the Traeger, skin-side down.
7. Cook for 25 to 30 minutes until the skin is well-browned, then flip. Continue to grill chicken until the internal temperature of the breast reaches 165°F and the thigh reaches 175°F, about 5 to 15 minutes longer. Grill: 350 °F Probe: 165 °F
8. Let rest 10 minutes before carving. Enjoy!

Buffalo Wings

Servings: 2-3
Cooking Time: 35 Minutes

Ingredients:
- 1 pound chicken wings
- 1 batch Chicken Rub
- 1 cup Frank's Red-Hot Sauce, Buffalo wing sauce, or similar

Directions:
1. Supply your smoker with wood pellets and follow the start-up procedure. Preheat the grill, with the lid closed, to 300°F.
2. Season the chicken wings with the rub. Using your hands, work the rub into the meat.
3. Place the wings directly on the grill grate and smoke until their internal temperature reaches 160°F.
4. Baste the wings with the sauce and continue to smoke until the wings' internal temperature reaches 170°F.

Spatchcocked Chicken With White Barbecue Sauce

Servings: 4
Cooking Time: 60 Minutes

Ingredients:
- 1 whole chicken, about 4 to 4½lb (1.8 to 2kg), preferably organic or farm raised
- extra virgin olive oil
- White Barbecue Sauce
- chopped fresh chives (optional)
- for the brine
- ½ gallon (1.9 liters) distilled water
- ½ cup kosher salt
- 2 tbsp light brown sugar or low-carb substitute
- for the rub
- ¼ cup coarse salt
- ¼ cup granulated light brown sugar or low-carb substitute
- ¼ cup sweet or smoked paprika
- 2 tbsp freshly ground black pepper
- 1 tbsp granulated garlic
- 2 tsp dried thyme
- ½ tsp ground cayenne

Directions:
1. In a large stockpot on the stovetop over medium-high heat, make the brine by combining the ingredients. Bring the mixture to a boil. Stir until the salt and sugar dissolve. Remove the pot from the stovetop and let the brine cool to room temperature. Cover and refrigerate until cool.
2. Remove the backbone of the chicken by using a sharp knife, starting at the tail and cutting through the rib bones. Repeat on the other side of the backbone. Fold the two halves backward to release the cartilaginous breastbone. (You might have to use a knife to slice through the thin skin on either side.) Remove the breastbone. Turn the chicken over and gently flatten it with the palm of your hand. Submerge the chicken in the brine. If it floats, place a resealable bag of ice on top. Refrigerate for 4 to 6 hours.

3. Supply your smoker with wood pellets and follow the start-up procedure. Preheat the grill, with the lid closed, to 325° F.
4. In a small bowl, make the rub by combining the ingredients.
5. Rinse the chicken with cold running water and dry with paper towels. (Discard the brine.) Coat the skin with olive oil. Lightly dust the chicken on both sides with the rub. (Save the remainder for another grill session.) Tuck the wingtips behind the chicken's back.
6. Place the chicken ribs side down on the grate and grill until the skin is nicely browned and the internal temperature in a thigh reaches 170°F (77°C), about 1 hour.
7. Transfer the chicken to a platter. Spoon the white barbecue sauce over the chicken. Spread the sauce with a basting brush, letting it pool in places. Lightly scatter the chives over the top. Carve the chicken and serve with extra sauce on the side.

Bbq Chicken Tostada

Servings: 4
Cooking Time: 50 Minutes

Ingredients:
- 4 Whole boneless, skinless chicken thighs
- salt and pepper
- 8 Whole Corn Tostada
- Refried Beans
- lettuce
- green onion, coarsely chopped
- cilantro, chopped
- guacamole

Directions:
1. Supply your smoker with wood pellets and follow the start-up procedure. Preheat the grill, with the lid closed, to 350° F.
2. While grill heats, trim excess fat and skin from chicken thighs.
3. Season with a light layer of salt and pepper.
4. Place chicken thighs on the grill grate and cook for 35 minutes.
5. Check internal temperature; chicken is done when a thermometer inserted reads 175 degrees F. Remove from the grill and let rest for 10 minutes before shredding.
6. Place tostadas on grill while chicken is resting for 5 minutes.
7. Build tostadas starting with refried beans, sliced lettuce, shredded chicken, tomatoes, green onions, cilantro, guacamole. Enjoy!

Smoked Turkey Wings

Servings: 2
Cooking Time: 60 Minutes

Ingredients:
- 4 turkey wings
- 1 batch Sweet and Spicy Cinnamon Rub

Directions:
1. Supply your smoker with wood pellets and follow the start-up procedure. Preheat the grill, with the lid closed, to 180°F.
2. Using your hands, work the rub into the turkey wings, coating them completely.
3. Place the wings directly on the grill grate and cook for 30 minutes.
4. Increase the grill's temperature to 325°F and continue to cook until the turkey's internal temperature reaches 170°F. Remove the wings from the grill and serve immediately.

Spatchcocked Turkey

Servings: 10-14
Cooking Time: 120 Minutes

Ingredients:
- 1 whole turkey
- 2 tablespoons olive oil
- 1 batch Chicken Rub

Directions:
1. Supply your smoker with wood pellets and follow the start-up procedure. Preheat the grill, with the lid closed, to 350°F.
2. To remove the turkey's backbone, place the turkey on a work surface, on its breast. Using kitchen shears, cut along one side of the turkey's backbone and then the other. Pull out the bone.
3. Once the backbone is removed, turn the turkey breast-side up and flatten it.
4. Coat the turkey with olive oil and season it on both sides with the rub. Using your hands, work the rub into the meat and skin.
5. Place the turkey directly on the grill grate, breast-side up, and cook until its internal temperature reaches 170°F.
6. Remove the turkey from the grill and let it rest for 10 minutes, before carving and serving.

Lemon Rosemary Beer Can Chicken

Servings: 4
Cooking Time: 60 Minutes

Ingredients:
- 1 (3 to 3-1/2 lb) whole chicken
- 1 lemon, halved
- 1 Teaspoon kosher salt
- 1 Teaspoon ground black pepper
- 1 Teaspoon fresh finely chopped rosemary
- 1 (12 oz) can beer

Directions:
1. Supply your smoker with wood pellets and follow the start-up procedure. Preheat the grill, with the lid closed, to 400° F.

2. Coat the chicken inside and out with the juice from one lemon. In a small bowl, combine salt, pepper and rosemary, and sprinkle on the inside and outside of chicken.

3. Empty half of the beer from the can and place the can on a solid surface. Place the chicken atop the beer can, tucking the legs in the front.

4. Carefully place the chicken directly on the grill grate using the legs to support if needed. Alternatively, place the chicken atop the beer can on a sheet tray for a more stable surface, then place the sheet tray directly on the grill grate.

5. Cook the chicken until an instant-read thermometer reads 165°F when inserted in the thickest part of the breast, about 60 minutes. Grill: 400 °F Probe: 165 °F

6. Let the chicken rest 10 minutes before carving. Serve with Chardonnay or any of your favorite medium body red or white wines. Enjoy!

Fig Glazed Chicken Stuffed Cornbread

Servings: 10
Cooking Time: 120 Minutes

Ingredients:

- Black Pepper
- 6 Tablespoons (For The Chicken) Butter, Unsalted
- 3 Chicken, Whole
- 2 1/5 Cups (Replace With Craisins For A Different Flavor) Dried Figs, Chopped
- 1 Egg
- 2 Tablespoon Extra-Virgin Olive Oil
- 1/2 Cup Heavy Cream
- 1/2 Cup Honey
- Kosher Salt
- 4 Tablespoon Lemon, Juice
- 1/2 Onion, Chopped
- Champion Chicken Seasoning
- 1 1/2 Teaspoon Finely Chopped Rosemary, Fresh
- 1 Pound Sweet Italian Sausage
- 3 Cups Water, Warm

Directions:

1. Mix figs, honey, lemon juice, and warm water. Cover with plastic wrap and let figs soften for 30 minutes. Strain the figs and reserve the liquid for glaze.

2. Heat olive oil over medium heat and sauté the onions with rosemary. Add the sausage. Cook until browned. Place into a large bowl, add the cornbread and figs. Season with Champion Chicken Seasoning. Stir. In a separate bowl, Stir together egg, heavy whipping cream, and chicken stock. Pour over the cornbread/fig mix and stir together. Set aside.

3. Rinse chickens and pat dry. Season liberally with Champion Chicken Seasoning, kosher salt and black pepper. Don't forget the cavity! Stuff cavities with Stuffing. Top each Chicken with 2 tablespoons butter.

4. Supply your smoker with wood pellets and follow the start-up procedure. Preheat the grill, with the lid closed, to 300° F. Place in a roasting tray and cook until internal temp reads 165°F.

5. While chickens cook, place the fig liquid, balsamic vinegar and butter over. Reduce to thicken and baste chickens with about 160°F or 10 minutes before finished. Rest for 10 minutes. Carve and serve!

Asian Chicken Sliders

Servings: 4
Cooking Time: 10 Minutes

Ingredients:

- 1½lb (680g) ground chicken, preferably a mix of breast and thigh meat
- 1 large egg, beaten
- ½ cup panko breadcrumbs or crushed chicharróns
- 2 scallions, trimmed, white and green parts finely minced
- 2 garlic cloves, peeled and finely minced
- ¼ cup loosely packed minced cilantro leaves
- 2 tbsp sambal oelek
- 1 tbsp light soy sauce
- 2 tsp peeled and minced fresh ginger
- 1 tsp coarse salt
- 1 tsp freshly ground black pepper
- vegetable oil
- for serving
- 8 slider buns
- reduced-fat mayo
- fresh baby arugula or spinach leaves
- pickled onions (optional)

Directions:

1. Supply your smoker with wood pellets and follow the start-up procedure. Preheat the grill, with the lid closed, to 450° F.

2. In a large bowl, combine all the ingredients except the vegetable oil. Wet your hands with cold water. Knead the mixture until it's somewhat sticky and the ingredients are incorporated. Form the mixture into 8 equal-sized patties. Lightly oil the patties on both sides with the oil.

3. Place the patties on the grate and grill until the internal temperature reaches 165°F (74°C), about 4 to 5 minutes per side.

4. Transfer each patty to the bottom half of each bun. Top with a dollop of mayo, a few arugula or spinach leaves, and drained pickled onions (if using). Top each slider with the top half of the bun. Run a knotted bamboo skewer through the top of each slider before serving.

Bbq Chicken Legs

Servings: 6
Cooking Time: 60 Minutes

Ingredients:
- 8 chicken drumsticks
- 2 Tablespoon Chicken Rub
- 1 Cup Apricot BBQ Sauce
- 1 Cup 'Que BBQ Sauce
- 1 Cup apple jelly, melted

Directions:
1. Pat drumsticks dry with a paper towel and season generously Traeger Chicken Rub.
2. Supply your smoker with wood pellets and follow the start-up procedure. Preheat the grill, with the lid closed, to 180° F.
3. Arrange the chicken legs on the grill grate and smoke for 30 minutes. Grill: 180 °F
4. Increase the grill temperature to 350 degrees F and cook for an additional 30 minutes. Grill: 350 °F
5. While the drumsticks are cooking, combine the two BBQ sauces and the jelly in a small sauce pan. Bring to a simmer over medium heat then set aside until ready to use.
6. Brush the BBQ sauce on the chicken legs. Cook for an additional 10 minutes, or until an instant-read meat thermometer inserted into the thickest part of the leg (but not touching the bone) reaches 165 degrees F. Enjoy! Grill: 350 °F Probe: 165 °F

Bbq Smoked Turkey Jerky

Servings: 4 - 6
Cooking Time: 120 Minutes

Ingredients:
- 2 Tablespoons Apple Cider Vinegar
- 2 Tablespoons (Any Kind) Barbecue Sauce
- 1 Tablespoon Quick Curing Salt
- ½ Cup Soy Sauce
- 4 Tablespoons Sweet Sweet Rib Rub
- 2 Pounds Boneless Skinless Turkey Breast
- ¼ Cup Water

Directions:
1. In a large bowl, combine the soy sauce, water, barbecue sauce, apple cider vinegar, quick curing salt, and 2 tablespoons of the Sweet Rib Rub. Whisk together until well combined and pour into a large, resealable plastic bag.
2. Using a sharp knife, slice the turkey into ¼ inch slices with the grain (this is easier if the meat is partially frozen). Trim off any fat, skin or connective tissue and discard.
3. Place the turkey slices into the plastic bag, seal, and massage the marinade into the turkey. Refrigerate for 24 hours.
4. Once the jerky is ready to go, remove the turkey from the refrigerator, drain the marinade and discard. Pat the turkey dry with paper towels and sprinkle all sides generously with the remaining Sweet Rib Rub.
5. Supply your smoker with wood pellets and follow the start-up procedure. Preheat the grill, with the lid closed, to 180° F. If you're using a sawdust or charcoal smoker, set it up for medium low heat.
6. Place the turkey slices directly onto the smoker grates and smoke for 2-4 hours, or until the jerky is chewy but still bends slightly.
7. Transfer the jerky to a resealable plastic bag while the jerky is still warm and allow it to sit at room temperature for 1 hour. Squeeze any air from the bag and place in the refrigerator. It will keep for several weeks.

Applewood-smoked Whole Turkey

Servings: 6-8
Cooking Time: 300 Minutes

Ingredients:
- 1 (10- to 12-pound) turkey, giblets removed
- Extra-virgin olive oil, for rubbing
- ¼ cup poultry seasoning
- 8 tablespoons (1 stick) unsalted butter, melted
- ½ cup apple juice
- 2 teaspoons dried sage
- 2 teaspoons dried thyme

Directions:
1. Supply your smoker with wood pellets and follow the start-up procedure. Preheat, with the lid closed, to 250°F.
2. Rub the turkey with oil and season with the poultry seasoning inside and out, getting under the skin.
3. In a bowl, combine the melted butter, apple juice, sage, and thyme to use for basting.
4. Put the turkey in a roasting pan, place on the grill, close the lid, and grill for 5 to 6 hours, basting every hour, until the skin is brown and crispy, or until a meat thermometer inserted in the thickest part of the thigh reads 165°F.
5. Let the bird rest for 15 to 20 minutes before carving.

Jalapeño- & Cheese-stuffed Chicken

Servings: 4
Cooking Time: 30 Minutes

Ingredients:
- 4 boneless, skinless chicken breasts, each about 6 to 8oz (170 to 225g)
- 8 strips of thin-sliced bacon
- for the filling
- 4oz (110g) light cream cheese, at room temperature

- ⅓ cup shredded pepper Jack or Cheddar cheese
- 2 jalapeños, destemmed, deseeded, and minced
- 2 tbsp reduced-fat mayo
- 1 tsp chili powder
- ½ tsp coarse salt

Directions:
1. Supply your smoker with wood pellets and follow the start-up procedure. Preheat the grill, with the lid closed, to 375° F.
2. In a large bowl, make the filling by combining the ingredients. Mix well.
3. Use a sharp, thin-bladed knife to cut a deep pocket in the side of each chicken breast, angling the knife toward the opposite side. (Don't cut all the way through.) Spoon ¼ of the cheese filling into the pocket of each breast and gently press the edges of the pocket together to enclose. Wrap 2 slices of bacon in a spiral pattern around each breast.
4. Place the chicken on the grate at an angle to the bars. Grill until the chicken is cooked through, the filling melts, and the bacon is golden brown, about 25 to 30 minutes.
5. Transfer the pockets to a platter. Let rest for 2 minutes before serving.

Smoked Whiskey Peach Pulled Chicken

Servings: 6-8
Cooking Time: 45 Minutes

Ingredients:
- 3-4 pound whole chicken
- 1 cup peach juice
- 1/4 cup whiskey
- 1/4 cup melted butter
- 1/4 cup Hey Grill Hey's Sweet BBQ Rub
- 1/2 cup Whiskey Peach BBQ sauce

Directions:
1. Supply your smoker with wood pellets and follow the start-up procedure. Preheat the grill, with the lid closed, to 225°F, using a mild fruit wood like a peach.
2. Remove any giblets or neck from inside of the chicken and pat dry.
3. In a jar, combine the peach juice, whiskey, and melted butter. Inject this mixture into your chicken in several spots. Be sure to inject in at least 3 different places in each breast, 2 places in the thighs, and 1 time in each leg.
4. Season your chicken generously on all sides with the Sweet BBQ Rub. Place in the middle of your grill and close the lid. Smoke for 45 minutes per pound of chicken.
5. Brush liberally with the whiskey peach BBQ sauce once the internal temperature of your meat reaches 150 degrees.
6. Check the temperature in both the thighs and the breasts and when your internal temperature reads consistently 160 degrees F, remove the chicken to a rimmed serving platter or baking sheet and cover tightly with foil to allow the chicken to come up to 165 degrees F and rest for 20 minutes.
7. Shred the chicken and set it onto your serving platter. Discard the carcass or save for homemade stock. Drizzle your smoked pulled chicken with more of the Whiskey Peach Barbecue Sauce and serve on toasted buns.

Italian Grilled Chicken Saltimbocca

Servings: 4
Cooking Time: 30 Minutes

Ingredients:
- 6 Chicken Breast
- olive oil
- Pork & Poultry Rub
- 6 Slices Prosciutto Slices
- 10 Sage, Leaves
- 1 Cup Parmesan cheese

Directions:
1. Supply your smoker with wood pellets and follow the start-up procedure. Preheat the grill, with the lid closed, to 350° F.
2. Using a sharp knife, carefully butterfly each chicken breast.
3. Oil the outside of each breast and season lightly with Traeger Pork and Poultry rub.
4. Wrap with a slice of prosciutto. Top with fresh sage and Parmesan cheese.
5. Arrange the chicken on a baking sheet or directly on the grill grate at an angle to the bars.
6. Roast until the chicken is cooked through, about 25 to 30 minutes or until it reaches an internal temperature of 165°F (75 C). Grill: 350 °F Probe: 165 °F
7. Let rest for 2 minutes before serving. Top with more fresh sage and parmesan. Enjoy!

Apple Bacon Lattice Turkey

Servings: 7
Cooking Time: 180 Minutes

Ingredients:
- 2 Apples
- Bacon
- 2 Celery, Stick
- (Parsley, Rosemary, Thyme) Herb Mix
- 1 Onion, Sliced
- Pepper
- Grills Champion Chicken Seasoning
- 1 Brined Turkey

Directions:

1. Supply your smoker with wood pellets and follow the start-up procedure. Preheat the grill, with the lid closed, to 300° F.
2. Be sure all the innards and giblets of the turkey have been removed.
3. Wash the external and internal parts of the turkey and pat the surface dry with a paper towel.
4. Slice fruit and veggies into large chunks and stuff inside turkey.
5. Liberally season the whole Turkey with Champion Chicken Seasoning.
6. Prep bacon into lattice design on a flexible cutting board. Flip onto top of turkey, covering the breasts.
7. Season with more Champion Chicken and black pepper
8. Season with more Champion Chicken and black pepper
9. Let the turkey rest for 30 minutes.

Buffalo Chicken Wraps

Servings: 4
Cooking Time: 20 Minutes

Ingredients:
- 2 teaspoons poultry seasoning
- 1 teaspoon freshly ground black pepper
- 1 teaspoon garlic powder
- 1 to 1½ pounds chicken tenders
- 4 tablespoons (½ stick) unsalted butter, melted
- ½ cup hot sauce (such as Frank's RedHot)
- 4 (10-inch) flour tortillas
- 1 cup shredded lettuce
- ½ cup diced tomato
- ½ cup diced celery
- ½ cup diced red onion
- ½ cup shredded Cheddar cheese
- ¼ cup blue cheese crumbles
- ¼ cup prepared ranch dressing
- 2 tablespoons sliced pickled jalapeño peppers (optional)

Directions:
1. Supply your smoker with wood pellets and follow the start-up procedure. Preheat, with the lid closed, to 350°F.
2. In a small bowl, stir together the poultry seasoning, pepper, and garlic powder to create an all-purpose rub, and season the chicken tenders with it.
3. Arrange the tenders directly on the grill, close the lid, and smoke for 20 minutes, or until a meat thermometer inserted in the thickest part of the meat reads 170°F.
4. In another bowl, stir together the melted butter and hot sauce and coat the smoked chicken with it.
5. To serve, heat the tortillas on the grill for less than a minute on each side and place on a plate.
6. Top each tortilla with some of the lettuce, tomato, celery, red onion, Cheddar cheese, blue cheese crumbles, ranch dressing, and jalapeños (if using).
7. Divide the chicken among the tortillas, close up securely, and serve.

Roasted Whole Chicken

Servings: 6-8
Cooking Time: 120 Minutes

Ingredients:
- 1 whole chicken
- 2 tablespoons olive oil
- 1 batch Chicken Rub

Directions:
1. Supply your smoker with wood pellets and follow the start-up procedure. Preheat the grill, with the lid closed, to 375°F.
2. Coat the chicken all over with olive oil and season it with the rub. Using your hands, work the rub into the meat.
3. Place the chicken directly on the grill grate and smoke until its internal temperature reaches 170°F.
4. Remove the chicken from the grill and let it rest for 10 minutes, before carving and serving.

Cider-brined Turkey

Servings: 8
Cooking Time: 180 Minutes

Ingredients:
- 1 whole turkey, about 12 to 14lb (4.5 to 5.4kg), thawed if frozen
- 1 white onion, peeled and sliced into quarters
- 1 apple, cut into wedges
- 2 celery stalks, sliced into 2-inch (5cm) pieces
- sprigs of fresh sage, rosemary, parsley, or thyme
- 8 tbsp unsalted butter, at room temperature
- coarse salt
- freshly ground black pepper
- for the brine
- 1 quart (1 liter) apple cider or apple juice
- 3 quarts (3 liters) cold distilled water
- ¾ cup coarse salt
- ½ cup light brown sugar or low-carb substitute
- 3 garlic cloves, peeled and smashed with a chef's knife
- 3 bay leaves

Directions:
1. In a large food-safe bucket, make the brine by combining the apple cider, water, salt, and brown sugar. Stir until the salt and sugar dissolve. Add the garlic and bay leaves. Submerge the turkey

in the brine. If it floats, place a resealable bag of ice on top. Refrigerate for at least 8 hours and up to 16 hours.

2. Supply your smoker with wood pellets and follow the start-up procedure. Preheat the grill, with the lid closed, to 350° F.

3. Remove the turkey from the brine and pat dry with paper towels. Discard the brine. Place the onion, apple, celery, and herbs in the main cavity. Tie the legs together with butcher's twine. Fold the wings behind the back. Rub the outside with butter. Lightly season with salt and pepper.

4. Place the turkey breast side up on a wire rack in a shallow roasting pan. Place the pan on the grate and roast the turkey until the internal temperature in the thickest part of a thigh reaches 165°F (74°C), about 2½ to 3 hours.

5. Transfer the turkey to a cutting board and let rest for 20 minutes. (Save the drippings to make from-scratch turkey gravy.) Carve the turkey and arrange the meat on a large platter before serving.

Chicken On A Throne

Servings: 6
Cooking Time: 75 Minutes

Ingredients:
- 1 can of low-carb beer or sugar-free dark-colored soda, about 12oz (350ml)
- 1 whole chicken, about 4lb (1.8kg)
- 3 tbsp barbecue rub, plus more

Directions:

1. Supply your smoker with wood pellets and follow the start-up procedure. Preheat the grill, with the lid closed, to 350° F.

2. Pour half the contents of the can into a glass for drinking. Set the half-full can aside.

3. Blot any juices off the chicken with paper towels. Sprinkle 2 teaspoons of the rub in the body and neck cavities. Sprinkle the remaining rub evenly on the outside. Tuck the wing tips behind the bird's back.

4. Carefully lower the chicken (body cavity side down) over the can. Place the chicken upright on its can on the grate. (For stability, pull the legs forward and rest them on the grate to essentially form a tripod.) Roast the chicken until the internal temperature in the thickest part of a thigh reaches 165°F (74°C), about 1 hour. (Check on your bird periodically to make sure it hasn't tipped over.) If it hasn't yet reached that temperature, continue cooking for about 15 minutes more.

5. Use heavy-duty insulated rubber gloves and tongs to carefully transfer the chicken to the kitchen. Let rest 5 minutes and then carefully ease the chicken off the can. Discard the can and its steaming liquid, being careful not to burn yourself. Carve the chicken and serve.

Roasted Christmas Goose

Servings: 8
Cooking Time: 120 Minutes

Ingredients:
- 5 1/2 Pound Goose
- 2 lemons
- 2 limes
- 2 Teaspoon salt
- 2 thyme sprigs
- 2 sage sprigs
- 1 Medium Apple, green
- 3 Tablespoon honey

Directions:

1. Supply your smoker with wood pellets and follow the start-up procedure. Preheat the grill, with the lid closed, to High heat.

2. Lightly score the breast and leg skin in a criss-cross pattern. This will help the fat to render down more quickly during cooking.

3. Grate the lemon and limes. Mix citrus zest with 2 teaspoons fine sea salt. Cut the lemons and lime into wedges.

4. Season cavity of the goose generously with salt, then rub the citrus mix well into the skin and sprinkle some inside the cavity.

5. Stuff goose with sage, thyme, lemons, limes and apples wedges. Place goose directly on the grill grate and cook for 40 minutes. Brush goose with honey and reduce temperature to 325°F.

6. Cook for 1-1/2 to 2 hours or until an instant read thermometer inserted in the thickest part of the breast reads 160°F. Grill: 325 °F Probe: 160 °F

7. Remove from grill, tent with foil and allow to rest for 30 minutes. Final internal temperature should be 165°F in the thickest part of the breast. Enjoy!

Bbq Turkey Drumsticks

Servings: 6
Cooking Time: 120 Minutes

Ingredients:
- 1/2 Tbsp Black Pepper
- 1 Tbsp Brown Sugar
- 1/2 Tsp Cayenne Pepper
- 1/2 Tbsp Coriander, Ground
- 1/2 Tbsp Granulated Garlic
- 1 Package, Approx 4 Lbs Honeysuckle White® Turkey Drumsticks
- 1 Tbsp Kosher Salt
- 2 Tbsp Olive Oil

Directions:

1. Supply your smoker with wood pellets and follow the start-up procedure. Preheat the grill, with the lid open, to 225° F. If using a gas or charcoal grill, set it up for low, indirect heat.
2. Place Honeysuckle White® Turkey Legs on a sheet tray, coat with olive oil, then season with a blend of salt pepper, cayenne, brown sugar, granulated garlic, and ground coriander.
3. Place turkey legs in the smoking cabinet and smoke for 1 ½ hours, checking the internal temperature after 1 hour.
4. Increase the temperature to 325°F, transfer the turkey legs to the bottom grill grate and cook for another 25 to 30 minutes, until the internal temperature reaches 170°F.
5. Remove turkey drumsticks from the grill, allow to rest for 10 minutes, then serve warm.

Smoked Honey Chicken Drumsticks

Servings: 4
Cooking Time: 30 Minutes

Ingredients:
- 1/2 Cup Apple Cider Vinegar
- 12 Chicken Drumsticks
- 2 Tablespoons Dijon Mustard
- 1/4 Cup Honey
- 1/4 Cup Ketchup
- 1 Tablespoon Sweet Heat Rub
- 1/2 Cup Soy Sauce

Directions:
1. Supply your smoker with wood pellets and follow the start-up procedure. Preheat the grill, with the lid open, to 225° F. Remove the wings from the marinade and place the drumsticks into the Buffalo Wing Rack.
2. Smoke for 60 minutes, or until a thermometer inserted into the thickest part of the drumstick registers at 170°F.
3. Turn the heat up to 350°F and cook for 5 to 10 minutes to make the skin crisp.
4. Remove from the smoker, serve immediately and enjoy!

Nashville Spiced Smoked Chicken

Servings: 6
Cooking Time: 40 Minutes

Ingredients:
- 6 drumsticks
- 1 quart Butter Milk
- 1 tbsp Louisiana Hot Sauce
- 1 tbsp Ground Cumin
- 1/2 tbsp Chili powder
- 1 tbsp Onion Powder
- 1 tbsp Garlic Powder
- 1/2 tbsp White Pepper
- 1 tbsp Red Cayenne Pepper
- 1 tbsp Black Pepper
- 2 tbsp Brown Sugar

Directions:
1. Soak wings overnight in marinade.
2. Remove chicken from marinade. Dry off chicken and wash off buttermilk.
3. Drizzle chicken with olive oil.
4. Apply dry rub to drumsticks by rubbing thoroughly.
5. Let drumsticks rest in dry rub for at least 30 minutes.
6. Supply your smoker with wood pellets and follow the start-up procedure. Preheat the grill, with the lid closed, to 325° F, using Apple Wood Pellets.
7. Cook chicken on 325 degrees for 30-40 minutes or until internal temperature reach 160 degrees F.
8. Let chicken rest for 10 minutes before serving.

Roasted Tin Foil Dinners

Servings: 4
Cooking Time: 25 Minutes

Ingredients:
- 4 boneless, skinless chicken breast
- Chicken Rub
- 1/2 Pound new potatoes, quartered
- 8 Ounce cremini mushrooms, cleaned and quartered
- salt and pepper
- 1/2 Pound green beans, ends trimmed
- 1 Medium lemon, cut into 3/4 inch slices

Directions:
1. Supply your smoker with wood pellets and follow the start-up procedure. Preheat the grill, with the lid closed, to 400° F.
2. Season chicken breast with salt, pepper and Traeger Chicken Rub. Place the potatoes, mushrooms and chicken in the middle of a large sheet of foil, season with more salt and pepper as needed, and wrap up tightly.
3. Place foil pack directly on the grill grate and cook for 15 minutes. Grill: 400 °F
4. Open up the foil pack and add green beans, lemon and additional salt and pepper, if needed. Wrap back up and return to the Traeger for an additional 10 minutes. Grill: 400 °F
5. Remove from the Traeger, open packet and enjoy!

Green Chile Chicken Enchiladas

Servings: 6
Cooking Time: 45 Minutes

Ingredients:
- 2 Cups Chicken, Shredded
- 1 (12 Oz) Package Colby Jack Cheese, Shredded
- 1 Enchilada Sauce, Can

- 1 Can Green Chile, Drained
- 1 Onion, Diced
- 1 Tablespoon Sweet Rib Rub
- 1 Cup Sour Cream
- 1 Package Flour Tortilla

Directions:

1. Supply your smoker with wood pellets and follow the start-up procedure. Preheat the grill, with the lid open, to 300° F.
2. In a bowl, mix - the chicken, green chiles, Sweet Heat seasoning, sour cream, diced onion, and half the bag of shredded cheese.
3. Place a large spoonful of the chicken mixture in the center of a tortilla and roll it up. Repeat with the remaining tortillas, then place in the baking pan, and pour the enchilada sauce over the tortilla pans. Top with the remainder of the shredded cheese.
4. Wrap the top of the pan tightly in aluminum foil and grill for 45 minutes or until the enchilada sauce is bubbly. Remove from the grill and serve.

Grilled Chipotle Chicken Skewers

Servings: 4
Cooking Time: 25 Minutes

Ingredients:

- BBQ Sauce
- 1 cup spicy BBQ sauce
- 3 chipotle peppers
- 1 Tbsp adobo sauce
- Skewers
- Olive oil
- 2 lbs boneless skinless chicken breasts
- 10 thick-cut bacon strips
- 1 large green bell pepper, cut into 3/4 to 1 inch pieces
- 1 medium red onion, peeled and cut into 3/4 to 1 inch pieces
- Bamboo skewers
- Garnish: freshly chopped garnish

Directions:

1. Supply your smoker with wood pellets and follow the start-up procedure. Preheat the grill, with the lid closed.
2. Soak the wooden skewers in water for at least 10 to 15 minutes before skewering to avoid them burning as much.
3. Add all ingredients for the sauce to a blender. Blend until they are combined well.
4. Cut chicken into 3/4-inch bite-sized pieces. Cut bacon into 3/4-inch strips.
5. Thread bacon (folding the bacon in half before skewering), chicken, peppers, and onion onto the skewers, alternating as you go.
6. Arrange the skewers on the grill grate and cook for 10 minutes, turning every few minutes. Baste the skewers with BBQ sauce on all sides. Continue to baste and turn the skewers every minute or so to caramelize.
7. The chicken is cooked through when it reaches an internal temperature of 165 °F. The bacon should be nice and crispy at this point.
8. Remove the skewers from the grill and sprinkle with freshly chopped parsley.

County Fair Turkey Legs

Servings: 4
Cooking Time: 90 Minutes

Ingredients:

- 4 turkey legs, each about 1lb (450g)
- for the brine
- ½ gallon (1.9 liters) distilled water
- ½ cup kosher salt
- ¼ cup light brown sugar or low-carb substitute
- 2½ tsp pink curing salt #1
- 1 tsp liquid smoke (optional)

Directions:

1. In a stockpot on the stovetop over medium-high heat, make the brine by combining the ingredients. Bring the mixture to a boil. Stir until the salts and sugar dissolve. Remove the pot from the stovetop and let the brine cool to room temperature. Cover and refrigerate until cool.
2. Submerge the turkey legs in the brine. If they float, place a resealable bag of ice on top. Refrigerate for 24 hours, turning from time to time so the legs cure evenly.
3. Supply your smoker with wood pellets and follow the start-up procedure. Preheat the grill, with the lid closed, to 325° F.
4. Remove the turkey legs from the brine and discard the liquid. Rinse the legs under cold running water and pat dry with paper towels.
5. Place the turkey legs on the grate and grill for 45 minutes. Turn and continue to cook until the turkey skin is nicely browned and the internal temperature in a leg reaches 170 to 175°F (77 to 79°C), about 45 minutes. (Turkey legs have a lot of connective tissue and they seem to turn out better when cooked to a slightly higher temperature.)
6. Remove the legs from the grill and serve warm or cold.

Smo-fried Chicken

Servings: 4-6
Cooking Time: 55 Minutes

Ingredients:

- 1 egg, beaten
- ½ cup milk
- 1 cup all-purpose flour
- 2 tablespoons salt

- 1 tablespoon freshly ground black pepper
- 2 teaspoons freshly ground white pepper
- 2 teaspoons cayenne pepper
- 2 teaspoons garlic powder
- 2 teaspoons onion powder
- 1 teaspoon smoked paprika
- 8 tablespoons (1 stick) unsalted butter, melted
- 1 whole chicken, cut up into pieces

Directions:
1. Supply your smoker with wood pellets and follow the start-up procedure. Preheat, with the lid closed, to 375°F.
2. In a medium bowl, combine the beaten egg with the milk and set aside.
3. In a separate medium bowl, stir together the flour, salt, black pepper, white pepper, cayenne, garlic powder, onion powder, and smoked paprika.
4. Line the bottom and sides of a high-sided metal baking pan with aluminum foil to ease cleanup.
5. Pour the melted butter into the prepared pan.
6. Dip the chicken pieces one at a time in the egg mixture, and then coat well with the seasoned flour. Transfer to the baking pan.
7. Smoke the chicken in the pan of butter ("smo-fry") on the grill, with the lid closed, for 25 minutes, then reduce the heat to 325°F and turn the chicken pieces over.
8. Continue smoking with the lid closed for about 30 minutes, or until a meat thermometer inserted in the thickest part of each chicken piece reads 165°F.
9. Serve immediately.

Cajun Brined Maple Smoked Turkey Breast

Servings: 4
Cooking Time: 180 Minutes

Ingredients:
- 1 Gallon water
- 3/4 Cup canning and pickling salt
- 3 Tablespoon minced garlic
- 3 Tablespoon dark brown sugar
- 2 Tablespoon Worcestershire sauce
- 2 Tablespoon Cajun seasoning
- 1 (5-6 lb) bone-in turkey breast
- 3 Tablespoon extra-virgin olive oil
- 2 Tablespoon Cajun seasoning

Directions:
1. In a large food safe container or bucket, combine all of the ingredients for the brine with 1 gallon water. Stir until the salt is dissolved.
2. Place the turkey breast in the brine and weigh it down to ensure it is fully submerged. Cover and brine in a refrigerator for 1 to 2 days.
3. Remove the turkey breast from the brine and pat dry. Drizzle with the olive oil using your hands to cover all areas of the bird. Season liberally with Cajun seasoning. Probe: 165 °F
4. Supply your smoker with wood pellets and follow the start-up procedure. Preheat the grill, with the lid closed, to 225° F.
5. Place the turkey breast directly on the grill grate, close the lid and cook for 3 hours. After 3 hours, increase the temperature to 425°F and continue to cook for another 30 minutes or until the internal temperature reads 165°F when a thermometer is inserted into the thickest part of the breast. Grill: 225 °F Probe: 165 °F
6. Remove the turkey breast from the grill and allow to rest for at least 15 minutes before slicing. Slice and serve. Enjoy!

Cornish Game Hen

Servings: 4
Cooking Time: 180 Minutes

Ingredients:
- 4 Cornish game hens
- Extra-virgin olive oil, for rubbing
- 2 teaspoons salt
- 1 teaspoon freshly ground black pepper
- 1 teaspoon celery seeds

Directions:
1. Supply your smoker with wood pellets and follow the start-up procedure. Preheat, with the lid closed, to 275°F.
2. Rub the game hens over and under the skin with olive oil and season all over with the salt, pepper, and celery seeds.
3. Place the birds directly on the grill grate, close the lid, and smoke for 2 to 3 hours, or until a meat thermometer inserted in each bird reads 170°F.
4. Serve the Cornish game hens hot.

Mandarin Chicken Breast

Servings: 4
Cooking Time: 25 Minutes

Ingredients:
- 1/2 Cup kosher salt
- 1/4 Cup brown sugar
- 1/2 Cup soy sauce
- 8 (6 oz) boneless, skinless chicken breasts
- sweet chili sauce
- steamed rice, for serving
- thinly sliced scallions, for garnish

Directions:
1. Pour 2 quarts water into a large mixing bowl, then add salt, brown sugar, and soy sauce. Stir until sugar and salt dissolve. Grill: 350 °F Probe: 170 °F

2. Submerge chicken breasts in the brine, cover and refrigerate for 2 hours.
3. Drain the chicken, rinse and pat dry with paper towels. Discard the brine.
4. Supply your smoker with wood pellets and follow the start-up procedure. Preheat the grill, with the lid closed, to 350° F.
5. Arrange the chicken breasts on the grill grate and cook for 25 to 30 minutes or until the internal temperature on an instant-read thermometer is 170°F. Turn chicken breasts once halfway through the cooking time. Grill: 350 °F Probe: 170 °F
6. Brush chicken breasts with the sweet chili sauce during the last few minutes of cooking.
7. Remove to a platter or plates and serve with steamed rice. Sprinkle the chicken breasts with thinly sliced scallions for garnish. Enjoy!

Chicken Corn Fritters

Servings: 8
Cooking Time: 45 Minutes

Ingredients:
- 2 Tsp Baking Powder
- 1 Cup Cheddar Jack Cheese, Shredded
- 1 1/2 Lbs Chicken Breast, Bone-In
- 3/4 Cup Corn Kernels, Drained
- 2 Eggs
- 3/4 Cup Flour
- 1 1/2 Tsp Lemon Juice
- 3 Tbsp Mayonnaise
- Olive Oil
- 2 Tbsp Parsley, Chopped
- 2 Tsp Champion Chicken Seasoning, Divided
- 1 Tbsp Scallions, Chopped
- 2 Tbsp Sour Cream
- 1 Yellow Onion, Chopped
- 1/3 Cup Milk

Directions:
1. Supply your smoker with wood pellets and follow the start-up procedure. Preheat the grill, with the lid open, to 425° F. If using a gas or charcoal grill, set it up for medium-high heat.
2. Remove skin from chicken breast. Drizzle chicken with olive oil, then season with 1 teaspoon of Champion Chicken. Place directly on grill grate, over indirect heat and grill for 25 minutes, until internal temperature is 165° F. Remove from the grill and rest for 10 minutes, then pull chicken.
3. In a mixing bowl combine onion, corn, eggs, parsley, milk, cheese, and pulled chicken.
4. In a separate mixing bowl, whisk together remaining teaspoon of Champion Chicken, flour and baking powder. Combine with the wet ingredients, then cover with plastic wrap and refrigerate for 2 hours.
5. Prepare dip: whisk together mayonnaise, sour cream, scallions, parsley, and lemon juice. Refrigerate until fritters are ready to serve.
6. Preheat griddle over medium-low flame.
7. Drizzle vegetable oil on the griddle, then add ¼ cup of fritter mixture to the griddle and cook 3 to 4 minutes per side, adding additional oil if needed.
8. Transfer fritters to a wire rack lined sheet tray. Allow to cool for 2 minutes, then serve warm with dip.

Delicious Smoked Turketta

Servings: 6
Cooking Time: 180 Minutes

Ingredients:
- 1 Shady Brook Farms® Turketta

Directions:
1. Supply your smoker with wood pellets and follow the start-up procedure. Preheat the grill, with the lid closed, to 250° F. If using a gas or charcoal grill, set it up for low, indirect heat.
2. Place the Turketta directly on the grill grate and smoke for 2½ to 3 hours, or until an internal temperature of 165°F is reached.

Buffalo Chicken Wings

Servings: 4
Cooking Time: 20 Minutes

Ingredients:
- 1 1/2 Tbsp Apple Cider Vinegar
- 1/2 Cup Butter, Unsalted, Cubed
- 1/4 Tsp Cayenne Pepper
- 3 Lbs Chicken Wings, Split
- 2 Tsp Chives, Minced (Garnish)
- 1/8 Tsp Garlic, Granulated
- 2/3 Cup Hot Pepper Sauce
- 1 Tbsp Ranch Seasoning
- To Taste, Sweet Heat Rub
- 1/2 Tsp Sweet Heat Rub (For Sauce)
- 1/4 Tsp Worcestershire Sauce

Directions:
1. Supply your smoker with wood pellets and follow the start-up procedure. Preheat the grill, with the lid open, to 425° F. If using a gas or charcoal grill, set it up for medium-high heat.
2. Place chicken wings in a large mixing bowl. Season with Sweet Heat.
3. Prepare sauce: Set a small cast iron pan or saucepan on the grill. Add the hot pepper sauce, apple cider vinegar, Worcestershire sauce, Sweet Heat, cayenne, and granulated garlic

to the skillet, and whisk to combine. When the sauce begins to bubble, remove the skillet from the grill and whisk in butter. Transfer the sauce to a mason jar.

4. Combine 1 cup of the buffalo sauce with ranch seasoning. Set aside.

5. Place wings on the grill and cook for 20 minutes, flipping and rotating every 3 to 5 minutes.

6. Remove wings from the grill when an internal temperature of 165° F is reached. Transfer to a mixing bowl, then pour sauce over. Toss to evenly coat. Garnish with fresh chives and serve warm.

Roasted Honey Bourbon Glazed Turkey

Servings: 8
Cooking Time: 240 Minutes

Ingredients:
- 1 Whole (18-20 lb) turkey
- 1/4 Cup Fin & Feather Rub
- 1/2 Cup bourbon
- 1/2 Cup honey
- 1/4 Cup brown sugar
- 3 Tablespoon apple cider vinegar
- 1 Tablespoon Dijon mustard
- salt and pepper

Directions:
1. Supply your smoker with wood pellets and follow the start-up procedure. Preheat the grill, with the lid closed, to 375° F. Truss the turkey legs together. Season the exterior of the bird and the cavity with Traeger Fin and Feather Rub.

2. Place the turkey directly on the grill grate and cook for 20-30 minutes at 375°F or until the skin begins to brown. Grill: 375 °F

3. After 30 minutes, reduce the temperature to 325°F and continue to cook until internal temperature registers 165°F when an instant read thermometer is inserted into the thickest part of the breast, about 3-4 hours. Grill: 325 °F Probe: 165 °F

4. For the Whiskey Glaze: Combine all ingredients in a small saucepan and bring to a boil. Reduce the temperature and let simmer 15-20 minutes or until thick enough to coat the back of a spoon. Remove from heat and set aside.

5. During the last ten minutes of cooking, brush the glaze on the turkey while on the grill and cook until the glaze is set, about 10 minutes. Remove from grill and let rest 10-15 minutes before carving. Enjoy! *Cook times will vary depending on set and ambient temperatures.

Grilled Hand Pulled Chicken

Servings: 4
Cooking Time: 90 Minutes

Ingredients:
- 2 Tablespoons Apple Cider Vinegar
- 1 Clove Garlic, Minced
- Juice Of Half Of A Lemon
- 1 Cup Mayo
- 1 Tablespoon Olive Oil
- ½ Teaspoon Paprika, Powder
- 2 Tablespoons Sugar
- 1, 3-4 Pound Chicken, Giblets Removed And Patted Dry
- 4 Tablespoons Champion Chicken Seasoning

Directions:
1. Supply your smoker with wood pellets and follow the start-up procedure. Preheat the grill, with the lid open, to 350° F.

2. In a large bowl, mix all the ingredients for the sauce together. Divide the sauce between two bowls and set aside.

3. On a clean, flat surface, lay your chicken breast side down. Using the kitchen shears, remove the spine and discard. Open the chicken up and flip the chicken over so that it lays breast side up. Press the breastbone down with the heel of your hand to flatten the chicken.

4. Generously rub the chicken with the olive oil and Champion Chicken. Place on the grill, skin-side up, on the grates. Grill for 1 ½ hours, basting with half the reserved sauce every 20 minutes, until the internal temperature reaches 175°F. Remove the chicken from the grill and cover loosely for 10 minutes.

5. Shred the chicken with forks and discard the skin and bones. Serve the chicken with the remaining white BBQ sauce.

Beer Chicken

Servings: 4
Cooking Time: 75 Minutes

Ingredients:
- 1 Beer, Can
- 1 Chicken, Whole
- Lemon Pepper Garlic Seasoning

Directions:
1. Supply your smoker with wood pellets and follow the start-up procedure. Preheat the grill, with the lid open, to 400° F.

2. Season the chicken all over with spices. Open the can of your favorite pop/beer and place the opening of the chicken over the can. Make sure that the chicken can stand upright without falling over. Place on your Grill and barbecue until the internal temperature reaching 165 degrees F (about an hour).

3. Remove from grill, slice and serve hot.

Dry Brine Traeger Turkey

Servings: 6
Cooking Time: 360 Minutes

Ingredients:
- 1 farm fresh turkey, any size
- 1 Teaspoon kosher salt per pound of turkey
- fresh thyme
- fresh rosemary
- fresh sage
- fresh parsley

Directions:
1. Make sure to plan ahead, this recipe requires multiple days of brine time.
2. Combine desired amounts of thyme, rosemary, sage and/or parsley with kosher salt. Rub kosher salt and spice mixture over entire surface of the turkey, including the cavity.
3. Place turkey in a bag or plastic wrap and seal tight. Place turkey in the fridge for 2 days. On day 3, take the turkey out of the bag or unwrap plastic wrap. Place the turkey back in the fridge, uncovered for 24 hours.
4. Supply your smoker with wood pellets and follow the start-up procedure. Preheat the grill, with the lid closed, to 180° F.
5. Place the turkey on grill, breast up. Smoke the turkey for 3 to 4 hours. Grill: 180 °F
6. After 3 to 4 hours, increase the grill temperature to 325°F and continue to cook turkey until it reaches an internal temperature of 165°F. Enjoy!

Cornish Game Hens

Servings: 4
Cooking Time: 60 Minutes

Ingredients:
- 4 Cornish game hens
- 4 Tablespoon butter, melted
- Chicken Rub
- 4 Sprig rosemary or sage, plus more for garnish

Directions:
1. Rinse the Cornish game hens under cold running water, inside and out. (Game hens do not usually come with giblets, but check the cavity for them before rinsing. If you find giblets, freeze them for chicken stock, if desired.)
2. Dry thoroughly with paper towels. Tuck the wings behind the backs and tie the legs together with butcher's string.
3. Rub the outside of each hen with the melted butter. Season with Traeger Chicken Rub. Slip a sprig of rosemary into the main cavity of each hen.
4. Supply your smoker with wood pellets and follow the start-up procedure. Preheat the grill, with the lid closed, to 375° F.
5. Roast the hens for 50 to 60 minutes, or until the juices run clear and the internal temperature of the thigh, when read on an instant-read meat thermometer, is 165°F. Grill: 375 °F Probe: 165 °F
6. Transfer the hens to a platter or plates and let rest for 5 minutes.
7. Garnish with a sprig of rosemary before serving. Enjoy!

Jamaican Jerk Chicken Quarters

Servings: 4
Cooking Time: 120 Minutes

Ingredients:
- 4 chicken leg quarters, scored
- ¼ cup canola oil
- ½ cup Jamaican Jerk Paste
- 1 tablespoon whole allspice (pimento) berries

Directions:
1. Supply your smoker with wood pellets and follow the start-up procedure. Preheat, with the lid closed, to 275°F.
2. Brush the chicken with canola oil, then brush 6 tablespoons of the Jerk paste on and under the skin. Reserve the remaining 2 tablespoons of paste for basting.
3. Throw the whole allspice berries in with the wood pellets for added smoke flavor.
4. Arrange the chicken on the grill, close the lid, and smoke for 1 hour to 1 hour 30 minutes, or until a meat thermometer inserted in the thickest part of the thigh reads 165°F.
5. Let the meat rest for 5 minutes and baste with the reserved jerk paste prior to serving.

Turkey & Bacon Kebabs With Ranch-style Dressing

Servings: 8
Cooking Time: 25 Minutes

Ingredients:
- 1½lb (680g) skinless turkey tenders or boneless, skinless turkey breasts, cut into 1-inch (2.5cm) chunks
- 8 strips of thick-cut bacon
- 12 fresh bay leaves (optional)
- for the dressing
- 1 cup reduced-fat mayo
- 1 cup light sour cream
- ½ cup buttermilk or whole milk, plus more
- 2 tbsp minced fresh parsley
- 2 tbsp minced fresh chives
- 1 tbsp minced fresh dill
- 2 tsp freshly squeezed lemon juice
- 1 tsp Worcestershire sauce

- 1 tsp garlic salt
- 1 tsp onion powder
- ½ tsp coarse salt, plus more
- ½ tsp freshly ground black pepper, plus more

Directions:
1. In a large bowl, make the dressing by whisking together the mayo, sour cream, and buttermilk until smooth. Whisk in the remaining ingredients. Pour half the mixture into a small bowl. Cover and refrigerate.
2. Add the turkey to the mixture remaining in the bowl and toss to coat thoroughly. If the dressing seems too thick (dip-like), add more buttermilk 1 tablespoon at a time. Cover and refrigerate for 2 to 4 hours.
3. Supply your smoker with wood pellets and follow the start-up procedure. Preheat the grill, with the lid closed, to 375° F.
4. Place the bacon on the grate and cook until some of the fat has rendered and the bacon begins to brown, about 15 minutes. Remove the bacon from the grill to cool. Cut the bacon into 1-inch (2.5cm) squares. Set aside.
5. Drain the tenders and discard any excess dressing. Alternate threading the turkey, bacon pieces, and 3 bay leaves on a bamboo skewer. Repeat the threading with 3 more skewers.
6. Place the kebabs on the grate and grill until the turkey is cooked through, about 4 to 5 minutes per side, turning as needed.
7. Transfer the skewers to a platter. Serve with the reserved dressing.

Bbq Chicken Thighs

Servings: 4
Cooking Time: 35 Minutes

Ingredients:
- 6 bone-in, skin-on chicken thighs
- salt and ground black pepper
- Big Game Rub

Directions:
1. Supply your smoker with wood pellets and follow the start-up procedure. Preheat the grill, with the lid closed, to 350° F.
2. While grill is heating, trim excess fat and skin from chicken thighs. Season with a light layer of salt and pepper then a layer of Traeger Big Game Rub.
3. Place chicken thighs on the grill grate and cook for 35 minutes. Check internal temperature, chicken is done at 165°F, but there is enough fat that they will stay moist at an internal temperature of 180°F and the texture is better. Grill: 350 °F Probe: 165 °F
4. Remove from the grill and let rest for 5 minutes before serving. Enjoy!

Smoked Maple Syrup Thanksgiving Turkey

Servings: 8
Cooking Time: 375 Minutes

Ingredients:
- 1 Cup Butter, Room Temp
- 1/2 Cup Maple Syrup
- 2 Tablespoons Champion Chicken Seasoning
- 1, (Pre-Brined) Turkey, Whole

Directions:
1. Supply your smoker with wood pellets and follow the start-up procedure. Preheat the grill, with the lid closed, to 250° F.
2. Combine the melted butter and maple syrup in a bowl. With the Marinade Injector, fill with the butter and syrup mixture and pierce the meat with the needle while pushing on the plunger, injecting the flavor. You want to inject the marinade into the thickest part of the breast, thigh, and wings.
3. Next, combine the room temperature butter and Champion Chicken seasoning and spread all over the turkey, making sure that you get it under the skin as well.
4. Place the turkey in an aluminum pan to catch all the drippings (this makes incredible gravy) and place on the grill.
5. When the breast and thigh meat of the turkey reaches 165°F to 170°F, remove from grill and let rest 15 minutes before carving. Happy Thanksgiving!

Grilled Chicken Wings

Servings: 6
Cooking Time: 50 Minutes

Ingredients:
- 4 Lbs Chicken Wings, Whole
- 1 Cup Cornmeal
- 2 Eggs
- 1 Cup Flour
- 2 Tbsp Champion Chicken Rub
- 1 Cup Milk

Directions:
1. Supply your smoker with wood pellets and follow the start-up procedure. Preheat the grill, with the lid open, to 300° F. If using a gas or charcoal grill, set it up for medium-low heat.
2. Place chicken wings on a sheet tray, then cut off the tip of each wing with a knife, or scissors. Pat dry with a paper towel.
3. In a mixing bowl, whisk together flour, cornmeal, and Champion Chicken. Set aside.
4. In another mixing bowl, whisk together milk and eggs. Set aside.
5. Form "breading" station: wings, egg wash, seasoned flour, sheet tray. Dunk each wing in egg wash, then coat in seasoned flour. Set aside on a sheet tray, while coating the remaining wings.
6. Place wings directly on the grill rack. Flip/rotate wings every 10 minutes for 45-55 minutes, until golden and "fried crisp."
7. Remove from the grill, rest for 10 minutes, then serve warm.

Smoked Drumsticks

Servings: 2-4
Cooking Time: 25 Minutes

Ingredients:
- 1 pound chicken drumsticks
- 2 tablespoons olive oil
- 1 batch Sweet and Spicy Cinnamon Rub

Directions:
1. Supply your smoker with wood pellets and follow the start-up procedure. Preheat the grill, with the lid closed, to 350°F.
2. Coat the drumsticks all over with olive oil and season with the rub. Using your hands, work the rub into the meat.
3. Place the drumsticks directly on the grill grate and smoke until their internal temperature reaches 170°F. Remove the drumsticks from the grill and serve immediately.

Oktoberfest Pretzel Mustard Chicken

Servings: 4
Cooking Time: 25 Minutes

Ingredients:
- 1/4 Pound pretzel sticks
- 3 Tablespoon Dijon mustard
- 3 Tablespoon apple cider or brown ale
- 1 Tablespoon honey
- 1 1/2 Teaspoon fresh thyme, plus more for garnish
- 4 boneless, skinless chicken breasts

Directions:
1. Pulse the pretzel sticks in a food processor or crush by hand in a resealable bag until they've turned into a powder the texture of panko breadcrumbs.
2. Transfer the crumbs to a wide, shallow bowl.
3. In separate shallow bowl, whisk mustard, beer or cider, honey and thyme together.
4. Spray a wire rack with cooking spray and place atop a sheet tray. Dip each chicken breast in the mustard mixture, then dredge in the pretzel crumbs to coat evenly and place on the wire rack. Spray the top of each chicken breast lightly with cooking spray.
5. Supply your smoker with wood pellets and follow the start-up procedure. Preheat the grill, with the lid closed, to 375° F.
6. Place the pan on the Traeger and bake for about 20 to 25 minutes, until the chicken breasts are fully cooked and register 165°F on an instant-read thermometer. Grill: 375 °F Probe: 165 °F
7. Let chicken rest for 5 minutes. Garnish with fresh thyme if desired. Enjoy!

Grilled Whole Chicken Stuffed Sausage And Apple

Servings: 4
Cooking Time: 90 Minutes

Ingredients:
- ¼ Tbsp Black Pepper
- 1 Tbsp Butter, Unsalted
- 1 Celery, Stalk
- ¾ Cup Chicken Broth
- ¼ Tbsp Dried Sage
- 1 ½ Cup Dry Stuffing, Unseasoned
- 1 Granny Smith Apple, Chopped
- 8 Oz. Italian Sausage, Casings Removed
- ½ Tbsp Olive Oil
- 3 Tbsp Tennessee Apple Butter Rub
- ¼ Tbsp Salt
- ¼ White Onion, Chopped
- ½ White Onion, Sliced
- 3-4 Lb. Whole Chicken

Directions:
1. Supply your smoker with wood pellets and follow the start-up procedure. Preheat the grill, with the lid open, to 400° F. If using a gas or charcoal grill, set it up for medium-high heat.
2. Meanwhile, rinse chicken thoroughly and dry with paper towel. Place sliced onion in cast iron pan and set chicken on top. Place stuffing inside chicken cavity. Sprinkle Tennessee Apple Butter seasoning all over chicken and rub into skin. Tuck wings under.
3. Transfer to pellet grill and cook for 45 minutes. Add 1 cup chicken stock to pan, rotate and cook an additional 30 minutes. Remove from grill when internal temperature reaches 165° F and there is even browning. Allow chicken to rest for 15 minutes, then carve and serve.

Savory Grilled Chicken Burrito Bowls

Servings: 4
Cooking Time: 20 Minutes

Ingredients:
- 1 Avocado
- 1 Can Black Beans, Rinsed And Drained
- 1 ½ Pounds Boneless Skinless Chicken Strips
- 1 Tablespoon Cilantro, Chopped
- 1 Can Corn Kernels, Drained
- Juice From 1 Lime
- ½ Lime Lime Juice
- 1 ½ Cups Long Grain White Rice
- 2 Tablespoons Olive Oil
- 2 Tablespoons Sweet Heat Rub
- ¼ Cup Salsa
- 1 Teaspoon Salt
- ½ Cup Shredded Mexican Blend Cheese
- ¼ Cup Sour Cream

Directions:
1. Supply your smoker with wood pellets and follow the start-up procedure. Preheat the grill, with the lid open, to 350° F. If using a gas or charcoal grill, set it up for medium heat.
2. Place the rice in a fine mesh sieve and rinse under cold water for 2-5 minutes, or until the water runs clear. Add the rice to a pot with 2 cups of water and 1 teaspoon of salt and bring to a boil on the stove top. Once the rice boils, drop the temperature to a simmer, place the pot lid on top securely, and let the rice cook for 20-25 minutes.
3. Once the time is up, remove the rice from the heat, and allow it to steam with the lid on for a further 10 minutes. Remove the lid from the rice, add the lime juice and cilantro, and fluff the rice with a fork. Set aside.
4. Grill the chicken for 5-7 minutes, or until the chicken reaches an internal temperature of 165°F and is golden and charred in some spots. Remove the chicken from the grill and allow it to rest for 5 minutes before slicing into bite sized pieces.
5. To assemble the burrito bowls: place a large scoop of cilantro lime rice into a bowl. Top with slices of grilled chicken, a scoop of black beans, a scoop of corn, salsa, cheese, sour cream, and avocado. Serve immediately.

Chicken Tenders

Servings: 2-4
Cooking Time: 80 Minutes

Ingredients:
- 1 pound boneless, skinless chicken breast tenders
- 1 batch Chicken Rub

Directions:
1. Supply your smoker with wood pellets and follow the start-up procedure. Preheat the grill, with the lid closed, to 180°F.
2. Season the chicken tenders with the rub. Using your hands, work the rub into the meat.
3. Place the tenders directly on the grill grate and smoke for 1 hour.
4. Increase the grill's temperature to 300°F and continue to cook until the tenders' internal temperature reaches 170°F. Remove the tenders from the grill and serve immediately.

Smoked Boneless Chicken Thighs

Servings: 8 - 10
Cooking Time: 55 Minutes

Ingredients:
- 2 Tbsp Ginger Root, Grated
- 5 Lbs. Boneless Skinless Chicken Thighs
- ⅔ Cup Brown Sugar
- 2 Cups Chicken Broth
- 1 Tsp Chinese Five-Spice Powder
- 5 Garlic Cloves, Minced
- ¼ Cup Honey
- 1 Tbsp Sweet Heat Rub
- ½ Cup Soy Sauce
- 1 Yellow Onion, Minced

Directions:
1. Supply your smoker with wood pellets and follow the start-up procedure. Preheat the grill, with the lid closed, to 225° F. If using a gas or charcoal grill, set it up for low heat.
2. Remove chicken from marinade and place on a metal sheet tray. Using a mesh strainer, strain the marinade directly into a cast iron skillet.
3. Place skillet with marinade and chicken on the grill. Allow chicken to smoke for 10 minutes, then increase grill temperature to 400°F.
4. Grill an additional 15 minutes. Make sure to stir marinade periodically. The sauce will begin to reduce and thicken as it cooks.
5. After 15 minutes, baste chicken thighs with marinade, then flip and baste the other sides. Grill an additional 15 minutes, then baste again.
6. Cook until glaze has caramelized and thickened, then remove from grill and serve hot.

Crispy Spiced Chicken Wings

Servings: 10
Cooking Time: 75 Minutes

Ingredients:
- 5 pounds of chicken wings (flats and drumettes)
- 2 1/2 Tablespoons baking powder
- 1 teaspoon salt

Directions:
1. Dry your chicken wings thoroughly on all sides with a paper towel. Place them in a zip-top bag.
2. Add the baking powder and salt to the wings, close the bag, and toss to coat evenly.
3. Supply your smoker with wood pellets and follow the start-up procedure. Preheat the grill, with the lid closed, to 250° F, using your favorite wood. Place the wings directly on the grill grates, close the lid, and smoke for 30 minutes.
4. Increase the heat in your smoker to 425 degrees F and continue cooking for 45 more minutes, or until the internal temperature of the wing reads 175 degrees F. You can rotate or flip the wings as needed to maintain even cooking and avoid any hot spots on the grill.
5. Remove the wing from the grill and serve. You can serve plain, toss in your favorite BBQ seasoning, or hot sauce.

Chicken Breast Calzones

Servings: 4
Cooking Time: 24 Minutes

Ingredients:
- 4 boneless, skinless chicken breasts, each about 6 to 8oz (170 to 225g)
- coarse salt
- freshly ground black pepper
- 1 cup good-quality Italian tomato sauce or marinara
- 4oz (110g) thinly sliced pepperoni or diced smoked ham
- 4oz (110g) provolone, fontina, or mozzarella cheese
- 8 fresh basil leaves
- 4 thin slices of prosciutto
- extra virgin olive oil
- freshly grated Parmesan cheese

Directions:
1. Supply your smoker with wood pellets and follow the start-up procedure. Preheat the grill, with the lid closed, to 425° F.
2. Use a sharp, thin-bladed knife to cut a deep pocket in the side of each breast, angling the knife toward the opposite side. (Don't cut all the way through.) Season the inside of each breast with salt and pepper. Add a couple spoonfuls of tomato sauce to each pocket. Add 1 ounce (25g) of pepperoni, 1 ounce (25g) of provolone, and 2 basil leaves.
3. Wrap each breast crosswise with a slice of prosciutto and then pin each breast closed with two toothpicks. Lightly brush the breasts with olive oil and season the outside with salt and pepper.
4. Place the breasts on the grate at an angle to the bars. Grill for 10 to 12 minutes and then turn with a thin-bladed spatula. Dust the tops with grated Parmesan. Continue to cook until the chicken is cooked through and the cheese has melted, about 10 to 12 minutes more.
5. Transfer the chicken to a platter. Let rest for 3 minutes and then remove the toothpicks. Serve immediately.

Cheese Chicken Cordon Bleu

Servings: 8
Cooking Time: 75 Minutes

Ingredients:
- 8 Chicken, Boneless/Skinless
- 1 Cup Mozzarella Cheese, Shredded
- Lemon Pepper Garlic Seasoning
- 8 Prosciutto, Sliced

Directions:
1. Supply your smoker with wood pellets and follow the start-up procedure. Preheat the grill, with the lid closed, to 250° F.
2. Pound each chicken breast with a mallet or cast iron pan so that it's about ½ inch thick.
3. On a piece of prosciutto, sprinkle mozzarella cheese and roll up. Place in the middle of a chicken breast and wrap the chicken around the prosciutto roll. Sprinkle with Lemon Pepper seasoning.
4. Smoke for an hour to 75 minutes, or until internal temperature reaches 165 degrees F.

Chicken Nachos

Servings: 6-8
Cooking Time: 10 Minutes

Ingredients:
- 1 Can Black Beans, Rinsed And Drained
- 1 Cup Cheddar Cheese, Shredded
- 2 Cups Chicken, Diced
- (If Desired) Cilantro
- 1 Can Corn Kernels, Drained
- (If Desired) Pickled Jalapeno Peppers
- 1/2 Tablespoon Champion Chicken Seasoning
- 1/2 Red Onion, Diced
- 1/2 Cup Salsa
- 1/4 Cup Sour Cream

Directions:
1. On a large sheet pan, spread out half the tortilla chips, then cover with half the shredded cheese and one cup of chicken. Sprinkle with half of Champion Chicken seasoning. Top with the rest of the tortilla chips, cheese, chicken and remaining seasoning.
2. Supply your smoker with wood pellets and follow the start-up procedure. Preheat the grill, with the lid closed, to 350° F. Grill for 5-7 minutes, or until the cheese is melted and bubbly and everything is warmed all the way through. Remove the pan from the grill.
3. Top the nachos with the black beans, corn, diced red onion, sour cream, cilantro and pickled jalapenos. Serve and enjoy!

Lemon & Herb Chicken

Servings: 3-4
Cooking Time: 75 Minutes

Ingredients:
- 1 roaster chicken, about 4lb (1.8kg), preferably organic
- 1 large sweet onion, peeled and sliced lengthwise into 8 wedges
- ½ cup chicken stock or broth
- sprigs of fresh rosemary, thyme, parsley, tarragon, or chives (or a mix)
- lemon wedges
- for the butter
- 4 tbsp unsalted butter, at room temperature
- 1 garlic clove, peeled and finely minced
- 2 tbsp chopped fresh herbs, such as rosemary, thyme, parsley, tarragon, or chives (or a mix)

- 2 tsp lemon zest
- 2 tsp freshly squeezed lemon juice
- ½ tsp coarse salt
- ½ tsp freshly ground black pepper

Directions:
1. Supply your smoker with wood pellets and follow the start-up procedure. Preheat the grill, with the lid closed, to 400° F.
2. In a small bowl, make the herb butter by combining the ingredients.
3. Place the chicken on a rimmed sheet pan and tuck the lemon rinds from the butter into the main cavity. Rub the outside of the chicken with the herb butter. (Reserve any remainder.) Tuck the wings behind the back and tie the legs together with butcher's twine. Place the onion wedges in a shallow roasting pan to help form a natural rack for the chicken. (Alternatively, place several large carrots, trimmed and peeled, on the bottom of the pan.) Place the chicken on the onion rack. Add the chicken stock and any remaining herbed butter and lemon juice.
4. Place the roasting pan on the grate, roast the chicken for 30 minutes, and then baste with the juices from the bottom of the pan. Baste every 15 minutes until the chicken is golden brown and the internal temperature reaches 165°F (74°C), about 45 minutes more.
5. Transfer the chicken to a cutting board and let rest for 10 minutes. Carve the chicken and place the slices on a platter with a deep well. Spoon some of the juices over the chicken. Scatter fresh herbs over the top. Serve with the lemon wedges.

Grilled Parmesan Chicken Wings

Servings: 4
Cooking Time: 25 Minutes

Ingredients:
- 4 Tbsp Butter
- 4 Lbs Chicken Wings, Trimmed And Patted Dry
- 4 Garlic Cloves, Chopped
- 2 Tbsp Olive Oil
- 1/2 Cup Parmesan Cheese, Grated
- 2 Tbsp Parsley, Chopped
- Champion Chicken Seasoning

Directions:
1. Lay chicken wings out on a sheet tray, blot with paper towel, then season with Champion Chicken.
2. Supply your smoker with wood pellets and follow the start-up procedure. Preheat the grill, with the lid open, to 400° F. If using a gas or charcoal grill, set it up for medium-high heat.
3. Transfer wings to grill and cook for 20 to 25 minutes, turning every 5 minutes, until lightly browned. Remove wings from the grill and set on a sheet tray. Place in the smoking cabinet to keep warm while preparing the garlic butter.
4. Melt butter and olive oil in a cast iron skillet, then add garlic and simmer until fragrant. Remove from the grill.
5. Transfer chicken wings to a large bowl and pour garlic butter over the wings. Add cheese and parsley, then toss well to coat. Serve warm with additional sprinkling of parmesan cheese.

Roasted Beer Can Chicken

Servings: 4
Cooking Time: 60 Minutes

Ingredients:
- 1 Whole (3-5 lb) chicken
- Chicken Rub
- 1 Can beer

Directions:
1. Season chicken generously with Traeger Chicken Rub, including inside the cavity.
2. Tuck the wing tips back.
3. Supply your smoker with wood pellets and follow the start-up procedure. Preheat the grill, with the lid closed, to 350° F.
4. Open the can of beer and set the chicken on top of the beer. Make sure all but the bottom 1-1/2 inch of the beer can is in the cavity of the chicken. Tip: you can also place the beer can directly on the grill grates, then place the chicken on top.
5. Place the entire chicken and beer can directly on the grill grate. Cook for 60 to 75 minutes, or until the internal temperature registers 165°F in the thickest part of the breast. Grill: 350 °F Probe: 165 °F
6. Remove from the grill and onto a sheet tray and let rest 5 to 10 minutes. Before carving, lay the bird on its back and remove the beer can. Carve and enjoy!

Traeger Mandarin Wings

Servings: 2
Cooking Time: 30 Minutes

Ingredients:
- 1 Bottle (12 oz) mandarin orange sauce
- Beef Rub
- Chicken Rub
- 2 Pound chicken wings, flats and drumettes separated

Directions:
1. Coat chicken wings with mandarin sauce. Sprinkle Traeger Beef Rub and Traeger Chicken Rub onto wings. Marinate for at least 30 minutes.
2. Supply your smoker with wood pellets and follow the start-up procedure. Preheat the grill, with the lid closed, to 350° F.
3. Place wings directly on the grill grate and cook for 30 minutes. Enjoy! Grill: 350 °F Probe: 165 °F

Juicy Jerk Chicken Kebabs

Servings: 4
Cooking Time: 12 Minutes

Ingredients:

- 1 Tablespoon All Spice, Ground
- 2 Lbs Chicken, Boneless/Skinless
- 1 Tablespoon Cinnamon, Ground
- 1/4 Cup Extra-Virgin Olive Oil
- 3 Garlic, Cloves
- 2 Inch Piece Ginger, Fresh
- 3 Green Onion
- 1 Lime, Juiced
- 1 Tablespoon Nutmeg, Ground
- 1 Cup Orange Juice, Fresh
- Pepper
- 1 Red Onion, Chopped
- Salt
- Skewers
- 1/4 Cup Soy Sauce
- 1/4 Cup Thyme, Fresh Sprigs

Directions:

1. Soak the bamboo skewers in water for about 30 minutes (the longer the better).
2. In a food processor, combine orange juice, oil, soy sauce, thyme, allspice, nutmeg, cinnamon, garlic, onions, ginger, lime juice, salt and pepper. Puree until smooth.
3. In a large resealable bag, pour all but 1/4 cup of the mixture in along with the sliced up chicken breasts. Seal the bag and marinate in the fridge for 2 - 3 hours.
4. Supply your smoker with wood pellets and follow the start-up procedure. Preheat the grill, with the lid open, to 450° F. Skewer the chicken and grill for about 7 minutes. Flip and continue grilling for about 5 minutes, or until the chicken is cooked through and grill marks appear. Serve with the remaining 1/4 cup of marinade.

Chicken Egg Rolls With Buffalo Sauce

Servings: 4
Cooking Time: 75 Minutes

Ingredients:

- 1/4 Cup Bleu Cheese, Crumbled
- 1/4 Cup Buffalo Sauce
- 1 Lb Chicken Breasts - Boneless, Skinless
- 4 Oz Cream Cheese, Softened
- 8 Egg Roll Wrappers
- 1/2 Jalapeno Pepper, Minced
- Pinch Sweet Heat Rub
- 1/4 Red Bell Pepper, Chopped
- 4 Scallion, Sliced Thin
- 1/4 Cup Sour Cream
- 2 Cups Vegetable Oil

Directions:

1. Supply your smoker with wood pellets and follow the start-up procedure. Preheat the grill, with the lid open, to 200° F. If using a gas or charcoal grill, set it up for low, indirect heat.
2. Season chicken breasts with Sweet Heat Rub, then place on the grill. Smoke for 1 hour, then remove from the grill, cool, shred, and set aside.
3. Prepare the filling: In a mixing bowl, use a hand mixer to blend cream cheese, bleu cheese, Buffalo sauce and sour cream.
4. Fold in scallions, jalapeño, red bell pepper, and shredded chicken.
5. Prepare egg rolls: Lay an egg roll wrapper on a flat surface and add 3 tablespoons of filling to the middle.
6. Fold the bottom of the wrapper over the top of the filling, then fold over each side. Brush the top point of the wrapper with warm water, then roll the wrapper tight. Transfer to a tray while filling the remaining wrappers.
7. Increase the temperature of the grill to 425°F, then set a cast iron Dutch oven on the grill. Add vegetable oil and heat for 5 minutes.
8. Place 3 egg rolls in heated oil and fry until golden, 1 to 2 minutes per side.
9. Transfer to a wire rack to cool, then fry the remaining egg rolls, in batches.
10. Cool egg rolls for 2 minutes, then slice in half and serve warm with celery sticks and extra Buffalo sauce for dipping.

Traditional Smoked Thanksgiving Turkey

Servings: 8
Cooking Time: 240 Minutes

Ingredients:

- 1/2 Pound butter
- 6 Clove garlic, minced
- 8 Sprig fresh thyme
- 1 Sprig fresh rosemary
- 1 Tablespoon cracked black pepper
- 1/2 Tablespoon kosher salt
- 20 Pound Turkey, Whole Birds (18-20 lbs)

Directions:

1. Supply your smoker with wood pellets and follow the start-up procedure. Preheat the grill, with the lid closed, to 300° F.
2. In a small bowl, combine softened butter with minced garlic, thyme leaves, chopped rosemary, black pepper and kosher salt.
3. Prep the turkey by separating the skin from the breast creating a pocket to stuff the butter-herb mixture in. Cover the entire breast with 1/4" thickness of butter mixture.

4. Season the whole turkey with kosher salt and black pepper. Optional: Stuff turkey cavity with Traditional Stuffing recipe. When ready to cook, set the grill temperature to 300°F and preheat, lid closed for 15 minutes.
5. Place turkey on the grill and smoke for 3-4 hours. Check the internal temperature, the desired temperature is 175°F in the thigh next to the bone, and 160°F in the breast. Turkey will continue to cook once taken off grill to reach a final temperature of 165°F in the breast. Grill: 300 °F Probe: 160 °F
6. Let rest for 10-15 minutes before serving. Enjoy!

Savory Jerk Chicken Wings

Servings: 4
Cooking Time: 20 Minutes

Ingredients:
- 1 Tsp Allspice, Ground
- 3 Lbs Chicken Wings, Split
- 1/2 Tsp Cinnamon, Ground
- 4 Garlic Cloves, Smashed
- 2 Tsp Ginger, Grated
- 1 Habanero Pepper, Chopped
- 2 Tbsp Honey
- 2 Tbsp Lemon Juice
- 1/3 Cup Lime Juice
- 1/2 Tsp Nutmeg, Ground
- 1/2 Cup Olive Oil
- 1/4 Cup Poblano Pepper, Chopped
- 1 Tbsp Tamari
- 2 Tsp Thyme, Dried
- 1/2 Cup Yellow Onion, Chopped

Directions:
1. Add chicken to a large resealable plastic bag.
2. In the bowl of a food processor, add the garlic, onion, ginger, peppers, tamari, honey, lime juice, lemon juice, thyme, allspice, cinnamon, nutmeg, and oil. Process on low for 1 minute, then transfer marinade to the bag. Seal the bag and place in the refrigerator for at least 2 hours, up to overnight.
3. Supply your smoker with wood pellets and follow the start-up procedure. Preheat the grill, with the lid open, to 425° F. If using a gas or charcoal grill, set it up for medium-high heat.
4. Remove wings from the marinade, and discard remaining marinade. Place wings on the grill and cook for 15 to 20 minutes, flipping every 5 minutes, until an internal temperature of 165 F is reached.
5. Remove wings from the grill and serve warm.

Italian Grilled Barbecue Chicken Wings

Servings: 4
Cooking Time: 18 Minutes

Ingredients:
- 1 cup KRAFT Zesty Italian Dressing
- 2 pounds chicken wings/drummettes
- 1/2 cup barbecue sauce

Directions:
1. Pour dressing over chicken in large bowl; toss to coat.
2. Refrigerate at least 30 minutes to marinate.
3. Supply your smoker with wood pellets and follow the start-up procedure. Preheat the grill, with the lid closed, to 400° F. Drain chicken; discard marinade.
4. Grill chicken 8 minutes on each side or until done.
5. Brush with barbecue sauce; grill for another 2 minutes.
6. Remove from grill and serve.

Lemon Cajun Chicken Carbonara

Servings: 2
Cooking Time: 20 Minutes

Ingredients:
- 2 Slices Thick-Cut Bacon
- 1 Tbsp Cajun Seasoning
- 8 Oz. Chicken Breast
- 4 Egg, Yolk
- 1 Tbsp Garlic Clove, Minced
- 1 ¼ Cup Heavy Cream
- 2 Tbsp + 1 Tbsp Divided Italian Parsley
- 1 ½ Tbsp Divided Olive Oil
- ½ Cup Grated Parmesan Cheese
- ½ Tbsp Hickory Bacon Seasoning
- ¼ Tbsp Red Chili Flakes
- 1 Tbsp Scallions
- ½ Lb. Spaghetti

Directions:
1. Supply your smoker with wood pellets and follow the start-up procedure. Preheat the grill, with the lid open, to 400° F. If using a gas or charcoal grill, set the temp to medium-high heat. In a medium bowl, combine chicken, Hickory Bacon Seasoning, Cajun seasoning, and ½ tablespoon of olive oil. Toss to combine. Set aside or place in a bag and marinate in the refrigerator for 30 minutes to 1 hour.
2. Place tenders on preheated grill and cook for 3 minutes per side. Remove from grill and place on a cutting board to rest for 5 minutes. Slice thinly on the diagonal and set aside.
3. In a large stock pot, boil pasta per package instructions. Drain and set aside.
4. In a large skillet heat 1 tablespoon of oil over medium heat. Sauté bacon, stirring frequently, for 3 minutes or until crisp. Add garlic and cook for one minute. Lower heat to low and add in drained pasta. Using tongs, gently toss pasta to coat in oil and bacon.

5. In a mixing bowl, whisk together heavy cream, parmesan, egg yolks, and 2 tablespoons of parsley. Slowly pour over pasta, continuously stirring, as to not scramble eggs. After 2 minutes, the sauce will thicken. Add in chicken and lemon zest, and gently stir another minute. Transfer to serving dishes and garnish with additional parsley and red chili flakes.

Wild West Wings

Servings: 4
Cooking Time: 60 Minutes

Ingredients:
- 2 pounds chicken wings
- 2 tablespoons extra-virgin olive oil
- 2 packages ranch dressing mix (such as Hidden Valley brand)
- ¼ cup prepared ranch dressing (optional)

Directions:
1. Supply your smoker with wood pellets and follow the start-up procedure. Preheat, with the lid closed, to 350°F.
2. Place the chicken wings in a large bowl and toss with the olive oil and ranch dressing mix.
3. Arrange the wings directly on the grill, or line the grill with aluminum foil for easy cleanup, close the lid, and smoke for 25 minutes.
4. Flip and smoke for 20 to 35 minutes more, or until a meat thermometer inserted in the thickest part of the wings reads 165°F and the wings are crispy. (Note: The wings will likely be done after 45 minutes, but an extra 10 to 15 minutes makes them crispy without drying the meat.)
5. Serve warm with ranch dressing (if using).

Marinated Grilled Honey Chicken Wings

Servings: 4-6
Cooking Time: 30 Minutes

Ingredients:
- 1/2 Bottle Beer, Any Brand
- 2 Lbs Chicken Wings, Whole
- 2 Tablespoon Honey
- 1 Tablespoon Sweet Heat Rub
- 2 Tablespoon Rice Wine Vinegar
- 1/2 Tablesoon Sesame Oil
- 1/4 Cup Soy Sauce
- 1 Tablespoon Sriracha Hot Sauce

Directions:
1. In a large glass or plastic bowl, combine the beer, soy sauce, honey, rice wine vinegar, sriracha, sesame oil and Sweet Heat Seasoning. Whisk well to combine.
2. Add the chicken wings to the marinade and toss well to combine. Cover with plastic wrap and refrigerate for 2 hours and up to 24 hours.
3. Remove chicken wings from refrigerator, drain marinade and pat dry. Supply your smoker with wood pellets and follow the start-up procedure. Supply your smoker with wood pellets and follow the start-up procedure. Preheat the grill, with the lid open, to 350° F. Place the wings on a grill pan and grill for 20-25 minutes, or until the wings' internal temperature is 165F. Remove from the grill, serve and enjoy!

Smoked Beer Brine Hens

Servings: 4
Cooking Time: 150 Minutes

Ingredients:
- 2 Tbsp Ales Pepper
- 12 Cups Beer Brine
- 2 Cornish Game Hens
- 2 Lemons
- 6 Rosemary Sprigs
- Salt & Freshly Ground Black Pepper
- 12 Thyme Sprigs

Directions:
1. Supply your smoker with wood pellets and follow the start-up procedure. Preheat the grill, with the lid open, to 300° F. (I have found the setting the grill at 300 will keep the top smoker temp between 200°F and 215°F, this could vary depending on the air temp and general weather conditions. You want to keep the upper smoking cabinet between 200°F and 215°F) If you're using a vertical smoker, set temp to 200°F.
2. Stuff your hens with the rosemary, thyme, and lemons. Coat the skin with the ales pepper and freshly ground black pepper.
3. Truss your hens and tie a small loop at the legs so you can hang your birds. Hang them in the smoker and insert a probe thermometer, cook to an internal temp of 155°F.
4. Remove the hens to rest. Final temp should be 160°F.
5. Serve these with some great creamed kale or charred asparagus.

Green Goddess Chicken Legs

Servings: 4
Cooking Time: 40 Minutes

Ingredients:
- 2 Pound chicken legs
- 2 Cup Prepared "Green Goddess" Dressing
- 1/4 Cup parsley, chopped
- 1 Tablespoon paprika

Directions:

1. Place the chicken legs in a large resealable plastic bag. Combine the Green Goddess dressing as well as the parsley and paprika. Pour over the chicken legs. Refrigerate for 2 to 8 hours.
2. Supply your smoker with wood pellets and follow the start-up procedure. Preheat the grill, with the lid closed, to 350° F. Drain the chicken legs. Arrange the legs directly on the grill grate and grill, turning once, for 40 to 50 minutes, or until the legs are golden brown and cooked through. Serve at once. Grill: 350 °F

Baked Prosciutto-wrapped Chicken Breast With Spinach And Boursin

Servings: 4
Cooking Time: 60 Minutes

Ingredients:
- 1 Tablespoon olive oil
- 10 Ounce baby spinach leaves, washed and dried
- 2 Whole packs (5.2 oz) Boursin Garlic & Fine Herbs Gournay Cheese
- 2 Pound boneless, skinless chicken breasts
- Pork & Poultry Rub
- 14 Slices prosciutto

Directions:
1. Heat olive oil in a medium sauté pan. Add spinach and sauté until wilted, about 3 to 5 minutes. Transfer to a strainer and squeeze out excess liquid. Place spinach and cheese in a medium bowl. Mix well and set aside.
2. Butterfly each chicken breast and open like a book. Cover with plastic wrap and using a meat mallet, pound out thinly. Season the chicken with Pork & Poultry Rub.
3. Lay a sheet of plastic wrap about 2 feet long down on a flat, clean surface. Lay down slices of prosciutto, slightly overlapping and double-wide. Place the chicken on top of the prosciutto leaving a 1-1/2 inch border.
4. Spread the spinach mixture on top of the chicken. Roll it up tightly to create a log. Tie off the ends tightly and transfer to the refrigerator. Refrigerate 2 to 3 hours or overnight.
5. Supply your smoker with wood pellets and follow the start-up procedure. Preheat the grill, with the lid closed, to 300° F.
6. Carefully remove the plastic wrap and place directly on the grill grate. Bake for an hour and a half, or until the internal temperature reaches 162°F to 165°F. Remove from Traeger and let rest for 10 minutes before slicing. Enjoy! Grill: 300 °F Probe: 162 °F

Smoked Deviled Eggs

Servings: 4
Cooking Time: 30 Minutes

Ingredients:
- 7 hard boiled eggs, cooked and peeled
- 3 Tablespoon mayonnaise
- 3 Teaspoon diced chives
- 1 Teaspoon brown mustard
- 1 Teaspoon apple cider vinegar
- hot sauce
- salt and pepper
- 2 Tablespoon cooked bacon, crumbled
- paprika

Directions:
1. Supply your smoker with wood pellets and follow the start-up procedure. Preheat the grill, with the lid closed, to 180° F.
2. Place cooked and peeled eggs directly on the grill grate and smoke eggs for 30 minutes. Grill: 180 °F
3. Remove from grill and allow eggs to cool. Slice the eggs lengthwise and scoop the egg yolks into a gallon zip top bag.
4. Add mayonnaise, chives, mustard, vinegar, hot sauce, salt, and pepper to the bag. Zip the bag closed and, using your hands, knead all of the ingredients together until completely smooth.
5. Squeeze the yolk mixture into one corner of the bag and cut a small part of the corner off. Pipe the yolk mixture into the hard boiled egg whites. Top the deviled eggs with crumbled bacon and paprika. Chill until ready to serve. Enjoy!

Loaded Chicken Fries

Servings: 4
Cooking Time: 20 Minutes

Ingredients:
- 8 Slices Bacon, Cooked And Diced
- 1 12 Oz Bag Cheese, Shredded
- 1 Bag Fries, Frozen
- 2 Tablespoons Green Onions, Diced
- ¼ Cup White Barbecue Sauce

Directions:
1. Supply your smoker with wood pellets and follow the start-up procedure. Preheat the grill, with the lid open, to 400° F.
2. Bake the fries on the baking sheet in your according to the manufacturer's instructions. Once the fries are done, remove them from the grill and reduce the temperature to 350°F.
3. Top the fries with the cheese, chicken and bacon. Place the fries back on the grill and cook for another 5-7 minutes, or until the chicken is warmed through and the cheese is melted. Remove the fries from the grill.
4. Top the fries with the white barbecue sauce and green onions and serve immediately.

Grilled Greek Chicken With Garlic & Lemon

Servings: 4
Cooking Time: 60 Minutes

Ingredients:
- 2 Whole Roasting Chicken, 3.5-4lbs, each cut into 8 pieces
- 2 Whole lemons, quartered
- Cup extra-virgin olive oil
- 4 Clove garlic, minced
- 1 1/2 Tablespoon Oregano, fresh
- 1 As Needed Chicken Rub
- 1 Cup Broth, chicken

Directions:
1. Arrange the chicken pieces in a single layer in a large roasting pan. Squeeze the juice from each piece of lemon over the chicken, catching any seeds in your fingers. Tuck the lemon rinds in with the chicken. Drizzle the olive oil over all.
2. Sprinkle the garlic over the chicken. Dust the chicken with the fresh oregano, and season it generously with the Traeger Chicken rub, or salt and black pepper. Pour the chicken broth into the pan.
3. Supply your smoker with wood pellets and follow the start-up procedure. Preheat the grill, with the lid closed, to 350° F.
4. Roast the chicken for an hour, or until the juices run clear or the internal temperature reaches 165°F on an instant-read meat thermometer. Grill: 350 °F Probe: 165 °F
5. Transfer to a platter or plates and spoon some of the juices on top. Let rest 3 minutes before serving. Enjoy!

Peanut Butter Chicken Wings

Servings: 4
Cooking Time: 35 Minutes

Ingredients:
- 1 Tsp Black Peppercorns, Ground
- 2 Tbsp Brown Sugar
- 4 Lbs Chicken Wings, Trimmed And Patted Dry
- 2 Tbsp Honey
- 1/4 Cup Peanut Butter
- 10 Oz Peanuts, Whole
- 2 Tsp Sweet Rib Rub
- 1/2 Red Onion, Minced
- 1/2 Cup Strawberry Preserves
- 1 Tbsp Thai Chili Sauce
- 1/4 Cup Worcestershire Sauce

Directions:
1. Place chicken wings in a 9 x13 glass baking dish. Pour mixture over chicken, cover with plastic wrap, and refrigerate for 2 hours.
2. Supply your smoker with wood pellets and follow the start-up procedure. Preheat the grill, with the lid open, to 400° F. Preheat griddle to medium-low flame. If using a gas or charcoal grill, set it to medium-high heat.
3. Place wings directly on grill grate, over indirect heat, and cook for 20 to 25 minutes, rotating wings every 5 minutes.
4. Meanwhile, place shelled peanuts on the griddle, turning occasionally with a metal spatula for 5 to 7 minutes, to lightly roast. Remove from the griddle and set aside to cool.
5. Remove wings from grill and allow to rest for 5 minutes. While wings are resting, shell the peanuts, and transfer to a resealable plastic bag. Use a rolling pin to crush the peanuts, then scatter peanuts on top of the chicken wings. Serve warm.

Bbq Turkey Breast With Meat Church Holy Cow

Servings: 8
Cooking Time: 180 Minutes

Ingredients:
- 1 Large boneless, skinless turkey breast
- 1/4 Cup Duke's Mayonnaise
- Meat Church Holy Cow BBQ Rub
- 1/2 Cup honey
- 1/4 Cup Dijon mustard
- 2 Tablespoon Meat Church Holy Cow BBQ Rub

Directions:
1. Rinse off the breast and pat dry. Slather it liberally in mayonnaise, this will act as a binder for the seasoning. Apply Meat Church Holy Cow BBQ Rub generously to all sides.
2. Supply your smoker with wood pellets and follow the start-up procedure. Preheat the grill, with the lid closed, to 275° F.
3. Place the breast directly on the grill grate and cook for 2 to 3 hours, or until the internal temperature reaches 160°F in the thickest part. (The breast will continue to cook another 5° or so after it is removed from the grill.) Grill: 275 °F Probe: 160 °F
4. While the turkey is cooking you can go ahead and prepare your glaze (if using). Mix all glaze ingredients in a small saucepan and bring to a simmer. Reduce by 1/3. Remove from the heat and set aside.
5. Drizzle the glaze on the turkey during the last 15 minutes of the cook. I recommend doing this around 158 - 160°F, internal temperature. (This turkey is also delicious as-is, without the optional glaze.)
6. Remove from the grill and let the turkey breast rest 5 to 10 minutes before slicing. Enjoy!

BEEF LAMB AND GAME RECIPES

Brined Smoked Brisket

Servings: 4
Cooking Time: 420 Minutes

Ingredients:
- 1 (5-7 lb) flat cut brisket
- 1 Cup brown sugar
- 1/2 Cup kosher salt
- 1/4 Cup Beef Rub

Directions:
1. Dissolve salt and sugar in 6 quarts boiling water. Add 6 cups ice then let it cool. Place the brisket in the brine and cover. Leave brine in the refrigerator overnight.
2. Remove the brisket from the brine and pat it dry with a paper towel. Sprinkle evenly with Traeger Beef Rub.
3. Supply your smoker with wood pellets and follow the start-up procedure. Preheat the grill, with the lid closed, to 250° F.
4. Place the brisket on the Traeger, fat cap down and smoke for 3 hours. Grill: 250 °F
5. After 3 hours, double wrap the brisket in foil and turn the temperature up to 275°F. Cook meat until internal temperature reaches 204°F, about 3 to 4 hours. Grill: 275 °F Probe: 204 °F
6. Unwrap the brisket and place it unwrapped on the grill for 30 more minutes. Grill: 275 °F
7. Remove the brisket from the grill and let it rest for 15 minutes before slicing against the grain. Enjoy!

Pastrami

Servings: 6-8
Cooking Time: 960 Minutes

Ingredients:
- 1 (8-pound) corned beef brisket
- 2 tablespoons yellow mustard
- 1 batch Espresso Brisket Rub
- Worcestershire Mop and Spritz, for spritzing

Directions:
1. Supply your smoker with wood pellets and follow the start-up procedure. Preheat the grill, with the lid closed, to 225°F.
2. Coat the brisket all over with mustard and season it with the rub. Using your hands, work the rub into the meat. Pour the mop into a spray bottle.
3. Place the brisket directly on the grill grate and smoke until its internal temperature reaches 195°F, spritzing it every hour with the mop.
4. Pull the corned beef brisket from the grill and wrap it completely in aluminum foil or butcher paper. Place the wrapped brisket in a cooler, cover the cooler, and let it rest for 1 or 2 hours.
5. Remove the corned beef from the cooler and unwrap it. Slice the corned beef and serve.

Flavour Texas Smoke Beef

Servings: 8
Cooking Time: 315 Minutes

Ingredients:
- 1 Cup Strong Brewed Coffee or Espresso, Cold
- 1 Cup Cola
- 1/2 Cup Soy Sauce
- 1/4 Cup Worcestershire Sauce
- 1/4 Cup Brown Sugar
- 1 Tablespoon Morton Tender Quick Home Meat Cure
- 1 1/2 Teaspoon Freshly Ground Black Pepper
- 1 Tablespoon Hot Sauce
- 2 Pound Trimmed Beef Top Or Bottom Round

Directions:
1. Plan ahead! This recipe requires marinating time overnight. In a mixing bowl, combine the coffee, cola, soy sauce, Worcestershire sauce, brown sugar, curing salt (if using), pepper, and hot sauce.
2. With a sharp knife, slice the beef into 1/4" thick slices against the grain. (This is easier if the meat is partially frozen.)
3. Trim any fat or connective tissue.
4. Put the beef slices in a large resealable plastic bag.
5. Pour the marinade mixture over the beef, and massage the bag so that all the slices get coated with the marinade.
6. Seal the bag and refrigerate for several hours, or overnight.
7. Supply your smoker with wood pellets and follow the start-up procedure. Preheat the grill, with the lid closed, to 180 °F.
8. Remove the beef from the marinade and discard the marinade.
9. Dry the beef slices between paper towels. Arrange the meat in a single layer directly on the grill grate.
10. Smoke for 4 to 5 hours, or until the jerky is dry but still chewy and somewhat pliant when you bend a piece.

Bbq Brisket With Traeger Coffee Rub

Servings: 8
Cooking Time: 540 Minutes

Ingredients:
- 15 Pound whole packer brisket
- 2 Tablespoon Coffee Rub

- 1 1/2 Cup water
- 2 Tablespoon salt

Directions:

1. Trim excess fat off brisket leaving a 1/4" inch cap on the bottom.
2. Combine 2 Tbsp Coffee rub, 1 cup water, and 2 Tbsp salt in a small bowl stirring until most of the salt is dissolved. Inject the brisket every square inch or so with the coffee rub mixture. Season the exterior of the brisket with remaining rub and remaining salt.
3. Supply your smoker with wood pellets and follow the start-up procedure. Preheat the grill, with the lid closed, to 250° F.
4. Place brisket directly on the grill grate and cook for about 6 hours or until the internal temperature reaches 160°F. Grill: 250 °F Probe: 160 °F
5. Wrap the brisket in two layers of foil and pour in 1/2 cup of water. Secure tin foil tightly to contain the liquid. Increase temperature to 275°F and return to grill. Cook an additional 3 hours or until internal temperature reaches 204°F. Grill: 275 °F Probe: 204 °F
6. Remove brisket from the grill and slice. Enjoy!

Three Ingredient Pot Roast

Servings: 4
Cooking Time: 180 Minutes

Ingredients:

- 4 Pound chuck roast, cut into 4 inch chunks
- 2 yellow onions, finely sliced
- 2 Teaspoon kosher salt
- 1/4 Cup extra-virgin olive oil
- freshly ground black pepper

Directions:

1. Supply your smoker with wood pellets and follow the start-up procedure. Preheat the grill, with the lid closed, to 400° F. Place half of the chuck roast into a 3-to-4 quart Dutch oven. (Note: if using a roast that is smaller than 4 lbs, make sure to use a smaller Dutch oven as well.) Add half the onions, half the salt, pepper, and half the olive oil. Repeat with the remaining ingredients.
2. Place a tight-fitting lid on the Dutch oven and place on the grill. Cook for 2 to 3 hours, until the chuck roast can be easily shredded with a fork. Reduce the grill temperature to 350°F if the chuck roast is boiling and not simmering. Grill: 400 °F
3. Remove Dutch oven from the grill and remove the lid. Allow the meat to cool, then skim the fat off the top. Alternatively, allow the meat to cool, refrigerate overnight, then skim the fat cap off the meat before reheating the next day. It will keep for 2 days in the fridge.
4. When ready to serve, this pot roast can be topped with many things to make it your own, including my Preserved Lemon Gremolata, chimichurri, peperonata, horseradish cream (horseradish, sour cream and mayo) or a variety of salsas.

Garlic Leg Of Lamb Roast

Servings: 4
Cooking Time: 70 Minutes

Ingredients:

- 1/3 Cup Beef Stock
- 1 Tsp Black Pepper
- 2 Tsp Brown Sugar
- 1 Tsp Coriander, Ground
- 1 Tbsp Dijon Mustard
- 2 Tbsp Fresh Mint Leaves, Chopped
- 4 Garlic Cloves, Chopped
- 2 Leg Of Lamb Roasts, Bone-In (2 Lbs. Each)
- 1 Lemon, Juice
- 1/2 Cup Olive Oil
- 1/2 Red Onion, Chopped (For Marinade)
- 1 Red Onion, Sliced
- 1/4 Cup Red Wine
- 1 1/2 Tbsp Rosemary Leaves
- To Taste, Rosemary Sprigs
- 1 1/2 Tbsp Sage Leaves, Chopped
- 2 Tsp Salt
- To Taste, Thyme Sprigs
- 2 Tsp Worcestershire Sauce

Directions:

1. Blot lamb legs dry with paper towel, then place in a resealable plastic bag.
2. In the bowl of a food processor, combine olive oil, beef stock, red wine, lemon, mint, rosemary, sage, red onion, garlic, Dijon, Worcestershire sauce, brown sugar, salt, pepper, and coriander. Process for 1 minute, then pour the marinade over the lamb. Seal the bag and refrigerate for 4 hours.
3. Remove the lamb from the refrigerator 30 minutes prior to roasting,
4. Supply your smoker with wood pellets and follow the start-up procedure. Preheat the grill, with the lid opened, to 375° F. If using a gas or charcoal grill, set it up for medium-high heat.
5. Place sliced red onion, rosemary and thyme sprigs in a cast iron skillet [preferably oblong], then set the lamb on top. Add 1 cup of water to the skillet.
6. Roast on the grill for 55 to 70 minutes, until an internal temperature of 135° to 140° F is reached.
7. Remove the lamb and let it rest for 15 minutes on a cutting board, then slice lamb and serve warm.

Flavour Bbq Brisket Burnt Ends

Servings: 6-8
Cooking Time: 420 Minutes

Ingredients:
- 1 Brisket Point
- Georgia Style BBQ Sauce (Mustard Base)
- As Needed Chop House Steak Rub

Directions:
1. Supply your smoker with wood pellets and follow the start-up procedure. Preheat the grill, with the lid closed, to 250° F.
2. Place your brisket on the grates, cook for 6 to 7 hours or until the internal temperature reaches 190°F
3. Remove from the grill and cut into 1-inch cubes. Toss brisket cubes with seasoning and your favorite BBQ sauce into a pan.
4. Place the pan in the grill for 2 hours, stirring half-way through.

Texas Pepper Beef Ribs

Servings: 16
Cooking Time: 360 Minutes

Ingredients:
- 8 lbs beef ribs (two 4 bone racks of plate ribs)
- 8 tbsp salt, pepper, garlic
- 4 tbsp olive oil

Directions:
1. Supply your smoker with wood pellets and follow the start-up procedure. Preheat the grill, with the lid closed, to 250 °F.
2. Pour two tbsp of olive oil on each rack of ribs and rub into meat on all sides.
3. Season the ribs on all sides using the salt, pepper, and garlic seasoning.
4. Set ribs in the smoker and cook for 3 hours before checking for color. Insert a temperature probe into the thickest part of the ribs.
5. Continue cooking until it reaches an internal temperature of around 170 °F.
6. Wrap ribs tightly with two layers of Peach Butcher Paper. Replace the probe into the ribs.
7. Continue cooking until it reaches an internal temperature of 205 °F(usually takes about 2 hours). Use a toothpick or the probe to check for doneness. Meat should be tender like butter. If meat is still tough, continue to cook until it becomes tender.
8. Once meat is tender, leave ribs wrapped and rest until the temperature lowers to around 160-170 °F(about 1 hour).
9. Slice and serve.

Reverse Seared Rib-eye Caps

Servings: 4
Cooking Time: 45 Minutes

Ingredients:
- 1 1/2 Pound rib-eye cap
- 2 Tablespoon Coffee Rub
- 2 Tablespoon Beef Rub

Directions:
1. Trim the rib-eye cap of excess silverskin and fat, if needed. Cut the cap into 4 equal portions and roll into steaks. Tie with butcher's twine to secure.
2. In a small bowl, combine both rubs. Season the steaks liberally with the rub mixture and set aside while the grill heats up.
3. Supply your smoker with wood pellets and follow the start-up procedure. Preheat the grill, with the lid closed, to 225° F.
4. Place the steaks directly on the grill grate, and smoke for 30 to 45 minutes until the internal temperature reaches 120°F. Grill: 225 °F Probe: 120 °F
5. Remove from the grill and set aside to rest.
6. Increase the grill temperature to 450°F. Grill: 450 °F
7. Place the steaks directly on the grill grate and cook 3 to 4 minutes per side, or until the internal temperature reaches 130°F. Grill: 450 °F Probe: 130 °F
8. Remove from grill and let rest 5 minutes before serving. Enjoy!

Flavour Memphis Bbq Beef Brisket

Servings: 10
Cooking Time: 600 Minutes

Ingredients:
- 1 Cup Beef Broth
- 1, 10-12 Pound Brisket
- 1 Bottle Sweet Rib Rub

Directions:
1. Cut away any silver skin or excess fat from the flat muscle and discard. Next, there will be a large, crescent shaped fat section on the flat of the meat.
2. Trim that fat until it is smooth against the meat so that it looks like a seamless transition between the point and flat. Flip the brisket over and trim the fat cap to ¼ inch thick. Slice between the point and the flat and save the flat for later.
3. Generously season the trimmed brisket point on all sides with the Sweet Rib Rub. Allow the brisket to sit for 30 minutes to marinate.
4. Pour the beef broth in the spray bottle and set aside.
5. Supply your smoker with wood pellets and follow the start-up procedure. Preheat the grill, with the lid closed, to 225° F. Place the brisket in the smoker, insert the smoker's attached temperature probe, if you have one, and set the brisket to cook for about 6-8 hours or until the internal temperature reaches 165°F. Spray the brisket with the beef broth every 2 hours to keep it moist.

6. Once the brisket reaches 165°F, remove from the smoker, wrap in peach butcher paper, folding the edges over to form a leakproof seal, and return to the smoker seam-side down for another 3-4 hours, or until the brisket reaches 200°F.
7. Remove the brisket from the smoker and allow it to rest for at least one hour before serving.

Smoked New York Steaks

Servings: 4
Cooking Time: 120 Minutes

Ingredients:
- 4 (1-inch-thick) New York steaks
- 2 tablespoons olive oil
- Salt
- Freshly ground black pepper

Directions:
1. Supply your smoker with wood pellets and follow the start-up procedure. Preheat the grill, with the lid closed, to 180°F.
2. Rub the steaks all over with olive oil and season both sides with salt and pepper.
3. Place the steaks directly on the grill grate and smoke for 1 hour.
4. Increase the grill's temperature to 375°F and continue to cook until the steaks' internal temperature reaches 145°F for medium-rare.
5. Remove the steaks and let them rest 5 minutes, before slicing and serving.

Ancho Pepper Rubbed Brisket

Servings: 12
Cooking Time: 720 Minutes

Ingredients:
- 2 ancho peppers, dried
- 1/2 cup apple cider vinegar
- 9 arbol chilies, dried
- 12 lbs beef brisket, packer cut
- 2 tsp coriander
- 1 tbsp cumin seed, whole
- 2 tsp garlic, granulated
- 1/4 cup kosher salt
- 2 tsp oregano, dried
- 2 tsp smoked paprika
- 3 cups water

Directions:
1. Supply your smoker with wood pellets and follow the start-up procedure. Preheat the grill, with the lid closed, to 350° F. Let it come to temperature. If using a gas or charcoal grill, set it up for medium heat.
2. Place the dried peppers in a large cast iron skillet, then transfer to the grill and cook for 5 minutes, or until fragrant and hot to the touch. Remove from the skillet, and set aside to cool.
3. Add cumin and coriander to the hot skillet, and toast for 1 minute. Remove seeds from the skillet and cool.
4. Remove stems from ancho peppers, then transfer all chilies to a food processor. Pulse a few times to get going, then process on high for 2 minutes, until coarse-ground.
5. Add in garlic, oregano, smoked paprika, and salt. Pulse 10 times to incorporate, then transfer mixture to a bowl.
6. Remove brisket from packaging, set on a cutting board, and blot dry with paper towels.
7. Use a sharp knife to trim the brisket. Start trimming with the fat side down. Trim the silver skin from the flat side, then remove the sides and corners. Remove the fat from around the point. Turn the brisket over and trim any excess fat, leaving around ¼-inch fat thickness.
8. Season the whole brisket with chili pepper rub, then set aside.
9. Fire up your and preheat to Smoke setting. If using a gas or charcoal grill, set it up for low, indirect heat.
10. Place the brisket on the grill, then increase the temperature to 250 F, and smoke until the internal temperature reaches 165°F. After 2 hours, start spraying the brisket every 30 minutes to help retain moisture.
11. Wrap the brisket tightly in butcher paper, then return to the grill and continue to smoke until the internal temperature reaches 200°F.
12. Remove the brisket from the gill and rest for 1 to 2 hours in an insulated cooler before slicing.

Braised Mediterranean Beef Brisket

Servings: 8
Cooking Time: 720 Minutes

Ingredients:
- 3 Tablespoon dried rosemary
- 2 Tablespoon ground cumin seeds
- 2 Tablespoon Coriander, Dried
- 1 Tablespoon dried oregano
- 2 Teaspoon ground cinnamon
- 1/2 Teaspoon salt
- 8 Pound beef brisket
- 1 Cup beef stock

Directions:
1. For a 6 to 8 lb brisket, plan for 8 to 12 hours of cook time, roughly 90 minutes per pound. A remote probe thermometer is critical to use for brisket.
2. Mix all seasoning together and coat brisket liberally. Wrap in plastic wrap. Let the wrapped brisket sit 12 to 24 hours in the refrigerator. Allow plenty of time for cooking.

3. Supply your smoker with wood pellets and follow the start-up procedure. Preheat the grill, with the lid closed, to 180° F.
4. Place brisket fat side down on the grill grate, insert thermometer probe and smoke for 4 hours.
5. After 4 hours, turn grill up to 250°F and preheat. Grill: 250 °F Probe: 250 °F
6. When internal meat temperature reaches 160°F, remove brisket from the grill and wrap in foil along with beef stock - DO NOT remove thermometer probe.
7. Place foiled brisket back on grill and cook until internal temperature reaches 204°F. Grill: 250 °F Probe: 204 °F
8. Remove brisket and allow it to rest in the foil for at least 30 minutes before slicing. Enjoy!

Garlic Standing Rib Roast

Servings: 4
Cooking Time: 240 Minutes

Ingredients:
- 1 tbsp cracked black pepper
- 1/2 tbsp granulated garlic
- 1/2 tbsp granulated onion
- 2 tbsp kosher salt
- 1 tbsp olive oil
- 2 tsp oregano, dried
- 1/2 tbsp parsley, dried
- 5 1/2 lbs prime rib roast, bone-in
- 2 tsp smoked paprika

Directions:
1. Place the roast in a glass baking dish. In a small mixing bowl, combine the salt, pepper, granulated garlic, granulated onion, parsley, oregano and smoked paprika. Season the entire roast with the spice blend, then cover and refrigerate overnight.
2. One hour prior to cooking, remove roast from the refrigerator, uncover, and let it sit out at room temperature.
3. Supply your smoker with wood pellets and follow the start-up procedure. Preheat the grill, with the lid closed, to 225° F. If using a gas or charcoal grill, set it up for low, indirect heat.
4. Place seasoned roast on a cast iron skillet, drizzle with olive oil, and transfer to the grill. Smoke the roast for 1 hour 45 minutes, or until internal temperature reaches 120° F. Remove from the grill and allow roast to rest for 15 minutes.
5. Increase the grill temperature to 450 F, then return roast to grill for an additional 10 to 15 minutes. Allow roast to rest for 15 minutes, slice and serve warm.

Traditional Tomahawk Steak

Servings: 4-6
Cooking Time: 120 Minutes

Ingredients:
- 1 tomahawk ribeye steak (2 1/2 to 3 1/2 lbs)
- 5 garlic cloves, minced
- 2 tbsp kosher salt
- 1 bundle fresh thyme
- 2 tbsp ground black pepper
- 8 oz butter stick
- 1 tbsp garlic powder
- 1/8 cup olive oil

Directions:
1. Mix rub ingredients (salt, black pepper, and garlic powder) in a small bowl. Use this mixture to season all sides of the ribeye steak generously. You can also substitute your favorite steak seasoning. After applying seasoning, let the steak rest at room temperature for at least 30 minutes.
2. While the steak rests, preheat your pellet grill to 450°F - 550°F for searing
3. Sear the steak for 5 minutes on each side. Halfway through each side (so after 2 1/2 minutes), rotate the steak 90° to form grill marks on the tomahawk
4. After the tomahawk steak has seared for 5 minutes on each side (10 minutes total), move the steak to a raised rack
5. Adjust your pellet grill's temperature to 250°F and turn up smoke setting if applicable. Leave the lid open for a moment to help allow some heat to escape
6. Stick your probe meat thermometer into the very center of the cut to measure internal temperature.
7. Place butter stick, garlic cloves, olive oil, and thyme in the aluminum pan. Then place the aluminum pan under the steak to catch drippings. After a few minutes, the steak drippings and ingredients will mix together
8. Baste the steak with the aluminum pan mixture every 10 minutes until the tomahawk steak reaches your desired doneness
9. Once the steak reaches its desired doneness, remove from the grill and place on a cutting board or serving dish. The steak should rest for 10-15 minutes before cutting/serving.

Bbq Beef Sandwich

Servings: 4
Cooking Time: 360 Minutes

Ingredients:
- 1 (4-6 lb) chuck roast
- 1/4 Cup Coffee Rub
- 1 Cup beef broth
- 6 hamburger buns
- 1 white onion, sliced
- dill pickles
- 1/2 Cup Special Sauce
- Sweet & Heat BBQ Sauce

Directions:

1. Supply your smoker with wood pellets and follow the start-up procedure. Preheat the grill, with the lid closed, to 250° F.
2. Trim excess fat from chuck roast. Rub roast with Traeger Coffee Rub. Place roast on Traeger and cook for 3-1/2 hours or until roast reaches an internal temperature of 160°F. Grill: 250 °F Probe: 160 °F
3. Remove roast from grill and wrap in a double layer of aluminum foil, add beef broth and place roast back in grill. Continue to cook for 1-1/2 hours while checking the temperature. The roast is done when the internal temperature reaches 204°F. Check every 30 minutes if internal temperature has not been reached. Grill: 250 °F Probe: 204 °F
4. Remove roast from grill and pull or shred the meat. Add the drippings back into the meat to help keep it moist.
5. Serve pulled roast in buns and top with sliced onions, pickles Traeger Special Sauce and Traeger Sweet & Heat BBQ Sauce.

Beef Brisket With Chophouse Steak Rub

Servings: 12
Cooking Time: 480 Minutes

Ingredients:
- As Needed, Chop House Steak Rub
- 1, 10 To 12 Lb Whole Beef Brisket

Directions:
1. Supply your smoker with wood pellets and follow the start-up procedure. Preheat the grill, with the lid closed, to 250° F.
2. While the grill is heating up, trim your brisket of excess fat, score the meat against the grain and season with Chop House Steak Rub or your favorite seasoning.
3. Place your brisket on the grates, fat side up and cook for 7-8 hours or until the internal temperature reaches 190°F. If the meat is not probe tender, keep cooking until your temperature probe can easily slide into the meat with little to no resistance.
4. Remove from the grill and allow to rest for 20-30 minutes.
5. Slice against the grain and enjoy!

Savory Whiskey Grilled Elk Steaks

Servings: 4
Cooking Time: 10 Minutes

Ingredients:
- ¼ Cup Brown Sugar
- 1 Tbsp Chop House Steak Seasoning
- 1 Tbsp Coarse Ground Pepper
- 4 Elk Steaks
- ½ Cup Olive Oil
- ½ Cup Soy Sauce
- ½ Cup Whiskey, Such As Jack Daniel'S
- ¼ Cup Yellow Mustard

Directions:
1. In a large mixing bowl, add the whiskey, soy sauce, olive oil, brown sugar, yellow mustard, and Chophouse Steak seasoning to a large mixing bowl and whisk until everything is well combined. Pour the marinade into a large, resealable plastic bag or glass baking dish, then add the elk steaks. Seal the bag and turn the steaks once to coat. Place the bag in the refrigerator and marinate for 4-12 hours.
2. Supply your smoker with wood pellets and follow the start-up procedure. Preheat the grill, with the lid open, to 425° F. If you're using a gas or charcoal grill, set it up for medium heat. Remove the elk steaks from the bag and discard the excess marinade. Insert a temperature probe into one of the elk steaks and place on the grill.
3. Grill the steaks for 7-10 minutes per side, or until the steaks reach an internal temperature of 135°F. Remove the steaks from the grill and allow the steaks to rest for 10 minutes before serving.

Sweetheart Steak

Servings: 2
Cooking Time: 12 Minutes

Ingredients:
- 1 (20 Oz) Boneless Strip Steak Or Rib Steak, Butterflied Into Heart Shape
- 2 Teaspoon Jacobsen Salt Co. Pure Kosher Sea Salt
- 2 Teaspoon black pepper
- 2 Tablespoon Raw Dark Chocolate, finely chopped
- 1/2 Tablespoon extra-virgin olive oil

Directions:
1. Draw a large heart on a piece of cardboard, shape to size of meat selected. Cut out cardboard heart shape, then trim meat into heart shape.
2. Combine all ingredients on the cut steak.
3. Supply your smoker with wood pellets and follow the start-up procedure. Preheat the grill, with the lid closed, to 450° F.
4. Grill steak for 5 to 7 minutes per side, or until you've reached desired doneness. Remove from grill. Let rest for 5 minutes. Enjoy!

Smoked Red Wine Beef Roast

Servings: 8
Cooking Time: 180 Minutes

Ingredients:
- 12 oz beef broth
- 6 lbs eye of round beef roast
- 2 tbsp black pepper
- ½ tbsp celery salt
- ½ tbsp garlic powder
- 2 tbsp kosher salt
- ½ tbsp onion powder

- 2 cups red wine
- 1/3 cup Worcestershire sauce

Directions:
1. Supply your smoker with wood pellets and follow the start-up procedure. Preheat the grill, with the lid closed, to 225 °F.
2. Mix the beef broth, red wine, and Worcestershire sauce in a mixing bowl. Fill your meat injector with the mixture.
3. Mix the seasonings in a spice bottle and apply the rub all over the roast, making sure to coat the whole roast evenly.
4. Place the beef roast in the foil pan, fat side up. Using the meat injector, inject the liquid into all areas of the beef roast. Fill the bottom of the pan with the remaining liquid.
5. Place the pan in the smoker and let it cook for 3 hours, basting with the juices in the pan every hour or so.
6. After 3 hours, start checking the roast for the desired internal temperature (Rare: 135 °F, Medium Rare: 145 °F, Medium: 155 °F, Well Done: 170 °F).
7. Remove from the grill and the pan, and let the roast rest for 20 to 30 minutes before slicing.
8. Slice against the grain and enjoy!

Pulled Beef

Servings: 5-8
Cooking Time: 840 Minutes

Ingredients:
- 1 (4-pound) top round roast
- 2 tablespoons yellow mustard
- 1 batch Espresso Brisket Rub
- ½ cup beef broth

Directions:
1. Supply your smoker with wood pellets and follow the start-up procedure. Preheat the grill, with the lid closed, to 225°F.
2. Coat the top round roast all over with mustard and season it with the rub. Using your hands, work the rub into the meat.
3. Place the roast directly on the grill grate and smoke until its internal temperature reaches 160°F and a dark bark has formed.
4. Pull the roast from the grill and place it on enough aluminum foil to wrap it completely.
5. Increase the grill's temperature to 350°F.
6. Fold in three sides of the foil around the roast and add the beef broth. Fold in the last side, completely enclosing the roast and liquid. Return the wrapped roast to the grill and cook until its internal temperature reaches 195°F.
7. Pull the roast from the grill and place it in a cooler. Cover the cooler and let the roast rest for 1 or 2 hours.
8. Remove the roast from the cooler and unwrap it. Pull apart the beef using just your fingers. Serve immediately.

Reuben Sandwich

Servings: 4
Cooking Time: 10 Minutes

Ingredients:
- 2 Cup mayonnaise
- 1/2 Cup ketchup
- 1/4 Cup pickle relish
- 2 Tablespoon Chicken Rub
- 4 Pound leftover corned beef, thinly sliced
- 2 1/2 Cup sauerkraut
- 10 Slices Swiss cheese
- 10 Slices marble rye bread
- 6 Tablespoon butter, room temperature

Directions:
1. See Traeger Smoked Corned Beef Brisket recipe for corned beef instructions.
2. Supply your smoker with wood pellets and follow the start-up procedure. Preheat the grill, with the lid closed, to 350° F.
3. Place a large griddle directly on the grill grate to heat up while the sandwiches are being assembled.
4. Combine the mayonnaise, ketchup, relish and Traeger Chicken Rub in a bowl and stir until well mixed.
5. Butter the outsides of the bread (the side that goes on the grill). Place a layer of sauce on the other side of the bread and top with the corned beef, sauerkraut and 2 Swiss cheese slices. Top with another slice of sauced bread.
6. Place sandwiches on the hot griddle in the Traeger and cook for 5 minutes. Using a spatula, flip the sandwiches and cook for an additional 5 minutes, or until toasted with melty cheese and warm meat. Grill: 350 °F
7. Remove sandwiches from the Traeger. Enjoy!

The Perfect T-bones

Servings: 4
Cooking Time: 30 Minutes

Ingredients
- 4 (1½- to 2-inch-thick) T-bone steaks
- 2 tablespoons olive oil
- 1 batch Espresso Brisket Rub or Chili-Coffee Rub

Directions:
1. Supply your smoker with wood pellets and follow the start-up procedure. Preheat the grill, with the lid closed, to 500°F.
2. Coat the steaks all over with olive oil and season both sides with the rub. Using your hands, work the rub into the meat.
3. Place the steaks directly on a grill grate and smoke until their internal temperature reaches 135°F for rare, 145°F for medium-rare, and 155°F for well-done. Remove the steaks from the grill and serve hot.

Reverse-seared Tri-tip

Servings: 4
Cooking Time: 180 Minutes

Ingredients:
- 1½ pounds tri-tip roast
- 1 batch Espresso Brisket Rub

Directions:
1. Supply your smoker with wood pellets and follow the start-up procedure. Preheat the grill, with the lid closed, to 180°F.
2. Season the tri-tip roast with the rub. Using your hands, work the rub into the meat.
3. Place the roast directly on the grill grate and smoke until its internal temperature reaches 140°F.
4. Increase the grill's temperature to 450°F and continue to cook until the roast's internal temperature reaches 145°F. This same technique can be done over an open flame or in a cast-iron skillet with some butter.
5. Remove the tri-tip roast from the grill and let it rest 10 to 15 minutes, before slicing and serving.

Chorizo Cheese Stuffed Burgers

Servings: 2
Cooking Time: 45 Minutes

Ingredients:
- 2 Pound ground beef, 80% lean
- 4 Ounce Prime Rib Rub
- 12 Ounce Chorizo
- 2 Slices cheddar cheese
- 4 Whole Brioche Bun
- Tomatoes, sliced
- red onion, sliced
- lettuce, sliced

Directions:
1. Mix 2 lb of 80/20 ground beef in mixing bowl with Traeger Prime Rib Rub.
2. Divide the ground beef into eight 1/4 lb patties. Make one patty the base, lay down 1/4 of a cheese slice, add 3 oz. of chorizo and top with another 1/4 cheese slice. Apply another patty on top and pinch the ends all the way around the burger to seal together the two patties.
3. Repeat until all 4 patties are done.
4. Supply your smoker with wood pellets and follow the start-up procedure. Preheat the grill, with the lid closed, to 325° F.
5. Place burgers on the Traeger for 15 minutes on each side. If desired, top each burger with slice of Cheddar cheese, let melt. Remove from Traeger and let rest for 10 minutes tented with foil.
6. While burgers are resting, brush the brioche buns with melted better and toast for 30-45 seconds on the grill.
7. Remove buns from grill and assemble burger with toppings. Enjoy!

Smoked Pheasant

Servings: 4-6
Cooking Time: 240 Minutes

Ingredients:
- 1 gallon hot water
- 1 cup salt
- 1 cup packed brown sugar
- 2 (2- to 3-pound) whole pheasants, cleaned and plucked
- ¼ cup extra-virgin olive oil
- 2 tablespoons onion powder
- 2 tablespoons freshly ground black pepper
- 2 tablespoons cayenne pepper
- 1 tablespoon minced garlic
- 2 teaspoons smoked paprika
- 1 cup molasses

Directions:
1. In a large container with a lid, combine the hot water, salt, and brown sugar, stirring to dissolve the salt and sugar. Let cool to room temperature, then submerge the pheasants in the brine, cover, and refrigerate for 8 to 12 hours.
2. Remove the pheasants from the brine, then rinse them and pat dry. Discard the brine.
3. Supply your smoker with wood pellets and follow the start-up procedure. Preheat, with the lid closed, to 250°F.
4. In a small bowl, combine the olive oil, black pepper, cayenne pepper, onion powder, garlic, and paprika to form a paste.
5. Rub the pheasants with the paste and place breast-side up on the grill grate. Close the lid and smoke for 1 hour.
6. Open the smoker and baste the pheasants with some of the molasses. Close the lid and continue smoking for 2 to 3 hours, basting with the molasses every 30 minutes, until a meat thermometer inserted into the thigh reads 160°F.
7. Remove the pheasants from the grill and let rest for 20 minutes before serving warm or cold.

Smoked Spiced Pulled Beef Chuck Roast

Servings: 6-8
Cooking Time: 360 Minutes

Ingredients:
- 1 chuck roast (3-4 pounds)
- 1 yellow or white onion (sliced)
- 3 cups beef stock (divided use)
- SIMPLE BEEF RUB
- 2 Tablespoons kosher salt
- 2 Tablespoons coarse black pepper
- 2 Tablespoons garlic powder

Directions:
1. Supply your smoker with wood pellets and follow the start-up procedure. Preheat the grill, with the lid closed, to 225 °F.
2. Combine all of the ingredients for the rub in a small bowl and rub liberally onto your beef roast, using your hands to press the rub into every surface of the meat.
3. Put the roast directly on your grill grate, fat-side up, and cook for 3 hours. Spray with 1 cup of the beef stock every hour (reserve the other 2 cups of stock).
4. Turn up the heat after 3 hours. Place the sliced onions in the bottom of a large disposable aluminum foil pan and pour the remaining 2 cups of stock in the bottom of the pan. Transfer the roast into the pan on top of the onions and place the pan into the grill.
5. Increase your grill temperature to 250 degrees F, and cook until the internal temperature reaches 165 degrees F (about 3 more hours).
6. Cover the pan tightly with aluminum foil once your roast hits 165 degrees F, and continue cooking until thermometer inserted in the thickest part of the meat reads 200 to 202 degrees F (this step can take another 3 hours). Every roast will be done at a slightly different temperature, so look for your probe to slide into the meat like it is sliding into softened butter.
7. Remove the pan from the smoker and let rest for a few minutes. Separate the roast from the cooking liquid. Shred the roast and separate the fat from the cooking liquid. Moisten the roast with the remaining cooking liquid, or make it into jus for dipping, or turn it into gravy.

Cheddar Bacon Beef Burgers

Servings: 12
Cooking Time: 30 Minutes

Ingredients:
- Bacon Cheddar Burger Seasoning
- 3/4 Cup Bacon, Chopped
- 3 Lbs Beef, Ground
- 1 Jalapeno, Chopped
- Pepper
- 1/2 Cup Ranch Dressing
- Salt
- 1 1/2 Cups Shredded Cheddar Cheese

Directions:
1. Supply your smoker with wood pellets and follow the start-up procedure. Preheat the grill, with the lid closed, to 350° F.
2. In a small bowl, combine cheese, bacon, jalapeno and ranch dressing.
3. In a clean, large bowl, combine ground beef with enough salt and pepper to taste.
4. Form meat into patties and place on a pan. A good rule of thumb is for each patty to be about the size of the palm of your hand.
5. Using a clean glass, press into each patty, leaving the imprint of the bottom of the glass in the patty. Stuff the filling into the indent. Grill for 25 minutes or until the ground beef reaches an internal temperature of 160°F. Serve hot.

Smoked Tri-tip

Servings: 4
Cooking Time: 300 Minutes

Ingredients:
- 1½ pounds tri-tip roast
- Salt
- Freshly ground black pepper
- 2 teaspoons garlic powder
- 2 teaspoons lemon pepper
- ½ cup apple juice

Directions:
1. Supply your smoker with wood pellets and follow the start-up procedure. Preheat the grill, with the lid closed, to 180°F.
2. Season the tri-tip roast with salt, pepper, garlic powder, and lemon pepper. Using your hands, work the seasoning into the meat.
3. Place the roast directly on the grill grate and smoke for 4 hours.
4. Pull the tri-tip from the grill and place it on enough aluminum foil to wrap it completely.
5. Increase the grill's temperature to 375°F.
6. Fold in three sides of the foil around the roast and add the apple juice. Fold in the last side, completely enclosing the tri-tip and liquid. Return the wrapped tri-tip to the grill and cook for 45 minutes more.
7. Remove the tri-tip roast from the grill and let it rest for 10 to 15 minutes, before unwrapping, slicing, and serving.

Smoked Duck Breast Bacon

Servings: 6
Cooking Time: 30 Minutes

Ingredients:
- 4 Cup water
- 2 Cup freshly brewed strong coffee
- 1 Cup kosher salt
- 1/2 Cup dark brown sugar
- 2 1/2 Tablespoon curing salt
- 1/4 Cup molasses
- 3 Cup ice
- 3 Pound skin-on duck breasts

Directions:
1. Stir together 4 cups water with coffee, kosher salt, brown sugar, and curing salt in a container with a lid. Mix until solids are dissolved. Add the molasses and stir until completely dissolved. Add 3 cups ice and stir until cure is cold. (It's ok if all the ice doesn't melt completely.)
2. Add duck breasts to cure and weigh them down with a large plate to keep submerged. Place covered container in refrigerator for a minimum of 6 hours.
3. Remove from refrigerator, take breasts out of brine and discard brine. Rinse duck breasts under cold running water and pat dry.
4. Supply your smoker with wood pellets and follow the start-up procedure. Preheat the grill, with the lid closed, to 165° F.
5. Place duck breasts on grill grate and smoke for 2 hours. Grill: 165 °F
6. Cool duck completely, wrap in plastic wrap and place in refrigerator until ready to use.
7. To cook, slice breast thinly and fry in a pan just like you would pork bacon. Or slice breast thinly, place on Traeger set to 350°F and cook for 10 minutes per side. Enjoy! Grill: 350 °F

Smoked Chicken Steak Sandwiches

Servings: 6
Cooking Time: 270 Minutes

Ingredients:
- 1 1/2 tsp black pepper, ground
- 3 lbs brisket flat
- 1 tbsp butter
- 1 1/2 cups chicken stock
- 1/4 cup chop house steak rub
- for topping, dill pickles
- 2 tsp garlic powder
- 8 oz maple cure
- 2 tsp mustard powder
- 1 onion, sliced
- 1 1/2 tbsp pickling spice
- pumpernickel rye, sliced
- to taste, sauerkraut
- to taste, spicy brown mustard
- 6 swiss cheese, sliced
- 2 qts water, cold

Directions:
1. Set the brisket flat on a cutting board, then trim off excess fat and silver skin.
2. Whisk together water and maple cure, until dissolved.
3. Lay brisket in a large container, season with pickling spice, then cover with brine/cure. The meat must be completely immersed. Cover and place in the refrigerator for 3 to 4 days.
4. Remove brisket flat from brine/cure. It will be pale grey in color, which is normal. Discard the cure and replace with plain water. Allow brisket to soak 1-2 hours.
5. Combine all ingredients for the rub in a bowl. Remove the brisket from the water and blot dry with paper towel.
6. Season the brisket well with the rub, pushing and massaging it into the surface. Place the brisket back into the refrigerator, uncovered, overnight.
7. Supply your smoker with wood pellets and follow the start-up procedure. Preheat the grill, with the lid closed, to 250° F. If using a gas or charcoal grill, set it up for low, indirect heat.
8. Transfer the brisket flat directly on the grill grate, fat side down, over indirect heat. Smoke for 2 hours, flipping after 1 hour.
9. Remove the brisket from the grill and place it in a cast iron skillet, or foil-lined aluminum pan with chicken stock and onions. Cover with a lid, or foil and return to the grill.
10. Increase temperature to 275° F, and cook an additional 1 hour, then check the brisket to see if enough liquid remains. If reducing too quickly, add 1 cup of water. Cook the brisket for another 1 hour, or until the brisket is probe tender
11. Remove from the grill and rest for at least 30 minutes, prior to slicing thin.
12. Preheat the griddle over low flame.
13. Grease griddle with 1 tablespoon of butter, then spread mustard on 4 slices of rye, then set on griddle. Add 2 portions of sliced pastrami. Warm pastrami 1 to 2 minutes, then flip. Top pastrami with sauerkraut and cheese, then close the griddle lid for 1 minute to crisp up the underside of the pastrami and melt the cheese.
14. Brush rye with mustard then set pastrami on every other slice. Set remaining toasted rye on top complete the smoked pastrami sandwich.
15. Remove from the griddle, then repeat. Slice each sandwich on the bias and serve warm with dill pickles.

Whiskey Bourbon Bbq Cheeseburger

Servings: 4
Cooking Time: 45 Minutes

Ingredients:
- 3 Pound ground beef
- Rub
- 1/2 Cup brown sugar
- 1 To Taste hot sauce
- 1/2 Cup bourbon whiskey
- 1 Pound bacon
- 4 Slices cheddar cheese

Directions:

1. In a medium bowl, combine ground beef and Traeger Rub and mix well using caution not to overwork or allow the beef to get too warm.
2. Divide the ground beef in quarters and put each quarter in a 6" cake ring. Press down and form the beef into a patty.
3. With a skewer, poke about 40 holes about ¾" of the way through each patty. Spread brown sugar all over the top of the patties then drizzle with hot sauce. Pour whiskey over each burger, transfer to the fridge and let sit for about a half hour.
4. Supply your smoker with wood pellets and follow the start-up procedure. Preheat the grill, with the lid closed, to 225° F.
5. Remove burgers from the cake rings. When the grill is to temp, place bacon and burgers directly on the grill grate and cook until burgers internal temperature reaches 165 °F. In the last ten minutes of cooking, top with cheddar cheese to melt. Grill: 225 °F Probe: 165 °F
6. Remove burgers and bacon from the grill and build your burger to your liking. Enjoy!

Grilled Tomahawk Steak

Servings: 4
Cooking Time: 60 Minutes

Ingredients:
- 2 Large tomahawk steaks
- 2 Tablespoon kosher salt
- 2 Tablespoon ground black pepper
- 1 Tablespoon paprika
- 1/2 Tablespoon garlic powder
- 1/2 Tablespoon onion powder
- 1/2 Tablespoon brown sugar
- 1 Teaspoon ground mustard
- 1/4 Teaspoon cayenne pepper

Directions:
1. In a small bowl, combine all ingredients for the rub. Season the steaks liberally with the rub and set steaks aside while the grill preheats.
2. Supply your smoker with wood pellets and follow the start-up procedure. Preheat the grill, with the lid closed, to 225° F.
3. Place the steaks directly on the grill grate and smoke for 45 minutes to 1 hour, until the internal temperature reaches 120°F. Grill: 225 °F
4. Remove steaks from the grill and set aside to rest.
5. Increase the grill temperature to 450°F. Grill: 450 °F
6. Place the steaks directly on the grill grate and cook 7 to 10 minutes per side, or until the internal temperature reaches 130°F. Grill: 450 °F Probe: 130 °F
7. Remove from grill and let rest 5 minutes before serving. Enjoy!

Roasted Prime Rib

Servings: 8
Cooking Time: 105 Minutes

Ingredients:
- 1 four-bone prime rib roast, about 8lb (3.6kg), trimmed
- extra virgin olive oil
- 1 cup beef stock or broth
- fresh coarsely ground black pepper
- Horseradish Sauce
- for the seasoned salt
- ¼ cup coarsely chopped fresh rosemary leaves
- 5 fresh sage leaves, coarsely chopped
- 1 tbsp granulated garlic or 2 tsp garlic powder
- 2 tsp whole black peppercorns or fresh coarsely ground black pepper
- 1¼ cups coarse salt, divided

Directions:
1. Supply your smoker with wood pellets and follow the start-up procedure. Preheat the grill, with the lid closed, to 450° F.
2. In a coffee grinder, make the seasoned salt by combining the rosemary, sage, granulated garlic, peppercorns, and ½ cup of salt. Pulse until the herbs and peppercorns are finely ground and the coarse salt resembles table salt. (The mixture will be damp from the moisture in the herbs.)
3. Transfer the mixture to a bowl and stir in the remaining ¾ cup of salt. Reserve 3 to 4 teaspoons of the seasoned salt for the prime rib. Spread the remaining mixture on a rimmed sheet pan and let dry completely, stirring occasionally, before storing at room temperature in a covered jar. Set aside. (Place the mixture in a dehydrator or low-temperature oven or your smoker to hasten the drying time.)
4. Carve the bones off the roast in a single slab. Set aside. Use butcher's twine to tie the roast at 1½-inch (3.75cm) intervals. Lightly coat on all sides with olive oil and season with the reserved seasoned salt.
5. Place the bones convex (rounded) side up in an aluminum foil roasting pan. Place the prime rib atop the bones. Add the beef stock to the bottom of the pan.
6. Place the pan on the grate and roast until the exterior is nicely browned, about 30 minutes. Lower the temperature to 350°F (177°C) and continue to roast the meat until the internal temperature reaches 125°F (52°C) to 130°F (54°C), about 60 to 75 minutes, basting with the drippings every 20 minutes. (To avoid overcooking, check the internal temperature of the roast every 20 minutes.)
7. Transfer the roast to a cutting board and loosely tent with aluminum foil. Let rest for 15 minutes. Carve the prime rib into ¾-inch (2cm) slices and serve with the horseradish sauce.

Hickory Smoked Prime Rib

Servings: 6
Cooking Time: 240 Minutes

Ingredients:
- 1 (8-10 lb) 4-bone prime rib roast
- 3 Tablespoon Dijon mustard
- 2 Tablespoon Worcestershire sauce
- 4 Clove garlic, mashed to a paste
- 2 Teaspoon dried thyme
- 2 Teaspoon dried rosemary
- Prime Rib Rub or coarse salt and freshly ground black pepper
- prepared horseradish, for serving

Directions:
1. If the roast has a fat cap more than 1/4 inch thick, trim it with a sharp knife or ask your butcher to do it for you. Tie the roast between the bones with butcher's twine. This discourages the eye of the meat from separating from the cap.
2. In a small bowl, whisk together the Dijon mustard, Worcestershire sauce, garlic, thyme and rosemary. If the dried rosemary needles are long, finely chop them before adding.
3. Slather the outside of the roast with the mustard paste and season generously with Traeger Prime Rib Rub on all sides. Refrigerate uncovered for up to 8 hours.
4. Supply your smoker with wood pellets and follow the start-up procedure. Preheat the grill, with the lid closed, to 250° F. Place the prime rib directly on the grill grate, fat-side up. Roast for 3-1/2 to 4 hours, or until the internal temperature of the meat (the tip of the temperature probe should be in the center of the meat) reaches 125°F to 130°F for rare or for medium-rare, 135°F. Grill: 250 °F Probe: 125 °F
5. Transfer meat to a cutting board, preferably one with a deep well so you don't lose the juices, and loosely tent the meat with foil. Allow meat to rest for 30 minutes. Grill: 250 °F Probe: 135 °F
6. To carve, remove the twine. Use a sharp knife to remove the rack of bone following the curvature of the meat. Carve the meat across the grain into 1/2 inch thick slices. Serve with horseradish, if desired. Enjoy!

Beer Chili Bratwurst

Servings: 4
Cooking Time: 45 Minutes

Ingredients:
- 1 Chopped Chipotle In Adobo
- 3 - 4 Cans Of Beer, Any Brand
- 4 Bratwursts, Raw
- 4 Bratwurst Buns
- ½ Cup Prepared Nacho Cheese Sauce
- 1 Cup Chili, Prepared
- Caramelized Onions
- Sweet Rib Rub

Directions:
1. Supply your smoker with wood pellets and follow the start-up procedure. Preheat the grill, with the lid closed, to 350° F. If you're using charcoal or gas, set the temperature to medium high.
2. Place a pot filled with beer, Sweet Rib Rub, caramelized onions and raw brats. Place on grill and par-boil for 20 minutes.
3. Grill the brats for 7-10 minutes, or until internal temperature of the brats is 160°F. Remove the brats from the grill and allow them to rest for 5 minutes.
4. While the brats rest, place the chili in a sauce pan, and place the sauce pan on the grill. Heat the chili all the way through.
5. In a separate sauce pan, add the nacho cheese to the pan, add adobo chili peppers and a shake of Sweet Rib Rub. Place the saucepan on the grill and heat until warm all the way through.
6. Assemble the brats: place a brat in a bun, then top with a spoonful of chili and a spoonful of nacho cheese. Serve immediately.

Bistecca Alla Fiorentina With Mushroom Ragout

Servings: 3
Cooking Time: 25 Minutes

Ingredients:
- 2 sprigs of fresh sage
- 2 sprigs of fresh rosemary
- 2 sprigs of fresh thyme
- 1 porterhouse steak, about 2½lb (1.25kg)
- extra virgin olive oil
- coarse salt
- fresh coarsely ground black pepper
- for the ragout
- 3 tbsp unsalted butter
- 3 shallots or 1 white onion, peeled and chopped
- 2 garlic cloves, peeled and minced
- 2lb (1kg) wild mushrooms, cleaned, destemmed, and sliced or chopped
- coarse salt
- freshly ground black pepper
- 2 tbsp Cognac or brandy
- ½ cup low-salt beef broth, plus more
- 2 tsp light soy sauce
- 2 tsp chopped fresh thyme or 1 tsp dried thyme
- ½ cup heavy whipping cream, plus more
- freshly squeezed lemon juice
- freshly chopped chives

Directions:

1. Place a cast iron skillet or cast iron griddle on the grate. Supply your smoker with wood pellets and follow the start-up procedure. Preheat the grill, with the lid closed, to 450° F.
2. In a large skillet on the stovetop over medium heat, begin making the ragout by melting the butter. Add the shallots and sauté until they soften, about 2 to 3 minutes, stirring often. Add the garlic and mushrooms. Season with salt and pepper. Cook until the mushrooms give up their liquid and begin to brown, about 5 minutes. Add the Cognac and cook for 1 minute. Stir in the broth, soy sauce, and thyme. Cook until the liquid reduces slightly, about 5 minutes. Remove the skillet from the stovetop and set aside.
3. Tie the sprigs of sage, rosemary, and thyme together with butcher's twine. Place the steak on a rimmed sheet pan and use the herb brush to generously brush both sides with olive oil. Season with salt and pepper.
4. Place the steak on the skillet and grill until the internal temperature reaches 125°F (52°C), about 8 to 10 minutes per side, occasionally using the herb brush to brush the steak with olive oil. If your grill has enough clearance, stand the porterhouse upright, resting on the bone, and continue to cook for a few minutes more.
5. Transfer the meat to a cutting board and brush it one final time with olive oil. Let rest for 5 minutes.
6. Add the cream to the ragout and reheat over medium-high heat until the mixture boils. Taste for seasoning, adding salt and pepper. If the ragout seems dry, add more cream or broth. If the flavors need brightening, stir in 1 or 2 teaspoons of lemon juice. Transfer the ragout to an attractive serving bowl and top with chives.
7. Carve off the strip steak and filet mignon. Slice them on a diagonal, keeping the slices in order. Place the bone on a platter and then place the slices around the bone. Serve immediately with the mushroom ragout.

Italian Meatballs

Servings: 6
Cooking Time: 90 Minutes

Ingredients:

- 1lb (450g) ground beef (85/15), well chilled
- ½lb (225g) Italian sausage, well chilled
- 1 large egg, beaten
- ½ cup finely grated Parmesan, Asiago, or Romano cheese
- ½ cup panko or other breadcrumbs
- 1 tsp Italian seasoning
- 1 tsp coarse salt
- ½ tsp freshly ground black pepper
- 1lb (450g) thin-sliced bacon, halved crosswise
- low-carb barbecue sauce, (optional)

Directions:

1. Supply your smoker with wood pellets and follow the start-up procedure. Preheat the grill, with the lid closed, to 250° F.
2. Place the ground beef, Italian sausage, egg, cheese, breadcrumbs, Italian seasoning, and salt and pepper in a large bowl. Wet your hands with cold water. Form your hands into claw shapes and combine the ingredients using a light touch.
3. Form the mixture into 24 equal-sized balls. Wrap each with a half strip of bacon and secure the ends with a toothpick.
4. Place the meatballs on the grate and smoke until the bacon has rendered its fat and the internal temperature reaches 160°F (71°C), about 1 to 1½ hours. Brush the meatballs with barbecue sauce (if using) during the last 10 minutes of smoking.
5. Transfer the meatballs to a platter. Let rest for 5 minutes before serving.

Sweet Heat Burnt Ends

Servings: 8-10
Cooking Time: 360 Minutes

Ingredients:

- 1 (6-pound) brisket point
- 2 tablespoons yellow mustard
- 1 batch Sweet Brown Sugar Rub
- 2 tablespoons honey
- 1 cup barbecue sauce
- 2 tablespoons light brown sugar

Directions:

1. Supply your smoker with wood pellets and follow the start-up procedure. Preheat the grill, with the lid closed, to 225°F.
2. Using a boning knife, carefully remove all but about ½ inch of the large layer of fat covering one side of your brisket point.
3. Coat the point all over with mustard and season it with the rub. Using your hands, work the rub into the meat.
4. Place the point directly on the grill grate and smoke until its internal temperature reaches 165°F.
5. Pull the brisket from the grill and wrap it completely in aluminum foil or butcher paper.
6. Increase the grill's temperature to 350°F and return the wrapped brisket to it. Continue to cook until its internal temperature reaches 185°F.
7. Remove the point from the grill, unwrap it, and cut the meat into 1-inch cubes. Place the cubes in an aluminum pan and stir in the honey, barbecue sauce, and brown sugar.
8. Place the pan in the grill and smoke the beef cubes for 1 hour more, uncovered. Remove the burnt ends from the grill and serve immediately.

Texas Shoulder Clod

Servings: 16-20
Cooking Time: 960 Minutes

Ingredients:
- ½ cup sea salt
- ½ cup freshly ground black pepper
- 1 tablespoon red pepper flakes
- 1 tablespoon minced garlic
- 1 tablespoon cayenne pepper
- 1 tablespoon smoked paprika
- 1 (13- to 15-pound) beef shoulder clod

Directions:
1. In a small bowl, combine the salt, pepper, red pepper flakes, minced garlic, cayenne pepper, and smoked paprika to create a rub. Generously apply it to the beef shoulder.
2. Supply your smoker with wood pellets and follow the start-up procedure. Preheat, with the lid closed, to 250°F.
3. Put the meat on the grill grate, close the lid, and smoke for 12 to 16 hours, or until a meat thermometer inserted deeply into the beef reads 195°F. You may need to cover the clod with aluminum foil toward the end of smoking to prevent over-browning.
4. Let the meat rest for about 15 minutes before slicing against the grain and serving.

Hot Coffee-rubbed Brisket

Servings: 8
Cooking Time: 240 Minutes

Ingredients:
- aluminum foil
- 12 lbs beef brisket, packer cut
- java chop house rub

Directions:
1. Inject the brisket with 1 cup of beef broth, being sure to inject with the grain, spacing 1 inch apart.
2. Season the whole brisket with Java Chophouse, then set aside.
3. Supply your smoker with wood pellets and follow the start-up procedure. Preheat the grill, with the lid closed, to 350° F. If using a gas or charcoal grill, set it up for medium heat.
4. Place the brisket, directly on the grill grate, fat side down, and cook for 1 hour. Begin spraying with broth (1 cup total) every 15 minutes until the internal temperature reaches 160 to 165° F (about 30 to 60 min).
5. Remove brisket from the grill and set on a foil-lined tray. Bring up the sides of the foil, then slowly pour the remaining cup of broth over the top of the brisket, giving time to allow broth to seep into the brisket. Wrap with foil, then set on a sheet tray and return to the grill.
6. Reduce temperature to 275°F and cook for an additional 1 ½ to 2 1/2 hours.
7. Begin checking the brisket for tenderness after 1 hour. Punch thermometer probe or skewer into brisket. Desired tenderness is achieved when the probe or skewer easily slides into the brisket, like butter. If the brisket is slightly tough, repeat this test every 30 minutes. The target temperature is between 206 and 210° F.
8. Remove the brisket from the grill, and cut foil to vent. Allow the brisket to rest for 30 to 45 minutes before slicing. Separate the point from the flat. Slice the flat against the grain, then cube the brisket point for burnt ends. Serve warm.

Roasted Mustard Crusted Prime Rib

Servings: 6
Cooking Time: 180 Minutes

Ingredients:
- 1 3-bone prime rib roast
- 1 Tablespoon black pepper
- 2 Tablespoon kosher salt
- 2 Tablespoon garlic, minced to a paste
- 1 Cup whole grain mustard

Directions:
1. Combine salt, black pepper, whole grain mustard and garlic in a small bowl and mix well. Rub mixture all over the exterior of the roast making sure each section is evenly coated.
2. Supply your smoker with wood pellets and follow the start-up procedure. Preheat the grill, with the lid closed, to 450° F.
3. Place the roast directly on the grill grate with the ribs facing the back of the grill. Close the lid and cook for 45 minutes or until the exterior of the roast has an even layer of browning. Grill: 450 °F
4. Reduce the temperature to 325 degrees F and continue to cook for 2.5 hours or until the internal temperature reaches 125 degrees F. Grill: 325 °F Probe: 125 °F
5. Remove roast from grill and allow to rest 15 minutes before slicing. After roast has rested, remove trussing and bones and slice into 1" inch sections. Enjoy!

Rosemary-smoked Lamb Chops

Servings: 4
Cooking Time: 125 Minutes

Ingredients:
- 4½ pounds bone-in lamb chops
- 2 tablespoons olive oil
- Salt
- Freshly ground black pepper
- 1 bunch fresh rosemary

Directions:

1. Supply your smoker with wood pellets and follow the start-up procedure. Preheat the grill, with the lid closed, to 180°F.
2. Rub the lamb chops all over with olive oil and season on both sides with salt and pepper.
3. Spread the rosemary directly on the grill grate, creating a surface area large enough for all the chops to rest on. Place the chops on the rosemary and smoke until they reach an internal temperature of 135°F.
4. Increase the grill's temperature to 450°F, remove the rosemary, and continue to cook the chops until their internal temperature reaches 145°F.
5. Remove the chops from the grill and let them rest for 5 minutes before serving.

Santa Maria Tri-tip With Pico De Gallo

Servings: 4
Cooking Time: 68 Minutes

Ingredients:
- 1 tri-tip roast, about 2 to 2½lb (1 to 1.2kg)
- coarse salt
- freshly ground black pepper
- granulated garlic or garlic powder
- for the pico de gallo
- 8 Roma tomatoes, decored, deseeded, and diced
- 1 white onion, peeled and diced
- 1 serrano pepper, destemmed, deseeded, and minced, plus more
- 1 garlic clove, peeled and minced
- juice of 1 lime
- ½ cup loosely packed cilantro leaves, chopped
- 1 tsp coarse salt

Directions:
1. In a medium bowl, make the pico de gallo by combining the tomatoes, onion, serrano, garlic, lime juice, and cilantro. Stir gently with a rubber spatula and season with salt to taste. Cover and refrigerate for 2 hours.
2. Approximately 45 minutes before you're ready to cook, season the roast on all sides with salt and pepper and granulated garlic.
3. Supply your smoker with wood pellets and follow the start-up procedure. Preheat the grill, with the lid closed, to 180° F.
4. Place the roast on the grate and smoke until the internal temperature in the thickest part of the roast reaches 115°F (46°C), about 45 minutes to 1 hour. Transfer the roast to a plate.
5. Raise the temperature to 450°F (232°C). Place the roast on the grate and sear until the internal temperature in the thickest part of the roast reaches 130 to 135°F (54 to 57°C), about 3 to 4 minutes per side. For best results, don't cook beyond medium rare. (The thinner tail should satisfy any diner who prefers beef to be more well done.)
6. Remove the roast from the grill and thinly slice on a sharp diagonal against the grain. Serve with the pico de gallo.

Slow Smoked Rib-eye Roast

Servings: 6
Cooking Time: 240 Minutes

Ingredients:
- 1 (4-6 lb) rib-eye roast
- 4 Tablespoon yellow mustard
- 1 Tablespoon Worcestershire sauce
- 1 Clove garlic, minced
- Prime Rib Rub
- 4 Sprig fresh thyme

Directions:
1. Supply your smoker with wood pellets and follow the start-up procedure. Preheat the grill, with the lid closed, to 250° F.
2. While the Traeger is warming up, prepare roast. Trim excess fat from the top of the roast down to 1/4 inch thick.
3. In a small bowl, combine the mustard, Worcestershire sauce and garlic. Cover entire roast with the mustard mixture and season liberally with Traeger Prime Rib rub.
4. Lay the sprigs of fresh thyme on the top of the roast.
5. Place the roast directly on the grill grate and smoke until the internal temperature of the roast reaches 135°F for rare or 145°F for medium, about 3 to 4 hours. Grill: 250 °F Probe: 135 °F
6. Remove roast from grill. Tent with foil and rest for 20 minutes before carving. Enjoy!

Savory Reverse Seared Ny Steak

Servings: 4
Cooking Time: 68 Minutes

Ingredients:
- 4 Tbsp Butter
- Steak Seasoning
- 4 - 1 1/2" Steak, New York Strip

Directions:
1. Supply your smoker with wood pellets and follow the start-up procedure. Preheat the grill, with the lid closed, to 250° F.
2. As the grill is preheating to the perfect temperature, spice the steaks with the Chop House steak rub.
3. Lay the steaks on the grill for roughly 60 minutes or until the steaks reach an internal temperature of 105 to 110 degrees F. Remove the steaks and set aside.
4. Crank up the heat to 500°F, open the Flame Broiler plate and let the grill preheat.

5. Place the steaks back on the grill and sear for 4 minutes. Don't forget to add 1 TBSP of butter for flavor to each steak. You know when your steak is done once the internal temperature reaches 130 to 135°F (for medium-rare). Follow the below internal temperature for your cooking preference:
6. Rare: 125°F
7. Medium Rare: 130°F
8. Medium: 140°F
9. Well Done: 160°F
10. Once reached for personal preference, take the steaks off the grill and let them rest for 5 to 10 minutes before eating. ENJOY!

Grilled Loco Moco Burger

Servings: 4
Cooking Time: 10 Minutes

Ingredients:
- Ounce ground beef, 80% lean
- 3 Tablespoon kosher salt
- 2 Tablespoon black pepper
- Cup Beef Gravy
- 2 Cup Rice, Cooked
- 4 eggs
- burger buns
- 2 Cup Hawaiian Pasta Salad

Directions:
1. Supply your smoker with wood pellets and follow the start-up procedure. Preheat the grill, with the lid closed, to 375° F.
2. Divide the ground beef into four, 6 oz portions and shape into patties. Season the patties with salt and pepper.
3. Place the patties on the grill and flip after six minutes cook time.
4. Check the internal temperature of the patties. Burgers are done when they reach an internal temperature of 165°F. Probe: 165°F
5. While the patties are cooking, heat the gravy and the rice. Cook the eggs over easy.
6. To assemble the burger: Start with the bottom of the bun, 1/4 cup rice, 1/4 cup pasta salad, a hamburger patty, gravy, a fried egg, and the top of the bun.
7. Serve while hot. Enjoy!

Smoked Prime Rib

Servings: 8
Cooking Time: 180 Minutes

Ingredients:
- 1 (8-10 lb) boneless rib-eye roast, choice grade or higher
- kosher salt
- Meat Church Holy Cow BBQ Rub
- Meat Church Gourmet Garlic and Herb Seasoning
- Worcestershire sauce
- beef stock or water, optional
- 3 Tablespoon butter

Directions:
1. Supply your smoker with wood pellets and follow the start-up procedure. Preheat the grill, with the lid closed, to 275° F.
2. Truss your prime rib, since using the boneless option. This will help keep its shape and cook evenly.
3. Apply a very heavy coat of salt to the entire roast. Let the salt sit for one hour, then wash it off and pat it dry. Apply Meat Church Holy Cow BBQ Rub liberally on all sides of the meat. It's hard to put too much on as we want to form a great bark. Remember, this cut is so big that there will not be much crust in many bites.
4. Next, come back over the entire rib roast with a heavy coat of Meat Church Gourmet Garlic and Herb seasoning. Let these two rubs sit and adhere for 15 to 20 minutes.
5. Place your rib roast on the Traeger. Grill: 275 °F
6. If you'd like, you can baste it every 45 minutes with Worcestershire sauce, beef stock or even water.
7. We are targeting a medium-rare cook in the middle which is 130°F to 135°F. Therefore, continue to cook your rib roast until you reach an internal temperature of 125°F in the middle. Keep in mind the outer edges will be further along. The ends will be closer to medium. Remove the meat from the grill when that temperature is obtained. Grill: 275 °F Probe: 125 °F
8. Tent the meat with aluminum foil and allow it to rest for at least 10 to 15 minutes. I prefer to top the rib roast with a high-quality butter. Let this butter melt down over your prime rib as it rests. The meat will continue to rise another 5°F to a final temperature of 130°F.

Savory Bacon Mac And Cheese Stuffed Sliders

Servings: 5
Cooking Time: 20 Minutes

Ingredients:
- 16 Oz Lean Beef, Ground
- Hawaiian Rolls
- 1 Box Mac And Cheese, Prepared
- Mustard, Ground
- Smoke Infused Applewood Bacon Rub

Directions:
1. Cook your favorite prepared mac and cheese. Follow the instructions on the box.
2. Supply your smoker with wood pellets and follow the start-up procedure. Preheat the grill, with the lid closed, to 400° F.
3. Put the ground beef into a bowl and generously add the Applewood Bacon Rub. Mix with your hands until the meat looks evenly coated.

4. Separate the meat out into 3oz balls, disperse or toss the remnants.
5. Split the balls in half, and add half of the meat to the bottom of the 3-in-1 Burger Press, then add a tablespoon of mac and cheese (it works better if you kind of make a bowl in the center of the meat). Then add the remaining half of the 3oz ball on top of the mac and cheese.
6. Use the 3-in-1 Burger press to create the perfect patty!
7. Add the sliders to the grill, flip every 5 minutes for about 15-20 minutes depending on how cooked you like your burgers.
8. You can also toast your buns at this time if you'd like.
9. Pull the sliders (and the buns) from the grill, add the stone ground mustard and whatever else your tummy may desire – and dig in!

Smoked Sirloin Roast Beef

Servings: 2
Cooking Time: 10 Minutes

Ingredients:
- 1 top sirloin beef roast (5-6 pounds)
- 3 tbsp sea salt
- 1/4 cup Montreal steak spice

Directions:
1. Trim the roast of any excess fat. Tie the roast up with kitchen twine if desired.
2. Rub the roast down with the sea salt and then rub the roast with the Montreal steak spice.
3. Supply your smoker with wood pellets and follow the start-up procedure. Preheat the grill, with the lid closed, to 250 °F.
4. Lay the roast on the grill grate and smoke until 135 degrees F, or until the desired doneness.
5. Remove the roast from the pellet smoker and let rest for 10 minutes. Slice and serve.

Smoked Corned Beef & Cabbage

Servings: 6
Cooking Time: 300 Minutes

Ingredients:
- 1 (3-5 lb) corned beef brisket
- 1 Quart chicken stock
- 12 Ounce (12 oz) beer, preferably pilsner or lager
- 1/4 Teaspoon garlic salt
- 1/2 Cup (1 stick) butter, cut into slices
- 2 Cup baby carrots
- 1 Pound baby or fingerling potatoes
- 1 Head cabbage, cut into wedges
- 2 Tablespoon fresh chopped dill

Directions:

1. Soak the corned beef in water for about 8 hours, changing water every 2 hours.
2. Supply your smoker with wood pellets and follow the start-up procedure. Preheat the grill, with the lid closed, to 180 °F.
3. Remove brisket from water and pat dry. Place directly on the grill grate and smoke for 2 hours. Grill: 180 °F
4. Transfer brisket from grill and place in a roasting pan. Increase grill temperature to 325°F and preheat, lid closed. Grill: 325 °F
5. Sprinkle seasoning packet on top of brisket and pour chicken stock and dark beer over the roast.
6. Cover roasting pan with foil and place on the grill. Cook for 2 hours or until beef is fork tender. Grill: 325 °F
7. Remove foil and add carrots and potatoes to the roasting pan. Cover meat and vegetables with garlic salt and butter slices. Grill: 325 °F
8. Recover with foil and cook for an additional hour or until carrots and potatoes are just tender. Add cabbage, cover and return to grill for 20 minutes more. Grill: 325 °F
9. Remove vegetables from the pan to a bowl or serving platter. Slice beef and serve with potatoes, cabbage and carrots. Garnish with fresh dill and thyme if desired. Enjoy!

Texas Smoked Beer Leftover Rib Meat

Servings: 4
Cooking Time: 30 Minutes

Ingredients:
- 1 Can Beer, Any Brand
- 1 Can Black Beans, Rinsed And Drained
- 1 Tablespoon Chili Powder
- 1 Can Corn Kernels, Drained
- 1/2 Teaspoon Cumin
- 1 Can Kidney Beans, Drained And Rinsed
- 2 Cups Pulled From The Bone Leftover Rib Meat
- 2 Tablespoons Louisiana Grills Pulled Pork Rub
- 1 Tablespoon Olive Oil
- 1 Can Tomato Sauce
- 1/2 White Onion, Diced

Directions:
1. Supply your smoker with wood pellets and follow the start-up procedure. Preheat the grill, with the lid closed, to 250° F. In a pan sauté your diced onions in olive oil and 1 tablespoon of beer until they turn a mild yellow color.
2. In the disposable aluminum pan, combine the sautéed onions and the rest of the ingredients, including the leftover beef rib meat.
3. Mix the ingredients well and cover tightly with aluminum foil.
4. Place on the grill and close the lid. Let smoke for 2 - 3 hours or until the chili is bubbling and tender.

Bbq Bacon Meatballs

Servings: 4
Cooking Time: 60 Minutes

Ingredients:

- 1 Pound ground beef
- 1 egg
- 1/4 Cup milk
- 1/2 Cup breadcrumbs
- 2 Tablespoon Beef Rub
- 4 Strips bacon, cut in half
- 1/4 Cup Rub
- 1/2 Cup Apricot BBQ Sauce

Directions:

1. Mix beef, egg, milk, breadcrumbs and Traeger Beef Rub in a large bowl by hand. Once well mixed, make 2 ounce meatballs until complete.
2. Wrap each meatball with a half slice of bacon and slide toothpick all the way through.
3. Put Traeger Rub in a small bowl and roll each meatball in the rub until well coated.
4. Supply your smoker with wood pellets and follow the start-up procedure. Preheat the grill, with the lid closed, to 180° F.
5. Place the meatballs on the grate, close the lid and smoke for 1 hour. Grill: 180 °F
6. Increase the Traeger temperature to 350°F and preheat, lid closed for 15 minutes. Cook meatballs for another 20 to 30 minutes or until the internal temperature reaches 160°F to 165°F. Grill: 350 °F Probe: 160 °F
7. About 10 minutes before the meatballs are ready, brush with Traeger Apricot BBQ Sauce and allow it to caramelize.
8. Remove from grill and allow to rest for 5 minutes. Enjoy!

Citrus Grilled Lamb Chops

Servings: 4 - 6
Cooking Time: 15 Minutes

Ingredients:

- 2 Tablespoons Chophouse Steak Seasoning
- 4 Finely Garlic Clove, Minced
- 2 Pounds Thick Cut Rib Chops Or Lamb Loin
- Juice From 1/2 Lemon
- Juice From 1/2 Lime
- ¼ Cup Olive Oil
- 3 Tablespoons Orange Juice
- ¼ Cup Red Wine Vinegar

Directions:

1. In a mixing bowl, whisk together all the ingredients and 2 tbsp Chophouse Steak. Place the lamb chops in a glass baking pan and pour the marinade over the top. Flip the chops over a few times to make sure that they are completely coated.
2. Cover the glass pan in aluminum foil and allow the lamb chops to marinade for 4-12 hours. Once the meat has finished marinating, drain off the excess marinade and discard.
3. Supply your smoker with wood pellets and follow the start-up procedure. Preheat the grill, with the lid closed, to 400° F. If you're using a gas or charcoal grill, set it up for medium high heat. Grill the chops for 5-7 minutes per side, then lower the temperature to 350°F or medium heat, and flip and grill for another 5-7 minutes.
4. Remove the lamb chops from the grill, cover in foil, and allow to rest for 5 minutes before serving.

Moked Christmas Crown Roast Of Lamb

Servings: 4
Cooking Time: 120 Minutes

Ingredients:

- 2 racks of lamb, trimmed, frenched, and tied into a crown
- 1¼ cups extra-virgin olive oil, divided
- 2 tablespoons chopped fresh basil
- 2 tablespoons chopped fresh rosemary
- 2 tablespoons ground sage
- 2 tablespoons ground thyme
- 8 garlic cloves, minced
- 2 teaspoons salt
- 2 teaspoons freshly ground black pepper

Directions:

1. Set the lamb out on the counter to take the chill off, about an hour.
2. In a small bowl, combine 1 cup of olive oil, the basil, rosemary, sage, thyme, garlic, salt, and pepper.
3. Baste the entire crown with the herbed olive oil and wrap the exposed frenched bones in aluminum foil.
4. Supply your smoker with wood pellets and follow the start-up procedure. Preheat, with the lid closed, to 275°F.
5. Put the lamb directly on the grill, close the lid, and smoke for 1 hour 30 minutes to 2 hours, or until a meat thermometer inserted in the thickest part reads 140°F.
6. Remove the lamb from the heat, tent with foil, and let rest for about 15 minutes before serving. The temperature will rise about 5°F during the rest period, for a finished temperature of 145°F.

Green Chile Cheese Beef Sliders

Servings: 8 - 10
Cooking Time: 480 Minutes

Ingredients:

- Aluminum Foil Aluminum Foil

- 1 Can Beef Broth
- 1 Package Slider Buns
- Cheddar Cheese, Slices
- 1 5-6Lbs Trimmed Beef Chuck Roast
- 1 Can Green Chiles, Diced
- 7 Oz Jar Salsa Verde
- 2 Tablespoons Sweet Heat Rub

Directions:
1. Supply your smoker with wood pellets and follow the start-up procedure. Preheat the grill, with the lid closed, to 300° F. If you're using a gas or charcoal grill, set the temperature to medium heat.
2. Remove the beef chuck roast from its packaging, drain any excess fluid, and pat it dry with paper towels.
3. Place the chuck roast in a disposable aluminum pan. Pour the salsa verde, diced green chiles, Sweet Heat Rub, and beef broth over the top of the roast.
4. Place a temperature probe into the thickest part of the chuck roast and tightly wrap the top of the pan in aluminum foil to seal it.
5. Grill for 5-6 hours, or until the beef is at an internal temperature of 202°F and is tender and falling apart.
6. Remove the chuck roast from the grill and allow it to rest for 30 minutes.
7. Once the chuck roast has finished resting, use the Meat Claws to shred the beef, discarding any fatty parts.
8. Top the slider buns with a slice of Cheddar cheese and a spoonful of the Green Chile Shredded Beef, and serve immediately.

Savory Teriyaki Smoked Steak Bites

Servings: 2
Cooking Time: 90 Minutes

Ingredients:
- Sirloin steak
- Teriyaki sauce
- Light brown sugar
- Garlic powder
- Garlic salt
- Soy sauce
- Apple cider vinegar
- Pepper

Directions:
1. Mix all ingredients for the marinade.
2. Trim steak and cut into 2 inches pieces.
3. Place in a zip lock bag and pour marinade over the steak. Squeeze as much air out as possible and tightly seal the bag.
4. Freeze the steak for at least 8 hours or overnight.
5. Supply your smoker with wood pellets and follow the start-up procedure. Preheat the grill, with the lid closed, to 225 °F.
6. Place the steak bites directly on the rack. Discard remaining marinade.
7. Smoke for 1 hour and 30 minutes or until the internal temp is 135-140 degrees F.

3-2-1 Bbq Beef Cheeks

Servings: 8
Cooking Time: 480 Minutes

Ingredients:
- 2 (2 lb) beef cheeks, silverskin trimmed
- Beef Rub
- 1/4 Cup liquid of choice (beef stock, dark beer, etc.)
- 2 Tablespoon honey, brown sugar or other sweetener

Directions:
1. Make sure the beef cheeks are trimmed of all silverskin. Season liberally with Traeger Beef rub.
2. Supply your smoker with wood pellets and follow the start-up procedure. Preheat the grill, with the lid closed, to 180° F.
3. Place beef cheeks directly on the grill grate and cook until they reach an internal temperature of 165°F, about 3 hours. Remove from grill and place the cheeks in a small rimmed baking dish. Grill: 180 °F Probe: 165 °F
4. Increase grill temperature to 225°F.
5. In a small bowl, combine liquid and sweetener and stir until sweetener is dissolved. Pour mixture into the baking dish and return the cheeks to the grill to cook for an additional two hours. Grill: 225 °F
6. Remove cheeks from the grill and cover with foil. Return to the grill to cook for an additional hour or until the internal temperature reaches 205°F. Grill: 225 °F Probe: 205 °F
7. Remove from the grill and allow the steam to escape. Wrap with foil again and let rest for 30 minutes before shredding or slicing. Enjoy!

Standing Venison Rib Roast

Servings: 6
Cooking Time: 30 Minutes

Ingredients:
- 1 (2 To 2-1/2 Lb) 8-Bone Venison Roast
- 1 Tablespoon extra-virgin olive oil
- Prime Rib Rub
- Blackened Saskatchewan Rub
- Coffee Rub

Directions:
1. Supply your smoker with wood pellets and follow the start-up procedure. Preheat the grill, with the lid closed, to 375° F.

2. Rub the olive oil over the roast coating evenly. Then season with Traeger Prime Rib Rub liberally.
3. Place the roast directly on the grill grate bone side down.
4. Cook for 20-25 minutes or until the internal temperature reaches 125°F when an instant read thermometer is inserted into the thickest part of the roast. Grill: 375 °F Probe: 125 °F
5. Remove from the grill and let rest 5-10 minutes before carving. Enjoy!

Reverse-seared Steaks

Servings: 4
Cooking Time: 120 Minutes

Ingredients:
- 4 (4-ounce) sirloin steaks
- 2 tablespoons olive oil
- Salt
- Freshly ground black pepper
- 4 tablespoons butter

Directions:
1. Supply your smoker with wood pellets and follow the start-up procedure. Preheat the grill, with the lid closed, to 180°F.
2. Rub the steaks all over with olive oil and season both sides with salt and pepper.
3. Place the steaks directly on the grill grate and smoke until their internal temperature reaches 135°F. Remove the steaks from the grill.
4. Place a cast-iron skillet on the grill grate and increase the grill's temperature to 450°F.
5. Place the steaks in the skillet and top each with 1 tablespoon of butter. Cook the steaks until their internal temperature reaches 145°F, flipping once after 2 or 3 minutes. (I recommend reverse-searing over an open flame rather than in the cast-iron skillet, if your grill has that option.) Remove the steaks and serve immediately.

Bison Meatballs

Servings: 8 - 10
Cooking Time: 30 Minutes

Ingredients:
- 1 Cored, Peeled, And Chopped Apple
- 2 Tablespoons Beef & Brisket Rub
- 2 Cups Beef Broth
- 2 Pounds Ground Bison
- ¼ Cup Breadcrumbs
- 3 Tablespoons Cornstarch
- 2 Tablespoons Dijon Mustard
- 2 Beaten Eggs
- 1 Finely Garlic Clove, Minced
- 2 Cups Hard Cider
- 3 Tablespoons Pure Maple Syrup
- 2 Tablespoons Olive Oil
- ½ Cup Pureed Onion
- ¼ Pound Pancetta
- 3 Tablespoons Water
- 1 Thinly Sliced Yellow Onion

Directions:
1. First, make the mustard sauce. In a large saucepan, add the olive oil over medium heat, then add the onion and apple. Cook the apple and onion until soft and caramelized, about 10-12 minutes. Once the onion and apple are soft, add in the hard cider, beef broth, maple syrup and Dijon mustard to the pan. Whisk everything together and bring the sauce to a boil.
2. Once the sauce comes to a boil, reduce it to a simmer and cook, stirring and scraping the bottom of the pot occasionally until the sauce reduces by half, about 30 minutes. Remove the sauce from the heat and allow it to cool.
3. Pour the sauce into a blender, place the lid on top, and blend the sauce until completely smooth. Return the sauce into the saucepan and bring it back to a boil. In a small bowl, mix together the cornstarch and water, then pour into the sauce. Cook the sauce until thickened, whisking the entire time, about 2 minutes. Set the sauce aside.
4. Make the meatballs. In a food processor, blend the pancetta until it becomes a smooth paste. Scrape the pancetta into large mixing bowl, and mix it with the ground bison, pureed onion, eggs, breadcrumbs, garlic, and Beef and Brisket Rub. Gently mix the meat together and, using a cookie scoop, scoop into meatballs. Place the meatballs on a baking sheet. Repeat with the remaining meat mixture.
5. Supply your smoker with wood pellets and follow the start-up procedure. Preheat the grill, with the lid closed, to 350° F. If you're using a gas or charcoal grill, set it up for medium heat. Place a large cast iron skillet on the grill and add the olive oil to it. Place the meatballs in an even layer in the skillet and grill, turning the meatballs occasionally until they are browned on all sides. Insert a temperature probe into one of the meatballs and continue grilling them until the internal temperature reaches 160°F.
6. Remove the meatballs from the grill, toss them with the mustard sauce, and serve immediately.

Smoked Beer Corned Beef

Servings: 6
Cooking Time: 240 Minutes

Ingredients:
- 6 lb corned beef brisket raw
- 2 tbsp black pepper
- 8 oz light beer

Directions:

1. Supply your smoker with wood pellets and follow the start-up procedure. Preheat the grill, with the lid closed, to 275 °F.
2. Cut open packaging of corned beef and drain off liquid. Be sure to grab the spice packet included with the brisket. Gently rinse off corned beef and then pat dry with a paper towel.
3. Open the spice packet included with your corned beef and sprinkle contents over the brisket, then sprinkle a light dusting of black pepper according to your preference.
4. Once pellet grill has reached temperature, insert probes into corned beef brisket pieces. If you only have a single probe, insert that probe in the center of the smallest piece because it will cook the fastest.
5. Smoke for 3 to 4 hours until corned beef reaches an internal temperature of 175 degrees F. Next transfer briskets to an aluminum pan and pour just enough beer in to cover the bottom of the pan. Cover with foil leaving one corner open to let out steam.
6. Continue cooking for another 2-3 hours until internal temperature reaches about 205 degrees F. Use an instant read thermometer and poke different parts of the brisket checking for tenderness. If probe goes into the meat with very little tension than it is done. If not, continue cooking until it becomes tender.
7. Once meat is tender and fully cooked, remove pan from pellet grill and let the corned beef rest for about 30 minutes still covered with one corner open to prevent overcooking.
8. Slice corned beef into 1/8 inch slices cutting against the grains of the brisket. If brisket crumbles make slices a little thicker.

Beer Braised Beef Sandwiches

Servings: 4
Cooking Time: 180 Minutes

Ingredients:
- 12 oz beer, porter or stout
- 1/2 black pepper
- 2 1/2 lbs chuck roast
- 4 hoagie rolls, sliced lengthwise
- 1/4 cup horseradish sauce
- 1 tbsp kosher salt
- 1 tbsp parsley, chopped
- 1 red onion, cut into thick rings
- 1/2 tbsp worcestershire sauce
- 1 yellow onion, cut into thick rings

Directions:
1. Supply your smoker with wood pellets and follow the start-up procedure. Preheat the grill, with the lid open, to 450° F. If using a gas or charcoal grill, set it up for high heat.
2. Set the chuck roast on a sheet tray, then season with salt and pepper. Place onions in a cast iron skillet or Dutch oven with a lid. Set aside.
3. Sear the chuck roast on the grill, 3 minutes per side, then transfer to the skillet set on top of the onions. Add the Worcestershire sauce and beer to the skillet, along the side of the roast. Cover and reduce the temperature to 325°F. Braise the roast for 2 ½ to 3 hours, until tender.
4. Remove the roast from the grill, add parsley, then pull apart and toss in reduced pan jus and onions.
5. Serve warm on hoagie rolls with horseradish sauce.

Venison Carne Asada

Servings: 4
Cooking Time: 8 Minutes

Ingredients:
- 1½lb (680g) venison steak, such as sirloin, about ¾ inch (2cm) thick
- southwestern-style rub
- 12 large scallions or spring onions, cleaned and trimmed
- for the marinade
- 2 garlic cloves, peeled and smashed with a chef's knife
- 1 jalapeño or serrano pepper, destemmed and thinly sliced
- juice of 1 orange
- juice of 1 lime
- 1 tbsp distilled white vinegar
- 1 tsp ground cumin
- 1 tsp coarse salt
- ⅓ cup vegetable oil
- ¼ cup chopped fresh cilantro
- for serving
- warmed flour or corn tortillas (optional)
- lime wedges
- sprigs of fresh cilantro
- Salsa de Molcajete or another salsa

Directions:
1. In a small bowl, make the marinade by combining the garlic, jalapeño, orange juice, lime juice, white vinegar, cumin, and salt. Whisk until the salt dissolves. Whisk in the vegetable oil and stir in the cilantro. Place the venison in a resealable plastic bag and add the marinade, massaging the bag to thoroughly coat the meat. Refrigerate for 2 to 4 hours.
2. Supply your smoker with wood pellets and follow the start-up procedure. Preheat the grill, with the lid closed, to 450° F.
3. Drain the venison and remove any solids. (Discard the marinade.) Pat dry with paper towels. Lightly dust on both sides with the rub. Place the venison and scallions on the grate and sear until the internal temperature reaches 135°F (57°C), about 3 to 4 minutes per side. Grill the scallions until the bulbs are browned and tender, about 4 to 6 minutes, turning as needed.
4. Remove the meat and scallions from the grill. Place the venison on a cutting board and let rest for 3 minutes. Slice thinly

on a sharp diagonal. Shingle the meat on a platter. Scatter the scallions and cilantro over the top. Serve with tortillas (if using), lime wedges, cilantro, and salsa.

Bbq Beef Short Ribs With Traeger Prime Rib Rub

Servings: 6
Cooking Time: 480 Minutes

Ingredients:
- 2 (4 bone) beef short rib racks
- Prime Rib Rub
- 1 Cup beef broth

Directions:
1. Clean and trim beef short ribs. Season generously with Traeger Prime Rib Rub.
2. Supply your smoker with wood pellets and follow the start-up procedure. Preheat the grill, with the lid closed, to 225° F.
3. Place ribs directly on the grill grate and cook for 5 hours or until the internal temperature reaches 160°F. Grill: 250 °F Probe: 160 °F
4. Stack two sheets of foil on a flat surface. Place 1 rack of ribs directly in the center of the foil sheets and wrap up like a packet leaving one end open. Pour in 1/2 cup beef broth and close packet. Repeat with remaining rack.
5. Place ribs back on grill, meat side down for 2-3 more hours or until the internal temperature reaches 204°F. Remove from grill and allow to rest 10 minutes before slicing. Grill: 250 °F Probe: 204 °F
6. Cut into individual ribs and serve with your favorite sides. Enjoy!

Baked Venison Tater Tot Casserole

Servings: 4
Cooking Time: 40 Minutes

Ingredients:
- 2 Pound Venison, ground
- 2 Can Peas, canned
- 2 Can cream of mushroom soup
- 28 Ounce frozen tater tots

Directions:
1. Cook ground venison in a medium sauté pan over medium high until browned. Drain off excess fat and set venison aside.
2. In a 13x9 pan, combine venison, peas and soup. Top with tater tots.
3. Supply your smoker with wood pellets and follow the start-up procedure. Preheat the grill, with the lid closed, to 350° F.
4. Place casserole dish directly on grill grate and cook for 30 minutes. Serve hot, enjoy!

Mustard Garlic Crusted Prime Rib

Servings: 8
Cooking Time: 195 Minutes

Ingredients:
- 1 (3 Rib) Beef, Prime Rib Roast
- 1 Tbsp Black Pepper
- 2 Tbsp Garlic, Crushed
- 1 Cup Mustard, Whole Grain
- 2 Tbsp Salt, Kosher

Directions:
1. Supply your smoker with wood pellets and follow the start-up procedure. Preheat the grill, with the lid closed, to 450° F.
2. Combine salt, black pepper, mustard and garlic in a bowl. Evenly rub the seasoning all over coating the entire surface of the roast.
3. Once your grill is preheated, place the roast on the grates, ensuring the ribs are facing the back end of the grill. Once the roast is placed on the grill, shut the lid to the grill.
4. After 45 minutes, lower the temperature of the grill to 325°F. Cook for an additional 2.5 hours or until the internal temperature reaches 125°F. Remove the roast, letting it rest for about 15 minutes. Slice and enjoy!

Bbq Brisket Tacos

Servings: 6
Cooking Time: 45 Minutes

Ingredients:
- 5 Pound leftover beef brisket
- 1/2 Cup beef broth
- 5 avocados
- 4 diced Roma tomatoes
- 1 jalapeño, minced
- 1/2 Cup sour cream
- 1 lime juice
- salt and pepper
- 20 flour tortillas

Directions:
1. Supply your smoker with wood pellets and follow the start-up procedure. Preheat the grill, with the lid closed, to 300° F.
2. If not already sliced, slice brisket against the grain to 1/4 inch slices. Place sliced brisket in a double layer of foil and add beef broth. Seal foil and place on grill for 45 to 60 minutes until warm. Grill: 300 °F
3. If not using leftover brisket, see here for our favorite brisket recipe.
4. While brisket is warming up, make the guacamole. Mash the avocados and mix with tomatoes, jalapeño, onion, sour cream, lime juice and salt and pepper. Set aside.

5. Wrap the tortillas in foil and place in grill for 15 minutes or until warm. Grill: 300 °F
6. Remove brisket and tortillas from grill and assemble. Top with guacamole and your favorite toppings. Enjoy!

Pan Seared Parsley Ribeye Steak

Servings: 2
Cooking Time: 20 Minutes

Ingredients:
- , 4 tbsp butter, room temp
- 1 tsp olive oil
- 1 tsp parsley, chopped
- tt   chop house steak rub
- 1 ribeye steak, 1 to 1.5 inch thick
- 1 tsp scallion, sliced thin

Directions:
1. Season steak with   Chop House Rub, then refrigerate for 1 hour.
2. In a small bowl, use a fork to mash up butter and 1 teaspoon of   Chop House Rub. Transfer compound butter to a sheet of parchment paper, roll, and refrigerate for 1 hour.
3. Remove steak from the refrigerator, then place a covered cast iron skillet on the grill.
4. Supply your smoker with wood pellets and follow the start-up procedure. Preheat the grill, with the lid open, to 400° F.
5. If using a gas or charcoal grill, set it up for medium-high heat.
6. Remove the lid from the skillet. Open the sear slide. Add oil, then sear steak 1 to 2 minutes per side.
7. Add 3 tablespoons of butter ½ to 1 tablespoon at a time, tilting the pan, and using a spoon to baste the steak.
8. Continue searing, adding and basting with butter for an additional 3 to 5 minutes.
9. Remove steak from the skillet, rest for 5 minutes, then serve warm with additional compound butter and fresh herbs.

Classic Poor Man's Burnt Ends

Servings: 6
Cooking Time: 480 Minutes

Ingredients:
- 1/2 Cup BBQ Sauce
- 1/4 Cup Brown Sugar
- 3 Pound Chuck Roast
- 4 Tablespoons Sweet Heat Rub

Directions:
1. Supply your smoker with wood pellets and follow the start-up procedure. Preheat the grill, with the lid closed, to 275° F.
2. Season your chuck roast liberally on all sides with Sweet Rib Rub. Insert a temperature probe into the thickest part of the chuck roast and place the roast on the smoker.
3. Smoke the roast until the internal temperature reaches 165°F. Wrap the chuck roast in aluminum foil and return to the smoker until the internal temperature is 195°F, about 1 hour.
4. Remove the wrapped roast from the smoker and allow to rest for 15-20 minutes. Cut into 3/4 inch cubes and transfer to a disposable aluminum pan. Sprinkle with 1/4 cup brown sugar and drizzle with most of the BBQ sauce, reserving a couple of tablespoons for later. Toss to coat all the burnt ends with the sauce.
5. Place the pan on the grill, close the lid and cook for an additional 1 1/2 to 2 hours, or until the sauce is thickened and the burnt ends are tender. Remove from the smoker and serve.

Venison Steaks

Servings: 4
Cooking Time: 80 Minutes

Ingredients:
- 4 (8-ounce) venison steaks
- 2 tablespoons extra-virgin olive oil
- 4 garlic cloves, minced
- 1 tablespoon ground sage
- 2 teaspoons sea salt
- 2 teaspoons freshly ground black pepper

Directions:
1. Supply your smoker with wood pellets and follow the start-up procedure. Preheat, with the lid closed, to 225°F.
2. Rub the venison steaks well with the olive oil and season with the garlic, sage, salt, and pepper.
3. Arrange the venison steaks directly on the grill grate, close the lid, and smoke for 1 hour and 20 minutes, or until a meat thermometer inserted in the center reads 130°F to 140°F, depending on desired doneness. If you want a better sear, remove the steaks from the grill at an internal temperature of 125°F, crank up the heat to 450°F, or the "High" setting, and cook the steaks on each side for an additional 2 to 3 minutes.

Traeger Tri-tip Roast

Servings: 6
Cooking Time: 240 Minutes

Ingredients:
- 1 tri-tip roast
- 'Que BBQ Sauce
- Prime Rib Rub
- 1/2 Cup beef broth

Directions:

1. Plan ahead, this recipe marinates overnight. Marinade the tri-tip in Traeger 'Que BBQ Sauce overnight in refrigerator.
2. Remove tri-tip from marinade and discard marinade. Lightly season with Traeger Prime Rib Rub.
3. Supply your smoker with wood pellets and follow the start-up procedure. Preheat the grill, with the lid closed, to 180° F.
4. Place tri-tip on the grill and smoke for 3 to 4 hours. Grill: 180 °F
5. Remove tri-tip from grill and place in aluminum foil with 1/2 cup beef broth. Close aluminum foil, and increase grill temperature to 350°F. Grill: 350 °F
6. Place meat back on the grill for 45 minutes. Remove from grill and let rest for 15 minutes before slicing. Enjoy! Grill: 350 °F

Beef Caldereta Stew

Servings: 12
Cooking Time: 240 Minutes

Ingredients:

- 1/2 cup cheddar cheese, grated
- 2 lbs, cut into 1 1/2" cubes chuck roast
- 4 garlic cloves, chopped
- 1 tsp kosher salt
- 2 tbsp olive oil
- 2 large yukon gold potatoes
- 5 chopped serrano peppers
- 2 tbsp tomato paste
- 2 cups tomato sauce
- 2 cups water

Directions:

1. Place beef in a cast iron skillet, then transfer to smoking cabinet. Make sure that the sear slide and side dampers are open, then supply your smoker with wood pellets and follow the start-up procedure. Preheat the grill to 375° F, to ensure the cabinet maintains temperature between 225°F and 250°F (If you're cooking on a different Pellet Grill, set the temperature to 225°F).
2. Smoke beef for 1½ hours, then turn cubed beef, and smoke an additional 1½ hours.
3. Place cast iron Dutch oven on the grill, over flame. Add olive oil, potatoes, and carrots. Cook for 3 to 5 minutes, stirring occasionally. Then add leeks and garlic and cook for 2 minutes, until fragrant.
4. Remove skillet from smoking cabinet and add beef pieces to potato mixture.
5. Add tomato sauce, tomato paste, water, and serrano peppers. Bring to a boil, then cover with lid. Set temperature to 275°F, and allow stew to simmer for 1 hour, until beef and potatoes are tender.
6. Add liver and cheese, and gently stir to combine, until the sauce thickens and cheese has melted.

7. Add bell peppers and olives. Stir, cover and cook an additional 2 minutes. Season with salt, and serve hot.

Bbq Sweet Pepper Meatloaf

Servings: 8
Cooking Time: 180 Minutes

Ingredients:

- 5 Pound ground beef, 80% lean
- 2 eggs
- 1 Cup plain panko breadcrumbs
- 1 Tablespoon kosher salt
- 1 Tablespoon black pepper
- 2 Tablespoon Rub
- 1 Cup diced sweet red peppers
- 1 Cup green onion, finely chopped
- 1 Cup ketchup

Directions:

1. Thoroughly mix together the ground beef, eggs, plain panko bread crumbs, kosher salt, black pepper, Traeger Rub, red sweet peppers and green onion.
2. Supply your smoker with wood pellets and follow the start-up procedure. Preheat the grill, with the lid closed, to 225° F.
3. Mold the meat mixture into a loaf and season exterior with the Traeger Rub.
4. Place meatloaf directly on the grill grate and cook for 2 hours and 15 minutes. Grill: 225 °F
5. Increase the grill temperature to 375°F and cook until an internal temperature of 155°F. Grill: 375 °F Probe: 155 °F
6. Glaze the meatloaf with ketchup and cook an additional 15 minutes. Grill: 375 °F
7. Allow to rest for 15 minutes before slicing. Enjoy!

Smoked Meatball Egg Sandwiches

Servings: 4
Cooking Time: 25 Minutes

Ingredients:

- 3/4 Cup Breadcrumbs
- 2 Cloves Garlic, Minced
- 1 & 1/2 Lb. Ground Chuck
- 1 Jar Of Your Favorite Marinara Sauce
- 1 Large Eggs
- ¼ Cup Onion
- ¼ Cup Parsley, Minced Fresh
- ½ Tsp Pepper
- 1 Tbsp Chop House Steak Seasoning
- Provolone Cheese, Sliced
- ½ Tsp Salt
- Shredded Mozzarella Cheese
- 4 Sub Rolls Or Baguettes (6"), Sliced

- 2 Tbsp Worcestershire

Directions:
1. In a larger mixing bowl, combine the ground chuck, onions, garlic, Chop House Steak seasoning, salt, pepper, fresh parsley, Worcestershire, and egg. Add the breadcrumb mixture and parmesan cheese to the bowl and fold it into meat until well combined.
2. Supply your smoker with wood pellets and follow the start-up procedure. Preheat the grill, with the lid closed, to 400° F. If you're using a gas or charcoal grill, set it up for medium high heat and add your cast iron pan to the grill to warm up.
3. Roll the meat mixture into balls about 1 ½ inches wide, roughly the size of golf balls. Place meatballs into the cast iron skillet. Cook for 15 minutes or until meatballs are fully cooked and beginning to brown.
4. Pour full jar of marinara into the cast iron pan and gently stir to coat meatballs. Let simmer for 10-15 minutes.
5. Tear off four sheets of aluminum foil and place a sliced bun in the center of each. Divide the meatballs with sauce among the rolls. Top each roll with provolone cheese slices and mozzarella, and wrap entire sandwich tightly in foil. Return to the grill and cook an additional 10 minutes or until cheese is melty and bread has toasted. Serve immediately and enjoy!

Savory Chili Mac And Cheese

Servings: 4
Cooking Time: 25 Minutes

Ingredients:
- 4 Cups Beef Stock
- 2 Teaspoons Chili Powder
- 2 Tbsp Chopped Fresh Parsley Leaves
- 2 Cloves Garlic, Minced
- 1 1/2 Teaspoon Cumin
- 10 Oz. Elbow Macaroni / Noodles
- 8 Oz Ground Beef
- 3/4 Cup Kidney Beans, Drained And Rinsed
- And Freshly Ground Black Pepper Kosher Salt
- 1 Tbs Olive Oil
- 1 Onion, Diced
- 1 Tbs Sweet Heat Rub
- 3/4 Cup Shredded Cheddar Cheese
- 1 (14.5-Ounce) Tomatoes, Canned And Diced

Directions:
1. Supply your smoker with wood pellets and follow the start-up procedure. Preheat the grill, with the lid open, to 350° F. If you're using a gas or charcoal grill, set it up for medium heat.
2. Heat olive oil in a Dutch oven or cast iron pan over medium-high heat. Add garlic, onion and ground beef, and cook until browned, about 3-5 minutes. Break up the beef as it cooks with a large wooden spoon or fork.
3. Stir in beef broth, tomatoes, beans, Sweet Heat, chili powder and cumin. Add salt and pepper to taste. Bring to a simmer and stir in pasta.
4. Transfer pot to the preheated grill and cover. Cook until pasta is cooked through, about 15-20 minutes. Remove from heat and top generously with shredded cheese, replace the cover to allow cheese to melt, about 2 minutes. Garnish with fresh parsley and serve immediately!

Lemon Tomahawk Steak

Servings: 2 – 4
Cooking Time: 215 Minutes

Ingredients:
- Apple Corer Or Metal Spoon
- 3 Lbs Gala Apples
- 1 Lemon
- Chop House Steak Rub
- 1 Tbsp Tennessee Apple Butter Rub
- Sugar
- 4 Cups Water

Directions:
1. Supply your smoker with wood pellets and follow the start-up procedure. Preheat the grill, with the lid closed, to 400° F. If using a gas or charcoal grill, set heat to medium-high heat.
2. Core and halve the apples. Place apples skin-side down on a sheet tray and season with Tennessee Apple Butter and set aside.
3. In a cast iron pot, combine the apple cores with the juice and zest from one lemon. Cover the mixture with water, transfer to the grill and bring to a boil. Reduce heat to 225° F. Place the apples directly on the grill grate (skin-side down) and cook for 1 hour.
4. After 1 hour, remove cast iron pot from the grill. Strain liquid, discard cores, return liquid to pot, and whisk in sugar. Cover with lid and return to grill. Allow to simmer for another hour.
5. Add smoked apples to the pot and continue to simmer for 20 minutes. Remove pot from grill and purée apple mixture in a blender. Pour apple purée back into pot and return to grill. Increase heat to 375° F and simmer for 20 minutes. Remove from grill and allow to cool slightly.
6. Reduce heat on grill to 225° F. Season the tomahawk steak with Chop House Steak Rub on both sides. Place the steak on the grill grates, insert a temperature probe, and grill, undisturbed, for 45 minutes, or until the steak reaches an internal temperature of 120°F
7. Remove steak from grill and set aside. Open the Sear Slide on your and increase temperature to 400°F. Return tomahawk to grill and sear over open flames, about 2-3 minutes per side.
8. Pull the steak off the grill and allow it to rest for 10 minutes. Ladle reserved apple butter over steak and serve.

Herb Grilled Venison Stew

Servings: 4 - 6
Cooking Time: 210 Minutes

Ingredients:
- 2 Bay Leaves
- 2 Cups Beef Stock
- 3 Carrots, Chopped
- 2 Cups Cauliflower Florets
- ¼ Tsp Cayenne Pepper
- 2 Celery Stalks, Chopped
- 4 Garlic Cloves, Minced
- 1 Tbsp Italian Parsley
- ¼ Tsp Marjoram, Dried
- 2 Tbsp Olive Oil
- 1 Onion, Chopped
- 1 Tsp Pulled Pork Rub
- 1 Cup Red Wine
- 1 Tsp Chopped Rosemary, Fresh
- (To Taste) Salt And Pepper
- 2 Cups Chopped Spinach
- 2 Sweet Potatoes, Diced
- 2 Tbs Tomato Paste
- ½ Cup Tomatoes, Canned And Diced
- 2 Lbs. Venison Stew Meat, Cut Into 1" Cubes
- 1 Cup Zucchini, Largely Diced

Directions:
1. Supply your smoker with wood pellets and follow the start-up procedure. Preheat the grill, with the lid open, to 400° F. If using a gas or charcoal grill, set heat to medium-high heat.
2. Place cast iron Dutch oven directly on grill grates and heat olive oil until shimmering. Add onion, celery, carrot, and garlic and cook, stirring constantly, for about 5-10 minutes or until onion is translucent.
3. Increase heat on the grill to 500° F. Add venison to the pot and cook until browned on all sides. Add the red wine and allow to simmer for 2 minutes.
4. Add tomato paste, beef stock, mushrooms, sweet potato, tomatoes, rosemary, Pulled Pork Rub, sage, marjoram, cayenne, salt, pepper and bay leaves and mix well to combine. Cover pot, reduce temperature to 300° F and let the stew simmer for at least 2.5 to 3 hours.
5. Remove lid and stir in the cauliflower, spinach, and zucchini. Return cover to pot and simmer an additional 15 minutes. Stir in parsley and serve hot.

Fajita Style Mexican Hot Dogs

Servings: 4
Cooking Time: 10 Minutes

Ingredients:
- 1 Green Bell Pepper, Sliced
- 1 Package Hot Dog Bun(S)
- 1 Package High Quality Ballpark Hot Dog(S)
- 1 Tbsp Olive Oil
- 1 Tsp Beef And Brisket Rub
- 1 Yellow Bell Pepper, Sliced
- 1 Yellow Onion, Sliced

Directions:
1. Supply your smoker with wood pellets and follow the start-up procedure. Preheat the grill, with the lid closed, to 350° F.
2. In a large bowl, toss the peppers and onions with the olive oil and Beef and Brisket Rub. Place the vegetables on the mesh grilling basket.
3. Remove from the grill and assemble the hot dogs. Top the buns with a hot dog and a generous scoop of the onion and pepper mixture. Serve immediately.

Spicy Smoked Chili Beef Jerky

Servings: 6
Cooking Time: 240 Minutes

Ingredients:
- 1 Cup chili sauce
- 1/3 Cup beer
- 2 Tablespoon soy sauce
- 1 Tablespoon Worcestershire sauce
- 2 Tablespoon Morton Tender Quick Home Meat Cure
- 1 Tablespoon minced pickled jalapeño peppers
- 2 Pound flank steak, cut into 1/4 inch thick slices

Directions:
1. In a mixing bowl, combine the chili sauce, beer, soy sauce, Worcestershire sauce, curing salt and pickled jalapeño peppers.
2. Put the beef slices in a large resealable bag. Pour the marinade mixture over the beef, and massage the bag so that all the slices get coated with the marinade. Seal the bag and refrigerate for several hours, or overnight.
3. Supply your smoker with wood pellets and follow the start-up procedure. Preheat the grill, with the lid closed, to 165° F.
4. Remove the beef from the marinade, discarding the marinade. Dry beef slices between paper towels.
5. Arrange the meat in a single layer directly on the grill grate or smoke shelf.
6. Smoke for 4 to 5 hours, or until the jerky is dry but still chewy and somewhat pliant when bending a piece. Grill: 165 °F
7. Transfer to a resealable bag while the jerky is still warm.
8. Let the jerky rest for an hour at room temperature. Squeeze any air from the bag, and refrigerate the jerky.
9. Pro Tip: you can use this recipe for any cut of beef or wild game. Enjoy!

Smoked Beer Brisket

Servings: 16
Cooking Time: 420 Minutes

Ingredients:
- 1 15 lb brisket
- Brisket Baste:
- 1 cup beer
- 1/4 cup apple cider vinegar
- 1/4 cup beef stock
- 5 tbsp butter, melted
- Brisket Rub:
- 2 tbsp garlic powder
- 2 tbsp onion powder
- 2 tbsp paprika
- 2 tbsp chili powder
- 2 tbsp kosher salt
- 2 tbsp coarse ground black pepper
- 1 tbsp brown sugar

Directions:
1. Supply your smoker with wood pellets and follow the start-up procedure. Preheat the grill, with the lid closed, to 225 °F.
2. In a small bowl, mix together garlic powder, onion powder, paprika, chili pepper, kosher salt, and pepper.
3. Rub the seasonings on all sides of the brisket.
4. Place the brisket on the grill grate, fat side down.
5. Cook the brisket until it reaches an internal temperature of 160 °F (about 3 to 4 hours).
6. When brisket reaches an internal temperature of 160 °F, remove it from the grill.
7. Double wrap the meat in aluminum foil and add the beef broth to the foil packet.
8. Return brisket to the grill grate and cook until it reaches an internal temperature of 204 °F (about 3 hours more).
9. Once finished, remove the brisket from the grill, unwrap from foil and let it rest for 15 minutes.
10. Cut against the grain and serve. Enjoy!

Smoked Corned Beef Reuben

Servings: 4
Cooking Time: 255 Minutes

Ingredients:
- aluminum foil
- 1 tbsp butter
- 1 cup chicken stock
- 3 lbs corned beef brisket
- 3 tbsp dijon mustard
- 1/2 cup russian dressing
- 1 cup sauerkraut
- 6 slices sourdough bread
- 6 swiss cheese, sliced
- vegetable oil

Directions:
1. Supply your smoker with wood pellets and follow the start-up procedure. Preheat the grill, with the lid closed, to 250° F. If using a gas or charcoal grill, set it up for low, indirect heat.
2. Coat all sides of corned beef brisket flat generously in mustard. Insert a temperature probe into the middle of the brisket flat, then transfer the brisket flat directly on grill grate, fat cap up, and cook for 2 hours.
3. Remove the brisket from the grill and place it in a pan lined with foil, or a disposable aluminum pan. Add chicken stock, then cover with foil and return to the grill.
4. Increase grill temperature to 300°F, and cook an additional 1 ½ to 2 hours, or until brisket is tender and reaches 190°F.
5. Remove from grill and allow brisket to rest for 15 minutes, then slice thin for Reuben sandwiches.
6. Preheat KC Combo griddle to medium-low flame. If using a gas or charcoal grill, preheat a cast iron skillet on medium-low heat.
7. Grease griddle with butter, then set 4 slices of sourdough on griddle, followed by 2 portions of sliced corned beef brisket. Warm brisket 1 to 2 minutes, then flip. Add sauerkraut and 1 ½ slices of Swiss cheese per portion. Close griddle lid for 2 to 3 minutes to melt cheese and crisp up underside of brisket.
8. Spoon dressing on sourdough, then set brisket on every other slice. Set remaining toasted sourdough on top of cheese to complete the Reuben sandwich.
9. Remove from griddle, then repeat with remaining 2 portions. Slice each sandwich on the bias and serve warm with extra dressing for dipping.

Smoked Longhorn Brisket

Servings: 8
Cooking Time: 420 Minutes

Ingredients:
- 1 (12-14 lb) whole packer brisket, trimmed
- 1/4 Cup Prime Rib Rub
- 2 Tablespoon coffee grounds

Directions:
1. Supply your smoker with wood pellets and follow the start-up procedure. Preheat the grill, with the lid closed, to 250° F.
2. Rub brisket with Traeger Prime Rib Rub and coffee grounds.
3. Place brisket on the grill grate fat-side down and smoke until it reaches an internal temperature of 160°F, this should take about 4 to 5 hours. Grill: 250 °F Probe: 160 °F
4. Remove brisket from grill and double wrap in foil. Return wrapped brisket to grill and cook until brisket reaches an internal temperature of 204°F, about 2-1/2 to 3 hours. Grill: 250 °F Probe: 204 °F
5. Once finished, remove from grill, unwrap and let rest for 15 minutes. Slice against the grain and serve. Enjoy!

Bacon Burger

Servings: 8
Cooking Time: 180 Minutes

Ingredients:
- 1 Pack Bacon
- 2 Lbs Beef, Ground
- 1 Fresh Bread, French Loaf
- Condiments (Ketchup, Mustard, Relish, Etc.)
- 2 Egg
- Lettuce
- 2 1/2 Cups Mac And Cheese, Prepared
- 2 Tbsp Mandarin Habanero Spice
- 1/2 Cup Original BBQ Sauce
- 1 Lb Pork, Ground
- Red Onion, Chopped
- Tomato, Sliced

Directions:
1. Place plastic wrap on a clean surface and lay the mac cheese in the middle. Wrap the plastic wrap around the mac cheese so that it becomes a tube. Freeze for 30 minutes or until you're ready to put the burger together.
2. Supply your smoker with wood pellets and follow the start-up procedure. Preheat the grill, with the lid closed, to 250° F.
3. In a large pan or a clean working surface, combine the ground beef, pork, eggs, barbecue sauce, and seasoning. Mix with your hands until everything is combined.
4. Next, you're going to make a bacon weave. There are many strategies for making a bacon weave, so use whatever method you're most comfortable with. Take half of the pack of bacon and lay each strip vertically next to each other. Starting at the top left corner, lay a piece of bacon horizontally on top of the first strip of bacon. Place it under the second piece of bacon and over the third piece. Repeat this pattern until you finish the row. Now, flip the first, third, fifth, and seventh vertical strip of bacon from the end closest to you over the entire bacon weave. Lay another piece of bacon horizontally over the pieces that are still lying flat (the second, fourth, sixth, and eighth piece). Return the odd pieces of bacon back to their original vertical placement. Flip the second, fourth, sixth, and eighth vertical strip of bacon from the end closest to you over the entire bacon weave. Lay another piece of bacon horizontally over the pieces that are still lying flat (the first, third, fifth, and seventh pieceReturn the even pieces of bacon back to their original vertical placement. Continue this pattern until the bacon weave is complete.
5. On top of your bacon weave, spread out the ground beef mixture so that it completely covers the bacon. Remove the mac cheese from the plastic wrap and lay in the middle of the meat spread. Roll the bacon weave and ground beef mixture around the mac cheese tube to form a log. Ensure that the mac cheese is completely surrounded and place on the grill. Smoke for 2 1/2 to 3 hours or until the internal temperature of the meat is 145°F. If you're using a meat probe, make sure that the meat probe is in the center of the MEAT, not in the mac cheese center.
6. Prepare the French loaf by slicing it in half, topping the bottom with lettuce, red onion, tomato and any condiments you prefer. Place the burger directly on to your toppings. Top with the second half of the loaf, cut into slices and enjoy!

Smoked Cheese Beef Burgers

Servings: 4
Cooking Time: 66 Minutes

Ingredients:
- 1 ½ pounds ground beef chuck 80/20
- 4 slices cheddar cheese optional
- 4 burger buns
- Assorted burger toppings
- Smoked Burger Seasoning
- 1 Tablespoon Kosher salt
- 1 Tablespoon coarse ground black pepper
- 1 Tablespoon garlic powder

Directions:
1. Supply your smoker with wood pellets and follow the start-up procedure. Preheat the grill, with the lid closed, to 225 °F.
2. Shape your ground beef into 4 patties, about 1/2 inch larger in diameter than your burger buns.
3. In a small bowl combine the burger seasoning and sprinkle on both sides of your burger patties.
4. Place the seasoned patties on the grill and smoke for up to 1 hour, or until the internal temperature of your burgers reads 135 °F.
5. Increase the heat of your grill to the high setting (at least 400 °F). Sear the burger patties for about 2-3 minutes on both sides. Add cheese after the first flip, if desired.
6. Check the temperature of your burger patties for desired doneness. The FDA recommends 165 °F for a well done burger.
7. Remove the burger patties and toast the buns over high heat. Assemble your smoked burgers on your toasted buns with any desired toppings and serve immediately.

Duck Fat Fries (confit)

Servings: 6
Cooking Time: 180 Minutes

Ingredients:
- 1/4 Cup sea salt
- 12 Whole black peppercorn
- 2 Sprig thyme sprigs
- 2 Clove garlic, crushed
- 1 Whole bay leaves

- 6 Whole Duck Leg Quarters, (leg with thigh attached), preferallb moulard
- olive oil

Directions:
1. Combine the salt and the water in a large resealable plastic bag (or a large bowl) and stir until the salt crystals dissolve.
2. Add the peppercorns, thyme, garlic, bay leaf, coriander, if using, and duck leg quarters. Seal the bag, put in a pan or bowl (to contain any potential leaks) and refrigerate for 24 hours.
3. Drain the duck leg quarters (discard the brine) and rinse under cold running water. Pat dry with paper towels. Prick the skin all over with a darning needle or sharp fork, being careful not to nick the meat. (It helps if you go in at an angle.) This creates channels for the fat to escape, making for crispier skin.
4. Supply your smoker with wood pellets and follow the start-up procedure. Preheat the grill, with the lid closed, to 400° F.
5. Meanwhile add enough olive oil to a large cast iron skillet or roasting pan to film the bottom. Arrange the duck leg quarters in the skillet or roasting pan in a single layer, skin-side down.
6. Put the skillet or roasting pan on the grill grate. Roast the duck for 30 minutes, or until the duck fat begins to render. Reduce the temperature to 300F (150C). Turn the duck legs so they are skin-side up. Cover the skillet or roasting pan tightly with foil. Grill: 300 °F
7. Continue to roast the duck for 2 hours. Uncover the duck and roast for an additional hour, or until the skin is crisp and golden brown. Remove the duck, shred, and serve immediately. (Alternatively, you can refrigerate the duck for up to a week. Re-crisp the skin by grilling the duck, skin-side down, in a hot cast iron skillet or on your Traeger.) Serve with brown butter french fries.
8. Strain the remaining duck fat through cheesecloth or a fine-mesh kitchen strainer and transfer to a covered container; refrigerate for up to 6 months. Use the flavorful fat to saut potatoes or sturdy greens.

Smoked Longhorn Cowboy Tri-tip

Servings: 6
Cooking Time: 240 Minutes

Ingredients:
- 1 (2-3 lb) tri-tip
- 1/8 Cup coffee grounds
- 1/4 Cup Beef Rub

Directions:
1. Supply your smoker with wood pellets and follow the start-up procedure. Preheat the grill, with the lid closed, to 180° F.
2. Rub tri-tip with Traeger Beef Rub and coffee grounds. Place on the grill grate and smoke at 180°F for 3 hours. Grill: 180 °F
3. Remove tri-tip and increase the grill temperature to 275°F. Grill: 275 °F
4. Double wrap the tri-tip in foil, return to grill and let cook for 45 to 90 minutes, or until the internal temperature reaches 130°F to 135°F. Grill: 275 °F Probe: 135 °F
5. Remove from the grill, unwrap foil and let it rest for 10 minutes before slicing. Enjoy!

Garlic Beef Meatballs

Servings: 6
Cooking Time: 15 Minutes

Ingredients:
- 1 1/2 Pounds Beef, Ground Round
- 1/2 Cup Breadcrumb, Dry
- 2 Cloves Garlic, Crushed
- 3/4 Tsp Italian Seasoning, Dried
- 1 Tsp Mustard, Dry
- 1/4 Cup Parmesan Cheese, Shredded
- 1/3 Cup Parsley, Minced Fresh
- 1/4 Tsp Crushed Red Red Bell Peppers
- 1/4 Tsp Salt
- 1/4 Cup Tomato Sauce

Directions:
1. Start your Grill on "smoke" with the lid open until a fire is established in the burn pot (3-7 minutes).
2. Supply your smoker with wood pellets and follow the start-up procedure. Preheat the grill, with the lid closed, to 400° F.
3. Place all ingredients in a bowl, combine them and stir well. Shape the mixture into 30 meatballs (1 ½ inches in width).
4. Spray a broiler pan with cooking spray, place on the grill, and bake for 15 minutes until fully cooked and browned.
5. Remove from grill, cool for 5 minutes, and serve.

Smoked Corned Beef Brisket

Servings: 4
Cooking Time: 300 Minutes

Ingredients:
- 1 (3 lb) flat cut corned beef brisket, fat cap at least 1/4 inch thick
- 1 Bottle Apricot BBQ Sauce
- 1/4 Cup Dijon mustard

Directions:
1. Remove the corned beef brisket from its packaging and discard the spice packet, if any. Soak the corned beef in water for at least 8 hours changing the water every 2 hours.
2. Supply your smoker with wood pellets and follow the start-up procedure. Preheat the grill, with the lid closed, to 275° F.

3. Put the brisket directly on the grill grate, fat side up and cook for 2 hours. Grill: 275 °F
4. Meanwhile, combine the Traeger Apricot BBQ Sauce and the Dijon mustard in a medium bowl, whisking to mix.
5. Pour half of the BBQ sauce-mustard mixture in the bottom of a disposable aluminum foil pan. With tongs, transfer the brisket to the pan, fat-side up. Pour the remainder of the BBQ sauce-mustard mixture over the top of the brisket, using a spatula to spread the sauce evenly. Cover the pan tightly with aluminum foil.
6. Return the brisket to the grill and continue to cook for 2 to 3 hours, or until the brisket is tender. The internal temperature should be 203°F on an instant-read meat thermometer. Probe: 203 °F
7. Remove from the grill and allow the meat to rest for 15 to 20 minutes at room temperature. Slice across the grain into 1/4 inch slices with a sharp knife and serve immediately. Enjoy!

Flavour Smoked Corned Beef Brisket Hash

Servings: 4
Cooking Time: 195 Minutes

Ingredients:

- 6 slices, chopped bacon
- 1 tsp black pepper
- 2 cups chicken stock
- 1, 2 lb. corned beef brisket
- 2 tbsp Italian parsley
- 1 ½ tsp hickory bacon rub
- 1, chopped red bell pepper
- 1 tsp thyme, fresh, chopped
- 1, chopped yellow onion
- 1 ½ lbs yukon gold potatoes

Directions:

1. Remove corned beef brisket from packaging, rinse under cold water, and pat dry with paper towel.
2. Season brisket with included seasoning packet and coarse black pepper, then rest for 30 minutes.
3. Supply your smoker with wood pellets and follow the start-up procedure. Preheat the grill, with the lid closed, to 225° F. If using a gas or charcoal grill, set it up for low indirect heat.
4. Lay brisket directly on the grill grate and smoke for 2 ½ to 3 hours or until the internal temperature reaches 165°F.
5. Once this temperature is achieved, place the brisket in a 9 x 13 metal pan with potatoes and chicken stock.
6. Cover with foil and cook until brisket reaches an internal temperature of 202°F.
7. Remove brisket from grill and refrigerate overnight or until brisket and potatoes have fully cooled.
8. When ready to cook, peel and dice potatoes then chop up 1 lb. of brisket, reserving the remainder for future use.
9. Place a cast-iron skillet on the pellet grill and preheat to 400°F.
10. Once skillet is heated, add bacon and sauté for 8 to 10 minutes, until brown.
11. Remove with slotted spoon and place on paper towel-lined tray.
12. Add onion and red bell pepper to skillet with rendered bacon fat and sauté for 3 minutes, then add cooked brisket.
13. Add Hickory Bacon Rub, parsley and thyme and sauté another 3 minutes.
14. Add diced potatoes. Gently stir to incorporate and serve hot.

Smoked Garlic Meatloaf

Servings: 8
Cooking Time: 180 Minutes

Ingredients:

- 2 Tsp Apple Cider Vinegar
- 2 Lbs Beef, Ground
- 1/2 Tsp Chipotle Pepper Flakes
- 3 Cups Crushed Chips Corn Tortillas
- 2 Grated Garlic, Cloves
- 2/3 Cup Ketchup
- 1 Small Grated Onion, Chopped
- 4 Oz Into Sticks Pepper Jack Cheese, Sliced
- 2 Tbsp Competition Smoked Rub
- 1 Lbs Pork, Ground
- 1/4 Cup Tomato Paste
- 1 Tsp Worcestershire Sauce

Directions:

1. Supply your smoker with wood pellets and follow the start-up procedure. Preheat the grill, with the lid closed, to 250° F.
2. First make the glaze: in a bowl, combine the ketchup, tomato paste, vinegar, Worcestershire, chipotle flakes and Competition Smoked Seasoning. Whisk well to combine and set aside.
3. In a large bowl, mix together the crushed corn chips, eggs, onion and garlic. Add 2/3rds of the glaze to this mixture, reserving the rest for glazing the meatloaf. Mix well to combine and allow to sit until the corn chips have hydrated.
4. Add the ground beef and pork to the corn chip mixture and mix until everything is well distributed.
5. Form the meatloaf into a log and push the sticks of pepper jack cheese into the center of the meatloaf and cover with the meat mixture. Loosely wrap in tin foil and poke holes in the foil with a knife to allow smoke to penetrate.
6. Grill for 1 ½ hours covered, then remove the top half of the tin foil, glaze with reserved glaze, and grill for another 1 ½ hours or until the internal temperature is 165F.

APPETIZERS AND SNACKS

Chicken Wings With Teriyaki Glaze

Servings: 4
Cooking Time: 50 Minutes

Ingredients:
- 16 large chicken wings, about 3lb (1.4kg) total
- 1 to 1½ tbsp toasted sesame oil
- for the glaze
- ½ cup light soy sauce or tamari
- ¼ cup sake or sugar-free dark-colored soda
- ¼ cup light brown sugar or low-carb substitute
- 2 tbsp mirin or 1 tbsp honey
- 1 garlic clove, peeled, minced or grated
- 2 tsp minced fresh ginger
- 1 tsp cornstarch mixed with 1 tbsp distilled water (optional)
- for serving
- 1 tbsp toasted sesame seeds
- 2 scallions, trimmed, white and green parts sliced sharply diagonally

Directions:
1. Supply your smoker with wood pellets and follow the start-up procedure. Preheat the grill, with the lid closed, to 350° F.
2. Place the chicken wings in a large bowl, add the sesame oil, and turn the wings to coat thoroughly.
3. Place the wings on the grate at an angle to the bars. Grill for 20 minutes and then turn. Continue to cook until the wings are nicely browned and the meat is no longer pink at the bone, about 20 minutes more.
4. To make the glaze, in a saucepan on the stovetop over medium-high heat, combine the ingredients and bring the mixture to a boil. Reduce the glaze by 1/3, about 6 to 8 minutes. If you prefer your glaze to be glossy and thick, add the cornstarch and water mixture to the glaze and cook until it coats the back of a spoon, about 1 to 2 minutes more.
5. Transfer the wings to an aluminum foil roasting pan. Pour the glaze over them, turning to coat thoroughly. Place the pan on the grate and cook the wings until the glaze sets, about 5 to 10 minutes.
6. Transfer the wings to a platter. Scatter the sesame seeds and scallions over the top. Serve with plenty of napkins.

Bacon-wrapped Jalapeño Poppers

Servings: 12
Cooking Time: 30 Minutes

Ingredients:
- 8 ounces cream cheese, softened
- ½ cup shredded Cheddar cheese
- ¼ cup chopped scallions
- 1 teaspoon chipotle chile powder or regular chili powder
- 1 teaspoon garlic powder
- 1 teaspoon salt
- 18 large jalapeño peppers, stemmed, seeded, and halved lengthwise
- 1 pound bacon (precooked works well)

Directions:
1. Supply your smoker with wood pellets and follow the start-up procedure. Preheat, with the lid closed, to 350°F. Line a baking sheet with aluminum foil.
2. In a small bowl, combine the cream cheese, Cheddar cheese, scallions, chipotle powder, garlic powder, and salt.
3. Stuff the jalapeño halves with the cheese mixture.
4. Cut the bacon into pieces big enough to wrap around the stuffed pepper halves.
5. Wrap the bacon around the peppers and place on the prepared baking sheet.
6. Put the baking sheet on the grill grate, close the lid, and smoke the peppers for 30 minutes, or until the cheese is melted and the bacon is cooked through and crisp.
7. Let the jalapeño poppers cool for 3 to 5 minutes. Serve warm.

Bacon Pork Pinwheels (kansas Lollipops)

Servings: 4-6
Cooking Time: 20 Minutes

Ingredients:
- 1 Whole Pork Loin, boneless
- To Taste salt and pepper
- To Taste Greek Seasoning
- 4 Slices bacon
- To Taste The Ultimate BBQ Sauce

Directions:
1. When ready to cook, start the smoker and set temperature to 500F. Preheat, lid closed, for 10 to 15 minutes.
2. Trim pork loin of any unwanted silver skin or fat. Using a sharp knife, cut pork loin length wise, into 4 long strips.
3. Lay pork flat, then season with salt, pepper and Cavender's Greek Seasoning.
4. Flip the pork strips over and layer bacon on unseasoned side. Begin tightly rolling the pork strips, with bacon being rolled up on the inside.
5. Secure a skewer all the way through each pork roll to secure it in place. Set the pork rolls down on grill and cook for 15 minutes.
6. Brush BBQ Sauce over the pork. Turn each skewer over, then coat the other side. Let pork cook for another 5-10 minutes, depending on thickness of your pork. Enjoy!

Bayou Wings With Cajun Rémoulade

Servings: 8
Cooking Time: 40 Minutes

Ingredients:
- 16 large whole chicken wings or 32 drumettes and flats, about 3lb (1.4kg) total
- for the rub
- 1 tbsp kosher salt
- 1 tsp freshly ground black pepper
- 1 tsp paprika
- ½ tsp ground cayenne, plus more
- ½ tsp garlic powder
- ½ tsp celery salt
- ½ tsp dried thyme
- 2 tbsp vegetable oil
- for the rémoulade
- 1¼ cups reduced-fat mayo
- ¼ cup Creole-style or whole grain mustard
- 2 tbsp horseradish
- 2 tbsp pickle relish
- 1 tbsp freshly squeezed lemon juice
- 1 tsp paprika, plus more
- 1 tsp hot sauce, plus more
- 1 tsp Worcestershire sauce
- coarse salt
- for serving
- lemon wedges
- pickled okra (optional)

Directions:
1. Supply your smoker with wood pellets and follow the start-up procedure. Preheat the grill, with the lid closed, to 350° F.
2. If using whole wings, cut through the two joints, separating them into drumettes, flats, and wing tips. (Discard the wing tips or save them for chicken stock.) Alternatively, leave the wings whole. Place the chicken in a resealable plastic bag.
3. In a small bowl, make the rub by combining the ingredients. Mix well. Pour the rub over the wings and toss them to thoroughly coat. Refrigerate for 2 hours.
4. In a small bowl, make the Cajun rémoulade by whisking together the mayo, mustard, horseradish, pickle relish, lemon juice, paprika, hot sauce, and Worcestershire. Season with salt to taste. The mixture should be highly seasoned. Transfer to a serving bowl and lightly dust with paprika. Cover and refrigerate until ready to serve.
5. Remove the wings from the refrigerator and allow the excess marinade to drip off. Place the wings on the grate at an angle to the bars. Grill for 20 minutes and then turn. (They'll brown more evenly but will also have less of a tendency to stick.) Continue to cook until the wings are nicely browned and the meat is no longer pink at the bone, about 20 minutes more.
6. Remove the wings from the grill and pile them on a platter. Serve with the Cajun rémoulade, lemon wedges, and pickled okra (if using).

Pulled Pork Loaded Nachos

Servings: 4
Cooking Time: 10 Minutes

Ingredients:
- 2 cups leftover smoked pulled pork
- 1 small sweet onion, diced
- 1 medium tomato, diced
- 1 jalapeño pepper, seeded and diced
- 1 garlic clove, minced
- 1 teaspoon salt
- 1 teaspoon freshly ground black pepper
- 1 bag tortilla chips
- 1 cup shredded Cheddar cheese
- ½ cup The Ultimate BBQ Sauce, divided
- ½ cup shredded jalapeño Monterey Jack cheese
- Juice of ½ lime
- 1 avocado, halved, pitted, and sliced
- 2 tablespoons sour cream
- 1 tablespoon chopped fresh cilantro

Directions:
1. Supply your smoker with wood pellets and follow the start-up procedure. Preheat, with the lid closed, to 375°F.
2. Heat the pulled pork in the microwave.
3. In a medium bowl, combine the onion, tomato, jalapeño, garlic, salt, and pepper, and set aside.
4. Arrange half of the tortilla chips in a large cast iron skillet. Spread half of the warmed pork on top and cover with the Cheddar cheese. Top with half of the onion-jalapeño mixture, then drizzle with ¼ cup of barbecue sauce.
5. Layer on the remaining tortilla chips, then the remaining pork and the Monterey Jack cheese. Top with the remaining onion-jalapeño mixture and drizzle with the remaining ¼ cup of barbecue sauce.
6. Place the skillet on the grill, close the lid, and smoke for about 10 minutes, or until the cheese is melted and bubbly. (Watch to make sure your chips don't burn!)
7. Squeeze the lime juice over the nachos, top with the avocado slices and sour cream, and garnish with the cilantro before serving hot.

Citrus-infused Marinated Olives

Servings: 6
Cooking Time: 30 Minutes

Ingredients:
- 1½ cups mixed brined olives, with pits
- ½ cup extra virgin olive oil
- 1 tbsp freshly squeezed lemon juice
- 1 garlic clove, peeled and thinly sliced
- 1 tsp smoked Spanish paprika
- 2 sprigs of fresh rosemary
- 2 sprigs of fresh thyme
- 2 bay leaves, fresh or dried
- 1 small dried red chili pepper, deseeded and flesh crumbled, or ¼ tsp crushed red pepper flakes
- 3 strips of orange zest
- 3 strips of lemon zest

Directions:
1. Supply your smoker with wood pellets and follow the start-up procedure. Preheat the grill, with the lid closed, to 180° F.
2. Drain the olives, reserving 1 tablespoon of brine. Spread the olives in a single layer in an aluminum foil roasting pan. Place the pan on the grate and cook the olives for 30 minutes, stirring the olives or shaking the pan once or twice.
3. In a small saucepan on the stovetop over low heat, warm the olive oil. Whisk in the lemon juice and the reserved 1 tablespoon of brine. Stir in the garlic and paprika. Add the rosemary, thyme, bay leaves, chili pepper, and orange and lemon zests. Warm over low heat for 10 minutes. Remove the saucepan from the heat.
4. Transfer the olives and olive oil mixture to a pint jar. Tuck the aromatics around the sides of the jar. Let cool and then cover and refrigerate for up to 5 days. Let the olives come to room temperature before serving.

Chorizo Queso Fundido

Servings: 4-6
Cooking Time: 20 Minutes

Ingredients:
- 1 poblano chile
- 1 cup chopped queso quesadilla or queso Oaxaca
- 1 cup shredded Monterey Jack cheese
- ¼ cup milk
- 1 tablespoon all-purpose flour
- 2 (4-ounce) links Mexican chorizo sausage, casings removed
- ⅓ cup beer
- 1 tablespoon unsalted butter
- 1 small red onion, chopped
- ½ cup whole kernel corn
- 2 serrano chiles or jalapeño peppers, stemmed, seeded, and coarsely chopped
- 1 tablespoon minced garlic
- 1 tablespoon freshly squeezed lime juice
- 1 teaspoon ground cumin
- 1 teaspoon salt
- 1 teaspoon freshly ground black pepper
- 1 tablespoon chopped fresh cilantro
- 1 tablespoon chopped scallions
- Tortilla chips, for serving

Directions:
1. Supply your smoker with wood pellets and follow the start-up procedure. Preheat, with the lid closed, to 350°F.
2. On the smoker or over medium-high heat on the stove top, place the poblano directly on the grate (or burner) to char for 1 to 2 minutes, turning as needed. Remove from heat and place in a closed-up lunch-size paper bag for 2 minutes to sweat and further loosen the skin.
3. Remove the skin and coarsely chop the poblano, removing the seeds; set aside.
4. In a bowl, combine the queso quesadilla, Monterey Jack, milk, and flour; set aside.
5. On the stove top, in a cast iron skillet over medium heat, cook and crumble the chorizo for about 2 minutes.
6. Transfer the cooked chorizo to a small, grill-safe pan and place over indirect heat on the smoker.
7. Place the cast iron skillet on the preheated grill grate. Pour in the beer and simmer for a few minutes, loosening and stirring in any remaining sausage bits from the pan.
8. Add the butter to the pan, then add the cheese mixture a little at a time, stirring constantly.
9. When the cheese is smooth, stir in the onion, corn, serrano chiles, garlic, lime juice, cuvmin, salt, and pepper. Stir in the reserved chopped charred poblano.
10. Close the lid and smoke for 15 to 20 minutes to infuse the queso with smoke flavor and further cook the vegetables.
11. When the cheese is bubbly, top with the chorizo mixture and garnish with the cilantro and scallions.
12. Serve the chorizo queso fundido hot with tortilla chips.

Grilled Guacamole

Servings: 6
Cooking Time: 30 Minutes

Ingredients:
- 3 large avocados, halved and pitted
- 1 lime, halved
- ½ jalapeño, deseeded and deveined
- ½ small white or red onion, peeled
- 2 garlic cloves, peeled and skewered on a toothpick
- 1 tsp coarse salt, plus more
- 1½ tbsp reduced-fat mayo

- 2 tbsp chopped fresh cilantro
- 2 tbsp crumbled queso fresco (optional)
- tortilla chips

Directions:
1. Supply your smoker with wood pellets and follow the start-up procedure. Preheat the grill, with the lid closed, to 225° F.
2. Place the avocados, lime, jalapeño, and onion cut sides down on the grate. Use the toothpicks to balance the garlic cloves between the bars. Smoke for 30 minutes. (You want the vegetables to retain most of their rawness.)
3. Transfer everything to a cutting board. Remove the garlic cloves from the toothpick and roughly chop. Sprinkle with the salt and continue to mince the garlic until it begins to form a paste. Scrape the garlic and salt into a large bowl.
4. Scoop the avocado flesh from the peels into the bowl. Squeeze the juice of ½ lime over the avocado. Mash the avocados but leave them somewhat chunky. Finely dice the jalapeño. Dice 2 tablespoons of onion. (Reserve the remaining onion for another use.) Add the jalapeño, onion, mayo, and cilantro to the bowl. Stir gently to combine. Taste for seasoning, adding more salt, lime juice, and jalapeño as desired.
5. Transfer the guacamole to a serving bowl. Top with the queso fresco (if using). Serve with tortilla chips.

Pigs In A Blanket

Servings: 4-6
Cooking Time: 15 Minutes

Ingredients:
- 2 Tablespoon Poppy Seeds
- 1 Tablespoon Dried Minced Onion
- 2 Teaspoon garlic, minced
- 2 Tablespoon Sesame Seeds
- 1 Teaspoon salt
- 8 Ounce Original Crescent Dough
- 1/4 Cup Dijon mustard
- 1 Large egg, beaten

Directions:
1. When ready to cook, start your smoker at 350 degrees F, and preheat with lid closed, 10 to 15 minutes.
2. Mix together poppy seeds, dried minced onion, dried minced garlic, salt and sesame seeds. Set aside.
3. Cut each triangle of crescent roll dough into thirds lengthwise, making 3 small strips from each roll.
4. Brush the dough strips lightly with Dijon mustard. Put the mini hot dogs on 1 end of the dough and roll up.
5. Arrange them, seam side down, on a greased baking pan. Brush with egg wash and sprinkle with seasoning mixture.
6. Bake in smoker until golden brown, about 12 to 15 minutes.
7. Serve with mustard or dipping sauce of your choice. Enjoy!

Simple Cream Cheese Sausage Balls

Servings: 5
Cooking Time: 30 Minutes

Ingredients:
- 1 pound ground hot sausage, uncooked
- 8 ounces cream cheese, softened
- 1 package mini filo dough shells

Directions:
1. Supply your smoker with wood pellets and follow the start-up procedure. Preheat, with the lid closed, to 350°F.
2. In a large bowl, using your hands, thoroughly mix together the sausage and cream cheese until well blended.
3. Place the filo dough shells on a rimmed perforated pizza pan or into a mini muffin tin.
4. Roll the sausage and cheese mixture into 1-inch balls and place into the filo shells.
5. Place the pizza pan or mini muffin tin on the grill, close the lid, and smoke the sausage balls for 30 minutes, or until cooked through and the sausage is no longer pink.
6. Plate and serve warm.

Deviled Eggs With Smoked Paprika

Servings: 6
Cooking Time: 30 Minutes

Ingredients:
- 6 large eggs
- 3 tbsp reduced-fat mayo, plus more
- 1 tsp Dijon or yellow mustard
- ½ tsp Spanish smoked paprika or regular paprika, plus more
- dash of hot sauce
- coarse salt
- freshly ground black pepper
- for garnishing
- small sprigs of fresh parsley, dill, tarragon, or cilantro
- chopped chives
- minced scallions
- Mustard Caviar
- sliced green or black olives
- celery leaves
- sliced radishes
- diced bell peppers
- sliced cherry tomatoes
- fresh or pickled jalapeños
- sliced or diced pickles
- slivers of sun-dried tomatoes
- bacon crumbles
- smoked salmon
- Hawaiian black salt
- Caviar

Directions:
1. Supply your smoker with wood pellets and follow the start-up procedure. Preheat the grill, with the lid closed, to 180° F.
2. On the stovetop over medium-high heat, bring a saucepan of water to a boil. (Make sure there's enough water in the saucepan to cover the eggs by 1 inch [5cm].) Use a slotted spoon to gently lower the eggs into the water. Lower the heat to maintain a simmer. Set a timer for 13 minutes.
3. Prepare an ice bath by combining ice and cold water in a large bowl. Carefully transfer the eggs to the ice bath when the timer goes off.
4. When the eggs are cool enough to handle, gently tap them all over to crack the shell. Carefully peel the eggs. Rinse under cold running water to remove any clinging bits of shell, but don't dry the eggs. (A damp surface will help the smoke adhere to the egg whites.)
5. Place the eggs on the grate and smoke until the eggs take on a light brown patina from the smoke, about 25 minutes. Transfer the eggs to a cutting board, handling them as little as possible.
6. Slice each egg in half lengthwise with a sharp knife. Wipe any yolk off the blade before slicing the next egg. Gently remove the yolks and place them in a food processor. Pulse to break up the yolks. Add the mayo, mustard, paprika, and hot sauce. Season with salt and pepper to taste. Pulse until the filling is smooth. Add additional mayo 1 teaspoon at a time if the mixture is a little dry. (It shouldn't be too loose either.)
7. Spoon the filling into each egg half or pipe it in using a small resealable plastic bag. You can also use a pastry bag fitted with a fluted tip.
8. Place the eggs on a platter and lightly dust with paprika. Accompany with one or more of the suggested garnishes.

Smoked Cashews

Servings: 6
Cooking Time: 60 Minutes

Ingredients:
- 1 pound roasted, salted cashews

Directions:
1. Supply your smoker with wood pellets and follow the start-up procedure. Preheat the grill, with the lid closed, to 120°F.
2. Pour the cashews onto a rimmed baking sheet and smoke for 1 hour, stirring once about halfway through the smoking time.
3. Remove the cashews from the grill, let cool, and store in an airtight container for as long as you can resist.

Pig Pops (sweet-hot Bacon On A Stick)

Servings: 24
Cooking Time: 30 Minutes

Ingredients:
- Nonstick cooking spray, oil, or butter, for greasing
- 2 pounds thick-cut bacon (24 slices)
- 24 metal skewers
- 1 cup packed light brown sugar
- 2 to 3 teaspoons cayenne pepper
- ½ cup maple syrup, divided

Directions:
1. Supply your smoker with wood pellets and follow the start-up procedure. Preheat, with the lid closed, to 350°F.
2. Coat a disposable aluminum foil baking sheet with cooking spray, oil, or butter.
3. Thread each bacon slice onto a metal skewer and place on the prepared baking sheet.
4. In a medium bowl, stir together the brown sugar and cayenne.
5. Baste the top sides of the bacon with ¼ cup of maple syrup.
6. Sprinkle half of the brown sugar mixture over the bacon.
7. Place the baking sheet on the grill, close the lid, and smoke for 15 to 30 minutes.
8. Using tongs, flip the bacon skewers. Baste with the remaining ¼ cup of maple syrup and top with the remaining brown sugar mixture.
9. Continue smoking with the lid closed for 10 to 15 minutes, or until crispy. You can eyeball the bacon and smoke to your desired doneness, but the actual ideal internal temperature for bacon is 155°F
10. Using tongs, carefully remove the bacon skewers from the grill. Let cool completely before handling.

Chuckwagon Beef Jerky

Servings: 6
Cooking Time: 300 Minutes

Ingredients:
- 2½lb (1.2kg) boneless top or bottom round steak, sirloin tip, flank steak, or venison
- 1 cup sugar-free dark-colored soda
- 1 cup cold brewed coffee
- ½ cup light soy sauce
- ¼ cup Worcestershire sauce
- 2 tbsp whiskey (optional)
- 2 tsp chili powder
- 1½ tsp garlic salt
- 1 tsp onion powder
- 1 tsp pink curing salt

Directions:
1. Slice the meat into ¼-inch-thick (.5cm) strips, trimming off any visible fat or gristle. (Slice against the grain for more tender jerky and with the grain for chewier jerky.) Place the meat in a large resealable plastic bag.

2. In a small bowl, whisk together the soda, coffee, soy sauce, Worcestershire sauce, whiskey (if using), chili powder, garlic salt, onion powder, and curing salt (if using). Whisk until the salt dissolves. Pour the mixture over the meat and reseal the bag. Refrigerate for 24 to 48 hours, turning the bag several times to redistribute the brine.

3. Supply your smoker with wood pellets and follow the start-up procedure. Preheat the grill, with the lid closed, to 150° F.

4. Drain the meat and discard the brine. Place the strips of meat in a single layer on paper towels and blot any excess moisture.

5. Place the meat in a single layer on the grate and smoke for 4 to 5 hours, turning once or twice. (If you're aware of hot spots on your grate, rotate the strips so they smoke evenly.) To test for doneness, bend one or two pieces in the middle. They should be dry but still somewhat pliant. Or simply eat a piece to see if it's done to your liking.

6. For the best texture, when you remove the meat from the grill, place the still-warm jerky in a resealable plastic bag and let rest for 30 minutes. (You might see condensation form on the inside of the bag, but the moisture will be reabsorbed by the meat.) Or let the meat cool completely and then store in a resealable plastic bag or covered container. The jerky will last a few days at room temperature but will last longer (up to 2 weeks) if refrigerated.

Smoked Cheese

Servings: 4
Cooking Time: 150 Minutes

Ingredients:

- 1 (2-pound) block medium Cheddar cheese, or your favorite cheese, quartered lengthwise

Directions:

1. Supply your smoker with wood pellets and follow the start-up procedure. Preheat the grill, with the lid closed, to 90°F.

2. Place the cheese directly on the grill grate and smoke for 2 hours, 30 minutes, checking frequently to be sure it's not melting. If the cheese begins to melt, try flipping it. If that doesn't help, remove it from the grill and refrigerate for about 1 hour and then return it to the cold smoker.

3. Remove the cheese, place it in a zip-top bag, and refrigerate overnight.

4. Slice the cheese and serve with crackers, or grate it and use for making a smoked mac and cheese.

Roasted Red Pepper Dip

Servings: 8
Cooking Time: 45 Minutes

Ingredients:

- 4 red bell peppers, halved, destemmed, and deseeded
- 1 cup English walnuts, divided
- 1 small white onion, peeled and coarsely chopped
- 2 garlic cloves, peeled and smashed with a chef's knife
- ¼ cup extra virgin olive oil, plus more
- 1 tbsp balsamic vinegar or balsamic glaze
- 1 tsp honey (eliminate if using balsamic glaze)
- 1 tsp coarse salt, plus more
- 1 tsp ground cumin
- 1 tsp smoked paprika
- ½ to 1 tsp Aleppo red pepper flakes, plus more
- ¼ cup fresh white breadcrumbs (optional)
- distilled water (optional)
- assorted crudités or wedges of pita bread

Directions:

1. Supply your smoker with wood pellets and follow the start-up procedure. Preheat the grill, with the lid closed, to 400° F.

2. Place the peppers skin side down on the grate and grill until the skins blister and the flesh softens, about 30 minutes. Transfer the peppers to a bowl and cover with plastic wrap. Let cool to room temperature. Remove the skins with a paring knife or your fingers. Coarsely chop or tear the peppers.

3. Place ¾ cup of walnuts in an aluminum foil roasting pan. Place the pan on the grate and toast for 10 to 15 minutes, stirring twice. Remove the pan from the grill and let the walnuts cool.

4. Place the peppers, onion, garlic, and walnuts in a food processor fitted with the chopping blade. Pulse several times. Add the olive oil, balsamic vinegar, honey, salt, cumin, paprika, and red pepper flakes. Process until the mixture is fairly smooth. Taste for seasoning, adding more salt or red pepper flakes (if desired). (If the mixture is too loose, add breadcrumbs until the texture is to your liking. If it's too thick, add olive oil or water 1 tablespoon at a time.)

5. Transfer the dip to a serving bowl. Use the back of a spoon to make a shallow depression in the center. Top with the remaining ¼ cup of walnuts and drizzle olive oil in the depression. Serve with crudités or pita bread.

Delicious Deviled Crab Appetizer

Servings: 30
Cooking Time: 10 Minutes

Ingredients:

- Nonstick cooking spray, oil, or butter, for greasing
- 1 cup panko breadcrumbs, divided
- 1 cup canned corn, drained
- ½ cup chopped scallions, divided
- ½ red bell pepper, finely chopped
- 16 ounces jumbo lump crabmeat
- ¾ cup mayonnaise, divided
- 1 egg, beaten
- 1 teaspoon salt

- 1 teaspoon freshly ground black pepper
- 2 teaspoons cayenne pepper, divided
- Juice of 1 lemon

Directions:
1. Supply your smoker with wood pellets and follow the start-up procedure. Preheat, with the lid closed, to 425°F.
2. Spray three 12-cup mini muffin pans with cooking spray and divide ½ cup of the panko between 30 of the muffin cups, pressing into the bottoms and up the sides. (Work in batches, if necessary, depending on the number of pans you have.)
3. In a medium bowl, combine the corn, ¼ cup of scallions, the bell pepper, crabmeat, half of the mayonnaise, the egg, salt, pepper, and 1 teaspoon of cayenne pepper.
4. Gently fold in the remaining ½ cup of breadcrumbs and divide the mixture between the prepared mini muffin cups.
5. Place the pans on the grill grate, close the lid, and smoke for 10 minutes, or until golden brown.
6. In a small bowl, combine the lemon juice and the remaining mayonnaise, scallions, and cayenne pepper to make a sauce.
7. Brush the tops of the mini crab cakes with the sauce and serve hot.

Smoked Turkey Sandwich

Servings: 1
Cooking Time: 15 Minutes

Ingredients:
- 2 slices sourdough bread
- 2 tablespoons butter, at room temperature
- 2 (1-ounce) slices Swiss cheese
- 4 ounces leftover Smoked Turkey
- 1 teaspoon garlic salt

Directions:
1. Supply your smoker with wood pellets and follow the start-up procedure. Preheat the grill, with the lid closed, to 375°F.
2. Coat one side of each bread slice with 1 tablespoon of butter and sprinkle the buttered sides with garlic salt.
3. Place 1 slice of cheese on each unbuttered side of the bread, and then put the turkey on the cheese.
4. Close the sandwich, buttered sides out, and place it directly on the grill grate. Cook for 5 minutes. Flip the sandwich and cook for 5 minutes more. Remove the sandwich from the grill, cut it in half, and serve.

Sriracha & Maple Cashews

Servings: 10
Cooking Time: 60 Minutes

Ingredients:
- 2 tbsp unsalted butter
- 3 tbsp pure maple syrup
- 1 tbsp sriracha
- 1 tsp coarse salt (use only if nuts are unsalted)
- 2½ cups unsalted cashews

Directions:
1. Supply your smoker with wood pellets and follow the start-up procedure. Preheat the grill, with the lid closed, to 250° F.
2. In a small saucepan on the stovetop over low heat, melt the butter. Add the maple syrup, sriracha, and salt (if using). Stir until combined. Add the nuts and stir gently to coat thoroughly.
3. Spread the nuts in a single layer in an aluminum foil roasting pan coated with cooking spray. Place the pan on the grate and smoke the nuts until they're lightly toasted, about 1 hour, stirring once or twice.
4. Remove the pan from the grill and let the nuts cool for 15 minutes. They'll be sticky at first but will crisp up. Break them up with your fingers and store at room temperature in an airtight container, such as a lidded glass jar.

Jalapeño Poppers With Chipotle Sour Cream

Servings: 8
Cooking Time: 45 Minutes

Ingredients:
- 3 strips of thin-sliced bacon
- 12 large jalapeños, red, green, or a mix
- 8oz (225g) light cream cheese, at room temperature
- 1 cup shredded pepper Jack, Monterey Jack, or Cheddar cheese
- 1 tsp chili powder
- ½ tsp garlic salt
- smoked paprika
- for the sour cream
- 1¼ cups light sour cream
- juice of ½ lime
- ½ to 1 canned chipotle peppers in adobo sauce, finely minced, plus 1 tsp of sauce, plus more
- 1 tbsp minced fresh cilantro leaves
- ½ tsp coarse salt, plus more

Directions:
1. Supply your smoker with wood pellets and follow the start-up procedure. Preheat the grill, with the lid closed, to 375° F.
2. Line a rimmed sheet pan with aluminum foil and place a wire rack on top. Place the bacon in a single layer on the wire rack. Place the pan on the grate and grill until the bacon is crisp and golden brown, about 20 minutes. Transfer the bacon to paper towels to cool and then crumble. Set aside.
3. In a small bowl, make the chipotle sour cream by whisking together the ingredients. Add more salt, chipotle peppers, or adobe sauce to taste. Cover and refrigerate.

4. Slice the jalapeños lengthwise through their stems. Scrape out the veins and seeds with the edge of a small metal spoon.

5. In a small bowl, beat together the cream cheese, shredded cheese, chili powder, and garlic salt. Stir in the crumbled bacon. Mound the cream cheese mixture in the jalapeño halves. Line another rimmed sheet pan with aluminum foil and place a wire rack on top. Place the jalapeños filled side up in a single layer on the wire rack.

6. Place the sheet pan on the grate and roast the jalapeños until the filling has melted and the peppers have softened, about 20 to 25 minutes. (They should no longer look bright in color.) Remove the pan from the grill and let the peppers rest for 5 minutes.

7. Transfer the poppers to a platter and lightly dust with paprika. Serve with the chipotle sour cream.

Cold-smoked Cheese

Servings: 6
Cooking Time: 180 Minutes

Ingredients:
- 2lb (1kg) well-chilled hard or semi-hard cheese, such as:
- Edam
- Gouda
- Cheddar
- Monterey Jack
- pepper Jack
- goat cheese
- fresh mozzarella
- Muenster
- aged Parmigiano-Reggiano
- Gruyère
- blue cheese

Directions:

1. Unwrap the cheese and remove any protective wax or coating. Cut into 4-ounce (110g) portions to increase the surface area.

2. If possible, move your smoker to a shady area. Place 1 resealable plastic bag filled with ice on top of the drip pan. This is especially important on a warm day because you want to keep the interior temperature of the grill between 70 and 90°F (21 and 32°C) or below.

3. Place a grill mat on one side of the grate. Place the cheese on the mat and allow space between each piece.

4. Fill your smoking tube or pellet maze (see Cast Iron Skillets and Grill Pans) with pellets or sawdust and light according to the manufacturer's instructions. Place the smoking tube on the grate near—but not on—the grill mat. When the tube is smoking consistently, close the grill lid.

5. Smoke the cheese for 1 to 3 hours, replacing the pellets or sawdust and ice if necessary. Monitor the temperature and make sure the cheese isn't beginning to melt. Carefully lift the mat with the cheese to a rimmed baking sheet and let the cheese cool completely before handling.

6. Package the smoked cheese in cheese storage paper or bags or vacuum-seal the cheese, labeling each. (While you can wrap the cheese tightly in plastic wrap, the cheese will spoil faster.) Let the cheese rest for at least 2 to 3 days before eating. It will be even better after 2 weeks.

COCKTAILS RECIPES

Smoked Berry Cocktail

Servings: 2
Cooking Time: 15 Minutes

Ingredients:
- 1/2 Cup strawberries, stemmed
- 1/2 Cup blackberries
- 1/2 Cup blueberries
- 8 Ounce bourbon or iced tea
- 2 Ounce lime juice
- 3 Ounce simple syrup
- soda water
- fresh mint, for garnish

Directions:
1. Supply your smoker with wood pellets and follow the start-up procedure. Preheat the grill, with the lid closed, to 180° F.
2. Wash berries well, spread them on a clean cookie sheet and place on the grill. Smoke berries for 15 minutes. Grill: 180 °F
3. Remove berries from grill and transfer to a blender. Puree berries until smooth then pass through a fine mesh strainer to remove seeds.
4. To create a layered cocktail, pour 2 ounces of berry puree in the bottom of a glass. Next, pour 2 ounces of bourbon or iced tea over the back of a spoon into the glass, then 1/2 ounce lime juice and 1/2 ounce simple syrup, top with soda water and ice. Finish with mint or extra berries for garnish.
5. Repeat the same process for 3 more servings. Enjoy!

Smoking Gun Cocktail

Servings: 2
Cooking Time: 45 Minutes

Ingredients:
- 2 Jar vermouth soaked cocktail onions
- 3 Ounce vodka
- 1 Ounce dry vermouth

Directions:
1. Supply your smoker with wood pellets and follow the start-up procedure. Preheat the grill, with the lid closed, to 180° F.
2. To make the smoked onion vermouth: Pour jar of vermouth soaked cocktail onions onto a shallow sheet pan. Smoke for 45 minutes. Remove from grill and set aside to chill. Grill: 180 °F
3. To make the cocktail: Add vodka, 1 teaspoon liquid from the smoked onions and dry vermouth to a mixing glass. Shake and strain into a chilled martini glass.
4. Garnish with smoked cocktail onions on a skewer. Enjoy!

Traeger Smoked Daiquiri

Servings: 2
Cooking Time: 25 Minutes

Ingredients:
- 2 limes, sliced
- 2 Tablespoon granulated sugar
- 3 Ounce Rum
- 1 Ounce Smoked Simple Syrup
- 1 1/2 Ounce lime juice

Directions:
1. Supply your smoker with wood pellets and follow the start-up procedure. Preheat the grill, with the lid closed, to 350° F.
2. Toss the lime slices with granulated sugar and place directly on the grill grate. Cook 20-25 minutes or until grill marks form. Remove from grill and cool. Grill: 350 °F
3. In a mixing glass add rum, Traeger Simple Syrup, and fresh lime juice. Add ice to the mixing glass and shake. Strain contents into a chilled glass.
4. Garnish with a grilled lime wheel. Enjoy!

In Traeger Fashion Cocktail

Servings: 2
Cooking Time: 20 Minutes

Ingredients:
- 2 Whole orange peel
- 2 Whole lemon peel
- 3 Ounce bourbon
- 1 Ounce Smoked Simple Syrup
- 6 Dash Bitters Lab Charred Cedar & Currant Bitters

Directions:
1. Supply your smoker with wood pellets and follow the start-up procedure. Preheat the grill, with the lid closed, to 350° F.
2. Place the lemon and orange peel directly on the grill grate and cook 20 to 25 minutes or until lightly browned. Grill: 350 °F
3. Add bourbon, Traeger Smoked Simple Syrup and bitters to a mixing glass and stir over ice. Stir until glass is chilled and contents are well diluted.
4. Strain into a new glass over fresh ice and garnish with grilled lemon and orange peel. Enjoy!

Smoked Apple Cider

Servings: 2
Cooking Time: 30 Minutes

Ingredients:
- 32 Ounce apple cider
- 2 cinnamon sticks
- 4 whole cloves
- 3 star anise
- 2 Pieces orange peel
- 2 Pieces lemon peel

Directions:
1. Supply your smoker with wood pellets and follow the start-up procedure. Preheat the grill, with the lid closed, to 225° F.
2. Combine the cider, cinnamon stick, star anise, clove, lemon and orange peel in a shallow baking dish.
3. Place directly on the grill grate and smoke for 30 minutes. Remove from grill, strain and transfer to four mugs. Grill: 225 °F
4. Finish with a slice of apple and a cinnamon stick to serve. Enjoy!

Grilled Blood Orange Mimosa

Servings: 4
Cooking Time: 15 Minutes

Ingredients:
- 3 blood orange, halved
- 2 Tablespoon granulated sugar
- 1 Bottle sparkling wine
- thyme sprigs, for garnish

Directions:
1. Supply your smoker with wood pellets and follow the start-up procedure. Preheat the grill, with the lid closed, to 375° F.
2. When the grill is hot, dip the cut side of the orange halves in sugar and place cut side down directly on the grill grate. Grill: 375 °F
3. Grill the oranges for 10-15 minutes or until grill marks develop. Grill: 375 °F
4. Remove from the grill and let cool at room temperature.
5. When cool enough to handle, juice the oranges and strain through a fine strainer removing any pulp.
6. Pour 5 oz of sparkling wine into each glass and top with 1 oz blood orange juice.
7. Garnish with a sprig of thyme. Enjoy!

Sunset Margarita

Servings: 2
Cooking Time: 55 Minutes

Ingredients:
- 4 oranges
- 2 Cup plus 1 teaspoon agave
- 1/2 Cup water
- 1 Ounce burnt orange agave
- 3 Ounce reposado tequila
- 1 1/2 Ounce fresh squeezed lime juice
- Jacobsen Salt Co. Cherrywood Smoked Salt

Directions:
1. Supply your smoker with wood pellets and follow the start-up procedure. Preheat the grill, with the lid closed, to 350° F.
2. For the Burnt Orange Agave Syrup: Cut one orange in half and brush cut side with agave. Place cut side down directly on the grill grate and grill for 15 minutes or until grill marks develop. Grill: 350 °F
3. While the orange halves are grilling, slice the other orange and brush both sides of the slices with agave. Place slices directly on the grill grate next to the halves and cook for 15 minutes or until grill marks develop. Grill: 350 °F
4. Remove orange halves from grill grate and let cool. After they have cooled, juice halves and strain. Set aside.
5. Combine 1/4 cup water and agave in a shallow dish and mix well. Remove orange slices from the grill and place in the agave mixture, reserving a few for garnish.
6. Reduce the grill temperature to 180 degrees F and place the shallow dish with agave and oranges directly on the grill grate. Smoke for 40 minutes. Remove from heat and strain. Set aside. Grill: 180 °F
7. To Mix Drink: Rim glass with Jacobsen Smoked Salt. Combine tequila, fresh lime juice, grilled orange juice and burnt orange agave syrup in a glass. Add ice and shake well.
8. Strain into a rimmed glass over clean ice. Garnish with a grilled orange slice. Enjoy!

Ryes And Shine Cocktail

Servings: 2
Cooking Time: 30 Minutes

Ingredients:
- 2 lemon, cut into wheels for garnish
- 6 Tablespoon granulated sugar
- 2 Ounce rye
- 1 Ounce bourbon
- 3 Ounce lemon juice
- 1 Ounce Smoked Simple Syrup
- 6 Dash Fernet-Branca

Directions:
1. Supply your smoker with wood pellets and follow the start-up procedure. Preheat the grill, with the lid closed, to 325° F.
2. Toss lemon wheels with granulated sugar to coat on both sides. Place wheels directly on the grill grate and cook for 15 minutes on each side or until grill marks form. Grill: 325 °F

3. Add rye, bourbon, lemon juice, Traeger Smoked Simple Syrup and Fernet-Branca to a shaker and shake until slightly diluted (about 10 to 15 seconds).
4. Pour into a fresh glass, serve neat and garnish with a grilled lemon wheel. Enjoy!

Grilled Peach Sour Cocktail

Servings: 2
Cooking Time: 15 Minutes

Ingredients:
- 2 peach, sliced
- 2 Tablespoon sugar
- 1 1/2 Ounce Smoked Simple Syrup
- 4 Ounce bourbon
- 6 Dash Bitters Lab Apricot Vanilla Bitters
- 2 Sprig fresh thyme, for garnish

Directions:
1. Supply your smoker with wood pellets and follow the start-up procedure. Preheat the grill, with the lid closed, to 325° F.
2. Toss peach slices with granulated sugar and place directly on grill grate. Cook for 20 minutes or until grill marks form. Remove from grill and let cool. Grill: 325 °F
3. Place peaches and Traeger Smoked Simple Syrup into tin and muddle. Peaches should form about an ounce of juice during the muddling. Once completed, add remaining ingredients and shake.
4. Pour contents into glass over fresh ice and garnish with fresh thyme. Enjoy!

Zombie Cocktail Recipe

Servings: 2
Cooking Time: 45 Minutes

Ingredients:
- fresh squeezed orange juice
- pineapple juice
- 2 Ounce light rum
- 2 Ounce dark rum
- 2 Ounce lime juice
- 1 Ounce Smoked Simple Syrup
- 6 Ounce smoked orange and pineapple juice
- 2 grilled orange peel, for garnish
- 2 grilled pineapple chunks, for garnish

Directions:
1. Supply your smoker with wood pellets and follow the start-up procedure. Preheat the grill, with the lid closed, to 180° F.
2. Smoked Orange and Pineapple Juice: Pour equal parts fresh squeezed orange juice and pineapple juice into a shallow sheet pan and smoke for 45 minutes. Remove and let cool. Measure out 3 ounces of juice and reserve any remaining juice in the refrigerator for future use. Grill: 180 °F
3. Add dark and light rums, 3 ounces smoked orange and pineapple juice, lime juice and Traeger Smoked Simple Syrup to a mixing glass.
4. Add ice, shake and strain over clean ice into a Tiki glass.
5. Garnish with a grilled orange peel and grilled pineapple. Enjoy!

Smoked Hot Buttered Rum

Servings: 4
Cooking Time: 30 Minutes

Ingredients:
- 2 Cup water
- 1/4 Cup brown sugar
- 1/2 Stick butter, melted
- 1 Teaspoon ground cinnamon
- 1/4 Teaspoon ground nutmeg
- ground cloves
- salt
- 6 Ounce Rum

Directions:
1. Supply your smoker with wood pellets and follow the start-up procedure. Preheat the grill, with the lid closed, to 180° F.
2. In a shallow baking dish, combine 2 cups water with all ingredients except for the rum and place directly on the grill grate. Smoke for 30 minutes. Grill: 180 °F
3. Remove from the grill and pour into the pitcher of a blender. Process until somewhat frothy.
4. Pour 1.5 ounces of rum each into 4 glasses. Split hot butter mixture evenly between the four glasses.
5. Garnish with a cinnamon stick and freshly grated nutmeg. Enjoy!

Strawberry Mule Cocktail

Servings: 2
Cooking Time: 15 Minutes

Ingredients:
- 8 grilled strawberries, plus more for serving
- 3 Ounce vodka
- 1 Ounce Smoked Simple Syrup
- 1 Ounce lemon juice
- 6 Ounce ginger beer
- fresh mint leaves

Directions:
1. Supply your smoker with wood pellets and follow the start-up procedure. Preheat the grill, with the lid closed, to 400° F.

2. Place strawberries directly on the grill grate and cook 15 minutes or until grill marks appear. Grill: 400 °F
3. For the cocktail: Add vodka, grilled strawberries, Traeger Smoked Simple Syrup and lemon juice to a shaker. Shake vigorously.
4. Double strain into a fresh glass or copper mug with crushed ice.
5. Top with ginger beer and garnish with extra grilled strawberries and fresh mint. Enjoy!

Garden Gimlet Cocktail

Servings: 2
Cooking Time: 45 Minutes

Ingredients:

- 2 Cup honey
- 4 lemons, zested
- 4 Sprig rosemary, plus more for garnish
- 1/2 Cup water
- 4 Slices cucumber
- 1 1/2 Ounce lime juice
- 3 Ounce vodka

Directions:
1. Supply your smoker with wood pellets and follow the start-up procedure. Preheat the grill, with the lid closed, to 180° F.
2. To make smoked lemon and rosemary honey syrup, thin 1 cup honey by adding 1/4 cup water to a shallow pan. Add lemon zest and 2 sprigs rosemary.
3. Place the pan directly on the grill grate and smoke 45 minutes to an hour. Remove from heat, strain and cool. Grill: 180 °F
4. In a cocktail shaker, muddle the cucumbers and 1oz of the smoked lemon and rosemary honey syrup.
5. After muddling, add lime juice, vodka, and ice. Shake and double strain into a coup glass.
6. Garnish with a sprig of rosemary. Enjoy!

Grilled Hawaiian Sour

Servings: 2
Cooking Time: 15 Minutes

Ingredients:

- 2 Whole pineapple, trimmed and sliced
- 1/2 Cup palm sugar
- 3 Ounce bourbon
- 2 Ounce grilled pineapple juice
- 2 Ounce Smoked Simple Syrup
- 10 Ounce lemon juice
- 2 grilled pineapple chunk, for garnish
- 2 pineapple leaf, for garnish

Directions:
1. Supply your smoker with wood pellets and follow the start-up procedure. Preheat the grill, with the lid closed, to 350° F.
2. For the Grilled Pineapple Juice: Dust pineapple slices with palm sugar. Place directly on the grill grate and cook for 8 minutes per side. Grill: 350 °F
3. Remove from grill and let cool. Reserve a few pieces for garnish. Run remaining pineapple pieces through centrifugal juicer to extract juice.
4. To Make the Drink: Add bourbon, grilled pineapple juice, simple syrup and lemon juice to a cocktail strainer with ice. Shake vigorously. Double strain into a chilled coupe glass. Garnish with grilled pineapple chunk and pineapple leaf. Enjoy!

Smoked Pomegranate Lemonade Cocktail

Servings: 2
Cooking Time: 45 Minutes

Ingredients:

- 32 Ounce POM Juice
- 2 Cup pomegranate seeds
- 3 Ounce vodka
- 8 Ounce lemonade
- lemon wheel, for garnish
- fresh mint, for garnish

Directions:
1. Supply your smoker with wood pellets and follow the start-up procedure. Preheat the grill, with the lid closed, to 225° F.
2. For the Smoked Pomegranate Ice Cubes: Pour one small container of POM juice and 1 cup of pomegranate seeds into a shallow sheet pan. Smoke on the Traeger for 45 minutes. Pull off grill and let sit until cooled. Grill: 180 °F
3. Pour smoked POM juice into ice molds of your choice and put into freezer.
4. When ready to serve, place the frozen pomegranate cubes into a mason jar. Pour vodka and lemonade over the ice cubes.
5. Garnish with a lemon wheel and fresh mint. Enjoy!

Smoked Mulled Wine

Servings: 10
Cooking Time: 60 Minutes

Ingredients:

- 2 Bottle red wine
- 1/2 Cup whiskey
- 1/2 Cup white rum
- 1/2 Cup honey
- 1 cinnamon stick
- 2 pods star anise
- 4 whole cloves
- 1 (3 in) orange peel

Directions:
1. Supply your smoker with wood pellets and follow the start-up procedure. Preheat the grill, with the lid closed, to 180° F.
2. In a shallow baking dish, combine wine, whiskey, rum, honey, cinnamon stick, star anise, cloves and orange peel. Stir well until combined.
3. Place the dish directly on the grill grate and smoke for one hour until the mixture is warm. Grill: 180 °F
4. Remove from grill and ladle into mugs leaving the mulling spices behind. Garnish with fresh cinnamon sticks, anise, orange zest or a combination. Enjoy!

Batter Up Cocktail

Servings: 2
Cooking Time: 60 Minutes

Ingredients:
- 2 whole nutmeg
- 4 Ounce Michter's Bourbon
- 3 Teaspoon pumpkin puree
- 1 Ounce Smoked Simple Syrup
- 2 Large egg

Directions:
1. Supply your smoker with wood pellets and follow the start-up procedure. Preheat the grill, with the lid closed, to 180° F.
2. Place whole nutmeg on a sheet tray and place in the grill. Smoke 1 hour. Remove from grill and let cool. Grill: 180 °F
3. Add everything to a shaker and shake without ice. Add ice, then shake and strain into a chilled highball glass.
4. Garnish with grated, smoked nutmeg. Enjoy!

Smoked Ice Mojito Slurpee

Servings: 2
Cooking Time: 30 Minutes

Ingredients:
- water
- 1 Cup white rum
- 1/2 Cup lime juice
- 1/4 Cup Smoked Simple Syrup
- 12 Whole fresh mint leaves
- 4 Sprig mint
- 4 Whole lime wedge, for garnish

Directions:
1. Supply your smoker with wood pellets and follow the start-up procedure. Preheat the grill, with the lid closed, to 180° F.
2. For optimal flavor, use Super Smoke if available. Grill: 180 °F
3. Remove water from grill and pour smoked water into ice cube trays. Place in freezer until frozen.
4. Add rum, lime juice, Traeger Smoked Simple Syrup, mint and smoked ice to a blender.
5. Blend until a slushy consistency and pour into glasses.
6. Garnish with a mint sprig and lime wedge. Enjoy!

Grilled Frozen Strawberry Lemonade

Servings: 4
Cooking Time: 15 Minutes

Ingredients:
- 1 Pound fresh strawberries
- 1/2 Cup turbinado sugar
- 8 lemon, halved
- 1/4 Cup Cointreau
- 1/4 Cup simple syrup
- 2 Cup ice
- 1 Cup Titos Vodka

Directions:
1. Supply your smoker with wood pellets and follow the start-up procedure. Preheat the grill, with the lid closed, to High heat.
2. Dip the lemon halves in turbinado sugar and place directly on the grill grate. Toss the strawberries with remaining sugar and place next to the lemons.
3. Cook until grill marks develop on both, about 15 min for lemons and 10 min for strawberries.
4. Remove from heat and let cool.
5. Juice grilled lemons straining out any seeds or pulp. Pour into a blender pitcher.
6. Remove stems from grilled strawberries and place in blender pitcher with lemon juice. Add simple syrup, vodka, cointreau, and 2 cups of ice.
7. Puree until smooth and transfer to 4-6 glasses. Garnish with grilled strawberries and grilled lemon slices if desired. Enjoy!

Smoked Sangria

Servings: 6
Cooking Time: 45 Minutes

Ingredients:
- 1 (750 ml) medium-bodied red wine
- 1/4 Cup Grand Marnier
- 1/4 Cup Smoked Simple Syrup
- 1 Cup fresh cranberries
- 1 Whole apple, sliced
- 2 Whole limes, sliced
- 4 cinnamon stick
- soda water

Directions:
1. Supply your smoker with wood pellets and follow the start-up procedure. Preheat the grill, with the lid closed, to 180° F.

2. In a shallow dish, combine red wine, Grand Marnier, Traeger Smoked Simple Syrup and cranberries, and place directly on the grill grate.
3. Smoke for 30 to 45 minutes or until the liquid picks up desired amount of smoke. Remove from grill and place in the fridge to cool. Grill: 180 °F
4. When the mixture has cooled, place in a large pitcher. Add sliced apples, limes, cinnamon sticks and ice to pitcher.
5. Top with soda water, if desired. Enjoy!

Smoked Pumpkin Spice Latte

Servings: 4
Cooking Time: 45 Minutes

Ingredients:
- 1 Small sugar pumpkin
- olive oil
- 1 Can sweetened condensed milk
- 1 Cup whole milk
- 2 Tablespoon Smoked Simple Syrup
- 1 Teaspoon pumpkin pie spice
- pinch of salt
- cinnamon
- whipped cream
- shaved nutmeg
- 8 Ounce smoked cold brew coffee

Directions:
1. Supply your smoker with wood pellets and follow the start-up procedure. Preheat the grill, with the lid closed, to 325° F.
2. Cut the sugar pumpkin in half, scoop out the seeds and discard. Place the pumpkin halves cut side up on a baking sheet and brush lightly with olive oil.
3. Place the sheet tray directly on the grill grate and cook 45 minutes or until the flesh is tender. Remove from heat and place on the counter to cool. Grill: 325 °F
4. When the pumpkin is cool enough to handle, scoop out the flesh and mash until smooth.
5. Place 3 Tbsp of the pumpkin puree in a separate bowl and reserve the remaining for another use.
6. Add the sweetened condensed milk, whole milk, Traeger Smoked Simple Syrup, pumpkin pie seasoning and salt to the pumpkin puree. Whisk to combine.
7. Pour the cold brew over ice, add desired amount of pumpkin spice creamer and top with whipped cream, cinnamon, and shaved nutmeg if desired. Enjoy!

Fig Slider Cocktail

Servings: 2
Cooking Time: 15 Minutes

Ingredients:
- 2 peach, halved
- 4 oranges
- honey
- sugar
- 2 Teaspoon orange fig spread
- 1 Ounce fresh lemon juice
- 4 Ounce bourbon
- 3 Ounce honey glazed grilled orange juice

Directions:
1. Supply your smoker with wood pellets and follow the start-up procedure. Preheat the grill, with the lid closed, to 325° F.
2. Pit the peach and cut in half. Cut one of the oranges in half. Glaze the peach and orange cut sides with honey and set directly on the grill grate until the honey caramelizes and fruit has grill marks. Grill: 325 °F
3. Cut the second orange into wheels and coat with granulated sugar on both sides. Place directly on the grill grate and cook 15 minutes each side or until grill marks form. Grill: 325 °F
4. In a mixing tin, add grilled peaches, bourbon, orange fig spread, fresh lemon juice and honey glazed orange juice.
5. Shake vigorously to blend the juices and fig spread. Strain over clean ice. Garnish with grilled orange wheel. Enjoy!

Bacon Old-fashioned Cocktail

Servings: 2
Cooking Time: 20 Minutes

Ingredients:
- 16 Slices bacon
- 1/2 Cup warm water (110°F to 115°F)
- 1500 mL bourbon
- 1/2 Fluid Ounce maple syrup
- 4 Dash Angostura bitters
- 2 fresh orange peel

Directions:
1. Smoke bacon prior to making Old Fashioned using this recipe for Applewood Smoked Bacon.
2. To Make Bacon: Supply your smoker with wood pellets and follow the start-up procedure. Preheat the grill, with the lid closed, to 325° F.
3. Place bacon in a single layer on a cooling rack that fits inside a baking sheet pan. Cook in Traeger for 15-20 minutes or until bacon is browned and crispy. Reserve bacon for later. Let the fat cool slightly; you'll use the fat to infuse the bourbon. Grill: 325 °F
4. Combine 1/4 cup of warm (not hot) liquid bacon fat with the entire contents of a 750ml bottle of bourbon in a glass or heavy plastic container.
5. Use a fork to stir well. Let it sit on the counter for a few hours, stirring every so often.

6. After about four hours, put bourbon fat mixture into the freezer. After about an hour, the fat will congeal and you can simply scoop it out with a spoon. You can fine-strain the mixture through a sieve to remove all fat if desired.
7. Combine ingredients with ice and stir until cold. Strain over fresh ice in an Old Fashioned glass and garnish with reserved bacon and orange peel. Enjoy!

Smoked Salted Caramel White Russian

Servings: 4
Cooking Time: 20 Minutes

Ingredients:
- 16 Ounce half-and-half
- salted caramel sauce
- 6 Ounce vodka
- 6 Ounce Kahlúa

Directions:
1. Supply your smoker with wood pellets and follow the start-up procedure. Preheat the grill, with the lid closed, to 180° F.
2. Pour the half-and-half in a shallow baking dish and place directly on the grill grate. In another shallow baking dish, pour 2 to 3 cups of water and place on the grill next to the half-and-half.
3. Smoke both the half-and-half and water for 20 minutes. Remove from the grill and let cool. Grill: 180 °F
4. Place the half-and-half in the fridge until ready to use. Pour the smoked water into ice cube trays and transfer to the freezer until completely frozen.
5. Separate the smoked ice cubes into four glasses. Drizzle the salted caramel sauce around the inside of the glass.
6. Pour 1-1/2 ounce vodka and 1-1/2 ounce Kahlúa into each of the glasses and top with the smoked half-and-half. Enjoy!

Smoky Scotch & Ginger Cocktail

Servings: 2
Cooking Time: 60 Minutes

Ingredients:
- 1 Ounce ginger syrup
- 1/2 Ounce brandied cherry juice
- 1/2 Ounce agave nectar
- 4 Ounce scotch
- 1 1/2 Ounce lemon juice
- 2 Slices grilled lemon, for garnish
- 2 cherry, for garnish

Directions:
1. Supply your smoker with wood pellets and follow the start-up procedure. Preheat the grill, with the lid closed, to 180° F.
2. For the smoked ginger cherry syrup: Place ginger syrup, cherry juice and agave nectar in a shallow dish and place the dish directly on the grill grate.
3. Smoke for 60 minutes, or until the mixture has picked up the smoke flavor. Remove from grill and allow to cool for 30 minutes. Grill: 180 °F
4. Place smoked ginger cherry syrup, scotch and lemon juice into a shaker tin and shake with ice. Strain into a glass over fresh ice and garnish with a grilled lemon wheel and cherry. Enjoy!

A Smoking Classic Cocktail

Servings: 2
Cooking Time: 60 Minutes

Ingredients:
- 2 Bottle Angostura orange bitters
- 10 sugar cubes
- 8 Ounce Champagne
- lemon twist

Directions:
1. Supply your smoker with wood pellets and follow the start-up procedure. Preheat the grill, with the lid closed, to 180° F.
2. For the Smoked Orange Bitters: In a small skillet, combine 1 bottle of Angostura orange bitters with a splash of water and 4 sugar cubes.
3. Place skillet on the grill grate and smoke for 60 minutes. Cool the smoked bitters and put back into the bottle. Grill: 180 °F
4. Add a sugar cube to each Champagne flute and soak the sugar cubes with the smoked bitters.
5. Add champagne and a lemon twist in a flute glass. Enjoy!

Cran-apple Tequila Punch With Smoked Oranges

Servings: 2
Cooking Time: 15 Minutes

Ingredients:
- 6 Cup apple juice, chilled
- 6 Cup light cranberry cocktail
- 1 Cup cranberries, fresh or thawed
- 3 Large oranges, halved
- 1 Cup sugar, for rimming glasses
- 2 Tablespoon lemon juice
- 2 Cup reposado tequila
- 1 Cup orange-flavored liqueur, such as Grand Marnier or Cointreau
- 2 Bottle sparkling wine (such as prosecco) or sparkling water

Directions:

1. Combine 1 cup each of the apple and cranberry juices, then pour into ice cube trays. If the cube molds are big enough, place a few cranberries into each cube. Freeze for 6 hours to overnight.
2. Supply your smoker with wood pellets and follow the start-up procedure. Preheat the grill, with the lid closed, to 180° F.
3. Place the orange halves cut-side down on the grill and smoke for 15 minutes. Remove from the grill and juice oranges. Reserve smoked orange juice. Grill: 180 °F
4. When ready to serve, place the sugar on a flat plate. Pour the lemon juice into a bowl that will fit the rim of each glass.
5. Carefully dip the rim of each glass in the lemon juice, then dip in the sugar to create a 1/8" sugar rim. Turn the glass right-side up and allow to dry for a few minutes before using.
6. Just before serving, mix the remaining apple juice, cranberry cocktail and smoked orange juice with the tequila, orange liqueur, and sparkling wine in a large bowl or pitcher. Taste, adding more of any ingredient to meet your preference.
7. When ready to serve, place a few ice cubes in each glass, then pour a cup of the punch over the top. Alternatively, place all of the ice cubes in the punch bowl and allow guests to help themselves. Enjoy!

Smoked Cold Brew Coffee

Servings: 8
Cooking Time: 120 Minutes

Ingredients:
- 12 Ounce coarse ground coffee
- heavy cream or milk
- sugar

Directions:
1. Place half the coffee grounds in a plastic container and slowly pour 3-1/2 cups water over the top of the grounds. Add remaining grounds and pour another 3-1/2 cups water over the top in a circular motion.
2. Press the grounds down into the water using the back of a spoon. Cover and transfer to the refrigerator and let sit for 18 to 24 hours.
3. Remove from refrigerator and strain into a clean container through a fine mesh strainer or double layer of cheese cloth.
4. Supply your smoker with wood pellets and follow the start-up procedure. Preheat the grill, with the lid closed, to 180° F.
5. Pour cold brew into a shallow baking dish and place directly on the grill grate. Smoke for 1 to 2 hours depending on desired level of smoke. Grill: 180 °F
6. Remove from grill and place over an ice bath to cool. Drink as is over ice, with cream or sugar or use in your favorite coffee recipes. Enjoy!

Smoked Hibiscus Sparkler

Servings: 4
Cooking Time: 30 Minutes

Ingredients:
- 1/2 Cup sugar
- 2 Tablespoon dried hibiscus flowers
- 1 Bottle sparkling wine
- crystallized ginger, for garnish

Directions:
1. Supply your smoker with wood pellets and follow the start-up procedure. Preheat the grill, with the lid closed, to 180° F.
2. Place water in a shallow baking dish and place directly on the grill grate. Smoke the water for 30 minutes or until desired smoke flavor is achieved. Grill: 180 °F
3. Pour water into a small saucepan and add sugar and hibiscus flowers. Bring to a simmer over medium heat and cook until sugar is dissolved.
4. Strain out the hibiscus flowers and transfer your simple syrup to a small container and refrigerate until chilled.
5. Pour 1/2 ounce smoked hibiscus simple syrup in the bottom of a champagne glass and top with sparkling wine.
6. Drop in a few pieces of crystallized ginger to garnish. Enjoy!

Smoked Jacobsen Salt Margarita

Servings: 2
Cooking Time: 1 Day

Ingredients:
- kosher sea salt
- 3 Cup Jacobsen Co. Honey
- 6 Ounce tequila
- 4 Ounce fresh squeezed lime juice
- 1/2 Cup Jacobsen Salt Co. Cherrywood Smoked Salt or smoked kosher salt
- 2 Ounce simple syrup
- 2 Teaspoon orange liqueur

Directions:
1. If making your own smoked salt, take kosher sea salt (however much you want to smoke) and spread it out on a tray.
2. Supply your smoker with wood pellets and follow the start-up procedure. Preheat the grill, with the lid closed, to 165° F.
3. Place tray of salt directly on the grill grate and smoke for about 24 hours, stirring the salt every 8 hours. Once it has smoked for 24 hours, take off grill and use in all your favorite dishes. Note: If you want to skip the long smoke session, use Jacobsen Salt Co. Cherrywood Smoked Salt. Grill: 165 °F
4. Simple Syrup: Put the honey and 1 cup water in a small saucepan. Cook over low heat, stirring, for about 20 min.

5. Fill a cocktail shaker with ice. Add tequila, lime juice, simple syrup and orange liqueur. Cover and shake until mixed and chilled, about 30 seconds.
6. Place smoked salt on a plate. Press the rim of a chilled rocks glass into the salt to rim the edge. Strain margarita into the glass. Enjoy!

Smoked Barnburner Cocktail

Servings: 2
Cooking Time: 45 Minutes

Ingredients:
- 16 Ounce fresh raspberries
- 1/2 Cup Smoked Simple Syrup
- 1 1/2 Ounce smoked raspberry syrup
- 3 Ounce reposado tequila
- 1 Ounce lime juice
- 1 Ounce lemon juice
- 2 grilled lime wheel, for garnish

Directions:
1. Supply your smoker with wood pellets and follow the start-up procedure. Preheat the grill, with the lid closed, to 180° F.
2. For Smoked Raspberry Syrup: Place fresh raspberries on a grill mat and smoke for 30 minutes. After the raspberries have been smoked, reserve a few for garnish and place the remainder into a shallow sheet pan with Traeger Smoked Simple Syrup. Grill: 180 °F
3. Place sheet pan on the grill grate and smoke for 45 minutes. Remove from grill and let cool. Strain through a fine mesh sieve discarding solids. Transfer the syrup to the refrigerator until ready to use. Makes about 1/2 cup of smoked raspberry syrup. Grill: 180 °F
4. For cocktail: Add 3/4 ounce smoked raspberry syrup, tequila, lime juice and lemon juice with ice into a mixing glass. Shake and pour over clean ice. Garnish with smoked raspberries and a grilled lime wheel. Enjoy!

Smoked Pineapple Hotel Nacional Cocktail

Servings: 2
Cooking Time: 20 Minutes

Ingredients:
- 2 pineapple
- 1/2 Cup water
- 1/2 Cup sugar
- 3 Fluid Ounce white rum
- 1 1/2 Fluid Ounce lime juice
- 1 1/2 Fluid Ounce Pineapple Syrup
- 1 Fluid Ounce apricot brandy
- 2 Dash Angostura bitters

Directions:

1. For the Syrup: Supply your smoker with wood pellets and follow the start-up procedure. Preheat the grill, with the lid closed, to 180° F.
2. Trim both ends of the pineapple, discard the ends. Cut the pineapple into slices about 3/4" thick. Don't worry about the skin, it doesn't hurt to leave it on. Place the pineapple slices on the grill and smoke for about 15 minutes on each sideTrim both ends of the pineapple and discard the ends. Cut the pineapple into slices about 3/4 inch thick. Don't worry about the skin, it doesn't hurt to leave it on. Place the pineapple slices on the grill and smoke for about 15 minutes per side. Grill: 180 °F
3. While the pineapple is smoking, combine 1/4 cup water and sugar in a saucepan over low heat, stirring constantly, until sugar is dissolved. Pour syrup into a large bowl and set aside.
4. When the pineapple is done cooking, cut each slice into eight or so wedges and add the wedges to the bowl with the simple syrup, tossing to coat and cover.
5. Leave the mixture to macerate for at least 4 hours (or up to 24) in the refrigerator, stirring from time to time.
6. Strain the syrup into a clean bowl through a fine-mesh strainer and press on the pineapple with a ladle to extract as much liquid as possible. You can bottle and refrigerate the syrup for up to 4 days.
7. To make the cocktail: Combine the rum, lime juice, pineapple syrup, apricot brandy, and bitters in a cocktail shaker or mixing glass. Fill with ice cubes and shake until cold.
8. Strain into a chilled cocktail glass. Garnish with a lime wheel and serve. Enjoy!

Dublin Delight Cocktail

Servings: 2
Cooking Time: 20 Minutes

Ingredients:
- 2 orange, sliced
- 3 Fluid Ounce Teeling Whiskey
- 1 1/2 Fluid Ounce Smoked Simple Syrup
- 6 Dash aromatic bitters
- 6 Fluid Ounce Guinness beer
- 2 Amarena cherry, for garnish

Directions:
1. Supply your smoker with wood pellets and follow the start-up procedure. Preheat the grill, with the lid closed, to 450° F.
2. Place orange slices directly on the grill grate and cook 20 to 25 minutes. Remove from grill and let cool. Grill: 450 °F
3. In a mixing glass, add whiskey, Traeger Smoked Simple Syrup and bitters. Add ice and shake. Pour over a beer glass filled with ice and top off with cold Guinness.
4. Garnish with a grilled orange slice and Amarena cherry. Enjoy!

Grilled Peach Mint Julep

Servings: 2
Cooking Time: 45 Minutes

Ingredients:
- 2 Whole peach
- 4 Ounce whiskey
- 2 Cup sugar
- 4 Tablespoon pink peppercorns
- 20 Whole fresh mint leaves, plus more for garnish
- 2 lime wedge, for garnish
- 4 Ounce bourbon

Directions:
1. For the Grilled Whiskey Peaches: cut peach into slices, then soak peach slices in whiskey in the refrigerator for 4 to 6 hours.
2. For the Pink Peppercorn Simple Syrup: In a shallow pan, combine sugar, 1 cup water and pink peppercorns.
3. Supply your smoker with wood pellets and follow the start-up procedure. Preheat the grill, with the lid closed, to 180° F.
4. Cook syrup down on the grill for 30 minutes, or until desired smoke flavor has been reached. Remove from the grill. Grill: 180 °F
5. Increase Traeger temperature to 350°F and preheat. Place the whiskey peach slices directly on the grill grate and cook 10 to 12 minutes or until peaches soften and get grill marks. Grill: 350 °F
6. To make the Julep: Muddle 1/2 ounce Pink Peppercorn Simple Syrup with 10 fresh mint leaves and 4 slices of grilled whiskey peaches.
7. Add crushed ice over the rim of the glass. Pour bourbon over the crushed ice and stir. Garnish with 1 large sprig of mint and fresh lime. Enjoy!

Smoked Irish Coffee

Servings: 2
Cooking Time: 15 Minutes

Ingredients:
- 10 Ounce hot coffee
- 1/2 Cup heavy cream
- 1 Tablespoon sugar
- 2 Ounce Irish whiskey
- freshly grated nutmeg, for garnish (optional)

Directions:
1. Supply your smoker with wood pellets and follow the start-up procedure. Preheat the grill, with the lid closed, to 180° F.
2. Place the coffee and cream in separate shallow baking dishes and place both directly on the grill grate. Smoke for 10 to 15 minutes until the liquids pick up a slight smoke flavor. Grill: 180 °F
3. Remove from the grill and cool the cream. When the cream is cool, add sugar and whip in a stand mixer or by hand to soft peaks.
4. Pour the hot coffee into two mugs then add 2 ounces of whiskey to each.
5. Top with smoked whipped cream and finish with freshly grated nutmeg, if desired. Enjoy!

Smoked Texas Ranch Water

Servings: 4
Cooking Time: 60 Minutes

Ingredients:
- 3 Whole limes
- 1 Tablespoon Blackened Saskatchewan Rub
- 12 Ounce blanco tequila
- 24 Ounce Topo Chico or other sparkling mineral water
- 8 Slices jalapeño, optional

Directions:
1. Supply your smoker with wood pellets and follow the start-up procedure. Preheat the grill, with the lid closed, to 225° F.
2. Cut two of the limes in half and sprinkle with Traeger Blackened Saskatchewan Rub. Place the four lime halves on the edge of the grill grate and smoke for 1 hour. Remove from grill and set aside to cool. Grill: 225 °F
3. Pour some of the rub onto a small plate. Cut the third lime into 1/4 wedges and use the lime to rub the rim of 4 cocktail glasses, turn the glasses upside down, and into the rub to salt the rim.
4. Place several ice cubes into your rimmed glasses and pour 3 ounces tequila, 6 ounces Topo Chico, squeeze the juice of one smoked lime (discard after squeezing), and add one fresh lime wedge to each. If using the jalapeño, add one or two slices to each glass (muddle if desired).
5. Stir to combine and enjoy!

Traeger Old Fashioned

Servings: 2
Cooking Time: 60 Minutes

Ingredients:
- 2 orange
- 2 Cup cherries
- 3 Ounce bourbon
- 1 Ounce Smoked Simple Syrup
- 8 Dash Bitters Lab Apricot Vanilla Bitters

Directions:
1. Supply your smoker with wood pellets and follow the start-up procedure. Preheat the grill, with the lid closed, to 180° F.
2. While Traeger preheats, slice whole orange into wheels.

3. Place cherries on a small sheet pan and place in the Traeger. Place orange slices directly on the grill grate.
4. Smoke cherries for 1 hour and oranges for 25 minutes, depending on taste, before removing from the grill. Let oranges and cherries cool. Grill: 180 °F
5. Pour bourbon into glass, followed by Traeger Smoked Simple Syrup and bitters. Add ice and stir for 45 seconds or until drink is well-diluted.
6. Strain contents into new glass over fresh ice. Skewer orange wheel and add cherry for garnish. Enjoy!

Traeger Boulevardier Cocktail

Servings: 2
Cooking Time: 60 Minutes

Ingredients:
- 4 oranges
- 1/2 Cup honey
- 1500 mL rye whiskey
- 1 1/2 Ounce Campari
- 1 1/2 Ounce sweet vermouth
- 2 Tablespoon granulated sugar
- 3 Ounce grilled orange infused rye

Directions:
1. Supply your smoker with wood pellets and follow the start-up procedure. Preheat the grill, with the lid closed, to 350° F.
2. Slice 2 oranges in half and coat cut side with honey. Peel remaining orange and place peels on the grill. Cook 20 to 25 minutes. Grill: 350 °F
3. Remove from grill and let cool. Place orange halves cut side down directly on the grill grate and cook 20 to 30 minutes or until dark grill marks appear. Remove orange halves and allow to cool. Grill: 350 °F
4. Place orange halves into a bottle of rye whiskey and let steep for 10 to 12 hours. The longer they steep, the sweeter and more pronounced the orange flavor will be.
5. Add all ingredients into a mixing glass and stir until diluted. Strain into a fresh coupe glass and serve neat.
6. Garnish with grilled orange peel. Enjoy!

Grilled Rabbit Tail Cocktail

Servings: 2
Cooking Time: 25 Minutes

Ingredients:
- 1 1/2 Ounce lemon juice
- 4 Ounce Apple Brandy
- 1 Ounce orange juice
- 1 Ounce Smoked Simple Syrup

Directions:
1. Supply your smoker with wood pellets and follow the start-up procedure. Preheat the grill, with the lid closed, to 350° F.
2. Place lemon halves directly on the grill grate and cook for 20-25 minutes or until grill marks appear. Remove from grill and let cool. Once cool enough to handle, juice the lemons then chill and reserve the juice. Grill: 350 °F
3. Using the proportions listed above and considering the size and consumption rate of your tailgate crew or party, mix all the above ingredients in a large thermos and top with a bit of ice.
4. Using 6-8 oz glasses or cups, guests can serve themselves from the thermos and garnish each drink with a grilled apple slice. Enjoy!

RECIPE INDEX

3-2-1 Bbq Beef Cheeks 175

A

A Smoking Classic Cocktail 201
Alder Smoked Scallops With Citrus & Garlic Butter Sauce 91
Amazing Bacon Cheese Fries 49
Ancho Pepper Rubbed Brisket 160
Anytime Pork Roast 52
Anzac Coconut Biscuits 39
Apple & Bourbon Glazed Ham 49
Apple Bacon Lattice Turkey 138
Apple Bacon Smoked Ham 58
Apple-smoked Bacon 52
Applewood-smoked Whole Turkey 137
Asian Chicken Sliders 136

B

Bacon Burger 184
Bacon Chocolate Chip Cookies 44
Bacon Old-fashioned Cocktail 200
Bacon Onion Ring 48
Bacon Pork Pinwheels (kansas Lollipops) 187
Bacon Weave Smoked Country Sausage 68
Bacon Wrapped Asparagus 69
Bacon Wrapped Corn On The Cob 106
Bacon Wrapped Scallops 80
Bacon Wrapped Shrimp 76
Bacon-wrapped Jalapeño Poppers 187
Baked Artichoke Parmesan Mushrooms 124
Baked Bacon Green Bean Casserole 115
Baked Bourbon Maple Pumpkin Pie 30
Baked Breakfast Mini Quiches 109
Baked Brie 24
Baked Buttermilk Biscuits 20
Baked Candied Bacon Cinnamon Rolls 58
Baked Cast Iron Berry Cobbler 27
Baked Cheesy Parmesan Grits 42
Baked Chocolate Brownie Cookies With Egg Nog 35
Baked Chocolate Coconut Brownies 16
Baked Garlic Duchess Potatoes 123

Baked Green Chile Mac & Cheese By Doug Scheiding 28
Baked Heirloom Tomato Tart 111
Baked Honey Glazed Ham 46
Baked Irish Creme Cake 41
Baked Kale Chips 127
Baked Loaded Tater Tots 114
Baked Maple And Brown Sugar Bacon 59
Baked Molten Chocolate Cake 32
Baked Pear Tarte Tatin 29
Baked Potatoes & Celery Root Au Gratin 21
Baked Prosciutto-wrapped Chicken Breast With Spinach And Boursin 155
Baked Pumpkin Pie 34
Baked Sage & Sausage Stuffing 50
Baked Steelhead 89
Baked Stuffed Avocados 125
Baked Sweet And Savory Yams By Bennie Kendrick 124
Baked Sweet Potato Casserole With Marshmallow Fluff 120
Baked Sweet Potatoes 116
Baked Venison Tater Tot Casserole 178
Baked Whole Fish In Sea Salt 92
Baked Winter Squash Au Gratin 110
Baked Wood-fired Pizza 15
Balsamic Brussels Sprouts With Bacon 64
Bananas Rum Foster 31
Barbecued Scallops 92
Barbecued Shrimp 94
Basil Margherita Pizza 28
Batter Up Cocktail 199
Bayou Wings With Cajun Rémoulade 188
Bbq Bacon Meatballs 174
Bbq Beef Sandwich 161
Bbq Beef Short Ribs With Traeger Prime Rib Rub 178
Bbq Breakfast Sausage 129
Bbq Brisket Tacos 178
Bbq Brisket With Traeger Coffee Rub 157
Bbq Brown Sugar Bacon Bites 50
Bbq Chicken Breasts 132

Bbq Chicken Drumsticks 132
Bbq Chicken Legs 137
Bbq Chicken Thighs 147
Bbq Chicken Tostada 135
Bbq Oysters 99
Bbq Pork Belly 57
Bbq Pork Belly Burnt Ends 72
Bbq Pork Chops 71
Bbq Pork Shoulder Roast With Sugar Lips Glaze 75
Bbq Pulled Pork Hash 66
Bbq Pulled Pork With Sweet & Heat Bbq Sauce 48
Bbq Roasted Salmon 95
Bbq Smoked Turkey Jerky 137
Bbq Sweet & Smoky Ribs 73
Bbq Sweet Pepper Meatloaf 180
Bbq Turkey Breast With Meat Church Holy Cow 156
Bbq Turkey Drumsticks 140
Beef Brisket With Chophouse Steak Rub 162
Beef Caldereta Stew 180
Beer Braised Beef Sandwiches 177
Beer Bread 20
Beer Chicken 145
Beer Chili Bratwurst 168
Beer Pork Belly Chili Con Carne 74
Bison Meatballs 176
Bistecca Alla Fiorentina With Mushroom Ragout 168
Blt Pasta Salad 121
Blueberry Bread Pudding 40
Blueberry Pancakes 15
Blueberry Sour Cream Muffins 26
Bourbon Chile Glazed Ham 69
Braised Creamed Green Beans 121
Braised Mediterranean Beef Brisket 160
Braised Pork Carnitas 57
Brats In Beer 55
Brined Smoked Brisket 157
Broccoli-cauliflower Salad 104
Buffalo Chicken 131
Buffalo Chicken Wings 144
Buffalo Chicken Wraps 139
Buffalo Wings 134
Butter Braised Green Beans 119
Buttered Thanksgiving Turkey 129

Butternut Squash 110
Butternut Squash Macaroni And Cheese 35

C

Cajun Brined Maple Smoked Turkey Breast 143
Cajun Double-smoked Ham 68
Cajun-blackened Shrimp 76
Cake With Smoked Berry Sauce 37
Caramel Bourbon Bacon Brownies 19
Caramelized Bourbon Baked Pears 33
Carolina Baked Beans 123
Carrot Cake 18
Cast Iron Pineapple Upside Down Cake 41
Cast Iron Potatoes 128
Cedar Smoked Garlic Salmon 84
Championship Ribs With Kansas City Style 74
Charleston Crab Cakes With Remoulade 101
Cheddar Bacon Beef Burgers 165
Cheese Chicken Cordon Bleu 150
Chef Curtis' Famous Chimichurri Sauce 112
Chicken Breast Calzones 150
Chicken Corn Fritters 144
Chicken Egg Rolls With Buffalo Sauce 152
Chicken Lollipops 131
Chicken Nachos 150
Chicken On A Throne 140
Chicken Pot Pie 38
Chicken Tenders 149
Chicken Wings With Teriyaki Glaze 187
Chili Cheese Fries 25
Chinese Alcoholic Bbq Pork Tenderloin 47
Chocolate Almond Cake 45
Chocolate Lava Cake With Smoked Whipped Cream 15
Chocolate Peanut Cookies 44
Chorizo Cheese Stuffed Burgers 164
Chorizo Queso Fundido 189
Christmas Brussel Sprouts 126
Chuckwagon Beef Jerky 191
Cider Hot-smoked Salmon 88
Cider-brined Turkey 139
Cinnamon Pull-aparts 25
Citrus Grilled Lamb Chops 174
Citrus-infused Marinated Olives 189

Citrus-smoked Trout 87
Classic Poor Man's Burnt Ends 179
Coconut Shrimp Jalapeño Poppers 90
Cold-smoked Cheese 194
Cold-smoked Salmon Gravlax 79
Cornbread Chicken Stuffing 45
Cornish Game Hen 143
Cornish Game Hens 146
County Fair Turkey Legs 142
Cran-apple Tequila Punch With Smoked Oranges 201
Cranberry Turkey Breast 133
Crème Brûlée 43
Crescent Rolls 27
Crispy Spiced Chicken Wings 149
Crown Roast Of Pork 52
Cuban Onion Pork Sandwich 71
Cured Cold-smoked Lox 96

D
Dark Chocolate Brownies With Bacon-salted Caramel 40
Delicious Deviled Crab Appetizer 192
Delicious Peanut Butter Cookies 34
Delicious Pellet Grill Cornbread 34
Delicious Pulled Pork Poutine 52
Delicious Smoked Bone-in Pork Chops 64
Delicious Smoked Trout 96
Delicious Smoked Turketta 144
Deviled Eggs With Smoked Paprika 190
Donut Bread Pudding 27
Double Chocolate Chip Brownie Pie 32
Double Vanilla Chocolate Cake 18
Double-smoked Cheese Potatoes 117
Dry Brine Traeger Turkey 146
Dry Rub Grilled Ribs 53
Dublin Delight Cocktail 203
Duck Breast With Pomegranate Sauce 129
Duck Fat Fries (confit) 184

E
Eggs Ham Benedict 33
Everything Pigs In A Blanket 66
Eyeball Cookies 42

F
Fajita Style Mexican Hot Dogs 182
Fast Ribs 46
Fig Glazed Chicken Stuffed Cornbread 136
Fig Slider Cocktail 200
Flavour Bbq Brisket Burnt Ends 159
Flavour Fire Spiced Shrimp 103
Flavour Memphis Bbq Beef Brisket 159
Flavour Smoked Corned Beef Brisket Hash 186
Flavour Texas Smoke Beef 157
Florentine Shrimp Al Cartoccio 84
Focaccia 29

G
Garden Gimlet Cocktail 198
Garlic Bacon Wrapped Shrimp 101
Garlic Beef Meatballs 185
Garlic Blackened Catfish 88
Garlic Blackened Salmon 85
Garlic Cheese Pull Apart Bread 38
Garlic Leg Of Lamb Roast 158
Garlic Lemon Pepper Chicken Wings 38
Garlic Pepper Shrimp Pesto Bruschetta 86
Garlic Standing Rib Roast 161
Green Bean Casserole 126
Green Bean Casserole Circa 1955 18
Green Chile Cheese Beef Sliders 174
Green Chile Chicken Enchiladas 141
Green Goddess Chicken Legs 154
Grilled Albacore Tuna With Potato-tomato Casserole 78
Grilled Apple Pie 39
Grilled Artichoke Cheese Salmon 92
Grilled Asparagus & Honey-glazed Carrots 115
Grilled Asparagus And Hollandaise Sauce 106
Grilled Asparagus And Spinach Salad 109
Grilled Beer Cabbage 125
Grilled Beer Cheese Dip 23
Grilled Blackened Saskatchewan Salmon 97
Grilled Blood Orange Mimosa 196
Grilled Bourbon Pecan Pie 43
Grilled Broccoli Rabe 124
Grilled Cabbage Steaks With Warm Bacon Vinaigrette 127

Grilled Cheesy Chicken 133
Grilled Chicken Wings 147
Grilled Chili-lime Corn 122
Grilled Chipotle Chicken Skewers 142
Grilled Corn On The Cob With Parmesan And Garlic 107
Grilled Crab Legs With Herb Butter 81
Grilled Fingerling Potato Salad 119
Grilled Frozen Strawberry Lemonade 199
Grilled Garlic Lobster Tails 102
Grilled Greek Chicken With Garlic & Lemon 156
Grilled Guacamole 189
Grilled Hand Pulled Chicken 145
Grilled Hawaiian Sour 198
Grilled Honey Chicken Wings 133
Grilled Lasagna With Cold-smoked Mozzarella 46
Grilled Lemon Pepper Pork Tenderloin 61
Grilled Lemon Shrimp Scampi 81
Grilled Lobster Tails With Smoked Paprika Butter 87
Grilled Loco Moco Burger 172
Grilled Parmesan Chicken Wings 151
Grilled Peach Mint Julep 204
Grilled Peach Sour Cocktail 197
Grilled Pepper Lobster Tails 83
Grilled Pork Loin 58
Grilled Prosciutto Wrapped Asparagus 51
Grilled Rabbit Tail Cocktail 205
Grilled Raspberry Chipotle Pork Ribs 62
Grilled Ratatouille Salad 111
Grilled Salmon 102
Grilled Salmon Steaks With Dill Sauce 98
Grilled Shrimp Brochette 85
Grilled Street Corn 105
Grilled Stuffed Pork Chops 69
Grilled Sugar Snap Peas And Smoked Bacon 64
Grilled Sweet Pork Tenderloin 54
Grilled Tilapia With Blistered Cherry Tomatoes 90
Grilled Tomahawk Steak 167
Grilled Trout With Citrus & Basil 99
Grilled Tuna Steaks With Lemon & Caper Butter 78
Grilled Whole Chicken Stuffed Sausage And Apple 148
Grilled Whole Steelhead Fillet 80
Grilled Zucchini Squash Spears 112

H
Hawaiian Pulled Pork 47
Herb Grilled Venison Stew 182
Hickory Smoked Pork Shoulder 73
Hickory Smoked Prime Rib 168
Home-cured Picnic Ham With Mustard Caviar 61
Honey Balsamic Salmon 95
Honey Glazed Pork Chops 55
Honey-soy Garlic Salmon 98
Hot Coffee-rubbed Brisket 170

I
In Traeger Fashion Cocktail 195
Italian Grilled Barbecue Chicken Wings 153
Italian Grilled Chicken Saltimbocca 138
Italian Meatballs 169

J
Jalapeño- & Cheese-stuffed Chicken 137
Jalapeno Cheddar Smoked Sausages 54
Jalapeño Poppers With Chipotle Sour Cream 193
Jamaican Jerk Chicken Quarters 146
Juicy Jerk Chicken Kebabs 152

K
Kimi's Simple Grilled Fresh Fish 80
Kodiak Cakes Candied Bacon Crumble Brownies 68
Korean Pulled Pork Lettuce Wraps 54

L
Lemon & Herb Chicken 150
Lemon Cajun Chicken Carbonara 153
Lemon Chicken, Broccoli, String Beans Foil Packs 21
Lemon Herb Grilled Salmon 76
Lemon Lobster Rolls 85
Lemon Rosemary Beer Can Chicken 135
Lemon Shrimp Scampi 97
Lemon Tomahawk Steak 181
Lime Mahi Mahi Fillets 84
Lip-smackin' Pork Loin 73
Loaded Chicken Fries 155
Lobster Tail 77

M
Mandarin Chicken Breast 143
Mango Rice Wine Thai Shrimp 80

Maple Syrup Pancake Casserole 22
Marbled Brownies With Amaretto & Ricotta 22
Marinated Grilled Honey Chicken Wings 154
Mashed Red Potatoes 116
Mexican Mahi Mahi With Baja Cabbage Slaw 86
Mezcal Shrimp With Salsa De Molcajete 81
Mini Sausage Rolls 65
Mint Butter Chocolate Chip Cookies 16
Moked Christmas Crown Roast Of Lamb 174
Moules Marinières With Garlic Butter Sauce 101
Mustard Garlic Crusted Prime Rib 178

N
Nashville Spiced Smoked Chicken 141

O
Oktoberfest Pretzel Mustard Chicken 148
Old Fashioned Cornbread 19
Old-fashioned Roasted Glazed Ham 65
Oysters In The Shell 95
Oysters Margarita 91

P
Pacific Northwest Salmon 100
Pan Seared Parsley Ribeye Steak 179
Parmesan Roasted Cauliflower 110
Pastrami 157
Peanut Butter Chicken Wings 156
Peper Fish Tacos 97
Pig On A Stick With Buffalo Glaze 49
Pig Pops (sweet-hot Bacon On A Stick) 191
Pigs In A Blanket 190
Pineapple Cake 44
Pizza Bites 17
Planked Trout With Fennel, Bacon & Orange 94
Portobello Marinated Mushroom 116
Potluck Salad With Smoked Cornbread 113
Pound Cake 43
Pretzel Bun With Pulled Pork 50
Pretzel Rolls 24
Prosciutto Wrapped Dates With Marcona Almonds 62
Prosciutto-wrapped Scallops 100
Pull-apart Dinner Rolls 16
Pulled Beef 163
Pulled Pork Loaded Nachos 188

Pulled Pork Shoulder And Chicken 57
Pulled Pork Stew 51
Pulled Pork Taquitos With Sour Cream 60
Pumpkin Bread 33

Q
Quick Baked Dinner Rolls 34

R
Red Potato Grilled Lollipops 109
Reuben Sandwich 163
Reverse Seared Rib-eye Caps 159
Reverse-seared Steaks 176
Reverse-seared Tri-tip 164
Roasted Artichokes With Garlic Butter 111
Roasted Asparagus 105
Roasted Beer Can Chicken 151
Roasted Beet & Bacon Salad 118
Roasted Christmas Goose 140
Roasted Do-ahead Mashed Potatoes 128
Roasted Fall Vegetables 123
Roasted Garlic Herb Fries 112
Roasted Green Beans With Bacon 117
Roasted Halibut With Spring Vegetables 79
Roasted Ham With Apricot Sauce 57
Roasted Hasselback Potatoes By Doug Scheiding 104
Roasted Honey Bourbon Glazed Turkey 145
Roasted Jalapeno Cheddar Deviled Eggs 118
Roasted Jalapeño Poppers 117
Roasted Mashed Potatoes 104
Roasted Mustard Crusted Prime Rib 170
Roasted New Potatoes 115
Roasted New Potatoes With Compound Butter 125
Roasted Olives 109
Roasted Pickled Beets 119
Roasted Pork With Balsamic Strawberry Sauce 56
Roasted Potato Poutine 104
Roasted Prime Rib 167
Roasted Pumpkin Seeds 108
Roasted Red Pepper Dip 192
Roasted Red Pepper White Bean Dip 128
Roasted Rosemary Orange Chicken 134
Roasted Sheet Pan Vegetables 114
Roasted Sweet Potato Steak Fries 114

Roasted Tin Foil Dinners 141
Roasted Tomatoes 121
Roasted Tomatoes With Hot Pepper Sauce 126
Roasted Vegetable Napoleon 116
Roasted Whole Chicken 139
Rosemary Cranberry Apple Sage Stuffing 36
Rosemary-smoked Lamb Chops 170
Ryes And Shine Cocktail 196

S

S'mores Dip Skillet 41
Salmon Cakes With Homemade Tartar Sauce 77
Salt Crusted Baked Potatoes 105
Santa Maria Tri-tip With Pico De Gallo 171
Savory Bacon Mac And Cheese Stuffed Sliders 172
Savory Cheesecake With Bourbon Pecan Topping 26
Savory Chili Mac And Cheese 181
Savory Grilled Chicken Burrito Bowls 148
Savory Jerk Chicken Wings 153
Savory Reverse Seared Ny Steak 171
Savory Smoked Chicken Breasts 130
Savory Teriyaki Smoked Steak Bites 175
Savory Whiskey Grilled Elk Steaks 162
Seared Ahi Tuna Steak With Soy Sauce 98
Seared Bluefin Tuna Steaks 94
Shrimp Cabbage Tacos With Lime Cream 78
Sicilian Stuffed Mushrooms 126
Simple Cream Cheese Sausage Balls 190
Simple Glazed Salmon Fillets 76
Simple Smoked Baby Backs 74
Skillet Buttermilk Cornbread 24
Skillet Potato Cake 123
Slow Smoked Rib-eye Roast 171
Smo-fried Chicken 142
Smoked & Loaded Baked Potato 120
Smoked Apple Cider 196
Smoked Apple Pork Belly 62
Smoked Asparagus Soup 107
Smoked Baby Back Ribs 66
Smoked Bacon Roses 70
Smoked Barnburner Cocktail 203
Smoked Bbq Onion Brussels Sprout 127
Smoked Beer Brine Hens 154
Smoked Beer Brisket 183
Smoked Beer Corned Beef 176
Smoked Beet-pickled Eggs 122
Smoked Berry Cocktail 195
Smoked Blackberry Pie 27
Smoked Bologna 53
Smoked Boneless Chicken Thighs 149
Smoked Cashews 191
Smoked Cedar Plank Salmon 89
Smoked Cheese 192
Smoked Cheese Beef Burgers 184
Smoked Cheesy Alfredo Sauce 21
Smoked Chicken Steak Sandwiches 166
Smoked Chili Con Queso By Doug Scheiding 51
Smoked Chorizo & Arugula Pesto 65
Smoked Cold Brew Coffee 202
Smoked Corned Beef & Cabbage 173
Smoked Corned Beef Brisket 185
Smoked Corned Beef Reuben 183
Smoked Curry Ketchup Pork Ribs 60
Smoked Deviled Eggs 155
Smoked Drumsticks 148
Smoked Duck Breast Bacon 165
Smoked Fish Chowder 93
Smoked Garlic Meatloaf 186
Smoked Hibiscus Sparkler 202
Smoked Honey Chicken Drumsticks 141
Smoked Honey Salmon 79
Smoked Hot Buttered Rum 197
Smoked Ice Mojito Slurpee 199
Smoked Irish Coffee 204
Smoked Jacobsen Salt Margarita 202
Smoked Jalapeño Poppers 116
Smoked Lemon Cheesecake 42
Smoked Lemon Tea 31
Smoked Lobster Scampi 82
Smoked Longhorn Brisket 183
Smoked Longhorn Cowboy Tri-tip 185
Smoked Macaroni Salad 108
Smoked Mango Shrimp 99
Smoked Maple Syrup Thanksgiving Turkey 147
Smoked Mashed Potatoes 122
Smoked Meatball Egg Sandwiches 180

Smoked Mulled Wine 198
Smoked Mushrooms 115
Smoked New York Steaks 160
Smoked Parmesan Herb Popcorn 111
Smoked Pheasant 164
Smoked Pickled Green Beans 113
Smoked Pico De Gallo 107
Smoked Pig Shots 72
Smoked Pineapple Hotel Nacional Cocktail 203
Smoked Pomegranate Lemonade Cocktail 198
Smoked Porchetta 63
Smoked Porchetta With Italian Salsa Verde 59
Smoked Pork Loin 53
Smoked Pork Tenderloin 55
Smoked Pork Tomato Tamales 70
Smoked Prime Rib 172
Smoked Pumpkin Spice Latte 200
Smoked Rack Of Pork 69
Smoked Red Wine Beef Roast 162
Smoked Salt Cured Lox 77
Smoked Salted Caramel White Russian 201
Smoked Sangria 199
Smoked Sirloin Roast Beef 173
Smoked Spiced Pulled Beef Chuck Roast 164
Smoked Sugar Halibut 96
Smoked Texas Ranch Water 204
Smoked Traeger Pulled Pork 55
Smoked Tri-tip 165
Smoked Trout 99
Smoked Turkey Jerky 132
Smoked Turkey Sandwich 193
Smoked Turkey Wings 135
Smoked Whiskey Peach Pulled Chicken 138
Smoked, Salted Caramel Apple Pie 19
Smoker Wheat Bread 23
Smoke-roasted Halibut With Mixed Herb Vinaigrette 90
Smokin' Lemon Bars 30
Smoking Gun Cocktail 195
Smoky Apple Crepes 37
Smoky Crab Dip 97
Smoky Pimento Cheese Cornbread 20
Smoky Scotch & Ginger Cocktail 201

Sopapilla Cheesecake By Doug Scheiding 28
Sourdough Pizza 36
Southern Sugar-glazed Ham 56
Spatchcocked Chicken With White Barbecue Sauce 134
Spatchcocked Turkey 135
Spiced Carrot Cake 17
Spiced Grilled Pork Chops 62
Spiced Lemon Cherry Pie 25
Spiced Pork Belly 61
Spiced Smoked Chicken Quarters 130
Spiced Smoked Swordfish 83
Spicy Asian Brussels Sprouts 124
Spicy Crab Poppers 102
Spicy Lime Shrimp 82
Spicy Shrimp Skewers 86
Spicy Smoked Chili Beef Jerky 182
Sriracha & Maple Cashews 193
St Louis Style Bbq Ribs With Texas Spicy Bbq Sauce 66
St. Louis Bbq Ribs 48
Standing Venison Rib Roast 175
Steak Fries With Horseradish Creme 110
Strawberry Basil Daiquiri 23
Strawberry Mule Cocktail 197
Stuffed Jalapenos 108
Sunset Margarita 196
Sweet And Spicy Baked Pork Beans 22
Sweet And Spicy Pork Roast 72
Sweet Cheese Muffins 36
Sweet Heat Burnt Ends 169
Sweet Mandarin Salmon 87
Sweet Potato Marshmallow Casserole 113
Sweet Smoked Country Ribs 67
Sweet Smoked Salmon Jerky 85
Sweetheart Steak 162
Swordfish With Sicilian Olive Oil Sauce 83

T

Tarte Tatin 22
Tater Tot Bake 120
Tequila & Lime Shrimp With Smoked Tomato Sauce 82
Teriyaki Smoked Honey Tilapia 95
Texas Grilled Ribs 67

Texas Pepper Beef Ribs 159
Texas Shoulder Clod 170
Texas Smoked Beer Leftover Rib Meat 173
Thai-style Swordfish Steaks With Peanut Sauce 89
The Dan Patrick Show Pull-apart Pesto Bread 32
The Perfect T-bones 163
Three Ingredient Pot Roast 158
Traditional Smoked Thanksgiving Turkey 152
Traditional Tomahawk Steak 161
Traeger Baked Focaccia 39
Traeger Baked Potato Torte 107
Traeger Baked Protein Bars 35
Traeger Baked Rainbow Trout 101
Traeger Bbq Half Chickens 130
Traeger Boulevardier Cocktail 205
Traeger Crab Legs 100
Traeger Grilled Whole Corn 120
Traeger Jerk Shrimp 93
Traeger Mandarin Wings 151
Traeger Old Fashioned 204
Traeger Pork Chops 59
Traeger Pulled Pork Sandwiches 63
Traeger Smoked Coleslaw 106
Traeger Smoked Daiquiri 195
Traeger Smoked Salmon 92
Traeger Smoked Sausage 47

Traeger Tri-tip Roast 179
Turkey & Bacon Kebabs With Ranch-style Dressing 146
Turkey Stuffing Bacon Balls 53
Twice-smoked Potatoes 105

U
Ultimate Baked Garlic Bread 36
Unique Carolina Mustard Ribs 75

V
Vanilla Cheesecake Skillet Brownie 32
Vanilla Chocolate Bacon Cupcakes 40
Venison Carne Asada 177
Venison Steaks 179
Vodka Brined Smoked Wild Salmon 87

W
Whiskey- & Cider-brined Pork Shoulder 67
Whiskey Bourbon Bbq Cheeseburger 166
Whole Roasted Cauliflower With Garlic Parmesan Butter 118
Whole Vermillion Red Snapper 79
Wild West Wings 154
Wood-fired Halibut 93

Z
Zombie Cocktail Recipe 197